Bridge to Higher Mathematics

Sam Vandervelde

This book was produced using the LaTeX typesetting system.

The cover artwork was designed by Eunice Cheung. The image depicts a footbridge at the Olbrich Botanical Gardens in Madison, Wisconsin.

Soli Deo gloria

Contents

To the Student

Mathematics is a wonderful subject. Consequently, a mathematics course can and should be a rewarding experience. My primary purpose in writing this text was to create a book to accompany such a course; a book that would convey the splendid nature of mathematics while presenting a few topics within the subject in as clear a manner as possible. The book is designed to draw the reader into the subject; to encourage the student to participate in the development of the ideas. For mathematics is not a spectator sport—one must actively engage in the material to properly understand and enjoy it.

This book is intended for students who have completed a standard high school mathematics curriculum and have discovered in the process that they enjoy the subject and wish to pursue more advanced studies such as group theory or real analysis. The reader has presumably also taken a calculus course; however, the text does not assume any knowledge of calculus. This was done so that the material would also be accessible to high school students and so that a course based on this text could be taken concurrently with a calculus course. The examples and problems assume a familiarity with algebra, properties of common functions such as $\cos x$ or e^x, elementary Euclidean geometry, and sets of numbers such as the integers or real numbers.

From a pedagogical standpoint, the goal of this text is to equip students with the tools and background necessary to succeed in upper level math courses. In particular, a course utilizing this book will aim to develop a student's capacity for mathematical reasoning and ability to write a sound mathematical proof. Once an interesting result has been discovered (or assigned for homework), one is faced with the challenge of explaining why it is true. There is a standard set of tools, strategies and vocabulary for accomplishing such a task. For this reason the third chapter serves as the pivot point around which the remainder of the book is set. The first two chapters introduce the framework of logic and set theory necessary for the discussion of proof techniques that comes next. The subsequent four chapters then provide an opportunity to employ and practice these techniques while laying the foundation for further mathematical study.

There are a number of features sprinkled throughout the text that warrant a brief explanation. For starters, at regular intervals the reader will encounter elementary questions following new definitions or techniques. These are dubbed "Concept Checks" and look like this:

CONCEPT CHECK a) How is it possible that there is an interstate highway in Hawaii?

The reader is strongly encouraged to mentally answer these questions right away, in order to help cement new concepts in place as soon as they are introduced. Answers to all the Concept Checks within each section may be found at the conclusion of that section. Somewhat less frequently the reader will be asked to supply a step in an argument or otherwise participate in the development of an idea via a "Quick Query" such as

QUICK QUERY b) How can one most effectively utilize the answers to all the exercises included at the back of the book?

Answers to the Quick Queries are also located at the end of each section.

Another feature that will quickly become apparent are the Mathematical Outings. These self-contained activities are intended for group investigation during class time or as an entertaining exploration for individuals to undertake to complement the material presented in that section. Their purpose is to help reinforce particular concepts as well as to provide a regular reminder that mathematics is a delightful, intriguing subject. The wide boxes appearing on almost every page hardly need an explanation—they highlight important definitions and techniques within each section. Finally, there is a special reference section included at the end of each chapter which summarizes all the vocabulary, concepts, techniques, and proof strategies found in that chapter. These sections are meant to aid in review and serve as a resource while studying later chapters. Complete sample proofs also appear in the reference section. Results in the text for which a sample proof is available are indicated by a dagger. (†)

Hundreds and hundreds of creative, stimulating, accessible questions have been composed for this book. In some sense, a text is only as strong as its selection of questions, since it is through working on these questions that a student internalizes the ideas laid out on the preceding pages. The questions are grouped into exercises, which need only an answer or a brief explanation, and writing problems, which require a proof: a complete mathematical explanation written in full sentences. Answers to all the exercises and hints to all the writing problems are given in Chapter 8, along with a few thoughts on how to best take advantage of them.

I hope you enjoy the book. And now, on to the mathematics.

Sam Vandervelde
St. Lawrence University
July 2010

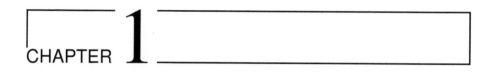

CHAPTER 1

Logical Foundations

1.1   Statements and Open Sentences

Certain words and phrases are ubiquitous in mathematical discourse because they convey the logical framework of the ideas being presented. For this reason they arise naturally in everyday language as well, although they may be used at times with a slightly different meaning in a conversational setting. Therefore our first task will be to introduce the standard terminology of logic and precisely define what these terms mean within the context of mathematics.

As a starting point, consider the following assertion:

> *"For all positive integers n, it is the case that $n^2 + 2$*
> *is a multiple of 3 or that $3n + 7$ is a perfect square."* $(*)$

Before going on, decide for yourself whether or not this assertion is true. How confident are you of your answer? Would you bet \$1 that you are correct? Would you bet \$100? Throughout this text we will discuss strategies for demonstrating the validity or falsehood of various statements such as the one made above. We will begin by analyzing their structure.

A **statement** is a mathematical assertion that can be assigned a **truth value**, either true or false.

Examples of statements include "The sum $3^3 + 4^3 + 5^3$ is equal to 6^3," or "A triangle with sides of length 3, 4 and 5 has an area of 6." Clearly questions and commands should not qualify as statements. At the risk of omitting interesting propositions like "The Patriots are the best football team of the decade," or "It's freezing outside," we will restrict ourselves primarily to mathematical statements. In this way we avoid issues such as personal opinion or imprecisely defined terms which make ambiguous the truth value of a statement.

1

Note that it is not necessary to be able to establish the veracity of a given mathematical sentence in order for it to qualify as a statement. For this reason "There is a prime number between any two consecutive perfect squares," is a perfectly valid statement, even though nobody is completely sure whether it is true or false. (Recall that a prime number is a positive integer that has exactly two positive divisors: itself and 1. The first six prime numbers are 2, 3, 5, 7, 11 and 13.) In case you were wondering, the aforementioned statement is almost certainly true, although a proof has yet to be found.

CONCEPT a) Which of the following are mathematical statements?
i. Seven trillion is the largest number.
ii. Please compute 38^2 in your head.
iii. Are all squares also rectangles?
iv. The integer 2^{1000} has 301 digits.
v. Both n and $2n + 1$ are primes.

One of the features of statement $(*)$ that makes it more complicated is the appearance of the variable n. Since the validity of a phrase such as "$3n + 7$ is a perfect square" depends on what value is assigned to the variable, we cannot immediately ascertain its truth value. Therefore it would be inappropriate to dub it a statement.

> An assertion involving one or more variables is called an **open sentence**. Choosing a value for each variable reduces the open sentence to a statement that is either true or false, depending upon the values selected. The set of values that a variable may assume is known as the **domain** of the variable and is usually indicated at the start of the open sentence.

Examining statement $(*)$ we discover that it contains two shorter open sentences; namely "$n^2 + 2$ is a multiple of 3," and "$3n + 7$ is a perfect square." We are also told that the domain of the variable n is the set of positive integers. For a given value of n in the domain each of these open sentences has a truth value. For example, when $n = 10$ we find that the first open sentence is true while the second is false. These two open sentences are joined into a single longer open sentence via the word OR. Common usage suggests that this compound sentence should be true when $n = 10$, since the first half is true.

> The **disjunction** of two statements or open sentences is obtained by joining them with the logical connective OR. A disjunction is true as long as at least one (and possibly both) of its components is true.

CONCEPT b) Is the disjunction "$n^2 + 2$ is a multiple of 3 or $3n + 7$ is a perfect square" true or false when $n = 6$? How about when $n = 8$, $n = 12$ and $n = 14$?

In lig.   he statement "100 is a perfect square or 101 is a prime" is   might differ from the common notion of OR for some peop.   neans that exactly one (but not both) of the individual sta   e is a mathematical term having this meaning, called 'exclu   i to XOR), but it arises relatively infrequently. Just remember that whenever the word OR appears in a mathematical setting, it always means that at least one of the component statements is true.

The logical companion to the word OR is the word AND.

> The **conjunction** of two statements or open sentences is obtained by joining them with the logical connective AND. A conjunction is true when both of its components are true.

In this case there is no disagreement between the common and mathematical usage of the term AND. Thus the statement "100 is a perfect square and 101 is a prime" is true, while "$5 < 6$ and $-5 < -6$" is false.

CONCEPT c) Create a conjunction of two open sentences involving a positive integer n that is false when $n = 1$ and $n = 2$ but true when $n = 3$.

In our quest to dissect statement $(*)$, we finally come to the first two words of the sentence. The phrase 'for all' is known as a **quantifier**, in the sense that it prescribes the quantity of values of the variable for which the ensuing open sentence should be true; in this case, all of them. The other commonly employed quantifier is 'there exists,' which specifies that the open sentence should be true for at least one value of the variable. It is not hard to imagine other quantifiers, most of which are self-explanatory. For instance we have 'there does not exist' and 'there exists a unique'. The latter means that the open sentence should be true for exactly one value of the variable.

CONCEPT d) Which of the following statements are true?
i. For all positive integers n the number $n^2 + 2n + 2$ is a multiple of 5.
ii. There exists a unique circle passing through two given points in the plane.

We can now say with certainty that statement $(*)$ is false, because the value $n = 12$ provides a counterexample. As we have already seen, when $n = 12$ both of the open sentences "$n^2 + 2$ is a multiple of 3" and "$3n + 7$ is a perfect square" are false; hence so is their disjunction. In other words, the open sentence "$n^2 + 2$ is a multiple of 3 or $3n + 7$ is a perfect square" is not true for all values of n, as asserted. Note that we need only find a single counterexample in order to conclude that the entire statement is false.[†]

a) The first and fourth sentences are mathematical statements. (Both happen to be false, though.) The second is a command, the third is a question, and the fifth is an open sentence.
b) The disjunction is true for $n = 6$, 8 and 14. However, it is false when $n = 12$ since $12^2 + 2 = 146$ is not a multiple of 3 nor is $3(12) + 7 = 43$ a perfect square.

c) A correct, but uninteresting conjunction is "$n > 2$ and $n < 10$." A more imaginative response might be "n is odd and $n^2 + 1$ is divisible by 5."

d) When $n = 3$ we find that $3^2 + 2(3) + 2 = 17$ is not a multiple of 5, thus the first statement is false. The second statement is also false, because there is always more than one circle passing through two given points.

EXERCISES

1. Decide whether the following statements are true or false.
a) The number 1776 is a perfect square.
b) It is the case that $3^3 + 4^3 + 5^3$ is equal to 6^3.
c) A triangle with sides of length 3, 4, and 5 has an area of 6.
d) There are at least two prime numbers between 11^2 and 12^2.
e) A cube has six faces, eight vertices, and ten edges.

2. Find an integer value of n for which the open sentence "$n^2 - n + 11$ is a prime number" is true. Find another value for n that makes it false.

3. Find all positive integers k for which the open sentence "$2^k + 1$ is a multiple of 3" is false. (Just check $k = 1, 2, \ldots, 8$ and describe the pattern.)

4. Find all real numbers x for which the open sentence $30(x - 20) = 20(x - 10)$ is true. By the way, this is commonly known as "solving the equation."

5. State the domain of the variables n, k and x in the previous three exercises.

6. In what way does the logical connective OR come into play when solving the equation $(x + 3)(x^2 - 9) = 0$?

7. Decide whether each statement is true or false.
a) There exists a real number x such that $e^x = 2$.
b) There exist positive integers p and q such that $p/q = \pi$.
c) There does not exist an integer k such that $k^2 + 2$ is divisible by 5.
d) For all real numbers m, the line having slope m and y-intercept 1 intersects the circle of radius 1 centered at the origin in exactly two points.
e) For every positive integer n, there exists a smaller positive integer.
f) There exists a unique two-digit number that is twice the product of its digits.
g) There exists a unique line passing through any two distinct points.

8. Find two positive integer values of n other than $n = 12$ which demonstrate that statement ($*$) is false.

WRITING

9. Twenty students attend a math class one morning. Each student arrives at a certain time, stays for some portion of the class, then departs without returning. Suppose that given any pair of students, they are both present in the classroom together for some part of the lecture. Prove that at some point in time all twenty students are simultaneously present in the classroom.

10. Twenty students are lined up for a math bee. Given any pair of adjacent students in the line, one or the other (or both) of them can recite the first fifty digits of π. Find an arrangement in which exactly ten students can recite π, including the third and fourteenth student. Then prove that for any such arrangement at least ten students know how to recite the first fifty digits of π.

11. Twenty math students are comparing grades on their first two quizzes of the year. The class discovers that whenever any pair of students consult with one another, these two students received the same grade on their first quiz or they received the same grade on their second quiz (or both). Prove that the entire class received the same grade on at least one of the two quizzes.

FURTHER EXPLORATION

12. It is standard in some programming languages for the number zero to represent one of the truth values (either true or false) and for positive numbers to represent the other truth value. If assigned correctly, the operations of addition and multiplication will then correspond to conjunction and disjunction, in some order. Figure out how to make this all work out neatly.

1.2   Logical Equivalence

The ultimatum "I will not both cook dinner and wash the dishes," is clearly equivalent to declaring that "I will not cook dinner or I will not wash the dishes." Notice that the first statement involves a conjunction while the second employs a disjunction. This observation is mildly troubling—apparently it is possible to say the same thing in two different ways! It is natural to wonder whether there is a systematic method for determining when two statements have the same logical meaning, especially since it is possible to construct far more complicated examples than the one given here. Happily, the answer is yes.

To describe this method efficiently we must first introduce some notation. We will commonly use the letters P, Q and R to represent statements. Thus a statement P has a truth value, either true (T) or false (F). Another statement Q also has two truth values, so there are four possible ways to assign truth values to both statements, listed in the **truth table** on the left below.

QUICK QUERY a) How many rows will a truth table for three statements have?

Next, we abbreviate "P OR Q" as $P \vee Q$. Recall that a disjunction is true unless both component statements are false. This definition is summarized by the truth table in the middle.

P	Q		P	Q	$P \vee Q$		P	Q	$P \wedge Q$
T	T		T	T	T		T	T	T
T	F		T	F	T		T	F	F
F	T		F	T	T		F	T	F
F	F		F	F	F		F	F	F

On the other hand, the conjunction "P AND Q," abbreviated as $P \wedge Q$, is only true when both P and Q are true. This fact is reflected by the truth table on the right. The **negation** "NOT P," written compactly as $\neg P$, has a particularly simple truth table. Thus if P is true then $\neg P$ is false, while if P is false then $\neg P$ is true. (Negation becomes more interesting when combined with other logical operations.) We introduce this notation because it is helpful to be familiar with these standard symbols. However, we will use symbolic notation outside of this chapter only rarely, such as when validating proof techniques.

CONCEPT CHECK b) The disjunction $P \vee \neg Q$ will be true except in one case. What truth values for P and Q make $P \vee \neg Q$ false?

CONCEPT CHECK c) Let P and Q be the statements "We won our first game," and "We won our second game," respectively. Translate the following statements into logical notation, using the symbols P, Q, $\wedge$, $\vee$ and $\neg$.

i. We won both of our first two games.
ii. We lost both of our first two games.
iii. We won at least one of our first two games.
iv. We lost at least one of our first two games.
v. We didn't win both of our first two games.

We are now in a position to show conclusively that the two statements made earlier mean the same thing, i.e. are logically equivalent.

> Suppose that two statements are constructed from the same set of component statements. The two statements are said to be **logically equivalent** if they have the same resulting truth value regardless of the manner in which truth values are assigned to the component statements.

To see how this plays out in practice, let P be the statement "I will cook dinner" and let Q be the statement "I will wash the dishes." Then "I will not both cook dinner and wash the dishes," can be translated as $\neg(P \wedge Q)$ while "I will not cook dinner or I will not wash the dishes," becomes $\neg P \vee \neg Q$. We next create a single truth table to compare the truth values of these two statements for all possible truth values for P and Q. Sure enough, in every case the outcomes are identical. We indicate their equivalence by writing $\neg(P \wedge Q) \equiv \neg P \vee \neg Q$.[†]

P	Q	$P \wedge Q$	$\neg(P \wedge Q)$	$\neg P$	$\neg Q$	$\neg P \vee \neg Q$
T	T	T	F	F	F	F
T	F	F	T	F	T	T
F	T	F	T	T	F	T
F	F	F	T	T	T	T

It should not come as a surprise to discover that the statements $\neg(P \vee Q)$ and $\neg P \wedge \neg Q$ are also logically equivalent, as you will confirm in the exercises.

These two rules for negating a conjunction or disjunction frequently come in handy, so we highlight them below.

DeMorgan's Laws indicate how negation distributes over conjunction and disjunction. They assert that

$$\neg(P \wedge Q) \equiv \neg P \vee \neg Q \qquad \text{and} \qquad \neg(P \vee Q) \equiv \neg P \wedge \neg Q.$$

Among other things, DeMorgan's Laws indicate how we should negate certain statements. Thus the opposite of "Let x be a real number such that $x \geq 0$ and $x^2 = 9$," would be "Let x be a real number such that $x < 0$ or $x^2 \neq 9$." (Note that the domain of the variable does not change.)

CONCEPT CHECK d) Determine the negative of the sentiment "Sink or swim."

The use of parentheses in the above examples was crucial to clarifying the scope of the NOT symbol. As you will discover in the exercises, $\neg(P \wedge Q)$ and $\neg P \wedge Q$ are not logically equivalent. Parentheses are also important when it comes to specifying order of operation, just as with algebraic expressions. For example, the statement $P \vee Q \wedge R$ is ambiguous—does this mean $(P \vee Q) \wedge R$ or $P \vee (Q \wedge R)$? The distinction is necessary, because these statements have different logical meanings. We may demonstrate this fact via a truth table.

P	Q	R	$(P \vee Q) \wedge R$	$P \vee (Q \wedge R)$
T	T	T	T	T
T	T	F	F	T
T	F	T	T	T
T	F	F	F	T
F	T	T	T	T
F	T	F	F	F
F	F	T	F	F
F	F	F	F	F

Since the right-hand columns are not identical we conclude that the two statements are not logically equivalent; that is, $(P \vee Q) \wedge R \not\equiv P \vee (Q \wedge R)$.

Certain statements, like "We'll get there when we get there," and "Either I'll pay you the money back, or I won't," are amusing because they manage to be undeniably true without really saying anything of note.

A statement that is always true is called a **tautology**, while a statement that is always false is known as a **contradiction**.

One can confirm that a given logical statement is a tautology by constructing its truth table and checking that every possible outcome is true; similarly, every entry in the truth table for a contradiction will be F. One example of a tautology is $P \vee \neg P$; for if P is true then so is $P \vee \neg P$, but if P is false then $\neg P$ is true, hence $P \vee \neg P$ is again true.

 e) Why is $P \wedge \neg P$ is a contradiction?

 f) What is the negation of a contradiction?

Tautologies and contradictions usually involve more than one statement, such as the tautology $(P \wedge \neg Q) \vee (\neg P \vee Q)$ appearing in the exercises. Bear in mind that these examples are relatively rare; most logical statements are sometimes true and sometimes false.

 a) A truth table for three statements has eight rows.
b) If P is false while Q is true then $P \vee \neg Q$ will be false.
c) The translations, in order, are $P \wedge Q$, $\neg P \wedge \neg Q$, $P \vee Q$, $\neg P \vee \neg Q$, and $\neg(P \wedge Q)$. Note that the last two statements actually mean the same thing.
d) "Don't sink and don't swim," or perhaps "Float."
e) It is impossible for P and $\neg P$ to both be true, hence $P \wedge \neg P$ will always be false.
f) The negation of a contradiction is a tautology.

EXERCISES

13. Let P be the statement "The cat is outside," let Q be the statement "The dog is outside," and let R be the statement "It is bright and sunny today." Translate the following statements into logical syntax.
a) The cat and dog are both inside, as it is raining today.
b) The cat is outside even though it is raining today.
c) At least one pet is outside on this sunny day.
d) It is not the case that the dog is outside in the sunshine.
e) The cat and dog are in different locations.

14. Establish that $\neg(P \wedge Q) \not\equiv \neg P \wedge Q$.

15. Consider the statements "It is not the case that I will run for president or stage a military coup," and "I will not run for president and I will not stage a military coup." Explain why these statements mean the same thing. Then translate both statements into compact logical notation.

16. Demonstrate that $\neg(P \vee Q) \equiv \neg P \wedge \neg Q$.

17. Negate each of the following statements.
a) Triangle ABC has a perimeter of 12 and an area of 6.
b) The number k is an integer such that k is even or $k \leq 10$.
c) I am older than Al but younger than Betty.
d) It is not the case that $2x < y$ and $2y < x$.
e) Jack will answer this question or the next one.
f) There is a new car behind at least one of the doors.

18. Which of the following gives a valid logical equivalent to $P \wedge (Q \vee R)$? Create a truth table to confirm that your choice is right. (Don't write out truth tables for the other two options, though.)

a) $P \wedge (Q \vee R) \equiv (P \wedge Q) \vee R$
b) $P \wedge (Q \vee R) \equiv (P \wedge Q) \vee (P \wedge R)$
c) $P \wedge (Q \vee R) \equiv (P \vee Q) \wedge (P \vee R)$

19. Create a truth table for the exclusive or operation "P XOR Q." Recall that this statement is true whenever exactly one of P and Q is true.

20. Write XOR in terms of OR, AND, NOT. In other words, create a statement involving only P, Q, $\vee$, $\wedge$, $\neg$, (, and) that is logically equivalent to "P XOR Q."

21. Show that the statement $P \wedge Q \vee R$ is ambiguous by demonstrating that the statements $(P \wedge Q) \vee R$ and $P \wedge (Q \vee R)$ are not logically equivalent.

22. Describe in words how to predict when the disjunction $P \vee Q \vee R$ is true. Then do the same for the conjunction $P \wedge Q \wedge R$.

23. Demonstrate that $(P \wedge \neg Q) \vee (\neg P \vee Q)$ is a tautology.

24. Verify that $((P \vee \neg Q) \wedge \neg R) \wedge (R \vee (Q \wedge \neg P))$ is a contradiction.

25. Suppose that statement P is a contradiction. Show that $(P \vee Q) \wedge (P \vee \neg Q)$ is also a contradiction.

WRITING

26. A father has 20 one dollar bills to distribute among his five sons. He declares that the oldest son will propose a scheme for dividing up the money and all five sons will vote on the plan. If a majority agree to the plan, then it will be implemented, otherwise dad will simply split the money evenly among his sons. Assume that all the sons act in a manner to maximize their monetary gain but will opt for evenly splitting the money, all else being equal. What proposal will the oldest son put forth, and why?

27. Imagine that in the scenario of the previous problem the father decides that after the oldest son's plan is unveiled, the second son will have the opportunity to propose a different division of funds. The sons will then vote on which plan they prefer. Assume that the sons still act to maximize their monetary gain, but will vote for the older son's plan if they stand to receive the same amount of money either way. What will transpire in this case, and why?

28. As part of an arithmetic exercise, Mr. Strump chooses two different digits from 1 to 9, tells Abby their product, then challenges Abby to figure out which two digits he has chosen. After a moment, Abby complains that there could be more than one answer. Realizing that she is correct, Mr. Strump helpfully mentions that the sum of the digits is not equal to 10. Abby is then able to correctly deduce the two digits. Explain how it is possible to precisely determine Mr. Strump's two digits based on this story.

1.3 The Implication

One of the aspects of mathematics that makes it such an exciting subject is the manner in which a given set of assumptions can lead to surprising or unexpected conclusions. For example, suppose that an ellipse is inscribed within a triangle, meaning that the ellipse is tangent to all three sides of the triangle. If we draw a segment joining each vertex of the triangle to the point of tangency on the opposite side as shown at right, then remarkably these three segments all intersect at a single point. This result is relatively simple to describe, but not nearly so easy to prove. The clearest explanation involves an operation on the diagram known as an affine transformation.

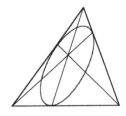

Or consider this delightful fact from number theory. Let $n \geq 2$ be a positive integer. Now multiply together all the numbers from $n-1$ down to 1 and then add 1 to the product. This quantity is written as $(n-1)! + 1$ in mathematical notation. If n is prime, the result will always be an exact multiple of n. For example, taking $n = 7$ we find that $6! + 1 = (6)(5)(4)(3)(2)(1) + 1 = 721$, which is a multiple of 7 as predicted. This result is known as Wilson's Theorem.

CONCEPT CHECK a) Confirm that Wilson's Theorem holds for $n = 3$ and $n = 5$.

Most mathematical results follow the format just described: if certain statements or conditions hold, then a result follows.

An **implication** has the form "If P then Q," where P and Q are statements or open sentences. We write $P \Rightarrow Q$ for short, and refer to P as the **hypothesis** or **premise**, whereas Q is known as the **conclusion**.

In practice, P encapsulates the facts we are given, while Q represents the result to be proved.

It is important to have a sound understanding of the logical meaning of implication, since it will inform the techniques we develop for proving mathematical statements. However, the implication has the potential to be confusing at first, for several reasons. To begin, there are many ways of expressing the implication in our language. Thus $P \Rightarrow Q$ can be written as "If P then Q" or "P implies Q" or "Q whenever P" or "Q follows from P," among many other possible ways to phrase this fundamental idea.

CONCEPT CHECK b) State the following implications in if-then form.
i. In order for photosynthesis to take place it is necessary to have light.
ii. We always have a great time when Laszlo comes over.
iii. For n^3 to be even it is sufficient for n to be a multiple of 6.

Another cause for the uncertainty that may accompany the implication is the fact that it is not immediately obvious how its truth table should be defined.

Of course, it makes sense that if P is true and the implication $P \Rightarrow Q$ is to hold, then Q must also be true. But other rows of the truth table would seem to be more debatable, at least on the surface. The following illustration will help to clarify the issue.

Suppose that Kate and Nate are playing a game of checkers. Nate promises that "If you beat me at checkers, then I will give you a chocolate bar." Let's consider each of four possible scenarios in turn and decide whether or not Nate has broken his promise.

- *Kate wins and Nate gives her a chocolate bar.*
  Clearly Nate has kept his promise, so his statement was true.

- *Kate wins but Nate does not give her a chocolate bar.*
  Just as clearly, Nate has broken his promise, thus his statement was false.

- *Kate loses but Nate gives her a chocolate bar anyway.*
  In this case Nate is being generous. (Perhaps he likes Kate.) At any rate, one can hardly claim that he has broken his promise.

- *Kate loses and Nate does not give her a chocolate bar.*
  Nate is not so generous here, but there are no grounds on which to accuse him of breaking his promise. Once again, his statement was valid.

Because of examples like the one above (and for various other good reasons), we define the truth table for $P \Rightarrow Q$ as shown at right. The final two rows are a bit counter-intuitive, where we declare that when P is false, the implication $P \Rightarrow Q$ is nonetheless true. These correspond to the final two scenarios above, in which we decided that Nate's statement was true, since he did not break his promise.

P	Q	$P \Rightarrow Q$
T	T	T
T	F	F
F	T	T
F	F	T

CONCEPT c) Consider the claim that "If quadrilateral $ABCD$ has right angles at vertices A and B, then it is a rectangle." Draw a quadrilateral which shows that this implication can be false. Which row of the truth table came into play?

When mathematical results are stated as implications they typically involve open sentences (i.e. one or more variables). This was the case for Wilson's Theorem mentioned earlier, which is restated below in several forms.

a. If n is prime, then $(n-1)! + 1$ is a multiple of n.

b. For all positive integers n, if n is prime then $(n-1)!+1$ is a multiple of n.

c. For all primes p, the number $(p-1)! + 1$ is a multiple of p.

The first version would seem to be adequate. Technically, though, this version is an open sentence, not a statement. Of course, it is understood that we are asserting that the implication is true for every positive integer n. Therefore a more precise wording is given by statement b. It is possible to streamline the wording without losing any of the meaning, as illustrated by the final version.

Mathematical Outing ★ ★ ★

Each of the four cards below has a digit printed on one side and a letter printed on the other side. Imagine that a classmate makes the assertion that "If there is a vowel on one side of a card then there is an odd number on the other side." Which cards *must* be turned over to check whether or not this is a true statement?

Now consider the following situation, concocted by psychologist Leda Cosmides and described by Malcolm Gladwell in his book *The Tipping Point*.

> Suppose four people are drinking in a bar. One is drinking Coke. One is sixteen. One is drinking beer and one is twenty-five. Given the rule that no one under twenty-one is allowed to drink beer, which of those people's IDs do we have to check to make sure the law is being observed?

If you felt that the first question was considerably harder than the second, you are not alone. But in fact they are equivalent puzzles. The point made by Gladwell is that as human beings most of us are hardwired to draw logical conclusions in relational as opposed to abstract contexts.

To convincingly argue that an implication such as the one above is true, we would in theory need to compute $(p-1)! + 1$ for each prime p and check that it is a multiple of p in every case. This is hardly feasible, since there are infinitely many primes. To circumvent this difficulty, mathematicians have developed general methods of argument that apply equally well to any prime. In this way a single proof can handle all the cases simultaneously. We shall develop some of these techniques in Chapter 4.

On the other hand, to demonstrate that such an implication is false, we need only find a single counterexample. According to our truth table, $P \Rightarrow Q$ fails to be true when P is true but Q is false. Therefore we should seek a value of the variable for which P holds but Q does not.

The **negation of the implication** "P implies Q" is given by "P and not Q." In symbolic notation we have $\neg(P \Rightarrow Q) \equiv P \wedge \neg Q$. Hence to find a counterexample to the statement "P implies Q," it suffices to find an instance for which P is true but Q is false.

CONCEPT d) State the negation of each implication.
i. If I eat another bite then I'll burst.
ii. If $(x-1)(x-3) = 3$ then $x-1 = 3$ or $x-3 = 3$.

Algebra instructors are accustomed to seeing claims such as "If $x^2 = 25$ then $x = 5$." This implication looks good, but is actually not always valid. To discover a counterexample, we must find a value of x for which the premise $x^2 = 25$ is true while the conclusion $x = 5$ is false. Put another way, we must find a value of x which satisfies the negation, which states that "$x^2 = 25$ and $x \neq 5$." The table below tests several values of x.

x-value	$x^2 = 25$	$x = 5$	$x^2 = 25 \Rightarrow x = 5$
$x = 5$	T	T	T
$x = 1$	F	F	T
$x = -5$	T	F	F

Therefore $x = -5$ provides a counterexample to the claim. This is the logical analysis behind the mistake known as overlooking a solution.[†]

CONCEPT e) For which value of x is the implication "If $(x-1)(x-3) = 3$ then $x-1 = 3$ or $x-3 = 3$" false?

a) For $n = 3$ we have $(2)(1) + 1 = 3$, which is divisible by 3. When $n = 5$ we have $(4)(3)(2)(1) + 1 = 25$, which is divisible by 5.
b) *i.* If photosynthesis takes place then light is present. *ii.* If Laszlo comes over then we have a great time. *iii.* If n is a multiple of 6 then n^3 is even.
c) One example would be a trapezoid having angles of $90°$, $90°$, $135°$, and $45°$, in that order. The second row of the table applies.
d) *i.* I ate another bite and I didn't burst. *ii.* We have $(x-1)(x-3) = 3$ and $x-1 \neq 3$ and $x-3 \neq 3$. (In other words, $(x-1)(x-3) = 3$ but $x \neq 4$ and $x \neq 6$.)
e) When $x = 0$ we have $(x-1)(x-3) = 3$, but neither $x-1 = 3$ nor $x-3 = 3$ holds.
▥ Two cards must be flipped over to verify the assertion: the E and the 2. (The latter because if there were a vowel on the reverse side then the assertion would be false.) Similarly, we must check IDs for the sixteen-year-old and the beer drinker.

EXERCISES

29. Write the following implications in "If P then Q" form.
a) When it rains, it pours.
b) I'll try escargot only if Al eats some first.
c) That a is even follows from the fact that $7a$ is even.
d) In order to start a fire it is necessary to light a match.
e) For triangle ABC to be isosceles it is sufficient to have $\angle A \cong \angle B$.
f) A positive discriminant implies that a quadratic has two distinct solutions.

30. Experimentation suggests that if p is a prime then $2^p - 1$ is also a prime. What would be required to show that this implication can be false?

31. Create a statement that is logically equivalent to $P \Rightarrow Q$ using only the symbols P, Q, $\wedge$, $\vee$, $\neg$. (Not necessarily all of them.)

32. Validate the definition of the negation of an implication by verifying that $\neg(P \Rightarrow Q) \equiv P \wedge \neg Q$ is a logical equivalence.

33. Write out the negation of each of the following implications.
a) If Cinderella marries the prince then I'll eat my hat.
b) If a^2 is divisible by 12 then a is even or a is a multiple of 3.
c) Quadrilateral $ABCD$ is a square whenever it has four congruent sides.
d) To bake bread it is necessary to use flour, water and yeast.

34. Let P and Q be the open sentences "$7n + 1$ is a perfect cube" and "n is a perfect square," respectively. Find positive integer values for n for which
    a) P and Q are both true,   b) P and Q are both false,
    c) P is true while Q is false,   d) P is false while Q is true.
In which cases is the implication $P \Rightarrow Q$ true?

35. For what value of x is the implication "If $|x - 3| = 1$ then $|x - 2| = 2$" false?

36. Find all values of y for which the implication "If $y < 2$ then $y^2 < 4$" is true. (In particular, note that it is *not* true for all values of y; in other words, squaring an inequality is not a valid algebraic step.)

37. In plain English, what does $(P \wedge (P \Rightarrow Q)) \Rightarrow Q$ say? This rule of inference in propositional logic is known as *modus ponens*. Construct a truth table for this statement. How does the truth table demonstrate that *modus ponens* is a valid rule of inference?

38. Repeat the previous exercise for $((P \Rightarrow Q) \wedge (Q \Rightarrow R)) \Rightarrow (P \Rightarrow R)$. This is another staple rule of inference in propositional logic, known as syllogism.

WRITING

While the following problems are not directly related to the material presented in this section, they represent a selection of classic problems with which every student should be familiar.

39. Six students get together to study for a math exam. Each pair of students are either acquainted with one another or else are unacquainted. Prove that it is possible to find three of the students all of whom are acquainted with one another, or else all of whom are unacquainted.

40. Seven mathematicians get together for a dinner party. Prove that it is not possible for each mathematician to shake hands with exactly three others.

41. Suppose that eight people attend a math mixer. Prove that if each person shakes hands with some (possible none) of the other guests, and no pair of individuals shakes hands more than once, then there must exist two guests who shook the same total number of hands.

1.4   The Biconditional

Let us return to the case of the student faced with the equation $x^2 = 25$. Imagine that instead of just writing $x = 5$, this student gave their answer as $x = 5, -5$ or 0; in other words, included an extraneous solution. We justifiably feel that this response should not receive full credit because $x = 0$ does not solve the equation. More precisely, a number should appear in the list of solutions *if* it satisfies $x^2 = 25$, which requires that we include both $x = 5$ and $x = -5$, but also *only if* it satisfies the equation, which rules out all other numbers.

A statement of the form "*P* if and only if *Q*," is a **biconditional**. For convenience, the phrase "if and only if" is often shortened to just **iff**. A biconditional essentially declares that two statements are **equivalent**, meaning that one statement is true exactly when the other is.

Incidentally, the popular abbreviation "iff" was invented by Paul Halmos, a beloved writer who is best known among budding mathematicians for his book *I Want to Be a Mathematician*.

CONCEPT CHECK   a) The following statements illustrate some of the different ways that the biconditional can be expressed. Determine a suitable way to complete each sentence to create valid statements.

i. A triangle has three congruent angles exactly when it has...

ii. For an integer n, a necessary and sufficient condition for n to be both odd and 1 greater than a multiple of 3 is that...

iii. That a real number x satisfies $x^2 < 4$ is equivalent to...

iv. Pigs can fly if and only if...

Since a biconditional asserts that one statement is true exactly when the other is true, the truth table for a biconditional has the entries shown at left.

P	Q	$P \Longleftrightarrow Q$
T	T	T
T	F	F
F	T	F
F	F	T

Although not immediately obvious, one way to express the notion that two statements P and Q are equivalent is to require that each statement imply the other. This explains the genesis of the term 'biconditional,' since the validity of each statement is conditional upon the validity of the other. It also explains the notation $P \Longleftrightarrow Q$ used for the biconditional—it's a combination of $P \Rightarrow Q$ and $P \Leftarrow Q$. This fundamental connection between implication and equivalence can be established by means of a truth table, as will be done in the exercises.

Whenever we discover that one statement implies another, it is natural to wonder whether the implication is true in the other direction.

The implication $Q \Rightarrow P$ is known as the **converse** of $P \Rightarrow Q$.

Mathematical Outing ★ ★ ★

We discovered earlier that when n is a prime the quantity $(n-1)! + 1$ is divisible by n. Let's see what happens when n is not a prime. Compute $(n-1)! + 1$ for $n = 6$, 8 and 9. What do you notice? Make a conjecture based on your findings. Does it appear that the given expression is divisible by n if and only if n is prime?

The next few questions will help to explain the pattern you just noticed. What would you predict will be the remainder when $47! + 1$ is divided by 48? Explain why your prediction should be true. Then repeat this exercise for the case in which $48! + 1$ is divided by 49.

CONCEPT b) Using if-then form, state the converse of each implication.
i. My flight is delayed whenever I reach the airport early.
ii. The angle measure $m\angle ACB = 90°$ implies that $(AC)^2 + (BC)^2 = (AB)^2$.

It is a common mistake to assume that just because an implication is true, then its converse will also be true. In reality, the converse is sometimes true and sometimes false; it depends on the particular implication under consideration. For example, we all know that a square has four sides of equal length. This can be phrased as an implication by saying "If quadrilateral $ABCD$ is a square, then it has four congruent sides." As mathematicians, we should immediately ask ourselves whether it is also true that "If $ABCD$ has four congruent sides, then it is a square." A moment's thought reveals that the converse if false, since a rhombus (diamond) has four sides of equal length but is not a square. We conclude that "$ABCD$ is a square" and "$ABCD$ has four congruent sides" are *not* equivalent statements.†

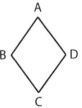

We are also familiar with the fact that if a positive integer a is even, then a^2 will also be even. The converse of this implication would read, "For any positive integer a, if a^2 is even then a is also even." In this case both the original statement and the converse happen to be true. According to our earlier discussion, we may now conclude that a is even if and only if a^2 is even. In general, whenever a statement and its converse are both true we have a pair of equivalent statements.

ALL THE ANSWERS a) *i.* ...when it has three congruent sides. *ii.* ...is that n is 1 greater than a multiple of 6. *iii.* ...is equivalent to $-2 < x < 2$. *iv.* ...elephants can jump (or any other situation that never occurs).
b) *i.* If my flight is delayed, then I reached the airport early. *ii.* If we have the equality $(AC)^2 + (BC)^2 = (AB)^2$ then $m\angle ACB = 90°$.
🕮 The value of $(n-1)! + 1$ is equal to 121, 5041 and 40321 when $n = 6$, 8 and 9. In each case the number is 1 more than a multiple of n, rather than equal to a multiple of n. Hence it appears that $(n-1)! + 1$ is divisible by n iff n is prime.

It makes sense that 47! would be a multiple of 48, since the product includes both 6 and 8. So adding 1 yields a number that is not a multiple of 48. Similarly, 48! is a multiple of 49 since this product includes 7 and 14.

Exercises

42. Briefly explain why these biconditional statements are true or false.
a) A necessary and sufficient condition for a triangle to have two congruent sides is for it to have two congruent angles.
b) For x a real number, $x^2 + x - 2 = 0$ if and only if $x = 1$ or $x = 2$.
c) Let a and b be positive integers. Then ab is a multiple of 10 exactly when a is a multiple of 10 or b is a multiple of 10.
d) We have that $x \neq y$ is equivalent to $x^2 \neq y^2$ for real numbers x and y.
e) A positive integer is divisible by 3 iff its reverse is. (The 'reverse' is obtained by writing the digits in the opposite order.)

43. Let P and Q be open sentences involving the variable x. What would a counterexample to the claim "For all x we have P iff Q," look like?

44. Create a truth table for the statement $(P \Rightarrow Q) \wedge (Q \Rightarrow P)$ and confirm that it is identical to the one given above for $P \Longleftrightarrow Q$.

45. Are the statements $(P \vee Q) \Longleftrightarrow R$ and $(P \Longleftrightarrow R) \vee (Q \Longleftrightarrow R)$ logically equivalent? Why or why not?

46. Write the converse of the following implications.
a) Let n be an integer. If n is not a multiple of 3, then $n^2 + 5$ is a multiple of 3.
b) When two rectangles are congruent it follows that they have the same area.
c) For positive real numbers x and y, if $x \geq y$ then $1/x \leq 1/y$.
d) Let R and L be points to the right and left of the y-axis, respectively. If line RL has positive y-intercept, then R is in quadrant I and L is in quadrant II.
e) For positive integers a and b, the number $a + b$ involves the digit 0 whenever both a and b use the digit 0.

47. For each of the implications in the previous problem, determine whether the implication is true or false and then decide whether its converse is true or false. Consequently, in which instances do we have a pair of equivalent statements?

48. Let P and Q be statements. Show that either $P \Rightarrow Q$ or its converse is true.

49. Show that the statements $Q \Rightarrow P$ and $\neg P \Rightarrow \neg Q$ are logically equivalent. Hence an equivalent way to state the converse of "P implies Q" is "not P implies not Q." (The statement $\neg P \Rightarrow \neg Q$ is known as the **inverse** of $P \Rightarrow Q$.)

50. Write out the inverse of each implication below. Which statement do you find to be more clear, the inverse or the converse?
a) Let k be a positive integer. If $3^k + 1$ is not a multiple of 4 then k is even.
b) Quadrilateral $ABCD$ is a square whenever it has four congruent sides.
c) For a real number a, the equation $2^x = a$ has no solution if a is not positive.

WRITING

51. The game of Snatch involves two players who take turns removing either 1, 2, 3 or 4 pennies from a pile of pennies. The winner is the player to take the last penny. Depending on the number n of pennies in the pile, the player about to move can either be guaranteed of eventually taking the last penny (a winning position) or cannot prevent the other player from doing so (a losing position). Which values of n constitute a losing position for the person about to play? Begin your answer with "A pile of n pennies represents a losing position if and only if n is..." Then explain why your answer is correct.

52. Suppose instead that in the game of Snatch players may only remove 1, 3 or 4 pennies on each turn. Now which values of n constitute a losing position? Write your answer and explanation as before.

FURTHER EXPLORATION

53. There are many possible ways to modify the game of Snatch. For instance, one might allow the players to remove 1, 2, 4, 8, 16, ... pennies on each turn. Or one might have two separate piles, with the stipulation that from 1 to 4 pennies may be removed, but only from one of the piles. Invent your own variation of Snatch and analyze your game by carefully describing the winning and losing positions and justifying your description.

1.5 Quantifiers

We briefly discussed quantified statement in the first section. At that point we were interested in positive integer values of n for which $n^2 + 2$ was a multiple of 3 or $3n + 7$ was a perfect square. Naturally we were curious as to how many values of n met these conditions. All values of n? At least one value of n? Exactly one value of n? No values of n?

> A phrase that indicates the number of values of a variable satisfying an open sentence is known as a **quantifier**. The two most common such phrases are the **universal quantifier** "for all x" ($\forall x$) and the **existential quantifier** "there exists an x" ($\exists x$).

Quantifiers are an indispensable part of our mathematical vocabulary. For example, theorems often assert that some result holds for all values of a variable. This is understood to be the case even when the phrase 'for all' is omitted. Thus it is the case that if $2^n - 1$ is a prime, then n itself must be a prime. A more precise rendering of this fact would state "For all positive integers n, if $2^n - 1$ is prime then n itself is prime." (Primes of the form $2^n - 1$ are known as *Mersenne primes*. The largest known primes are of this form. As of this writing the current record-holder is $2^{43,112,609} - 1$, a number having over ten million digits.)

Although the concept of quantified statements is intuitively clear, it takes some careful thought to keep track of what happens when we negate a quantified statement or analyze statements containing two variables and two quantifiers.

QUERY a) Determine a statement which asserts the exact opposite of the quantified statement "For every positive integer n, $n^2 - n + 41$ is prime."

An appealing but incorrect way to phrase the negative would be "For every positive integer n, it is the case that $n^2 - n + 41$ is not prime." The reason that this option does not suffice is that it swings from one extreme to the other rather than encompassing all possibilities not covered by the original statement. The given statement claims that there are no exceptions to the rule that $n^2 - n + 41$ is prime. The opposite stance would be that there is an exception to this rule; in other words, there does exist a value of n for which $n^2 - n + 41$ is not prime. (Observe that this is a considerably less stringent condition than requiring that $n^2 - n + 41$ is not prime for all n.)

> The **negation of a quantified statement** of the form "For all x, we have P," can be written as "There exists an x such that $\neg P$." Similarly, the negation of the statement "There exists an x such that P," takes the form "For all x, we have $\neg P$."

The negation of an existential quantifier might also be written "There does not exist x such that P." However, this is generally not as useful a way to convey the opposite meaning. Also, if P happens to be a conjunction, disjunction or implication one must also take care to write $\neg P$ correctly.

CONCEPT b) Write the negation of the statement "There exists a real number x such that $|x + 3| \le 1$ and $|x - 4| \le 2$."

A third quantifier occurs regularly in mathematical discussions, although perhaps not quite as frequently as the universal and existential quantifiers just discussed. It is the phrase 'there exists a unique,' also indicated by writing 'there is one and only one.' Uniqueness is one of the most elegant and appealing characteristics in mathematics. For instance, given a triangle, there exists a unique circle within the triangle that is tangent to all three sides, as illustrated at right. Or given any positive integer n, there is one and only one way to write n as a product of primes.

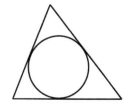

CONCEPT c) Given any three points in the plane, is it true that there exists a unique circle passing through all three points?

As a brief illustration, we argue that there is a unique solution to the equation $(x+4)(x-2) = -9$. This is because rearranging and factoring the given equation leads to $(x + 1)^2 = 0$. Clearly $x = -1$ is the one and only solution.

Mathematical Outing ★ ★ ★

Self-referential statements are a recipe for trouble when it comes to logical consistency. Consider

P_1) The other statement is true.
P_2) The other statement is false.

There is no consistent way to assign a truth value to each of these statements. For if P_1 is true then P_2 will be true, which means that P_1 is false, a contradiction. Likewise, if P_1 is false then P_2 will be also, implying that P_1 is true after all, so we again reach a contradiction.

Self-referential statements can form the basis for entertaining logic puzzles, though. See if you can deduce the unique way of assigning truth values to the following five statements in a logically consistent manner, and consequently determine whether or not I like spaghetti and meatballs.

P_1) I like spaghetti and meatballs.
P_2) All odd-numbered statements are false.
P_3) All even-numbered statements are true.
P_4) At least one of P_2 or P_3 is true.
P_5) If P_1 is false then P_2 is true.

The situation becomes even more exciting for open sentences involving two or more variables, since we can quantify each variable separately. For instance, Bertrand's Postulate states that for all positive integers $n \geq 2$, there exists a prime p between n and $2n$. It is important to understand that these quantifiers are *nested*, meaning that the second one ("there exists a prime p") falls within the scope of the first one ("For all positive integers $n \geq 2$"). We first select any permissible value of n, say $n = 13$. We are then guaranteed a prime between n and $2n$; in this case, between 13 and 26. Sure enough, such a prime does exist. In fact, there are a total of three such primes, namely $p = 17$, 19, and 23.

C⅁ᴺC⅁ᴾᵀ d) Confirm that Bertrand's Postulate holds for $n = 2, 3, \ldots, 10$.

The structure of Bertrand's Postulate is "For all $n \geq 2$, we have P," where P itself is the quantified statement "There exists a prime p such that Q," and Q is the statement "p is between n and $2n$." Identifying this structure permits us to determine the negation of the result. We begin by writing "There exists an $n \geq 2$ such that $\neg P$." The negation of P is "For all primes p we have $\neg Q$." Finally, the negation of Q is "p is not between n and $2n$." Putting this all together and writing the result smoothly, the negation states that "There exists an integer $n \geq 2$ such that there are no primes p between n and $2n$."

QUᴵᶜᴷᴱᴿʸ e) To appreciate how crucial the order of quantifiers can be, consider the claim "There exists a prime p such that for all integers $n \geq 2$ the prime p lies between n and $2n$." Is the new statement true? Why or why not?

The order in which quantifiers appear does not matter when they are of the same type. Thus we could claim that for all real numbers x, it is the case that for all real numbers y the quantity $(x - y)^2$ is positive. The meaning would remain unchanged if we were to place the "for all y" quantifier ahead of the "for all x" quantifier. Because of this fact, the given statement is usually shortened to just "For all real numbers x and y, we have $(x - y)^2 > 0$." In the same manner, rather than writing "There exists a positive integer m for which there is a positive integer n such that $m^2 + mn + n^2$ is a perfect square," we typically combine the two existential quantifiers to obtain "There exist positive integers m and n such that $m^2 + mn + n^2$ is a perfect square."

Finally, note that when the universal quantifier is applied to an implication, it makes sense to consider quantifying the converse of the implication. For instance, we claimed earlier that for all positive integers n, if $2^n - 1$ is prime then n is also prime. Quantifying the converse would read "For all n, if n is prime then $2^n - 1$ is also prime." If both of these statements were true, we could conclude that "For all n, $2^n - 1$ is prime if and only if n is prime." As one of the exercises will reveal, the converse does not hold for all values of n, so the statements "$2^n - 1$ is prime" and "n is prime" are not equivalent.

a) There is a positive integer n such that $n^2 - n + 41$ is not prime.
b) Every real number x satisfies $|x + 3| > 1$ or $|x - 4| > 2$.
c) No, it is not always true. If the three points are situated along a line, then there is no circle that passes through all three of them.
d) In each case there is a prime between n and $2n$.
e) The new statement is false; there is no such prime. Thus $p = 23$ won't do because 23 does not lie between n and $2n$ for all n—certainly not for $n = 10$, for instance.
▦ If P_3 is true then P_2 will be also, which leads to a contradiction. Hence P_3 is false. Now if P_4 is true then P_2 is also, contradicting the fact that P_3 is false. Thus P_4 is also false, which means that P_2 is false. Now suppose that P_1 is false. This would make P_5 false also, which contradicts P_2. So P_1 is true, hence P_5 is also. When the dust settles, it turns out that I do like spaghetti and meatballs.

EXERCISES

54. Determine the most accurate way to quantify each open sentence. Choose from among for all, there exists, there exists a unique, or there does not exist. Rewrite each quantified statement so that it reads nicely.

a) _____ (integer n): n contains every odd digit.
b) _____ (real number x): $x^2 + 4x + 5 = 0$.
c) _____ (point C): C lies on the lines $y = x$ and $y = 3x - 5$.
d) _____ (real number t): $|t - 4| \leq 3$ and $|t + 5| \leq 6$.
e) _____ (integer k): the number $6k + 5$ is odd.
f) _____ (point U): the distance from U to the origin is positive.

55. Find the negation of "There exists a real number x such that $\cos x = 3x$." Employ the universal quantifier in your statement.

56. Determine the negation of "For all positive integers n, if n is prime, then $2^n - 1$ is prime." Then find a value for n that satisfies your negation.

57. Write down the negation of the assertion "If $f(x)$ is a linear function then $f(1) + f(2) = f(3)$." Now use the linear function $f(x) = 2x + 5$ to show that the negation is true.

58. Decide whether or not it is true that given fixed points A and B, there exists a unique square having these points as two of its vertices.

59. Find the value of a for which the equation $(x - 3)(x + 5) = a$ has a unique solution; i.e. is satisfied by a unique real number x.

60. Determine the negation of the statement "For all rectangles in the plane there exists a circle inside the rectangle that is tangent to all four sides."

61. Consider the claim "For all real numbers x there exists a real number y such that $y > x$." Is this claim true or false? Explain.

62. Now consider the closely related claim "There exists a real number y such that for all real numbers x we have $y > x$." Is this claim true or false? Explain.

63. Write the negation of "There exists a positive integer N such that for all integers $n > N$ we have $\cos n < 0.99$."

64. Consider the statement "For all real numbers x and y, we have $(x - y)^2 > 0$." Is this assertion true or false?

65. Show that there exist positive integers m and n such that $m^2 + mn + n^2$ is a perfect square.

66. Let P and Q be open sentences involving a variable m. Suppose that it is the case that "There exists an integer m such that $P \Rightarrow Q$," and it is also true that "There exists an integer m such that $Q \Rightarrow P$." Does it necessarily follow that the statement "There exists an integer m such that $P \Longleftrightarrow Q$" is true?

WRITING

67. Show that for every positive integer a there exists a positive integer b such that $ab + 1$ is a perfect square.

68. Prove that for all positive real numbers r there exists a rectangle whose area is equal to r and whose perimeter is greater than $4r$.

69. Demonstrate that there exists an infinitely long path in the plane, starting at the origin, such that from any point (x, y) in the plane one can reach the path by moving a total distance of less than one unit.

70. Prove that there exists a polynomial of the form $f(n) = n^2 + bn + c$, where b and c are positive integers, such that $f(n)$ is composite (i.e. not prime) for all positive integers n.

71. Explain why given a finite collection of three or more points in the plane, no three of which are collinear, there exists a triangle having three of the points as its vertices, which contains none of the other points in its interior.

1.6 Reference

The purpose of this section is to provide a condensed summary of the most important facts and techniques from this chapter, as a reference when studying or working on material from later chapters.

• *Vocabulary* statement, truth value, open sentence, domain, disjunction, conjunction, truth table, negation, logically equivalent, DeMorgan's Laws, tautology, contradiction, implication, hypothesis, premise, conclusion, biconditional, iff, equivalent statements, converse, inverse, universal/existential quantifier

• *Compound statements* A statement is a mathematical sentence that is either true or false, while an open sentence is an assertion involving one or more variables. Given statements or open sentences P, Q we may form their conjunction $P \wedge Q$ ("P and Q"), their disjunction $P \vee Q$ ("P or Q"), the implication $P \Rightarrow Q$ ("P implies Q"), its converse $Q \Rightarrow P$ ("Q implies P"), its inverse $\neg P \Rightarrow \neg Q$, and the biconditional $P \Longleftrightarrow Q$ ("P if and only if Q").

• *Truth tables* A truth table contains one row for each possible set of truth values of its components. For complicated statements, create several columns to determine the truth value of each part of the statement first. Two statements are logically equivalent if they have identical truth tables. A tautology is a statement that is true in every case while a contradiction is false in every case.

• *Implication* The statement P implies Q may be expressed as Q whenever P, Q follows from P, when P we have Q, for P it is necessary to have Q, or P is sufficient for Q. This implication is true unless P is true while Q is false. The converse is written Q implies P. If an implication and its converse are both true then the component statements are equivalent, meaning that each is true or false exactly when the other is; in this case we say P if and only if Q.

• *Quantified statements* An open sentence contains variables. By inserting a quantifier such as 'For all' (universal quantifier $\forall$) or 'There exists' (existential quantifier $\exists$) or 'There exists a unique' ($\exists!$) or 'There does not exist' ($\nexists$) we obtain a statement. The statement "For all x there exists a y such that..." has a different meaning than "There exists a y such that for all x..."

• *Negation* The table below indicates how to negate a variety of statements.

Statement	Negation
P and Q	$\neg P$ or $\neg Q$
P or Q	$\neg P$ and $\neg Q$
if P then Q	P and $\neg Q$
for all x we have P	there exists x such that $\neg P$
there exists x such that P	for all x we have $\neg P$

Furthermore, the negation of "For all x there exists a y such that P," is written "There exists an x such that for all y we have $\neg P$." Similarly, the negation of the statement "There exists an x such that for all y we have P," is written "For all x there exists a y such that $\neg P$.

Sample Proofs

The following proofs provide concise explanations for results discussed within this chapter. They are meant to serve as an illustration for how proofs of similar statements could be phrased. The boldface numbers indicate the section containing each result; the location of that result within the section is marked by a dagger (†).

———◆———

1.1 Show that the following assertion is false: "For all positive integers n, it is the case that $n^2 + 2$ is a multiple of 3 or that $3n + 7$ is a perfect square."

Proof We exhibit a counterexample to show that the given assertion is false. Taking $n = 9$ we find that $n^2 + 2 = 83$, which is not a multiple of 3. Furthermore $3n + 7 = 34$, which is not a perfect square. Therefore it is not the case that $n^2 + 2$ is a multiple of 3 or that $3n + 7$ is a perfect square for all positive integers n.

———◆———

1.2 Show that the statements $\neg(P \wedge Q)$ and $\neg P \vee \neg Q$ are logically equivalent.

Proof To show that these statements are logically equivalent we construct a truth table for each, shown below.

P	Q	$P \wedge Q$	$\neg(P \wedge Q)$	$\neg P$	$\neg Q$	$\neg P \vee \neg Q$
T	T	T	F	F	F	F
T	F	F	T	F	T	T
F	T	F	T	T	F	T
F	F	F	T	T	T	T

Since the truth values for the two statements match in every case, they are logically equivalent.

———◆———

1.3 Explain why the implication "For all x, if $x^2 = 25$ then $x = 5$" is false.

Proof We will demonstrate a value of x for which the hypothesis is true but the conclusion is false. Consider $x = -5$; in this case $x^2 = 25$ holds, but $x = 5$ does not. Therefore this implication is not valid for all real numbers x.

———◆———

1.4 Determine whether the claim "If $ABCD$ is a square then $ABCD$ has four congruent sides" is true, whether the converse is true, and whether we have a pair a equivalent statements.

Proof We know from elementary geometry that a square has four congruent sides, so the given implication is true. The converse asserts that "If $ABCD$ has four congruent sides then $ABCD$ is a square." This claim is false, since a rhombus (diamond) has four congruent sides but is not a square. Therefore the two statements are not equivalent, since they do not each imply the other.

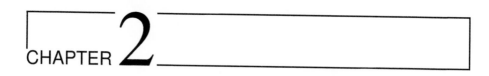

CHAPTER 2

Set Theory

2.1 Presenting Sets

Certain notions which we all take for granted are harder to define precisely than one might expect. In *Taming the Infinite: The Story of Mathematics,* Ian Stewart describes the situation in this way:

> The meaning of 'number' is a surprisingly difficult conceptual and philosophical problem. It is made all the more frustrating by the fact that we all know perfectly well how to use numbers. We know how they behave, but not what they are.

He goes on to outline Gottlob Frege's approach to putting the whole numbers on a firm footing. Thus one might define the concept of 'two' via the collection of all sets containing two objects. However, this practice of considering all sets satisfying a certain condition cannot be applied indiscriminately, as philosopher-mathematician Bertrand Russell subsequently pointed out. In the Mathematical Outing on the next page you will consider "Russell's paradox," which highlights the potential problems with Frege's approach.

We will be content with a relatively informal definition of a set.

A **set** is any unordered collection of distinct objects. These objects are called the **elements** or members of the set. The set containing no elements is known as the **empty set**.

A set may have finitely many elements, such as the set of desks in a classroom; or infinitely many members, such as the set of positive integers; or possibly no elements at all. The members of a set can be practically any objects imaginable, as long as they are clearly defined. Thus a set might contain numbers, letters,

Mathematical Outing ★ ★ ★

To obtain a sense of the sorts of pitfalls awaiting set theorists, consider the following classic paradox. In a certain town there is a single barber, who shaves exactly those men who do not shave themselves. Who shaves the barber? Try to appreciate the logical paradox that arises in this description of the barber, then find the clever trick answer that circumvents the paradox.

In a similar manner we could define a set which contains exactly those sets which do not contain themselves. Why does this lead to a logical inconsistency? And how is it possible for a set to contain itself in the first place?

polynomials, points, colors, or even other sets. In theory a set could contain any combination of these objects, but in practice we tend to only consider sets whose elements are related to one another in some way, such as the set of letters in your name, or the set of even numbers. As in the previous chapter, we will confine ourselves mainly to mathematical objects and examples.

We typically name sets using upper case letters, such as A, B or C. There are a variety of ways to describe the elements of a set, each of which has advantages. We could give a verbal description of a set, for example, by declaring that B is the set of letters in the title of this book. We might also simply list the elements of a set within curly brackets:

$$B = \{b, r, i, d, g, e, t, o, h, i, g, h, e, r, m, a, t, h\}.$$

Recall that a set only catalogs distinct objects, so the appearance of the second letter g is redundant and should be omitted, and similarly for other repeated letters. An equivalent but more appropriate list of the letters in this set is

$$B = \{b, r, i, d, g, e, t, o, h, a, m\}.$$

Since the order in which elements is listed is irrelevant, we could also write

$$B = \{a, b, d, e, g, h, i, m, o, r, t\} \quad \text{or} \quad B = \{m, o, t, h, b, r, i, g, a, d, e\}.$$

For a given set, it is natural to ask which objects are included in the set and how many objects there are in total. We indicate membership in or exclusion from a set using the symbols $\in$ and $\notin$. Thus it would be fair to say that $a \in B$ and $g \in B$, but $z \notin B$ and $\star \notin B$ either. We also write $|B|$ to indicate the size, or **cardinality** of set B. In the example above we have $|B| = 11$, of course. For the time being we will only consider the cardinality of finite sets.

CONCEPT a) What can we say about set A if $x \notin A$ for all objects x?

CONCEPT b) Think of a five letter word with the property that $|B| = 3$, where B is the set of letters appearing in your word.

Listing the elements of a set has its drawbacks when the set contains infinitely many members. However, when the pattern is clear it is acceptable to list the first four or five elements, followed by an ellipsis (...). Thus the set of all positive odd integers is $\{1, 3, 5, 7, \ldots\}$. The empty set can also be written using curly brackets as { }. However, this special set arises so frequently that it has been assigned its own symbol, which is $\emptyset$.

CONCEPT c) Let C be the set of positive integers which only contain the digits 3 or 4. List the elements of C using an ellipsis.

Another standard method for presenting a set is to provide a mathematical characterization of the elements in the set. Suppose we wish to refer to the set of all real numbers greater than 5. The following notation, which we shall call **bar notation** for lack of a more imaginative term, achieves this quite efficiently. Using the symbol $\mathbb{R}$ for the set of all real numbers, we could write

$$A = \{x \mid x \in \mathbb{R} \text{ and } x > 5\}.$$

The actual element (in this case a number x) is placed to the left of the bar, while the description (x is a real number greater than 5) appears to the right of the bar. A literal translation would be "A is the set of all x such that x is a real number and x is greater than 5." A less clunky rendition might read "Let A be the set of all real numbers greater than 5." Observe that x is only used internally in the definition of set A; it does not refer to anything beyond. Thus we would obtain the same result by defining $A = \{w \mid w \in \mathbb{R} \text{ and } w > 5\}$.

CONCEPT d) Let A be the set of all real numbers between 5 and 6, including 5 but not 6. Describe A with bar notation, using the variable y.

There is often more than one way to employ bar notation to describe a set. For example, suppose that B is the set of perfect squares. We could think of the elements of B as *numbers,* each of which is the square of an integer, in which case we would write $B = \{n \mid n = k^2, \ k \in \mathbb{Z}\}$. Or we might decide that the elements of B are *squares,* such that the number being squared is an integer. This interpretation leads to $B = \{n^2 \mid n \in \mathbb{Z}\}$. The latter approach is preferable in many ways, but either is correct.

CONCEPT e) Find two different ways to present the set C of all odd integers using bar notation.

Certain sets of numbers, such as the real numbers $\mathbb{R}$, are referred to regularly enough to merit their own special symbol. Other standard sets include the integers $\mathbb{Z}$, the positive integers $\mathbb{N}$ (also called the natural numbers), the rational numbers $\mathbb{Q}$ (the set of all fractions), and the complex numbers $\mathbb{C}$. Recall that a complex number is formed by adding a real number to a real multiple of i, where $i = \sqrt{-1}$. Thus we could write

$$\mathbb{C} = \{a + bi \mid a, b \in \mathbb{R}\}.$$

In case you were wondering, the letter $\mathbb{Z}$ for 'integers' comes to us compliments of the German root word *zahl,* meaning 'number.'

a) Set A must be the empty set: $A = \emptyset$.

b) Possible answers include radar, geese, queue or mommy.

c) $C = \{3, 4, 33, 34, 43, 44, 333, 334, \ldots\}$. It is probably a good idea to list at least seven elements of this set before the ellipsis, to make the pattern clear.

d) We could write $A = \{y \mid y \in \mathbb{R},\ 5 \le y < 6\}$.

e) Either $C = \{n \mid n = 2k + 1,\ k \in \mathbb{Z}\}$ or $C = \{2n + 1 \mid n \in \mathbb{N}\}$ will work, although the latter is more concise.

It appears at first that the question cannot be answered. If the barber shaves himself, then he is shaving a man who shaves himself, contrary to his job description. On the other hand, if he does not shave himself, then he neglects his mandate to shave all men who don't shave themselves. The way out of this quandary, of course, is to realize that the barber is a woman!

There is no similar clever fix for Russell's paradox, though. Our set S contains itself or it doesn't; either situation contradicts the definition of the set. However, it is possible for a set to contain itself. For instance, let $A = \{1, \{1, \{1, \{1, \ldots\}\}\}\}$. Then $A = \{1, A\}$. There are infinitely many nested sets in this example, although each set contains only two elements—the number 1 and the set A.

EXERCISES

1. What is the set of colors appearing on both the American flag and the Jamaican flag?

2. Give a verbal description of the set $\{1, 4, 8, 9, 16, 25, 27, 32, 36, \ldots\}$. (In other words, find the rule that determines which numbers are included on this list.)

3. Give a verbal description of the set {January, March, May, July, August, October, December}.

4. Give an example of a set B for which $|B| = 3$ and the elements of B are polynomials having even coefficients.

5. Give an example of a set C with $|C| = 2$ such that the elements of C are sets each of which contain four letters.

6. Let D be the set whose elements are equal to the product of two consecutive natural numbers, such as $12 = 3 \cdot 4$. Present set D using a list and also via bar notation. Which method is better suited for this set?

7. Briefly justify why the following statements are true or false.

a) If A is the set of letters in the word 'flabbergasted,' then $|A| = 13$.

b) For the set A in the previous part, we have $a \in A$ or $z \in A$.

c) If $B = \{n \mid n \in \mathbb{Z},\ 10 \le n \le 20\}$ then $|B| = 10$.

d) For the set B in the previous part we have $11 \in B$ and $\sqrt{200} \in B$.

e) If L is the set of letters in your full legal name, then $a \in L$.

f) Let $C = \{x \mid x \in \mathbb{R},\ x^2 \le 10\}$. If $\pi \notin C$ then $-3 \notin C$.

8. How many sets A are there for which $|A| = 5$ and the elements of A are states in New England?

9. Describe the following sets using bar notation.

a) A is the set of all integers divisible by 7

b) $B = \{3, 5, 9, 17, 33, 65, \cdots\}$

c) C is the set of all real numbers between $\sqrt{2}$ and π

d) $D = \{\frac{1}{2}, \frac{1}{3}, \frac{1}{4}, \frac{1}{5}, \ldots\}$

10. Using bar notation, describe the set of rational numbers between 0 and 1. Then describe the set of positive rationals whose denominator is a power of 2, such as $\frac{7}{2}$, $\frac{3}{4}$, 5 or $\frac{1}{16}$. (The powers of 2 are 1, 2, 4, 8, ...)

11. Consider the set $\{y = m(x - 1) \mid m \in \mathbb{R}\}$. Give a verbal description of the sorts of objects that are elements of this set.

12. Let $B = \{2m + 5n \mid m, n \in \mathbb{N}\}$. Is $10 \in B$? Is $13 \in B$? Explain.

WRITING

13. Let A be a set with $|A| \geq 3$, all of whose elements are integers. Show that one can find distinct elements $m, n \in A$ such that $m - n$ is even.

14. Let A, B and C be different sets containing letters of the alphabet. Explain why there must exist some letter that is either contained in exactly one of the sets or contained in exactly two of the sets.

15. Prove that it is impossible to split the natural numbers into sets A and B such that for distinct elements $m, n \in A$ we have $m + n \in B$ and vice-versa.

16. Set C consists of the thirty-six points of the form (a, b) where a and b are integers with $0 \leq a, b \leq 5$. Prove that no matter how we select five points from set C, two of them will be situated a distance of $2\sqrt{2}$ or less apart.

2.2 Combining Sets

Membership in the exclusive $\Delta\Pi$ club is not for everyone. Only those people whose first and last names both begin with the letter D and whose birthday is 3/14 are permitted to join. In other words, the $\Delta\Pi$ club is only interested in those rare individuals common to both categories. Lately the club president, Daphney Daly, has suggested that in order to boost the club's dwindling enrollment, membership restrictions should be relaxed to allow individuals in either category to apply. These two approaches to membership requirements correspond in a natural way to the two most basic means of combining sets.

> The set of elements common to two given sets A and B is known as their **intersection** and written as $A \cap B$. The set of elements appearing in at least one of these sets is called the **union**, denoted by $A \cup B$.

QUICK ERY a) Decide which elements ought to belong to each of $A \cup B \cup C$ and $A \cap B \cap C$. Then write a compact description of each set using bar notation.

| Mathematical Outing | ★ ★ ★

Imagine that a certain math class consists of both
male and female students, some of whom reside in
New York while others come from out of state. All
students are currently seated. You are permitted
to request that all the students within some broad category (boys, girls, in-state
or out-of-state) stand up. You may also ask all male students, or all female
students, to reverse their position by standing if they are currently seated or
vice-versa. However, you may not give instructions such as "All boys please
sit," or "All girls from out of state please stand." Figure out how to arrange
for the following sets of students to stand while all others are seated.

- All students who are either female or from out of state.

- All female students who are from New York.

- All students who are either female and from New York or male and from
  out of state.

Note that the set operation of intersection corresponds to the logical operation of conjunction. This relationship is made clear by the fact that

$$A \cap B = \{x \mid x \in A \text{ and } x \in B\}.$$

Similarly union corresponds to the logical operation of disjunction, since

$$A \cup B = \{x \mid x \in A \text{ or } x \in B\}.$$

Notice the resemblance between the symbols $\cap$, $\wedge$ and $\cup$, $\vee$ as well.

[CONCEPT] b) Suppose that $x \in A \cup B \cup C$ but $x \notin A \cap B \cap C$. Consequently,
how many of the sets A, B or C must x be an element of?

It would stand to reason that the set operation corresponding to NOT would
involve creating a new set consisting of all objects not contained in a set A. Some
care needs to be exercised here, though. For instance, if A is the set of students
registered for our course who are sophomores, then objects
not contained in A include the governor of Maine, the color
orange, and a golden retriever named Izzy, among many
other things. What we really have in mind when we imagine
"not A" is the set of all students who are *registered for
our course* who are not sophomores. There is a **universal
set** lurking in the background that indicates the set of all
objects under consideration; in our case, students registered
for this course. Working within a universal set also helps
to dodge the paradoxes implicit in dealing with "the set of all sets."

With this in mind, let U be a universal set, and let A be a set whose elements all belong to U. Then the **complement** of set A, denoted by $\overline{A}$, is comprised of all elements of U which are not in A. (The set $\overline{A}$ is sometimes referred to as the complement of A in U.) The universal set is often understood from context. Thus if B is the set of real numbers less than 5, then $\overline{B} = \{x \mid x \in \mathbb{R},\ x \geq 5\}$. It would be almost redundant to declare that U is the set of real numbers.

CONCEPT CHECK c) For any set A and universal set U, what is the complement of the complement of A?

CONCEPT CHECK d) Suppose that U is the English alphabet, $A = \{m, a, i, n, e\}$ and $B = \{w, y, o, m, i, n, g\}$. Compute $|A \cup B|$ and $|A \cap \overline{B}|$.

It is also standard practice to omit any reference to the universal set when discussing statements such as $\overline{A \cap B} = \overline{A} \cup \overline{B}$. It is assumed that the elements of A and B belong to a larger universal set in which all the action takes place.

The stage is almost set for our first major set theoretic result. However, before attempting it we need a strategy for showing that two sets are equal.

> We say that A and B are **equal sets**, written $A = B$, if these two sets contain precisely the same elements. One common technique for showing that two sets are equal is to show that every element of the first set must be an element of the second set, and vice-versa.

We employ this strategy to establish the **set identity** $\overline{A \cap B} = \overline{A} \cup \overline{B}$.

Step one: Let x be any element of the first set; i.e. let $x \in \overline{A \cap B}$. This means that $x \notin A \cap B$. Since $A \cap B$ consists of elements in both A and B, if x is not in the intersection then either $x \notin A$ or $x \notin B$, or both. In other words, $x \in \overline{A}$ or $x \in \overline{B}$, which means that $x \in \overline{A} \cup \overline{B}$.

Step two: On the other hand, if $x \in \overline{A} \cup \overline{B}$ then we know that $x \in \overline{A}$ or $x \in \overline{B}$, which means that $x \notin A$ or $x \notin B$. Since x is missing from at least one of the sets A or B, it cannot reside in their intersection, hence $x \notin A \cap B$. Finally, this is the same as $x \in \overline{A \cap B}$. Hence we conclude that the sets $\overline{A \cap B}$ and $\overline{A} \cup \overline{B}$ are indeed equal.[†]

You may have noticed that the steps in this paragraph were essentially the same as the steps in the previous paragraph, just in the opposite order. This will sometimes be the case, but more often it will not, especially as we tackle more sophisticated set identities.

There is a rather convenient means of picturing unions, intersections and complements of sets which greatly clarifies set identities such as $\overline{A \cap B} = \overline{A} \cup \overline{B}$. A **Venn diagram** for two sets A and B is shown below. Given an arbitrary element x of the universal set, there are four ways that x could be (or not be) a member of set A and set B. These possibilities correspond to the four regions in the Venn diagram. For example, we might have $x \notin A$ but $x \in B$, which corresponds to region *III*. Various combinations of these regions represent different sets. Thus set A is made up of regions *I* and *II*, while $A \cap B$ consists of region *II* alone. The remaining figures below illustrate how to shade in the portion of the Venn diagram corresponding to the sets $\overline{A \cap B}$, $\overline{A}$ and $\overline{B}$. It now becomes clear that $\overline{A} \cup \overline{B}$ will be identical to $\overline{A \cap B}$, so we conclude that these two sets are equal.

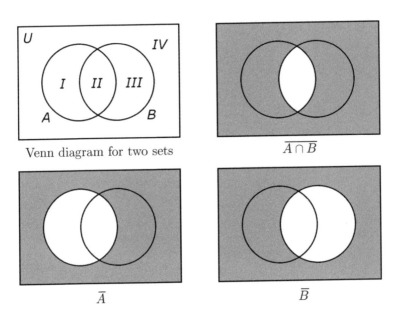

Venn diagram for two sets $\overline{A \cap B}$

$\overline{A}$ $\overline{B}$

A Venn diagram for three sets is shown at right, with the region corresponding to the set $(A \cup B) \cap C$ shaded. Because a Venn diagram for two or three sets includes regions for every possible combination of membership in the sets, they provide a rigorous means of confirming identities involving two or three sets. In other words, the pictures above (if presented in a more organized manner) serve to establish that $\overline{A \cap B} = \overline{A} \cup \overline{B}$ just as adequately as the two-paragraph proof that preceded them. For our purposes we will declare that the technique of Venn diagrams is valid as long as there are three or fewer sets involved, which are combined using only union, intersection, and complements.

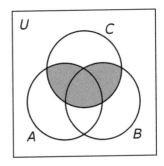

CᴏɴCᴇᴘᴛ e) How many regions does a Venn diagram for three sets have?

CᴏɴCᴇᴘᴛ f) Shade in the set $A \cup (B \cap C)$ in a Venn diagram for three sets. Compare it to the Venn diagram for $(A \cup B) \cap C$ above. What can you conclude based on these pictures?

a) We have that $A \cup B \cup C = \{x \mid x \in A \text{ or } x \in B \text{ or } x \in C\}$ and $A \cap B \cap C = \{x \mid x \in A \text{ and } x \in B \text{ and } x \in C\}$.

b) It is the case that x belongs to exactly one or two of A, B, C.

c) The answer is the original set A.

d) We have $|A \cup B| = 9$ and $|A \cap \overline{B}| = 2$.

e) A three-set Venn diagram has eight regions.

f) The Venn diagram for $A \cup (B \cap C)$ will resemble the one pictured for $(A \cup B) \cap C$, except that the remaining regions within set A will also be shaded in. Hence these two sets are not equal in general.

• In the first scenario, simply have the female students rise, then ask the out of staters to rise. • For the second situation, ask the boys to stand, request that the out-of-state students also stand, then have all boys and all girls reverse positions. • In the third case have the New Yorkers rise, then have all the boys reverse positions.

EXERCISES

17. Let A and B be the sets of students in a certain class who are sophomores and who are from New York, respectively. Write an expression that represents the set of students who are sophomores or who come from outside New York.

18. Define a universal set $U = \{a, b, c, d, e, f, g, h\}$. Using these elements, construct two sets A and B satisfying $|A| = 5$, $|B| = 4$ and $|A \cap B| = 2$. Using the sets you chose, compute $|\overline{A} \cap \overline{B}|$.

19. Why is it not possible for two sets to satisfy both $A \cap B = \{f, o, u, r\}$ and $A \cup B = \{f, o, r, t, y, s, i, x\}$?

20. Given the universal set $U = \{a, b, c, \ldots, z\}$, we define $A = \{b, r, i, d, g, e\}$, $B = \{f, o, r, t, y, s, i, x\}$ and $C = \{s, u, b, z, e, r, o\}$. Decide whether the following statements are true or false.

a) $|A \cup C| = 10$

b) $B \cap \overline{B} = \emptyset$

c) $|B \cup \overline{C}| = 23$

d) $(A \cup B) \cap C = \{s, o, b, e, r\}$

e) $|(A \cap B) \cup (B \cap C)| = 5$

f) $\overline{A} \cap \overline{B} \cap \overline{C} = \{a, c, h, j, k, l, m, n, p, q, v, w, y\}$

g) $|A \cup B \cup C| = 15$

21. Let $A = \{x \mid 1 < x < 3\}$, $B = \{x \mid 5 \leq x \leq 7\}$ and $C = \{x \mid 2 < x < 6\}$, where x represents a real number. Determine the sets $A \cup C$, $(A \cup B) \cap C$ and $B \cap \overline{C}$, writing your answers in bar notation.

22. List the four possible ways that x could be (or not be) an element of two given sets A and B. In each case identify the corresponding region in the labelled Venn diagram within this section.

23. Use Venn diagrams to prove that $\overline{A \cap B \cap C} = \overline{A} \cup \overline{B} \cup \overline{C}$.

24. Use Venn diagrams to prove that $A \cap (B \cup C) = (A \cap B) \cup (A \cap C)$.

WRITING

25. Explain why our set equality strategy is valid. In other words, prove that if every element of a set A is contained in another set B and vice-versa, then the two sets must contain precisely the same elements.

26. Without appealing to a Venn diagram, demonstrate that $\overline{A \cup B} = \overline{A} \cap \overline{B}$.

27. Without appealing to a Venn diagram, prove that for any three sets A, B and C we have $A \cup (B \cap C) = (A \cup B) \cap (A \cup C)$.

28. Prove that $\overline{A_1 \cap A_2 \cap A_3 \cap A_4} = \overline{A}_1 \cup \overline{A}_2 \cup \overline{A}_3 \cup \overline{A}_4$.

29. Let A and B be sets within the universal set $U = \{a, b, c, \ldots, z\}$. Working from the definitions, explain why $|\overline{A \cup B}| = 26 - |A| - |B| + |A \cap B|$.

30. Prove that $|A \cup B| + |A \cup C| + |B \cup C| \le |A| + |B| + |C| + |A \cup B \cup C|$ for any three finite sets A, B and C.

FURTHER EXPLORATION

31. Draw a configuration of four circles within a rectangle that creates as many regions as possible. Confirm that it is impossible to obtain the requisite sixteen regions necessary for a complete Venn diagram of four sets. Then figure out a way to create a Venn diagram for four sets using elliptical regions.

2.3   Subsets and Power Sets

We now introduce several concepts which concern the extent to which elements of one set are members of another set. At one extreme, it may be the case that *all* the elements of a set A also belong to another set B. At the other extreme, it could also be the case that *none* of the elements of A are contained in B.

Given sets A and B, whenever each element of A is also an element of B we say that A is a **subset** of B and write $A \subseteq B$. Therefore to prove that $A \subseteq B$ one must show that if $x \in A$, then $x \in B$.

On the other hand, if A and B have no elements in common then they are **disjoint**, which can be proved by showing that if $x \in A$ then $x \notin B$.

It makes sense that if A is a subset of B, then B contains A. More formally, we say that B is a **superset** of A, denoted by $B \supseteq A$. However, this perspective (and associated notation) arises fairly infrequently.

CONCEPT a) Give an example of two sets which are neither disjoint nor subsets of one another.

CONCEPT b) What can be said about sets A and B if we have $A \cap B = \emptyset$? if we have $A \cap B = A$? if we have $A \cap B = B$?

Mathematical Outing ★ ★ ★

According to the definition of subset, should the empty set be counted as a subset of $C_2 = \{1, 2\}$? Decide whether the definition supports an answer of yes or no before going on. The other three subsets are clearly $\{1\}$, $\{2\}$ and $\{1, 2\}$, so depending upon your answer, you would conclude that there are either three or four subsets of C_2.

Now list all the subsets of $C_1 = \{1\}$, $C_3 = \{1, 2, 3\}$ and $C_4 = \{1, 2, 3, 4\}$ and look for a pattern among the numbers of such subsets. Which decision regarding the empty set leads to a nicer, more natural answer? Based on your pattern, how many subsets will $C_n = \{1, 2, \ldots, n\}$ have?

To highlight the process by which we begin crafting a proof, let us show that if $A \subseteq B \cap \overline{C}$ then $C \subseteq \overline{A}$. There are two subsets here, so where do we begin? The key is to focus on the statement to be proved; namely, $C \subseteq \overline{A}$. (This is the part following the word 'then' in an if-then statement; i.e. the conclusion of the implication.) So we should apply our set inclusion strategy to $C \subseteq \overline{A}$: we begin by supposing that $x \in C$ and will attempt to prove that $x \in \overline{A}$.

QUICK QUERY c) Create a Venn diagram of two sets B and C, then draw set A inside $B \cap \overline{C}$. From the picture, is it feasible that $C \subseteq \overline{A}$?

Drawing on the intuition gained by the Venn diagram just constructed, we realize that since $x \in C$ it follows that $x \notin \overline{C}$. Hence by definition of intersection, $x \notin B \cap \overline{C}$ either. We can now make the key deduction in the proof: since x is outside the set $B \cap \overline{C}$ but all of A is contained within $B \cap \overline{C}$, we know that $x \notin A$. This means that $x \in \overline{A}$. Since $x \in C$ implies $x \in \overline{A}$ we may conclude that $C \subseteq \overline{A}$, as desired.[†]

CONCEPT CHECK d) Can you touch your tongue and your nose?

A set is considered to be a subset of itself, so it is true that $A \subseteq A$, in the same way that it is correct to write $5 \leq 5$. But should the empty set be counted as a subset of A? The definition requires that every element of $\emptyset$ be contained in A, but there are no elements of $\emptyset$ to which we may apply this condition. Technically, we say that the condition is *vacuously* satisfied. The Mathematical Outing above might provide a more compelling reason to declare that $\emptyset \subseteq A$.

At times we may wish to exclude the option of taking the empty set as a subset; in this case we use language like "Let A be a **nonempty** subset of B." On the other hand, to rule out the option of selecting all of B as a subset, we would say "Let A be a **proper subset** of B." We indicate this by writing $A \subset B$, in the same way that we use $<$ rather than $\leq$ when the two objects being compared are not permitted to be equal.

CONCEPT CHECK e) How many subsets of $\{1, 2, 3\}$ are both nonempty and proper?

As an illustration, let $A = \{2, 4, 6, 8, \ldots\}$ be the set of even natural numbers, let $B = \{1, 2, 4, 8, \ldots\}$ list the powers of 2, and let $C = \{6, 12, 18, 24, \ldots\}$ contain the multiples of six. Comparing the elements within the various sets, we quickly realize that every multiple of six is even but not vice-versa, hence $C \subset A$. In addition, no multiple of 6 is a power of 2, hence B and C are disjoint; that is, $B \cap C = \emptyset$. There is a single power of 2 that is odd, which is enough to prevent B from being a subset of A, a fact which may be conveyed succinctly as $B \not\subseteq A$. Deleting all the even numbers from set B singles out the lone offending odd number, which is 1.

> Removing all elements from a set B that belong to another set A creates a new set: the **set difference** $B - A$.

Therefore we may write $B - A = \{1\}$ for the sets described above. Alternately, we might consider $A - B = \{6, 10, 12, 14, 18, \ldots\}$, the even numbers that are not

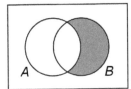

powers of 2. Note that it is not necessary for one set to be a subset of another to form their set difference. In general, a set difference $B - A$ may be described as "all B that are not A." A Venn diagram for the difference $B - A$ is shown at left. From this diagram it becomes clear that we may also define $B - A$ as $\overline{A} \cap B$.

CONCEPT CHECK f) Using the sets defined above, describe the set $A - C$ verbally and also list its elements using curly brackets and an ellipsis.

CONCEPT CHECK g) Suppose that for certain sets A, B and X we have $X \subseteq B - A$. What is the relationship between X and A? between X and B?

The collection of all subsets of A can be assembled into a single larger set.

> We define the **power set** $\mathcal{P}(A)$ of a set A to be the set of all subsets of A, including the empty set and the set A itself.

The motivation for this terminology stems from the fact that when A is a finite set, there are exactly $2^{|A|}$ subsets, so the cardinality of $\mathcal{P}(A)$ is a power of 2. To explain this phenomenon, imagine building a subset of A. There are two choices available for the first element of A: either include it in our subset or leave it out. Regardless of our decision, we are now faced with the same two possibilities for the second element—either include it in our subset or leave it out. Continuing this reasoning for each element of A, we find that there are $(2)(2) \cdots (2) = 2^{|A|}$ ways to build a subset of A, as claimed.

The power set of A is a set whose elements are themselves sets, which takes some getting used to. For starters, one has to pay attention not to mix up the symbols $\in$ and $\subseteq$. Thus if $A = \{b, a, l, o, n, e, y\}$ then it would be appropriate to write $\{n, o, e, l\} \subseteq A$, but not $\{n, o, e, l\} \subseteq \mathcal{P}(A)$. Since the subsets of A are *elements* of $\mathcal{P}(A)$, we should instead write $\{n, o, e, l\} \in \mathcal{P}(A)$. A subset of $\mathcal{P}(A)$ would look like $\{\{n, o, b, l, e\}, \{b, a, y\}\}$, for instance.

CᴏɴCᴇᴘᴛ h) For the set $A = \{b, a, l, o, n, e, y\}$, write down a subset of $\mathcal{P}(A)$ having three elements that are pairwise disjoint, but whose union is all of A.

QUɪᴄᴋ i) Let $A = \{c, d, e\}$ and let $B = \{a, b, c, d\}$. Determine the sets contained in $\mathcal{P}(B - A)$ and the sets contained in $\mathcal{P}(B) - \mathcal{P}(A)$.

Suppose that A and B are nonempty sets. As a slightly intricate but very instructive example, let us demonstrate that every element of the power set $\mathcal{P}(B - A)$ is contained in $\mathcal{P}(B) - \mathcal{P}(A)$, with one exception. In other words, we will show that $\mathcal{P}(B - A)$ is almost a subset of $\mathcal{P}(B) - \mathcal{P}(A)$. The exception is the empty set, for $\emptyset \in \mathcal{P}(B - A)$ but $\emptyset \notin \mathcal{P}(B) - \mathcal{P}(A)$. It is true that $\emptyset \in \mathcal{P}(B)$, but $\emptyset \in \mathcal{P}(A)$ as well, so it is removed when we subtract $\mathcal{P}(A)$.

Now let X be a non-empty subset of $B - A$, so that $X \in \mathcal{P}(B - A)$. (We write X instead of x, since we are referring to a set instead of an element.) We will show that $X \in \mathcal{P}(B) - \mathcal{P}(A)$ as well. Since $X \subseteq B - A$, each element of X is a member of B but not of A. In other words, X is a subset of B, but X and A are disjoint. It follows that $X \in \mathcal{P}(B)$ since $X \subseteq B$. But clearly $X \notin \mathcal{P}(A)$ since the elements of X are not in A. (Here is where we use the fact that X is non-empty.) So when we subtract $\mathcal{P}(A)$ from $\mathcal{P}(B)$, the element X of $\mathcal{P}(B)$ is not removed. Hence $X \in \mathcal{P}(B) - \mathcal{P}(A)$, as claimed.[†]

Aʟʟ ᴛʜᴇ Aɴsᴡᴇʀs a) The sets $\{m, a, i, n, e\}$ and $\{t, e, x, a, s\}$, for instance.
b) We have A and B disjoint, $A \subseteq B$, and $B \subseteq A$, respectively.
c) Assuming that the circle representing B is on the left, draw a smaller circle for A within the left circle but outside the right circle.
d) Of course you can! Just extend your hand so that one finger touches your tongue and another finger touches your nose. The point of this seemingly irrelevant exercise is to highlight the fact that we often use and interpret the word AND in a careless manner. If you tried to curl your tongue upwards to accomplish this activity, you were trying to touch your tongue *to* your nose.

In the same way, it is easy to slip up by attempting to prove that $C \subseteq \overline{A}$ by writing "Suppose that $x \in C$ and $x \in \overline{A}$." But a conjunction is logically quite different from an implication, dooming this proof from the outset. So be careful to phrase a set inclusion proof as an implication—"We wish to show that if $x \in C$ then $x \in \overline{A}$."
e) Six subsets of $\{1, 2, 3\}$ are both nonempty and proper.
f) The set $A - C$ consists of positive even numbers that are not multiples of 6, namely the numbers $\{2, 4, 8, 10, 14, \ldots\}$.
g) This means that X is a subset of B and that X and A are disjoint.
h) One answer could be $\{\{b, o, y\}, \{a, l, e\}, \{n\}\}$.
i) The sets $\{a, b\}$, $\{a\}$, $\{b\}$, $\emptyset$ make up $\mathcal{P}(B - A)$. On the other hand, $\mathcal{P}(B) - \mathcal{P}(A)$ consists of all sixteen subsets of B except for $\{c, d\}$, $\{c\}$, $\{d\}$, $\emptyset$.
▥ If we include the empty set, the subsets of C_3 are $\emptyset$, $\{1\}$, $\{2\}$, $\{3\}$, $\{1, 2\}$, $\{1, 3\}$, $\{2, 3\}$ and $\{1, 2, 3\}$. In this fashion we find that the number of subsets of C_1 to C_4 are 2, 4, 8 and 16 when we include the empty set. These powers of 2 are much more appealing than the alternative, which suggests that $\emptyset \subseteq C_2$ should be true. Including the empty set, there are 2^n subsets of C_n.

Exercises

32. Let $A = \{f, l, a, t\}$. To remove the letter l, do we write $A - l$ or $A - \{l\}$?

33. Suppose that $A \subseteq B$. What is the relationship between sets $\overline{A}$ and $\overline{B}$?

34. If A is a proper subset of B then what can be said of the set $B - A$?

35. Would it be correct to assert that $\emptyset \subseteq \mathcal{P}(A)$? Does it make sense to write $\emptyset \in \mathcal{P}(A)$? What is the difference between these two statements?

36. Let $A = \{x \mid -1 < x < 1\}$, $B = \{x \mid -2 \le x \le 2\}$ and $C = \{x \mid -2 < x < 3\}$, where $x \in \mathbb{R}$. Determine whether the following statements are true or false.
a) $A \subseteq B$ and $B \subseteq C$
b) $\overline{C} \subseteq \overline{B}$ or $\overline{B} \subseteq \overline{A}$
c) $A - C$ is the empty set
d) $C - B = \{x \mid x = -2 \text{ or } 2 < x < 3\}$
e) $\overline{A}$ and B are disjoint

37. Construct two finite sets A and B such that $|B| = 7$, $|A| = 5$ and $|B - A| = 4$. (Your example shows that in general $|B - A| \ne |B| - |A|$.)

38. Suppose that sets A and B satisfy $|A| = 101$, $|B| = 88$ and $|B - A| = 31$. Determine $|A - B|$. (HINT: Use a Venn diagram.)

39. Let $A = \{g, n, a, r, l, y\}$. What is the only set that is both a subset of A and disjoint from A?

40. Let $B = \{b, r, i, d, g, e\}$. How many nonempty subsets of B are disjoint from the set $\{s, t, r, e, a, m\}$?

41. If $C = \{s, a, t, i, n\}$, then how many sets $D \in \mathcal{P}(C)$ satisfy $|D| = 2$?

42. Suppose that $A = \{b, i, s, m, a, r, c\}$. How many subsets of A contain m?

43. Given sets $B = \{t, u, r, k, e, y\}$ and $A = \{b, r, u, t, e\}$, compute $|\mathcal{P}(B) - \mathcal{P}(A)|$.

Writing

44. For sets A and B, show that $A \cap B$ and $B - A$ are disjoint. Give a written proof that does not rely on a Venn diagram.

45. Given sets A, B and C, explain why $\overline{B \cup C}$ and $(A \cap B) \cup C$ are disjoint. Do not rely on a Venn diagram in your proof.

46. Prove that $(A \cup B) \cap C \subseteq A \cup (B \cap C)$. Give a written proof that does not rely on a Venn diagram, and also illustrate this result with a Venn diagram.

47. Prove that $(A - B) - C \subseteq A - (B - C)$. Give a written proof that does not rely on a Venn diagram, and also illustrate this result with a Venn diagram.

48. Demonstrate that if $B \subseteq C$ then $A \cup \overline{C} \subseteq A \cup \overline{B}$.

49. Suppose that A, B and C are sets such that $A - B \subseteq C$. Show that in this case $\overline{C} \subseteq \overline{A} \cup B$. Do not rely on a Venn diagram in your proof.

50. For sets A and B, explain why $\mathcal{P}(A) \cup \mathcal{P}(B) \subseteq \mathcal{P}(A \cup B)$.

51. For sets A and B, prove that $\mathcal{P}(A) \cap \mathcal{P}(B) = \mathcal{P}(A \cap B)$.

52. Establish that $\mathcal{P}(B) - \mathcal{P}(A) = \mathcal{P}(B) - \mathcal{P}(A \cap B)$ for any sets A and B.

53. Let C be a set of Halloween candies. Suppose that Aaron helps himself to some (possibly none) of the candies, and then Betty does the same with what remains. (There may well be candies left over at the end of this process.) Prove that there are $3^{|C|}$ ways for the candy distribution to take place.

2.4 Cartesian Products

It is not at all unusual for a single object, mathematical or otherwise, to have two or more numbers associated with it. For instance, at each visit a pediatrician will record both a child's height in inches and his weight in pounds. This information can be succinctly presented as an ordered pair of numbers, as in $(42, 57)$ for a solid seven-year old. We can think of the 42 as an element from the set of all possible heights, and the 57 as an element from the set of all possible weights.

Given two sets A and B, their **Cartesian product** $A \times B$ is the set consisting of all **ordered pairs** (a, b) with $a \in A$ and $b \in B$. When A and B are both finite sets, we have $|A \times B| = |A| \cdot |B|$.

Perhaps the most familiar example of a Cartesian product is the set of points in the Cartesian plane. Such a point has an x-coordinate and a y-coordinate, which are presented as the ordered pair (x, y). Each coordinate is a real number, so the Cartesian plane is the product $\mathbb{R} \times \mathbb{R}$, sometimes written as $\mathbb{R}^2$ for short.

Anyone who has played a game of Battleship has dealt with a Cartesian product. The square game board is divided into a grid, with rows labelled 'A' through 'J' and columns numbered 1 to 10. Each location on the board is referred to by a letter and a number, as in "Is (C,7) a hit?" From a mathematical perspective, the locations on the game board represent the Cartesian product of the sets $A = \{A, B, C, D, E, F, G, H, I, J\}$ and $B = \{1, 2, 3, 4, 5, 6, 7, 8, 9, 10\}$. The elements of this Cartesian product are the pairs

$$(A, 1) \quad (A, 2) \quad (A, 3) \quad \cdots \quad (J, 9) \quad (J, 10).$$

These ordered pairs are arranged in a 10×10 grid, so there are 100 of them, which agrees with the fact that $|A \times B| = |A| \cdot |B| = 10 \cdot 10 = 100$.

CᴼᴺCᴱᴾᵀ a) Let $A = \{10, 20, 30\}$ and let $B = \{1, 2, 3, 4\}$. Find an organized way to list all the elements of $A \times B$. Based on your list, why does it make sense that $|A \times B| = |A| \cdot |B|$?

Mathematical Outing ⋆ ⋆ ⋆

The game of PairMission is played using the ordered pairs of a Cartesian product. To begin, two players select disjoint finite sets A and B, such as $A = \{a, b, c, d\}$ and $B = \{1, 2, 3\}$. The players alternate turns writing down ordered pairs in a column, with the rule that a play is "pairmissible" as long as the letter and number in the pair have not *both* been used earlier in the game. The winner is the last person able to write down a legal ordered pair. For example, the sequence of moves

$$(a, 2)\ (b, 2)\ (a, 3)\ (c, 2)$$

is possible. The first player could now win the game by writing down $(d, 1)$, since there are no further legal moves.

Play a few rounds of PairMission to get a feel for the game. How can one quickly ascertain whether the game is over? Now explain how the first player can guarantee a win when $A = \{a, b, c\}$ and $B = \{1, 2, 3\}$. Then demonstrate that the second player can force a win for $A = \{a, b, c, d\}$ and $B = \{1, 2, 3\}$. After analyzing a few more games, make a conjecture concerning which player has a winning strategy for any pair of sets A and B.

To reinforce these ideas, suppose now that $A = \{x \in \mathbb{R} \mid 3 \leq x \leq 6\}$ and $B = \{y \in \mathbb{R} \mid 1 \leq y \leq 8\}$. Then $A \times B$ would consist of all ordered pairs (x, y) of real numbers for which $3 \leq x \leq 6$ and $1 \leq y \leq 8$. The most natural way to visualize the collection of all such ordered pairs is as a subset of the Cartesian plane. The points (x, y) in $A \times B$ constitute a solid rectangle with width 3 and height 7, pictured in the diagram.

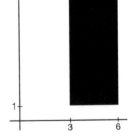

CHECK CONCEPT b) Use a diagram to help illustrate why the assertion $(A \times C) \cup (B \times D) = (A \cup B) \times (C \cup D)$ is false. How could one modify the left-hand side to create a valid set identity?

To indicate the sorts of steps needed to prove a statement about Cartesian products, we will show that $(A \times C) \cup (B \times D) \subseteq (A \cup B) \times (C \cup D)$. We must show that every element of the first set is also a member of the second one. But now the sets are Cartesian products, so we represent a generic element as (x, y) rather than just x. Thus we suppose that $(x, y) \in (A \times C) \cup (B \times D)$. This means that either $(x, y) \in (A \times C)$ or $(x, y) \in (B \times D)$, so we must consider two separate cases. On the one hand, if $(x, y) \in (A \times C)$ then by definition $x \in A$ and $y \in C$. But since $x \in A$ then clearly $x \in A \cup B$, and similarly $y \in C$ implies that $y \in C \cup D$. Therefore $(x, y) \in (A \cup B) \times (C \cup D)$. The case where $(x, y) \in (B \times D)$ is entirely analogous, so we are done.[†]

QUICK QUERY c) Suppose that $A = \{1, 2\}$ and $B = \{1, 2, 3\}$. Write out the elements of $A \times B$ and $B \times A$. Do we obtain the same ordered pairs in each case? In other words, is $A \times B = B \times A$?

Since the order in which elements are listed in an ordered pair matters, in general it is not the case that $A \times B$ and $B \times A$ are the same set. However, in a few special cases these two Cartesian products do consist of exactly the same set of ordered pairs. The first possibility is that $B = \emptyset$, for in this case both $A \times B$ and $B \times A$ are the empty set.

QUICK QUERY d) Why is it the case that if $B = \emptyset$ then $A \times B = \emptyset$ as well?

By the same reasoning, both Cartesian products are empty when $A = \emptyset$ as well.

If both A and B are nonempty, there is only one other way to ensure that $A \times B = B \times A$. To discover what this condition might be, let's take any elements $x \in A$ and $y \in B$. (This is possible since neither A nor B are the empty set.) So we would have $(x, y) \in A \times B$. But since $A \times B = B \times A$, we could then write $(x, y) \in B \times A$, which means that $x \in B$ and $y \in A$. In summary, we deduce that if x is any element of A then $x \in B$ also, and furthermore that if y is any element of B then $y \in A$. But this is exactly our criteria for showing that two sets are equal, so we conclude that we must have $A = B$. Clearly this condition works, for both sides of $A \times B = B \times A$ reduce to just $A \times A$.

By the way, taking the Cartesian product of a set with itself is a fairly common occurrence in mathematics; we have already seen one example above when we wrote the plane as $\mathbb{R} \times \mathbb{R}$. The set $A \times A$ will also play an important role when we discuss relations and functions in a later chapter.

 ALL THE ANSWERS a) List all the ordered pairs in a three by four table. The top row would contain $(10, 1)$ $(10, 2)$ $(10, 3)$ $(10, 4)$, and so on.

b) Replace the left-hand side by including two extra Cartesian products in the union: $(A \times C) \cup (A \times D) \cup (B \times C) \cup (B \times D)$.

c) The ordered pairs are not identical; for instance, $(1, 3) \in A \times B$ but $(1, 3) \notin B \times A$. Thus $A \times B \neq B \times A$ for these sets.

d) If there are no elements in B, then there is no way to create an ordered pair (x, y) with $y \in B$.

The game is over as soon as all available letters and numbers appear at least once somewhere in the list of moves. When $A = \{a, b, c\}$ and $B = \{1, 2, 3\}$, suppose the first player writes down $(a, 1)$. If the second player matches neither of these characters, say by playing $(b, 3)$, then the first player should take the remaining two characters, which are $(c, 2)$ to win the game. However, if the second player does match one of the characters, say by playing $(b, 1)$, then the first player should continue to match that character by playing $(c, 1)$. The game must now last for exactly two more moves, causing the first player to win in this scenario as well.

Analysis of the game with $A = \{a, b, c, d\}$ and $B = \{1, 2, 3\}$ is left to the reader. In general, it turns out that the second player has a winning strategy if at least one of $|A|$ and $|B|$ is even, while the first player can always win if both $|A|$ and $|B|$ are odd. (Can you figure out the winning strategies?) Finally, try to find a nice way to represent this game by putting markers on a rectangular grid whose rows are labeled with the letters in A and whose columns are labeled by the numbers in B.

EXERCISES

54. What can we deduce about sets A and B if $A \times B = \emptyset$?

55. Write the definition of the Cartesian product $A \times B$ using bar notation.

56. Explain how a standard deck of cards illustrates a Cartesian product.

57. Let $U = \{1, 2, \ldots, 9\}$ be the universal set, and let $A = \{n \mid n \in U, \ n \text{ is odd}\}$ and $B = \{n \mid n \in U, \ n \text{ is a perfect square}\}$. Compute the cardinality of
   a) $U \times U$ d) $\overline{A \times B}$
   b) $A \times B$ e) $(A \cup B) \times (A \cap B)$
   c) $\overline{A} \times \overline{B}$ f) $(A - B) \times (\overline{B} - \overline{A})$

58. Do you believe that $\overline{A \times B} = \overline{A} \times \overline{B}$ based on your answers to the previous exercise? Why or why not?

59. Let S be the subset $\{(x, y) \mid x^2 + 2y^2 = 10\}$ of $\mathbb{R}^2$. What is the common name for this mathematically defined set?

60. Suppose $C = \{w \mid 1 \le w \le 3\}$ and $D = \{w \mid 2 \le w \le 5\}$. Then $C \times D$ is a subset of the Cartesian plane $\mathbb{R} \times \mathbb{R}$.
a) Sketch the region corresponding to $C \times D$ and describe its shape.
b) Draw the subset $D \times C$ on the same set of axes.
c) Use your diagram to determine $(C \times D) \cap (D \times C)$.

61. Define the sets $A = \{s, c, a, m, p, e, r\}$, $B = \{p, r, a, n, c, e\}$, $C = \{1, 2, 3, 5, 8\}$ and $D = \{2, 3, 5, 7, 11, 13\}$. Describe the intersection $(A \times C) \cap (B \times D)$.

62. Craft a verbal description of the Cartesian product $A \times B \times C$.

63. Suppose that $A = \{1, 2, 3, 4, 5\}$, $B = \{a, b, c, d, e, f\}$ and $C = \{\bullet, \star, \diamond\}$. How many elements are there in the set $A \times B \times C$?

WRITING

64. Show that for two sets A and B within some universal set U, it is the case that $\overline{A} \times \overline{B} \subseteq \overline{A \times B}$.

65. Prove that $A \times (B \cup C) = (A \times B) \cup (A \times C)$ for any three sets A, B and C.

66. Make and prove a conjecture regarding the relationship between the sets $A \times (B - C)$ and $(A \times B) - (A \times C)$.

67. Demonstrate that $(A \times C) \cap (B \times D) = (A \times D) \cap (B \times C)$ for any four sets A, B, C and D.

68. The intersection $(A \times B) \cap (B \times A)$ can be written as the Cartesian product of a certain set with itself. Find, with proof, an expression for that set.

69. Let $A = \{1, 2, 3, \ldots, 10\}$. Prove that if we select any twenty ordered pairs from $A \times A$, then we can always find two of the chosen pairs that give the same sum when the numbers within the pair are added together.

70. Prove that the game of PairMission described in the Mathematical Outing for this section will end after at most $|A| + |B| - 1$ moves.

2.5 Index Sets

For sake of illustration, consider the set of all words that contain the letter 'a'. For our purposes a word may be formed from any finite string of lower case letters from our alphabet, such as 'gargantuan' or 'scrambleflopsy' or 'sjivkavl.' Naturally we would also be interested in the set of all words that contain the letter b, or the letter c, and so on. In this sort of situation it makes sense to name each set in a manner that reflects the letter on which it depends.

To accomplish this task we employ subscripts. Thus we let W_a be the set of all words containing the letter a, and similarly for W_b through W_z. The common variable name W reflects the fact that each set contains words.

The subscripts a, b, ... are known as **indices**; the set $I = \{a, b, c, \dots, z\}$ of all indices is called the **index set**. The collection of all the sets W_a through W_z comprises a **family** of sets, in the sense that they are related by a common definition. It may help to remember that each index *indicates* a particular set in the family.

CON**C**EPT a) The set $\{\dots, -10, -5, 0, 5, 10, \dots\}$ consists of all integers that are divisible by 5. Of course, there is a whole family of such sets. Decide on a name for these sets and identify the index set.

Observe that we are not introducing any new set operations in this section. Rather, we are describing a scheme for organizing related sets. But we are free to apply set operations to indexed sets—they are just sets, after all. Thus $\overline{W}_p$ is the set of words which do not contain the letter p, so 'rambunctious' $\in \overline{W}_p$, for instance. Furthermore, 'chocolate' $\in W_c \cap W_t$ and 'zamboni' $\in W_z - W_e$.

It may come as a surprise to learn that the intersection of all the sets W_α for $\alpha \in I$ is non-empty. As you might expect, the intersection of an indexed collection of sets consists of those elements that appear in every single set. We could write their intersection as $W_a \cap W_b \cap \cdots \cap W_z$, but this notation is cumbersome at best. Instead we adopt the notation $\bigcap_{\alpha \in I} W_\alpha$. Hence our definition of the intersection of the family of sets W_α can be shortened to

$$\bigcap_{\alpha \in I} W_\alpha = \{x \mid x \in W_\alpha \text{ for all } \alpha \in I\}.$$

If this intersection is to be non-empty, then there must exist a word that contains every letter of the alphabet at least once! This does seem surprising, until we remember that in the present setting 'words' are arbitrary strings of letters, not necessarily English words. For instance, we have

$$\text{'aquickfoxjumpsoverthelazybrowndog'} \in \bigcap_{\alpha \in I} W_\alpha.$$

CON**C**EPT b) What is $\bigcap_{\alpha \in I} \overline{W}_\alpha$?

In order to have other examples of indexed sets at our disposal, we now formally define two frequently encountered sets of real numbers.

An **open interval** is a set of real numbers of the form $\{x \in \mathbb{R} \mid a < x < b\}$, for fixed real numbers $a < b$, while a **closed interval** is a set of the form $\{x \in \mathbb{R} \mid a \leq x \leq b\}$. These sets are usually written compactly as (a, b) and $[a, b]$, respectively.

Although one might worry that the ordered pair $(3, 7)$ could be confused with the open interval $(3, 7)$, in practice this hardly ever occurs. Several examples of open and closed intervals are pictured below. It is often useful to have a mental picture such as this in mind when working with intervals.

c) What are the possible outcomes that may be obtained by intersecting two closed intervals? What are the possibilities when working with open intervals instead?

Having introduced the notion of an interval, we are now prepared to consider an entire family of open intervals. Let B_r be the set of all numbers between -1 and some positive real number r. In other words, define $B_r = (-1, r)$. The first two intervals pictured above are members of this family; namely, B_3 and $B_{4.5}$. In this case the index set is $J = \{r \mid r \in \mathbb{R}, \ r > 0\}$. It is important to make a distinction between the index set and the other sets belonging to the family. Think of the index set J as the master set: it catalogs all the other sets, since there is one set B_r for each $r \in J$.

d) Based on the definition of B_r, which of the following are correct?

i. $B_3 \subset B_7$ ii. $\sqrt{10} \in B_\pi$ iii. $B_{4.5}$ and $\overline{B}_{5.2}$ are disjoint.

In the same manner as before we can form the intersection $\bigcap_{r \in J} B_r$ of the entire family of open intervals. The challenge in this case is not so much understanding the notation as determining the answer. Clearly $-\frac{1}{2}$ is contained in every such interval, as is -0.1. In fact, every real number from -1 up to and including 0 is contained in the interval B_r for all $r \in J$. (Convince yourself of this fact.) But no positive real number is contained in every set B_r for all $r > 0$. For example, consider the number $.0001$. We need only select a smaller positive number, such as $r = .000001$, in order to find a set that does not contain $.0001$.

Mathematical Outing ★ ★ ★

For each $n \in \mathbb{N}$, let C_n be the set of counting numbers from 1 to n, so that

$$C_n = \{1, 2, \ldots, n\}.$$

To begin, show that $\bigcup_{n=1}^{\infty} C_n = \mathbb{N}$. (This is a set equality, so explain why every element of $\bigcup_{n=1}^{\infty} C_n$ is in $\mathbb{N}$ and vice-versa.) What do subsets of C_n look like? In other words, describe the elements of $\mathcal{P}(C_n)$. Next describe the set $\bigcup_{n=1}^{\infty} \mathcal{P}(C_n)$ in a single complete sentence. Now for the stumper: is this set the same as $\mathcal{P}(\mathbb{N})$? Why or why not?

And since $.0001 \notin B_{.000001}$, it is not contained in the intersection of all the B_r. We conclude that

$$\bigcap_{r \in J} B_r = \{x \mid -1 < x \le 0\}.^{\dagger}$$

Just as we can find the intersection of a family of sets, we can also find their union. For example, consider the union of the sets W_α, where α represents a letter of the alphabet. Predictably, such a union is written in the form $\bigcup_{\alpha \in I} W_\alpha$, and consists of those words that are members of at least one of the sets W_α. But every word is a member of some W_α, since every word contains at least one letter, so the union is the set of all words.

CONCEPT CHECK e) Determine $\bigcup_{r \in J} B_r$, writing your answer using bar notation.

It is quite common for a family of sets to be indexed by simply being numbered. Whenever our index set is the natural numbers (or a subset thereof) there is a more informative way of writing an intersection or union, reminiscent of sigma notation. For instance, imagine that we had a family A_1, A_2, A_3, ... of sets. We can express the intersection of sets A_3 through A_6 as

$$\bigcap_{n=3}^{6} A_n = A_3 \cap A_4 \cap A_5 \cap A_6.$$

Similarly, the union of sets A_1 through A_7 is written $\bigcup_{n=1}^{7} A_n$, so that

$$\bigcup_{n=1}^{7} A_n = A_1 \cup A_2 \cup A_3 \cup A_4 \cup A_5 \cup A_6 \cup A_7.$$

If we wish to take the intersection of all the sets in the family we employ the notation $\bigcap_{n=1}^{\infty} A_n$, just as is done for sigma notation when expressing an infinite series. Predictably, an infinite union is written as $\bigcup_{n=1}^{\infty} A_n$. This notation is quite versatile; thus the union of all the even-numbered sets can be written $\bigcup_{n=1}^{\infty} A_{2n}$, while the intersection of all odd-numbered sets is $\bigcap_{n=1}^{\infty} A_{2n-1}$.

a) Let M_n be the set of all integers that are multiples of n. The index set is $\mathbb{N}$, since we have one set M_n for each $n \in \mathbb{N}$.

b) The empty set, since no word omits every letter of the alphabet.

c) The intersection of two closed intervals is either a closed interval, a point, or the empty set. Two open intervals intersect in either an open interval or the empty set.

d) *i.* True *ii.* False, since $\sqrt{10} > \pi$ *iii.* True

e) Every real number $x > -1$, no matter how large, is a member of some set B_r. For example, 1000000 is an element of $B_{1000001}$. Hence $\bigcup_{r \in J} B_r = \{x \mid x > -1\}$.

▣ Argue that if $x \in \bigcup_{n=1}^{\infty} C_n$ then $x \in C_k$ for some k, which means that x is a counting number from 1 to k, so $x \in \mathbb{N}$. Conversely, if $x \in \mathbb{N}$ then x is a counting number, say $x = k$. But then $x \in C_k$ (and C_{k+1}, etc.), and hence $x \in \bigcup_{n=1}^{\infty} C_n$.

Elements of $\mathcal{P}(C_n)$ are subsets of $\{1, 2, \ldots, n\}$; i.e. sets all of whose elements are counting numbers from 1 to n. Hence $\bigcup_{n=1}^{\infty} \mathcal{P}(C_n)$ consists of all *finite* sets of counting numbers. And therein lies the rub, for $\mathcal{P}(\mathbb{N})$ contains *all* subsets of $\mathbb{N}$, including infinite ones. More concretely, $\{1, 3, 5, 7, \ldots\}$ belongs to $\mathcal{P}(\mathbb{N})$ but not to $\bigcup_{n=1}^{\infty} \mathcal{P}(C_n)$.

━━━━━━━━━━━━━━━ ❖ ━━━━━━━━━━━━━━━

EXERCISES

71. Consider the set of points in the plane a distance r from the origin, where r is a particular real number not smaller than 2. Create an appropriate name for this family of sets and identify the index set.

72. In the previous exercise, use compact notation to indicate the union of all the sets for which $3 \leq r \leq 5$. Also, draw a sketch of this union.

73. Let A_k be a family of sets, one set for each element $k \in I$ for some index set I. Write a definition for the union of this family using bar notation, as was done for intersection earlier in this section.

74. Let W_α be the family defined in this section. Give an example of an element in each of the following sets. (Any string of letters will do, but ordinary English words are cooler.)

a) $W_x - W_e$

b) $W_j \cup W_q \cup W_v$

c) $\overline{W_a} \cap \overline{W_e} \cap \overline{W_o} \cap \overline{W_u}$

d) $\bigcap_{\alpha \in I'} W_\alpha$, where $I' = \{a, b, c, d, e, f\}$

75. Give a description of the elements of $\bigcup_{\alpha \in I'} W_\alpha$, where $I' = \{a, b, c, d, e, f\}$.

76. Write the following sets using sigma-style notation.

a) $A_8 \cup A_9 \cup A_{10} \cup A_{11} \cup A_{12}$

b) $B_3 \cap B_6 \cap B_9 \cap \cdots$

c) $C_2 \cup C_3 \cup C_4 \cup \cdots$

d) $D_5 \cap D_6 \cap D_7 \cap D_8$

77. Let D_n be the set of positive divisors of a natural number n. Thus $D_1 = \{1\}$ and $D_{10} = \{1, 2, 5, 10\}$. Find the following sets, writing them in list form.

a) $\bigcup_{n=14}^{16} D_n$

b) $D_{100} - D_{50}$

c) $\bigcup_{n=1}^{100} D_n$

d) $\bigcap_{n=1}^{\infty} D_n$

78. Let $J = \{r \mid r \geq 1\}$, and for each real number $r \in J$ define C_r to be the closed interval $[r, 2r]$. Sketch the sets C_4, C_5 and C_6 on a number line. Based on your sketch, find $\bigcap_{k=4}^{6} C_k$ and $\bigcup_{k=4}^{6} C_k$, writing your answer in bar notation.

79. Using the notation of the previous exercise, determine $\bigcap_{r \in J} C_r$ and $\bigcup_{r \in J} C_r$.

80. Continuing the previous exercises, let $J' = \{x \mid 3 \leq x \leq 4.5\}$. Now determine $\bigcap_{r \in J'} C_r$ and $\bigcup_{r \in J'} C_r$.

81. Let M_n be the set of integers that are multiples of n, where n is a natural number. For instance, $M_5 = \{\ldots, -10, -5, 0, 5, 10, \ldots\}$ is the set appearing earlier in this section. Determine $M_3 \cap M_5$, $M_4 \cap M_6$ and $M_{10} \cap M_{15} \cap M_{20}$.

82. Continuing the previous exercise, find a succinct way to describe the intersection $M_a \cap M_b$, where a and b are positive integers. Also, what is $\bigcap_{n \in \mathbb{N}} M_n$?

83. Let $B_r = (r, 10)$ for $r \leq 8$ be a family of open intervals. Determine $\bigcap_{2 < r < 4} B_r$, writing your answer in bar notation.

84. For the sets B_r in the previous exercise, create an intersection which results in the open interval $(6, 10)$.

WRITING

85. Let A_t be a family of sets, where $t \in I$. Prove that $\overline{\bigcap_{t \in I} A_t} = \bigcup_{t \in I} \bar{A}_t$.

86. For each real number r in the open interval $(0, 1)$ let B_r be the open interval $(5 + r, 8 + r)$. Prove that $\bigcap_{r \in (0,1)} B_r = [6, 8]$.

87. Let M_n be the set of integers that are multiples of n, where n is a natural number. For instance, $M_5 = \{\ldots, -10, -5, 0, 5, 10, \ldots\}$. Determine the elements of the set $\mathbb{Z} - \bigcup_{n=1}^{\infty} M_{2n+1}$ and explain why your answer is correct.

2.6 Reference

As before, the purpose of this section is to provide a condensed summary of the most important facts and techniques from this chapter, as a reference when studying or working on material from later chapters. We also include a list of the various strategies we have developed for proving statements about sets.

- *Vocabulary* set, element, empty set, cardinality, bar notation, intersection, union, universal set, complement, equal sets, set identity, Venn diagram, subset, superset, disjoint, nonempty, proper subset, set difference, power set, Cartesian product, ordered pair, indices, index set, family, open interval, closed interval

- *Sets* Sets may be described via a verbal description or by listing their elements between curly brackets $\{\cdots\}$. The order in which elements are listed does not matter, as long as each element is listed only once. One can also employ bar notation, which involves writing down the objects in the set followed by a description of those objects, separated by a bar, as in $\{n^2 \mid n \in \mathbb{N},\ n\ \text{odd}\}$ for the squares of the odd numbers. The cardinality of a finite set is the number of elements in the set; hence $|\emptyset| = 0$. The symbols $\mathbb{N}$, $\mathbb{Z}$, $\mathbb{Q}$, $\mathbb{R}$ and $\mathbb{C}$ refer to the natural numbers, integers, rational, real, and complex numbers. Observe that $\mathbb{N} \subset \mathbb{Z} \subset \mathbb{Q} \subset \mathbb{R} \subset \mathbb{C}$.

• *Set Operations* We may take the union, intersection, difference or Cartesian product of two sets, denoted by $A \cup B$, $A \cap B$, $A - B$ and $A \times B$. We may also take the complement of a set relative to some universal set. Seemingly different combinations of sets may produce the same result, like $\overline{A - B} = \overline{A} \cup B$, giving a set identity. A Venn diagram provides a useful way to visualize combinations of sets and to prove set identities involving two or three sets.

• *Power Sets* The power set of A, written $\mathcal{P}(A)$, is the set of all subsets of A, including $\emptyset$ and A. When A is finite, there are $2^{|A|}$ subsets of A, and therefore $2^{|A|}$ elements of $\mathcal{P}(A)$. If X is a subset of A then we would write $X \subseteq A$ or $X \in \mathcal{P}(A)$, but not $X \subseteq \mathcal{P}(A)$. If the subset X is not equal to all of A then we call X a proper subset, and write $X \subset A$.

• *Cartesian Products* The Cartesian product $A \times B$ is the set of all ordered pairs (a, b) with $a \in A$ and $b \in B$. When A and B are both finite, there are $|A| \cdot |B|$ such ordered pairs. The Cartesian plane is $\mathbb{R} \times \mathbb{R}$, or $\mathbb{R}^2$ for short. One effective way to visualize a Cartesian product is to organize its elements into a two-dimensional array, with the rows and columns corresponding to the elements of A and B. The Cartesian product is not commutative, meaning that in general $A \times B \neq B \times A$.

• *Index Sets* When a collection of sets that depend on a particular quantity are defined in a common fashion we have a family of sets, such as A_k for $k \in I$. The index set I keeps track of all the possible values of the quantity. There is one set A_k for each element $k \in I$. We may form the intersection or union of the entire family by writing $\bigcap_{k \in I} A_k$ or $\bigcup_{k \in I} A_k$. When the sets are numbered, an alternate sigma-style notation may be employed, as in $\bigcup_{k=1}^{5} A_k$ or $\bigcap_{k=1}^{\infty} A_k$.

PROOF STRATEGIES

The paragraphs below briefly outline strategies for approaching various assertions involving sets, complete with a template for writing a proof. Keep in mind that no such list can possibly be comprehensive; the reader will need to adapt the strategies and templates here to suit the particular statement to be proved.

∗ *Unions and Intersections* To show that an element is contained in the union of two sets, it suffices to show that the element is in either set. However, to demonstrate that the element is in their intersection, you must prove that the element is contained in both sets.

On the flip side, if we are given an element in an intersection, we know it is contained in both sets. It is less helpful if we only know that an element is in the union of two sets, since then it may be in either set. In this situation we resort to a proof by cases. If the argument for the two cases is essentially the same, it is acceptable to omit the second case, as illustrated below. (But if the second case is *not* analogous to the first, be sure to write it out.)

> One could write "Since $x \in A \cup B$, we know that either $x \in A$ or $x \in B$. In the first case we have $x \in A$, so [main argument here], which shows that [conclusion]. The case $x \in B$ is analogous, again giving [conclusion]."

∗ Set Equality To prove that two sets are equal, show that each element in the first set is included in the second set, and vice-versa. These two arguments are usually given in separate paragraphs, unless the proofs are relatively short or very similar in nature.

> "We begin by showing that if $x \in$ [first set] then $x \in$ [second set]. [Proof of this statement.] Conversely, it is also true that if $x \in$ [second set] then $x \in$ [first set], because [proof of this statement]. Therefore we may conclude that [first set] = [second set]."

Note that for set identities involving two or three sets, it is also sufficient to create Venn diagrams for each set, justifying in full sentences why you shaded in particular regions, and then observe that the two diagrams are identical. This amounts to a proof by cases, presented visually. This approach applies to any identity involving three or fewer sets, unions, intersections, complements, and set differences. However, don't use Venn diagram proofs for statements involving four or more sets, power sets, or Cartesian products.

∗ Set Inclusion To prove that one set is contained in another, show that if some object is an element of the first set then it is also an element of the second set. Be aware that it is tempting to begin a proof that $A \subseteq B$ by writing "We must show that $x \in A$ and $x \in B$." *This is a logically invalid approach.* To demonstrate that $A \subseteq B$ we must prove an implication: if $x \in A$ then $x \in B$.

> A sample argument reads as follows "Suppose that $x \in$ [first set]. We must show that $x \in$ [second set]. [Main argument here], which shows that $x \in$ [second set]. It follows that [first set] $\subseteq$ [second set]."

∗ Set Inequality and Disjoint Sets To prove that two sets are not equal, it suffices to produce a single element that is in one of the sets but not the other.

> "To see that these sets are not necessarily equal, consider [give examples of sets]. Then the element $x =$ [counterexample] is in the first set, but not the second, because [reasons]. Therefore the sets are not equal."

To prove that two sets are disjoint, show that given any element of the first set, it cannot also be an element of the second set.

> "To prove that the given sets are disjoint, consider any $x \in$ [first set]. Then $x \notin$ [second set] because [reasons]. Therefore the sets are disjoint."

★ TIP ★ *When deciding what strategy to apply to a particular proof, you must focus on what you are being asked to prove.* (This is the statement following the word 'then' in most problems.) Don't get side-tracked by other information at this stage. For instance, suppose that we wish to prove that

CLAIM: For all sets A and B, if $A - B = \emptyset$ then $\mathcal{P}(A) \subseteq \mathcal{P}(B)$.

At first glance there are quite a few distracting features to this question: a set equality, a set inclusion, an empty set, power sets, and so forth. With practice, you will learn to immediately concentrate on the expression $\mathcal{P}(A) \subseteq \mathcal{P}(B)$ since it follows the word 'then.' We now recognize that we are being asked to prove a set inclusion, so we can safely write down the first sentence:

PROOF: We wish to prove that $\mathcal{P}(A) \subseteq \mathcal{P}(B)$. Therefore let $X \in \mathcal{P}(A)$; we wish to show that $X \in \mathcal{P}(B)$.

From our work with power sets we know how to interpret $X \in \mathcal{P}(A)$, so we can also safely write down the second sentence of the proof.

PROOF: We wish to prove that $\mathcal{P}(A) \subseteq \mathcal{P}(B)$. Therefore let $X \in \mathcal{P}(A)$; we wish to show that $X \in \mathcal{P}(B)$. Equivalently, we have $X \subseteq A$ and we wish to show that $X \subseteq B$.

The proof is now off to a promising start, which is at least a third of the battle. We leave the details of the remainder of the proof to the reader. There is a hint as to how to proceed in the answers at the back.

SAMPLE PROOFS

The following proofs provide concise explanations for results discussed within this chapter. They are meant to serve as an illustration for how proofs of similar statements could be phrased. The boldface numbers indicate the section containing each result; the location of that result within the section is marked by a dagger (†).

———◆———

2.2 For sets A and B prove that $\overline{A \cap B} = \overline{A} \cup \overline{B}$.

Proof We begin by showing that each element of $\overline{A \cap B}$ is contained in $\overline{A} \cup \overline{B}$. So suppose that $x \in \overline{A \cap B}$; this means that $x \notin A \cap B$. Since x is not in their intersection, it must lie outside of at least one of A or B, hence $x \notin A$ or $x \notin B$. This means that $x \in \overline{A}$ or $x \in \overline{B}$, giving $x \in \overline{A} \cup \overline{B}$.

On the other hand, suppose that we have $x \in \overline{A} \cup \overline{B}$. This means that $x \in \overline{A}$ or $x \in \overline{B}$, so $x \notin A$ or $x \notin B$. Since x is not contained in at least one of A or B, it does not reside in their intersection, thus $x \notin A \cap B$. It follows that $x \in \overline{A \cap B}$, as desired. Since the elements of each set are contained in the other, we conclude that $\overline{A \cap B} = \overline{A} \cup \overline{B}$.

———◆———

2.3 For any sets A, B and C, prove that if $A \subseteq B \cap \overline{C}$ then $C \subseteq \overline{A}$.

Proof We wish to prove that $C \subseteq \overline{A}$, so we will show that whenever $x \in C$ then $x \in \overline{A}$ as well. Thus suppose that $x \in C$, which means that $x \notin \overline{C}$. It follows that $x \notin B \cap \overline{C}$ either, since x does not belong to both sets. But if $x \notin B \cap \overline{C}$ while $A \subseteq B \cap \overline{C}$ then we may deduce that $x \notin A$, because x lies outside $B \cap \overline{C}$ while all of A is contained within $B \cap \overline{C}$. Therefore $x \in C$ implies that $x \notin A$, i.e. $x \in \overline{A}$, giving $C \subseteq \overline{A}$.

2.3 Given nonempty sets A and B, prove that every set in $\mathcal{P}(B-A)$ is contained in $\mathcal{P}(B) - \mathcal{P}(A)$, except for the empty set.

Proof To begin, we will consider the empty set. We know that $\emptyset \in \mathcal{P}(B - A)$ since the empty set is a subset of every set. However, the empty set is not in $\mathcal{P}(B) - \mathcal{P}(A)$. It is true that $\emptyset \in \mathcal{P}(B)$, but $\emptyset \in \mathcal{P}(A)$ as well, so it is removed when we subtract $\mathcal{P}(A)$ from $\mathcal{P}(B)$.

Now suppose that X is any nonempty set in $\mathcal{P}(B-A)$. We wish to argue that $X \in \mathcal{P}(B) - \mathcal{P}(A)$, which means we must prove that $X \in \mathcal{P}(B)$ but $X \notin \mathcal{P}(A)$. By definition of power set, this is the same as showing that if $X \subseteq B - A$ then $X \subseteq B$ but $X \nsubseteq A$. So suppose that $X \subseteq B - A$. This means that every element of X is in $B - A$, i.e. is in B but not in A. Since every element of X is in B we do have $X \subseteq B$. However, since all elements of X are not in A (of which there is at least one, since X is nonempty), we also have $X \nsubseteq A$. Hence if $X \in \mathcal{P}(B - A)$ it follows that $X \in \mathcal{P}(B) - \mathcal{P}(A)$, as claimed.

2.4 Prove that $(A \times C) \cup (B \times D) \subseteq (A \cup B) \times (C \cup D)$ for sets A, B, C and D.

Proof To prove this set inclusion we show that if $(x, y) \in (A \times C) \cup (B \times D)$ then $(x, y) \in (A \cup B) \times (C \cup D)$. So suppose that $(x, y) \in (A \times C) \cup (B \times D)$. Since (x, y) is an element of a union of sets, we know that either $(x, y) \in A \times C$ or $(x, y) \in B \times D$. We consider each possibility separately. In the first case we have $(x, y) \in A \times C$, hence $x \in A$ and $y \in C$. But this implies that $x \in A \cup B$ and $y \in C \cup D$ by definition of union. It follows that $(x, y) \in (A \cup B) \times (C \cup D)$, as desired. The proof of the second case in which $(x, y) \in B \times D$ is analogous, so we are done.

2.5 Let B_r represent the open interval $(-1, r)$ and let J be the set of positive real numbers. Describe, with proof, the set $\bigcap_{r \in J} B_r$.

Proof We claim that the intersection of this family consists of all $-1 < x \leq 0$. First, if $x \leq -1$ then $x \notin B_r$ for any r according to the definition of B_r, and thus x is clearly not in their intersection. Furthermore, if $-1 < x \leq 0$ then $x \in B_r$ for every positive real number r, since B_r consists of all real numbers between -1 and r, which certainly includes any x in the range $-1 < x \leq 0$. Hence these values of x belong to the intersection $\bigcap_{r \in J} B_r$. Finally, given any $x > 0$, choose $r = \frac{1}{2}x$. Then r is a smaller positive real number, so $x \notin B_r$ for this particular r. Since x is absent from at least one such set, it does not belong to their intersection. In summary, $\bigcap_{r \in J} B_r = \{x \in \mathbb{R} \mid -1 < x \leq 0\}$.

CHAPTER 3

Proof Techniques

3.1 A Case for Proof

Towards the end of the first chapter we met Bertrand's Postulate, which states that for all $n \geq 2$ there is a prime between n and $2n$. We verified this claim for values of n from $n = 2$ through $n = 10$. One could easily extend this list by hand to values of n in the hundreds or even thousands, or to much higher values with the aid of a computer. In fact, the further one goes, the more plausible the theorem becomes—for instance, there are no less than 135 primes between 1000 and 2000. The list looks like

$$1009, \ 1013, \ 1019, \ 1021, \ \ldots, \ 1987, \ 1993, \ 1997, \ 1999.$$

At this point most of us would happily agree that Bertrand's Postulate is undoubtedly correct. However, we would also concede that we have not really *proved* that Bertrand's Postulate is true; only *convinced* ourselves that it is. Before we consider what constitutes a mathematical proof, we should reflect for a moment on why one should pursue a proof of Bertrand's Postulate at all.

There are a number of answers to this question. One reason that is often forwarded goes along the lines of "You can never be sure." It is true that there are examples of simple, appealing open sentences that are true for a great many values of n, only to succumb to an unexpectedly large counterexample—the next Mathematical Outing reveals one such faulty conjecture. Examples such as this illustrate the importance of backing up assertions with proof. Besides, few would debate that a result must be rigorously established before it may attain the honored status of theorem. But to be honest, promising statements that turn out to be false occur relatively infrequently. And even professional mathematicians are willing to accept and implement unproven results when

Bernhard Riemann

Mathematical Outing ★ ★ ★

Make a list of the first twenty-four odd primes: 3, 5, 7, ..., 89, 97. Now go back through the list and circle all the primes that are one less than a multiple of four (such as 3 or 47) and box all the primes that are one more than a multiple of four (such as 5 or 29). Study the distribution of circles and boxes and make three conjectures based on the questions below.

- How many circled primes are there among all the positive integers?

- How do the number of primes of each type compare up to any point?

- How do the number of primes of each type compare in the long run?

Finally, guess which of your conjectures are in fact true.

there is overwhelming evidence in their favor. Perhaps the best known example is the Riemann Hypothesis, which predicts the nature of the solutions to

$$\zeta(s) = \frac{1}{1^s} + \frac{1}{2^s} + \frac{1}{3^s} + \frac{1}{4^s} + \cdots = 0,$$

where $\zeta(s)$ is the Riemann-zeta function. It is not uncommon for a published theorem to include a sentence along the lines of, "We assume that the Riemann Hypothesis is true." The mathematical community expectantly awaits a proof; the possibility of a disproof is more or less out of the question.

All of this brings us back to the issue of why we bother to prove statements that we already believe to be correct. The more compelling reason is that we, as mathematicians, are even more interested in understanding why numbers (or geometric diagrams, or other mathematical objects) behave in the way that they do than we are in discovering fascinating relationships in the first place. Coming up with an intriguing question or stumbling upon a nice result is exciting, but represents only the initial stage of an investigation. It is in the quest for an explanation that one begins to truly understand the principles governing fascinating mathematical observations, and it is in the careful writing of a proof that one certifies this understanding to oneself (and others). Individuals who are drawn to math often mention that they are attracted to the potential for absolute certainty; to the satisfaction that an irrefutable proof provides.

📖 The data suggests that there are infinitely many circled primes, that up to any given point there are at least as many circled primes as boxed primes, and that there are approximately "the same number" of each type. The first and the third conjectures are indeed true, although not particularly easy to prove. The second looks good for a very long time, but ultimately falls through. The smallest counterexample occurs for the prime $n = 26861$, at which point the boxed primes outnumber the circled primes for the first time.

3.2 Mathematical Writing

Mastering the craft of writing a good proof takes both practice and guidance. Just as with learning any new language, there is initially a high potential barrier to mathematical writing. One must become accustomed to certain conventions, learn how to use notation correctly, absorb a new vocabulary, master a set of proof techniques, increase ones level of rigor, and more. Nonetheless, this skill is well within the reach of the willing student.

The backbone of any good proof is a complete, watertight argument. Since the mathematical methods for achieving this depend a great deal on the type of problem under consideration, we will relegate the discussion of what constitutes a rigorous proof in each case to the corresponding section covering that topic. But we can at least comment upon how much detail to include with a proof. The general rule of thumb is to provide enough discussion to completely justify each step, but not so much as to obscure the overall thrust of the argument. In this respect excellent proofs resemble poetry, in that they say everything that is necessary in as few words as possible.

There are several ways to achieve brevity in proofs. For starters, effective use of mathematical notation helps to streamline a discussion. Rather than saying

VERSION 1: Let x be an element of one of the sets A_1 or A_2 or A_3, except that we don't want to have $x = 0$,"

it is preferable to write

VERSION 2: Let $x \in (A_1 \cup A_2 \cup A_3)$, $x \neq 0$.

It is possible to go to an extreme with dense notation, but this is not usually an issue when one first begins to write proofs. Where possible, one should build on previous work rather than reproving known results. It is also common for several cases of an argument to be so similar that it becomes redundant to write out all the steps for each. When this occurs, it is acceptable and even desirable to implement phrasing like "In the same manner it follows that. . ." or "In a similar fashion we have. . ." Finally, and most importantly, the strategy one employs in proving a statement can have a profound effect on the length and clarity of the proof. It is worth taking the time to look for a clean, elegant approach to a problem. Beautiful mathematics deserves an equally nice presentation.

Beyond mathematical content, it is important to use good style when writing a proof. Thus one should employ proper grammar, punctuate correctly, and so on. In particular, one should write in complete sentences. But there are a number of issues unique to mathematical writing, that curious blend of regular words, logical expressions, and mathematical notation which you have by now become accustomed to reading but which is still very unfamiliar to write. The list below highlights some points to bear in mind when writing a proof.

1. Structure your proof in the form of one or more paragraphs. It is not necessary to restate the assertion to be proved, although it does make the proof more readable. It makes sense to indicate that the claim has yet to be established, for instance by writing "We will prove that $A \cap B \subseteq A \cup B$,"

rather than by simply stating the assertion "For sets A and B we have $A \cap B \subseteq A \cup B$," as if the result is already known to be true. Regardless, it is helpful to then lead off with a sentence that summarizes the proof strategy, as in "We will show that if $x \in A \cap B$ then $x \in A \cup B$ also."

2. Take advantage of the abundance of synonyms for common mathematical terms to add flavor to your writing. For instance, the words establish, show, explain, and demonstrate may all be used in place of 'prove.' It is also handy to have alternatives for the word 'therefore.' Synonyms include thus, hence, it follows that, so, for this reason, and consequently.

3. The ubiquitous use of the pronoun 'we' has probably not escaped your notice. It is conventional to use 'we' instead of 'I,' presumably on the grounds that reading mathematics is intended to be an active rather than a passive activity. In other words, the reader joins the author as the proof unfolds, at least in principle. This same philosophy dictates that we write 'one' instead of 'you' when the writer wishes to refer to a third person.

4. From a grammatical point of view, a mathematical expression functions as a noun. It can serve as the subject of a sentence, as in "The equation $x^2 + 2x - 2 = 0$ plays an important role in today's discussion," or a direct object, as in "We complete the square to solve $x^2 + 2x - 2 = 0$," or the object of a preposition, as in "Add 3 to both sides of $x^2 + 2x - 2 = 0$."

5. Avoid beginning a sentence with a mathematical expression. Therefore it is preferable to write "The equation $x^2 + 2x - 2 = 0$ plays..." rather than just "$x^2 + 2x - 2 = 0$ plays..." Other examples include "We have $x \in A \cup B$ because we know $x \in A$," as opposed to "$x \in A \cup B$ because...," and saying "We know that n is not prime since n is even and $n \geq 4$," rather than "n is not prime..." There are a variety of other phrases to facilitate this practice, most of which one picks up by reading mathematics.

6. As much as possible one should avoid awkward line breaks that split mathematical expressions across separate lines. Reading "The equation $x^2 + 2x - 2 = 0$ plays an important role..." is unnecessarily difficult because the equation is cut in half. This problem occurs primarily when using software such as LaTeX to prepare a proof and can usually be remedied by the judicious insertion of a few filler words or a reordering of the sentence.

7. Mathematical definitions, expressions or equations which are particularly important or lengthy should be displayed by centering them on their own line. This practice circumvents the potential for bad line breaks, draws greater attention to the math, and allows more room for writing out bulky formulas. For these reasons we chose to display the expression

$$\bigcap_{r \in J} B_r = \{x \mid -1 < x \leq 0\}$$

in an earlier section, rather than write $\bigcap_{r \in J} B_r = \{x \mid -1 < x \leq 0\}$ in line with the text.

8. Meaning is clarified by using mathematical terms correctly. For instance, we *solve* the *equation* $x^2 + 2x - 2 = 0$, but we *evaluate* the *expression* $5n + 1$ when $n = 16$. (The difference being that in the former situation there is an $=$ sign, in the latter case there is not.)

9. Finally, a quick word is in order regarding the use of arabic numerals versus words for numbers. In general, one should write out the word for a number when it counts how many of a certain object we have, as in "Three French hens, two turtle doves and a partridge in a pear tree." However, utilize an arabic numeral when referring to a number as an arithmetic object, such as "Add 3 to both sides of $x^2 + 2x - 2 = 0$." In some instances either choice is acceptable—we could turn to page five or to p. 31, for example. But numerals are preferred for unwieldy numbers, like "101 Dalmatians."

We conclude this section by considering how to conclude a proof. Any number of phrases can be used to indicate that the final step has been reached and that the proof is complete. One might write "... as desired," or "... which was what we wanted," or simply "This completes the proof." Traditionally authors will also include a symbol to visually separate the proof from the ensuing discussion. Popular choices include the letters 'QED' (from the Latin *quod erat demonstratum,* 'that which was to be demonstrated'), a filled box ∎, or an open box □. But each person has a unique style and should not feel constrained by these options, at least initially. Feel free to use a diamond ♦, a star ★, a circled snowflake ❋, a boxed plus ⊞, or another symbol of your choosing.

EXERCISES

1. Rewrite the following sentences to address any short-comings in grammar or mathematical style that you notice.

a) The sum of 2 3's and 4 5's is twenty-six.

b) Let x be a positive real number. x could be ≤ -1 also. $x = 0$ is OK too.

c) I recommend using a truth table in order to show that $\neg(P \wedge Q \wedge R) \equiv \neg P \vee \neg Q \vee \neg R$ is a logical equivalence.

d) Their are 3 kinds of people those who can count or those who cant.

e) $A \supseteq B$ can also be written as $B \subseteq A$.

f) You should $\sqrt{}$ both sides of $x^2 = 36$ to solve the formula.

g) $f(x) = x^2$ and $g(x) = 3x + 4$ means $f(x) = g(x) = x = 4$.

h) $A \cup B$ contains more numbers than B as long as A is not a subset of B.

i) Did you know that $\sqrt{\frac{6}{1^2} + \frac{6}{2^2} + \frac{6}{3^2} + \frac{6}{4^2} + \cdots}$ equals π?

3.3   Sudoku Interlude

The purpose of this short section is partly to anticipate some of the techniques that will be introduced in subsequent sections, partly to engage in logical thinking, and partly to have fun with a clever puzzle.[1] Your goal is to fill in each square of the 5×5 grid below with one of the digits from 1 to 5 in such a way that each row, each column, and each *pentomino* contains all five digits exactly once. (A pentomino consists of five squares joined along their edges. Five different pentominoes are highlighted in the grid below.) The reader is invited to find the unique answer before reading the partial explanation that comes next.

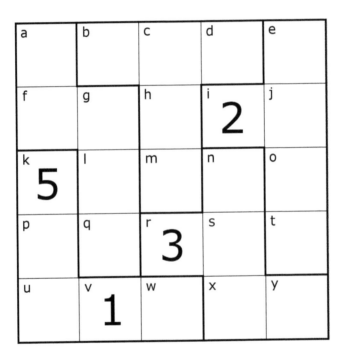

We'll do the first few steps together to illustrate the sorts of deductions that one might utilize in order to solve this puzzle. Although not immediately obvious, the square labeled y is a promising place to start. Since the pentomino along the right-hand side already contains a 2, we cannot place a 2 in the squares e, j, o nor t. But a 2 must appear in the fifth column, so it can only show up in square y. We will write y = 2 to indicate this fact.

Because a 5 and 1 already appear in the pentomino in the lower left corner, we can only have w = 2, 3 or 4. But there is already a 2 in the fifth row and a 3 in the third column, so by process of elimination we must have w = 4. Technically

---

[1]The author learned of this sort of miniature Sudoku puzzle from Scott Kim, one of the most creative designers of original puzzles around. Visit www.scottkim.com to enjoy more of his delightful work.

speaking, we are considering five separate cases for square w. Four of them lead to an "illegal" configuration of numbers, so if there is a solution it must involve writing a 4 in square w. Using process of elimination again, we can now easily find that $p = 2$, $u = 3$ and $x = 5$.

The stage is now set to demonstrate yet another strategy for solving Sudoku puzzles (or proving mathematical statements). We will argue that $b \neq 2$ by showing that if we do place a 2 in square b, then we are led to an illegal configuration. So suppose that $b = 2$. Now consider the third column. It must contain a 2, but due to the positions of the four 2's already placed we can only have $m = 2$. But this results in the middle top pentomino containing two 2's! Since $b = 2$ leads to trouble, we conclude that $b \neq 2$. We leave the enjoyable task of deducing the contents of the remaining squares to the reader.

EXERCISES

2. Finish solving the Sudoku puzzle that appears in this section.

3. Make a copy of the Sudoku board shown above but do not write any digits into the grid yet. Now find a way to fill in the squares, following the same rules as before, so that squares c, l, i, p and y do not all contain the same digit. (This will ensure that your solution is not equivalent to the previous one.)

WRITING

4. Complete the written solution begun in this section. You may utilize the notation introduced above, and do not need to repeat any steps already presented. You may also assume that your reader is an intelligent human being who is familiar with Sudoku. Your goal is to write as efficient a solution as possible without skipping any steps.

5. The Sudoku puzzle from this section has a unique solution. Explain why at least four squares had to be given as clues in order for the solution to be unique.

FURTHER EXPLORATION

6. Create your own 5×5 pentomino Sudoku puzzle. Convention dictates that your puzzle should have a unique solution. Try to give no more than five clues.

3.4 Indirect Proofs

The majority of the mathematical arguments seen thus far have been **direct proofs**. In this sort of proof each step builds on previous steps or on given facts, in an orderly and logical manner, until the desired conclusion is reached. The techniques used within a direct proof will vary widely from one type of problem to another, but the overall approach is the same: make a sequence of logical deductions starting with the premises, culminating in the result to be proved.

However, at times a direct argument is insufficient or undesirable, particularly when one wishes to prove a negative result; i.e. that something does not occur. To illustrate, consider the following assertion from set theory.

$$\textit{"For arbitrary sets } A, B \textit{ and } C, \textit{ if } A - C \not\subseteq A - B, \qquad (*)$$
$$\textit{then it follows that } B \not\subseteq C.\textit{"}$$

In this case an attempt at a direct proof becomes overly complicated at best, and flounders at worst. We have a strategy for approaching a statement such as $B \subseteq C$, but how do we deal with $B \not\subseteq C$? More generally, how do we deduce one negative statement from another? In this case the obstacle is not that we are lacking tools for dealing with set theory, but rather that we need a whole new proof technique for handling negative statements.

C̲O̲N̲C̲EPT a) Suppose that $A = \{1, 2, 3, 4, 5, 6\}$ and $C = \{1, 2, 3, 4\}$. Find a set B such that $A - C \not\subseteq A - B$. Is it the case that $B \not\subseteq C$ for your choice of B?

The key to proving $(*)$ is to utilize **proof by contrapositive**. This approach is motivated and justified by the observation that $P \Rightarrow Q$ is logically equivalent to $\neg Q \Rightarrow \neg P$. (The routine verification of this fact appears as an exercise.)

> The implication $\neg Q \Rightarrow \neg P$ is the **contrapositive** of $P \Rightarrow Q$. Since these statements are logically equivalent, to prove that $P \Rightarrow Q$ it suffices to demonstrate that $\neg Q \Rightarrow \neg P$.

Note that if the implication already contains negatives, then it may be clearer to think of the original statement as $\neg P \Rightarrow \neg Q$ and the contrapositive as $Q \Rightarrow P$.

This small logical sleight of hand makes a great deal of difference in our quest to understand $(*)$. That implication has the form $\neg P \Rightarrow \neg Q$, where P is "$A - C \subseteq A - B$" and Q stands for "$B \subseteq C$." According to the above discussion, it would be equivalent to prove that $Q \Rightarrow P$; in other words, that $B \subseteq C$ implies $A - C \subseteq A - B$. Now at least we can picture the statement to be proven with a Venn diagram, which is set up so that $B \subseteq C$. The dark gray region represents $A - C$, while the two gray regions together represent $A - B$.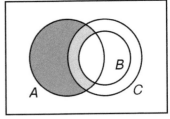
Although this diagram does not constitute a proof, it seems quite plausible now that $A - C \subseteq A - B$. The remainder of the proof is left to the reader.[†]

C̲O̲N̲C̲EPT b) Formulate the first sentence of a proof that for sets A, B and C, we have $B \subseteq C$ implies $A - C \subseteq A - B$.

To further illustrate how one might phrase a proof by contrapositive, let us examine the relatively simple assertion that if $C \not\subseteq A \cup B$ then $C \not\subseteq A$. We will prove the contrapositive of this statement; i.e. we will show that if $C \subseteq A$ then $C \subseteq A \cup B$. We focus on the conclusion of this if-then statement: we must

Mathematical Outing ★ ★ ★

Irrational numbers can behave in unexpected ways. Suppose that α and β are irrational numbers. Which of the following numbers *must* also be irrational, according to your intuition? As much as possible, give specific counterexamples in the remaining cases; in other words, find irrationals α and β such that the given expression is clearly rational.

$$7\alpha, \qquad \beta - 4, \qquad \alpha + \beta, \qquad \alpha^2, \qquad \sqrt{\beta}, \qquad \alpha\beta.$$

An intriguing fact, which is far from obvious, is that it is possible for α^β to be a rational number. The clever idea is to take $\alpha = \sqrt{2}^{\sqrt{2}}$ and $\beta = \sqrt{2}$. There are two options to consider. First suppose that α is irrational. What is the value of α^β? How does this prove the claim? On the other hand, why would it also be fine if α turned out to be rational?

show that $C \subseteq A \cup B$, which is a set inclusion. So take any element $x \in C$; since $C \subseteq A$ we deduce that $x \in A$ also. Since $x \in A$ we know that $x \in A \cup B$ by definition of union. Because $x \in C$ implies $x \in A \cup B$, we conclude that $C \subseteq A \cup B$, as desired.

The second indirect proof technique that we consider is often invoked when dealing with irrational numbers. Recall that a real number r is a rational number if it can be written in the form $r = \frac{m}{n}$ for integers m and n with $n \neq 0$. Thus $\frac{1}{3}$, $-7\frac{2}{5}$, 5 and 0 are all rational numbers. A real number that is not equal to the ratio of two integers is called irrational. In the language of set theory, the irrationals are the set $\mathbb{R} - \mathbb{Q}$. With varying amounts of effort one can prove that the numbers $\sqrt{7}$, π and e^2 are all irrational, among many others.

CONCEPT CHECK c) Decide whether or not $\log_7 14$ and $\log_8 16$ are irrational.

Our intuition suggests that if α is an irrational number, then 3α must be also. We employ the following strategy to establish this result.

> To prove an implication $P \Rightarrow Q$ using **proof by contradiction**, assume that the result (Q) to be proved is in fact false, then combine this assumption with given information (P) and any other useful true statements to arrive at a deduction which contradicts a known fact.

The point is that since the result to be proved can't be false, it must be true. As we shall see, this approach is particularly effective when attempting to prove a negative statement; that is, trying to show that some situation cannot occur. This technique may also be employed to prove a stand-alone statement Q; just show that $\neg Q$ leads to a deduction that contradicts standard known facts.

To see this technique in action, let us prove that if α is irrational, then 3α is also irrational. (Note that we wish to prove a negative statement—that 3α *cannot* be written as a fraction.) Suppose to the contrary that 3α is in fact a rational. Then we can write $3\alpha = \frac{m}{n}$ for integers m and n. Dividing through by 3 gives $\alpha = \frac{m}{3n}$. (We know to perform this step because we want to work our way back to α algebraically, because we already know something about α.) Since $\alpha = \frac{m}{3n}$ we see that α can be written as a ratio of integers, contradicting the fact that α is irrational. Therefore our assumption that 3α is rational cannot be true, so we conclude that 3α is irrational, as claimed.[†]

C⌊ᴏɴ⌉C⌊ᴇᴘᴛ⌉ d) It is the case that if β is irrational then $\sqrt{\beta}$ is also irrational. Write the first two sentences of a proof by contradiction of this fact.

Proof by contradiction is a powerful tool, applicable to a wide range of problems. To appreciate its versatility, consider the following curious arrangement of squares discovered in 1925 by a secondary school teacher in Poland named Zbigniew Moron.

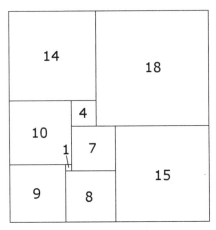

Such an arrangement is known as a *perfect square dissection*; it illustrates how to dissect a 32×33 rectangle into nine squares, each of which has a different side length. (It was long thought impossible to obtain a perfect square dissection of a square, until R. Sprague found a way to do so in 1939 using 55 squares.) Our purpose here is to explain why the smallest square of any perfect square dissection must always be situated somewhere in the middle of the arrangement.

Although it is not immediately obvious that we should do so, we employ proof by contradiction. Thus assume to the contrary that the smallest square is *not* located in the middle of the arrangement; that is, it rests against one of the edges. Now consider the squares immediately adjacent to the smallest square on either side. Because they are larger, their sides extend beyond that of the smallest square, as shown in the figure at right.

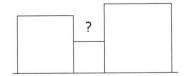

(The same is true if the smallest square happens to be situated in the corner.)

There must be another square to help fill the space above the smallest square. But now we reach our contradiction: the other squares are all larger, and so it is impossible to fit one into the space indicated by the '?'. This contradiction forces us to reject the possibility that the smallest square rests against an edge. Therefore we conclude that the smallest square must appear in the middle of the configuration of squares, as claimed.

 a) One possibility is $B = \{3,5\}$, since in this case $A - C = \{5,6\}$ while $A - B = \{1,2,4,6\}$, and clearly the former set is not a subset of the latter set. As expected, $B \not\subseteq C$.

b) "To prove $A - C \subseteq A - B$ we must show that for any $x \in A - C$ we have $x \in A - B$."

c) We calculate $\log_7 14 \approx 1.356207187108$ and $\log_8 16 \approx 1.333333333333$, so $\log_7 14$ appears to be irrational, while $\log_8 16$ seems to equal $\frac{4}{3}$.

d) "Assume to the contrary that $\sqrt{\beta}$ is rational. Then we may write $\sqrt{\beta} = \frac{m}{n}$ for integers m and n."

The numbers 7α, $\beta - 4$, and $\sqrt{\beta}$ must also be irrational. However, if we choose $\alpha = 3 + \sqrt{2}$ and $\beta = 3 - \sqrt{2}$, then $\alpha + \beta = 6$, which is rational. Similarly, taking $\alpha = \sqrt{7}$ gives $\alpha^2 = 7$, a rational. Finally, letting $\alpha = \pi$ and $\beta = \frac{1}{\pi}$ we find $\alpha\beta = 1$.

We compute $\alpha^\beta = \sqrt{2}^{\sqrt{2} \cdot \sqrt{2}} = \sqrt{2}^2 = 2$, using standard laws of exponents. Hence α^β is rational, as desired. If α happens to rational, then we would conclude that $\sqrt{2}^{\sqrt{2}}$ is rational, so either way we discover that it is possible for an irrational raised to an irrational power to be rational.

EXERCISES

7. Validate the technique of proof by contrapositive by showing that $P \Rightarrow Q$ is logically equivalent to $\neg Q \Rightarrow \neg P$.

8. State the contrapositive of each of the following implications. Then decide whether you would prefer to prove the original statement or the contrapositive. (You do *not* actually need to prove these statements.)

a) Let m and n be positive integers. Prove that if m^3 is not divisible by n^3, then m is not divisible by n.

b) Show that for a real number x, if $x > 1$ then $3^x > 3x$.

c) For finite sets A and B, prove that if $A \not\subseteq B$ then $|A| \geq 1$.

d) If all the sides of a triangle have different lengths, then all of its angles have different sizes.

9. How would a proof by contradiction of the following statements begin? Write at least the first sentence. Include more sentences where possible.

a) The number $\sqrt{7}$ is irrational.

b) There are infinitely many primes.

c) If five sisters split up 2000 grams of chocolate, then at least one of the sisters receives 400 or more grams of chocolate.

d) Given four non-collinear points in the plane, there exist three points which form an angle measuring $90°$ or more.

10. For each statement determine which type of proof is most likely to succeed: a direct proof, a proof by contrapositive, or a proof by contradiction.

a) Prove that there do not exist $a, b, c \in \mathbb{N}$ such that $a^3 + b^3 = c^3$.

b) For sets A and B, prove that if $A \cup B \neq \emptyset$ then either $A \neq \emptyset$ or $B \neq \emptyset$.

c) For $x, y \in \mathbb{R}$, prove that if $x + y = 7$ and $xy = 10$, then $x^2 + y^2 = 29$.

d) If $2^n - 1$ is not divisible by 7, then n is not a multiple of 3.

e) For sets A, B and C show that $\mathcal{P}(A) \cup \mathcal{P}(B) \cup \mathcal{P}(C) \subseteq \mathcal{P}(A \cup B \cup C)$.

f) If x and y are positive real numbers then $\frac{x}{x+2y} \geq \frac{1}{3}$ or $\frac{y}{y+2x} \geq \frac{1}{3}$.

WRITING

11. For sets A and B prove that if $A \times B = \emptyset$ then either $A = \emptyset$ or $B = \emptyset$.

12. For sets A, B and C demonstrate that if $A \not\subseteq B \cup C$ then $A - B \not\subseteq C$.

13. Let A, B and C be sets such that $A \subseteq B \cap C$. Prove that $\overline{B \cup C} \subseteq \overline{A}$.

14. Explain why stating that $B \not\subseteq C$ is equivalent to saying that there exists an element x such that $x \in B$ but $x \notin C$. Use this idea to find a direct proof of $(*)$.

15. Let x be a real number. Prove that if $x^3 + 5x = 40$ then $x < 3$. (Do not use a calculator to solve for x; rather, find a "pencil-and-paper" proof.)

16. Prove that for real numbers x and y, if $x \neq y$ then $\frac{x}{2x-1} \neq \frac{y}{2y-1}$.

17. Prove that if $x, y \in \mathbb{R}$ are positive then $\frac{x}{x+2y} \geq \frac{1}{3}$ or $\frac{y}{y+2x} \geq \frac{1}{3}$.

18. Let β be an irrational number. Use proof by contrapositive to prove that $\beta - 4$ is also irrational.

19. Let β be an irrational number. Employ proof by contradiction to prove that $\sqrt{\beta}$ is also irrational.

20. Prove that there is no positive rational number that is smaller than all other positive rational numbers.

21. Let A, B and C be finite nonempty sets such that $\mathcal{P}(A) \cup \mathcal{P}(B) = \mathcal{P}(C)$. Prove that either $A = C$ or $B = C$.

FURTHER EXPLORATION

22. Now that we have alluded to the fact that there exists a perfect square dissection of a square, it is natural to wonder whether or not there exists a perfect cube dissection of a cube. In other words, is it possible to begin with an $m \times m \times m$ cube, for some $m \in \mathbb{N}$, and dissect it into a finite collection of smaller cubes whose side lengths are distinct positive integers? Surprisingly, the answer is no! The proof relies on the ideas presented in this section. Once you understand the argument, adapt it to decide whether or not there exist perfect cube dissections of $l \times m \times n$ rectangular boxes.

3.5   Biconditional, Vacuous and Trivial Proofs

In this section we consider three more types of proof. The first is quite important, while the next two do not crop up very often. We begin with proofs of biconditional statements, written as $P \Longleftrightarrow Q$ in logical notation. Recall that these statements may be phrased as "P if and only if Q" or "P is necessary and sufficient for Q" or "P is equivalent to Q." Earlier we established the logical equivalence of $P \Longleftrightarrow Q$ and $(P \Rightarrow Q) \wedge (Q \Rightarrow P)$, which gives us the following proof strategy.

> To prove that two statements P and Q are equivalent, one must prove that each statement implies the other. Thus to prove a result of the form "P if and only if Q," one should show that $P \Rightarrow Q$ and that $Q \Rightarrow P$, utilizing whichever proof techniques are most applicable in each case.

CONCEPT CHECK a) Suppose that P, Q and R are statements such that $P \Longleftrightarrow Q$ and $Q \Longleftrightarrow R$. What can be said about statements P and R?

To illustrate the structure of a biconditional proof we will show that for sets A and B we have $A \cup B = B$ if and only if $A \subseteq B$.

Step one: We first show that $A \cup B = B$ implies $A \subseteq B$. We need to prove a set inclusion (namely, that $A \subseteq B$), so our strategy will be to prove that if $x \in A$ then $x \in B$. So suppose that $x \in A$. Then clearly $x \in A \cup B$ by definition of union. Since $A \cup B = B$, it follows that $x \in B$, which was what we wanted.

Step two: We prove the converse, which states that $A \subseteq B$ implies $A \cup B = B$. This time we must prove a set equality (namely, that $A \cup B = B$), so we must argue that if $x \in A \cup B$ then $x \in B$ and vice-versa. So suppose that $x \in A \cup B$; then either $x \in A$ or $x \in B$. In the former case, we deduce that $x \in B$ since $A \subseteq B$. Hence $x \in B$ in either case, as desired. It remains to show that if $x \in B$ then $x \in A \cup B$, but this is clear by definition of union. Hence $A \cup B = B$ as claimed, which completes the entire proof.[†]

Since the main challenge in constructing this argument is keeping track of where we are in the proof, we also present the overall flow of the proof in outline form in Figure 3.1, to help clarify its logical structure.

Biconditional statements provide the appropriate language when we wish to characterize a certain class of mathematical objects.

> A property is said to **characterize** a certain class of objects if the set of objects possessing the property is exactly the specified class of objects. To prove a characterization one must show that an object has the property if and only if it is a member of the designated class of objects.

I. $A \cup B = B \Rightarrow A \subseteq B$ II. $A \subseteq B \Rightarrow A \cup B = B$
   A. Proof that $A \subseteq B$ A. Proof that $A \cup B = B$
   B. Suppose $x \in A$ B. If $x \in A \cup B$ then $x \in B$
   C. Deduce $x \in A \cup B$ 1. Suppose $x \in A \cup B$
   D. Use $A \cup B = B$ 2. Case one: $x \in A$
   E. Conclude $x \in B$ a. Use $A \subseteq B$
                                            b. Deduce $x \in B$
                               3. Case two: $x \in B$
                               4. Either way $x \in B$
                      C. If $x \in B$ then $x \in A \cup B$
                         1. Clear by defn of union

Figure 3.1: Proof that $A \cup B = B \iff A \subseteq B$

For instance, the class of objects might be a certain set of numbers, such as primes, or a particular set of geometric figures, such as parallelograms. Although the concept of characterization might seem to be abstract, it is actually a very familiar idea. Thus taxonomists characterize birds as the set of animals having feathers. To arrive at this characterization, a taxonomist mentally reviews the collection of all birds and searches for a property or feature which every bird possesses but which no other animal shares. The property of having feathers is a suitable choice, since an animal has feathers if and only if it is a bird.

CONCEPT CHECK b) Give two different reasons why the property of being able to fly is not a valid means of characterizing animals that are birds.

Most students have also encountered the concept of characterization in their high school geometry course. A standard exercise involves showing that the class of quadrilaterals known as parallelograms may be characterized by the condition that each diagonal bisects the other. To prove that this condition does in fact characterize parallelograms one must show that if $ABCD$ is a parallelogram then diagonals $\overline{AC}$ and $\overline{BD}$

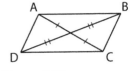

bisect one another, and conversely that if diagonals $\overline{AC}$ and $\overline{BD}$ bisect one another then $ABCD$ is a parallelogram.

CONCEPT CHECK c) What class of quadrilaterals is characterized by the property that the diagonals bisect one another and are also perpendicular?

In the same manner, Wilson's Theorem provides a characterization of primes. We have seen (although not proved) that an integer $n \geq 2$ is a prime if and only if $(n-1)! + 1$ is a multiple of n. Hence primes are characterized by the property that n divides evenly into $(n-1)! + 1$. (By the way, this is not an especially practical characterization of primes. There are far more efficient means of testing whether a number such as 2011 is prime than to compute $2010! + 1$.) To prove

Wilson's Theorem it turns out to be more convenient to prove that if n is prime then $(n-1)! + 1$ is a multiple of n, while if n is not prime then $(n-1)! + 1$ is not a multiple of n. This suggests the following alternate strategy to proving biconditional statements, whose validity we will confirm in the exercises.

> To prove that the biconditional statement $P \Longleftrightarrow Q$ holds, it suffices to prove both $P \Rightarrow Q$ and $\neg P \Rightarrow \neg Q$.

We will now dramatically change gears by considering two very different types of proofs. To illustrate them, consider the somewhat fanciful claims

1) If pigs can fly then I can run a six-minute mile.
2) If I'm on time for class then the pope is Catholic.

QUICK QUERY d) To review, what is the only way an implication can fail to be true? In light of this, which of the above statements are true, and why?

One means of ascertaining that a statement of the form "For all n we have $P \Rightarrow Q$" is true would be to make a list of the truth values of P and Q for each value of n and then to search for an instance in which P is true but Q is false. Such a list is shown at right for the statement "For all positive integers n, if n is a power of 2 then $8n - 7$ is a perfect square." (So P represents "n is a power of 2" and Q stands for "$8n-7$ is a perfect square.") It becomes apparent when we reach $n = 8$ that this statement is not true for all n.

n	P	Q	$P \Rightarrow Q$
1	T	T	T
2	T	T	T
3	F	F	T
4	T	T	T
5	F	F	T
6	F	F	T
7	F	T	T
8	T	F	F

However, suppose that in the process of investigating an implication $P \Rightarrow Q$ we were to discover that statement P is always false. Then clearly we would never encounter an instance in which P was true but Q was false.

> If the premise P of an implication $P \Rightarrow Q$ is always false then we say that the implication is vacuously true, and by showing that P is always false we provide a **vacuous proof** of the statement.

The word 'vacuous' literally means 'void' or 'empty.' Once we have determined that P is always false there is nothing left to prove; the conclusion Q is irrelevant. For this reason the first statement above is vacuously true.

We encountered a vacuously true statement when we first began studying subsets. At that point there was some debate over whether or not the empty set should count as a subset of a given set A. According to the definition, to prove that $\emptyset \subseteq A$ we must show that if $x \in \emptyset$, then $x \in A$. But the premise of this implication is always false (there are no elements in the empty set), therefore the statement is vacuously true.

Let's consider the seemingly remarkable claim that for $n \in \mathbb{N}$ it is the case that $3n + 4$ is a perfect square whenever $n^2 + 5n + 6$ is a prime. This fact seems astonishing, until we begin to try a few values of n and discover that $n^2 + 5n + 6$ seems to always factor. This observation affords the following explanation. We will prove that the statement is vacuously true by showing that $n^2 + 5n + 6$ is never prime. Observe that this expression factors as $(n + 2)(n + 3)$. Since each factor is 3 or more for $n \in \mathbb{N}$, their product cannot be a prime. Hence the statement is vacuously true.[†]

There is another situation in which an implication $P \Rightarrow Q$ is automatically true; namely, when statement Q is always true. Again, it is clear that we could never encounter an instance in which P was true but Q was false. For this reason the second statement above is true, since the pope is definitely Catholic.

> If the conclusion Q of an implication $P \Rightarrow Q$ is always true then we say that the implication is trivially true, and by showing that Q is always true we provide a **trivial proof** of the statement.

This sort of situation is even more rare than a vacuously true statement. The name also has the potential to misleading: when someone refers to a proof as 'trivial' they are usually referring to how easy it was to find rather than to its logical structure. We mention trivial proofs here for sake of completeness. A template for writing out a trivial proof may be found in the reference section at the end of this chapter.

a) It follows that $P \Longleftrightarrow R$; statements P and R are equivalent.
b) There are birds that don't fly (such as ostriches or penguins) and non-birds that do fly (such as bats or bumblebees).
c) A quadrilateral possesses this property if and only if it is a rhombus.
d) An implication $P \Rightarrow Q$ fails only if the premise P is true while the conclusion Q is false. Hence both statements are true, since the premise of the first statement is false while the conclusion of the second statement is true.

---   ❖   ---

EXERCISES

23. An alternate strategy for proving a biconditional statement $P \Longleftrightarrow Q$ is to prove that $P \Rightarrow Q$ and that $\neg P \Rightarrow \neg Q$. Explain why this approach is valid.

24. Determine whether each biconditional statement given below is true or false. Briefly justify your answers.
a) An integer a is divisible by 12 if and only if a^3 is divisible by 12.
b) Let $\triangle ABC$ be a triangle. We have $\overline{AB} \cong \overline{AC}$ exactly when $\angle B \cong \angle C$.
c) For nonempty sets A and B, having $A \subseteq B$ is a necessary and sufficient condition to ensure that $\mathcal{P}(A) \subseteq \mathcal{P}(B)$.
d) Let x and y be nonzero real numbers. Then $x < y$ iff $1/x > 1/y$.

25. Give a succinct description of those integers m which are characterized by the property that $m^2 - 1$ is a multiple of 8.

26. Which numbers are characterized by the property that their decimal expansions either terminate or eventually begin repeating?

27. Write down the two implications which must be proven in order to demonstrate that linear functions $f(x)$ are characterized by the condition that they satisfy $f(x - a) + f(x + a) = 2f(x)$ for all $a, x \in \mathbb{R}$.

28. Determine a property that characterizes the set of points in the plane situated on one of the lines $y = x$ or $y = -x$.

29. Each of the following statements is either vacuously true or trivially true. Determine which category each assertion belongs to.
a) For all $n \in \mathbb{N}$, if $n^2 + n + 1$ is a prime then $n^2 + 2n + 1$ is a perfect square.
b) For all $n \in \mathbb{N}$, if $4n + 5$ is even then $6n + 7$ is a perfect cube.
c) Let x be a real number. If $2^x = 0$ then $3^x = 0$ also.
d) For real numbers x and y, if $|x + 1| > |y - 2|$ then $|x + y + 1| > -2$.
e) If B is the midpoint of $\overline{AC}$ and C is the midpoint of $\overline{AB}$ then $BC = 4$.
f) If points A, B and C satisfy $(AB)(BC) = (AC)^2$ then $AB + BC \geq AC$.
g) For finite sets A and B, if $|A| < |B|$, then it follows that $A \subseteq A \cup B$.
h) For finite sets A and B, if $|A \times B| < |B \times A|$ then $|\mathcal{P}(A)| < |\mathcal{P}(B)|$.

WRITING

30. Let A and B be sets. Outline the logical structure of a proof that $A \subseteq B$ if and only if $A \cap B = A$, as done earlier in this section.

31. Let A and B be sets. Prove that $A \subseteq B$ if and only if $A \cap B = A$. (It will help to complete the previous exercise first.)

32. Given circles $\mathcal{C}_1$ and $\mathcal{C}_2$, prove that the circumference of $\mathcal{C}_1$ is twice the circumference of $\mathcal{C}_2$ exactly when the area of $\mathcal{C}_1$ is quadruple the area of $\mathcal{C}_2$.

33. Let x and y be nonzero real numbers. Prove that $\frac{2}{x} + \frac{3}{y} = 1$ is equivalent to $(x - 2)(y - 3) = 6$.

34. Show that a positive integer a is even if and only if a^2 ends with one of the digits 0, 4 or 6.

35. Prove that for a given nonempty set B, subsets of B are characterized by the condition that they are disjoint from $\overline{B}$.

36. Demonstrate that the real numbers in the interval $[-1, 1]$ are characterized by the condition that their squares are at least as close to 0 as they are.

37. Write a short, complete proof of each statement below.
a) For all $n \in \mathbb{N}$, if $n^2 + n + 1$ is a prime then $n^2 + 2n + 1$ is a perfect square.
b) For real numbers x and y, if $|x + 1| > |y - 2|$ then $|x + y + 1| > -2$.
c) If B is the midpoint of $\overline{AC}$ and C is the midpoint of $\overline{AB}$ then $BC = 4$.
d) For finite sets A and B, if $|A \times B| < |B \times A|$ then $|\mathcal{P}(A)| < |\mathcal{P}(B)|$.

3.6　Conjecture and Disproof

Searching for and discovering interesting results is one of the most exciting aspects of studying mathematics. The exact process by which this occurs can be difficult to pin down, though. Noticing patterns or unexpected connections is something of an art, as is the closely related skill of asking productive questions. At the risk of over-simplifying, we could say that successful mathematicians combine diligent exploration of new ideas with well-developed intuition in order to formulate appealing new results.

　　To gain some sense of how this process unfolds, let us focus our attention on a sequence of numbers that ought to contain some interesting mathematics: the perfect squares. The square numbers from 0^2 up to 20^2 are listed below.

$$0,\ 1,\ 4,\ 9,\ 16,\ 25,\ 36,\ 49,\ 64,\ 81,\ 100,\ 121,$$
$$144,\ 169,\ 196,\ 225,\ 256,\ 289,\ 324,\ 361,\ 400$$

Using what we already know about square numbers as a launching pad, we now search for patterns and ask ourselves questions, motivated by the conviction that there are nice relationships among the square numbers waiting to be found.

QUERY a) What facts concerning square numbers are you familiar with? What patterns do you notice among the numbers in the above list? What questions could you ask about the perfect squares?

For instance, we might already be aware that it is possible to add two squares and obtain a third square, as in $64 + 225 = 289$. Thus we might ask ourselves whether the sum of two squares can be equal to the sum of *two* other squares.

　　Of the many possible directions that this discussion could take us, we choose to pursue the idea of doubling squares. Experimentation suggests that multiplying a positive square by 2 never yields another square. This conjecture turns out to be true; however, in some cases one can come exceedingly close! For example we find that $2(25) = 50 = 49 + 1$ and, even more impressively, that $2(144) = 288 = 289 - 1$. The first five instances in which twice a square differs from another perfect square by only one are listed below. We organize our findings in a table to aid in our search for conjectures.

$2m^2 = n^2 \pm 1$	m	n
$2(1) = 1 + 1$	1	1
$2(4) = 9 - 1$	2	3
$2(25) = 49 + 1$	5	7
$2(144) = 289 - 1$	12	17
$2(841) = 1681 + 1$	29	41

At this point several nice patterns begin to emerge. For instance, the sum of the m and n values in any particular row gives the m value for the next row.

CONCEPT b) Make at least three other conjectures regarding the numbers appearing above. Use the patterns you notice to predict the next two rows of the table, then confirm that they do in fact work.

Mathematical Outing ★ ★ ★

The investigation described here illustrates a classic example of the process of making and testing a conjecture. To experience it for yourself, conduct the following experiment. Draw a circle, then plot n irregularly spaced points around its circumference. Next connect every pair of points with a line segment. For a given value of n, what is the largest number of regions created within the circle? For instance, using $n = 4$ points we can create eight regions, as illustrated at left.

a) Determine the maximum number of regions created by $n = 2$, 3, 4 and 5 points.

b) Make a conjecture based on your findings and predict the number of regions for $n = 6$ or $n = 7$.

c) Confirm or refute your conjecture by actually counting the regions for $n = 6$ and $n = 7$.

Observe that what has turned into an interesting investigation began with a fertile topic (perfect squares), germinated since we asked a good question (what happens if we double squares), and bore fruit in part due to a well-organized table. These conditions often accompany the discovery of nice results.

Intriguing, accessible conjectures usually attract enough attention that they are proven within a relatively short length of time. Occasionally such conjectures persist for many years before sufficiently powerful techniques or an exceptionally ingenious approach finally permits a proof. The most famous example concerns a generalization of our observation above that it is possible for two squares to sum to a third square. In algebraic terms, we have observed that there exist positive integers a, b and c such that $a^2 + b^2 = c^2$. One might ask whether the same is possible for higher powers—can we have $a^3 + b^3 = c^3$ or $a^4 + b^4 = c^4$, for example? In 1637 Fermat conjectured that there are no solutions involving higher powers and managed to prove that this is the case for fourth powers. Over a century later Euler supplied a proof for perfect cubes. However, it was not until the 1990's that Wiles and other mathematicians were finally able to establish "Fermat's Last Theorem" in full generality.

Pierre de Fermat

Once one has formulated and tested a promising conjecture, the next step is usually to find a proof. However, it is not unusual for conjectures to turn out to be false, in which case one supplies a disproof instead.

> To **disprove** a claim, write the negation of the conjectured statement and then prove that this negation is true.

Typically the (false) statement involves a universal quantifier; in other words, it asserts that "For all ..., if we have ... then ..." In this case the negation reads "There exists ... for which we have ... but not ..." Therefore a disproof amounts to finding a **counterexample**: a particular mathematical object satisfying the premise but not the conclusion of the implication.

We have already seen several promising conjectures succumb to counterexamples. We present one more in order to carefully apply the above principles. Consider the claim that "For all $n \in \mathbb{N}$, if n is prime then $6n + 1$ is also prime." To disprove this assertion we first state the negation, "There exists an $n \in \mathbb{N}$ such that n is prime but $6n + 1$ is not prime." Thus to find a counterexample we check each prime value for n in turn to see whether or not $6n + 1$ is prime. With a bit of patience we find that the smallest counterexample is $n = 19$, since $6n + 1 = 115$ is not prime.[†]

CONCEPT CHECK c) Describe what conditions a counterexample must satisfy in order to disprove the claim that "Given any four points in the plane, there exists a circle through three of the points containing the fourth point in its interior."

By the way, it would be inappropriate to begin a disproof with the sentence, "We will show that this proof is false." The proof should be sound; it's the *claim* that is false. We also mention that the best response to a conjecture that doesn't pan out would be to modify the conjecture and continue exploring, rather than to shelve the idea. There is hardly ever such a thing as a mathematical dead end. As we have seen, finding a counterexample often amounts to proving that there exists some number (or formula, or diagram) satisfying certain conditions. This task is an important enough mathematical activity that we will devote an entire section to it, coming up next.

 a) Common answers might include the fact that subtracting each square from the next gives the sequence of odd numbers, or the fact that squares may only end in the digits 0, 1, 4, 5, 6 or 9. Questions about squares are virtually limitless. We might ask how many square numbers are also Fibonacci numbers, or if there is a perfect square involving only the digits 3 and 4, or whether there is a function which crosses the x-axis precisely at the square numbers, to mention but a few possibilities.

b) For starters, it appears that the $+1$'s and -1's alternate down the first column. Furthermore, the sum of two consecutive m values seems to always give the adjacent n value. Finally, the sum of an m value and twice the next m value gives another m value. (The same pattern holds for n values as well.) The next two rows of the table are $m = 70$, $n = 99$ and $m = 169$, $n = 239$.

c) We must find four points in the plane such that the circle through any three of them does not contain the fourth in its interior. This can be accomplished by taking the points at the vertices of a square, for example.

a) The number of regions formed by $n = 2$, 3, 4 and 5 points is 2, 4, 8 and 16 regions, respectively. At this point it seems abundantly clear that the answers are given by powers of 2. More precisely, n points seem to yield 2^{n-1} regions, so there will be 32 regions for $n = 6$ points and 64 regions for $n = 7$ points. To our dismay, a carefully diagram reveals that this is not the case! In fact we can obtain at most 31 regions when $n = 6$ and at most 57 regions when $n = 7$.

EXERCISES

38. Find three pairs of positive integers m and n such that $3m^2 = n^2 \pm 1$. Thus tripling a square can produce a number that is very close to another perfect square. (The first three values of m are less than 20.)

39. Based on the values found in the previous question, make three conjectures regarding pairs of numbers (m, n) for which $3m^2 = n^2 \pm 1$, and predict the next two pairs of integers that satisfy this equation.

40. Choose any three positive real numbers x, y and z and compute the values of $x + y + z$ and $3\sqrt[3]{xyz}$. Repeat this process for three other triples. How do the two values compare in each case? Make a conjecture based on your results.

41. One of the most famous open conjectures is known as the $3x + 1$ problem. Beginning with any positive integer, divide by 2 if it is even or triple and add 1 if it is odd. Repeatedly apply this rule to obtain a sequence of numbers. The conjecture states that regardless of the initial number the sequence will eventually reach the number 1. For instance, starting with 17 gives

$$17 \rightarrow 52 \rightarrow 26 \rightarrow 13 \rightarrow 40 \rightarrow 20 \rightarrow 10 \rightarrow 5 \rightarrow 16 \rightarrow 8 \rightarrow 4 \rightarrow 2 \rightarrow 1.$$

Confirm the $3x + 1$ problem for all values of n from 10 to 20. (Observe that the above sequence already takes care of 10, 13, 16, 17 and 20.)

42. Which positive integers can be written as the difference of two squares? Make a list of all such numbers from 1 to 20. For instance we have

$$1 = 1^2 - 0^2, \quad 3 = 2^2 - 1^2, \quad 4 = 2^2 - 0^2, \quad \text{and} \quad 5 = 3^2 - 2^2.$$

Make a conjecture about which positive integers (such as 2) are left off this list.

43. Draw a triangle ABC and plot the midpoints L, M and N of sides $\overline{BC}$, $\overline{AC}$ and $\overline{AB}$. Next draw segments $\overline{AL}$ and $\overline{BM}$, crossing at point G. How does length AG compare to GL? What about BG and GM? Now draw segment $\overline{CN}$. What seems to occur? Make two conjectures based on your observations.

WRITING

44. Disprove the assertion that "For positive integers m, if $m + 1$ and $5m + 1$ are both perfect squares, then $m = 3$."

45. Show that the following assertion is false: for every quadrilateral $ABCD$, if $m\angle A > m\angle B$ then $BD > AC$.

46. Find a disproof of the statement, "For real numbers x and y, if $x^2 + 3x = y^2 + 3y$ then it follows that $x = y$.

47. A classmate claims that there exists a perfect square with two or more digits that immediately follows a prime. Show that he is mistaken.

48. Disprove the claim that there exist four points in the plane all of which are the same distance from one another.

Further Exploration

49. Goldbach's conjecture states that every even number from 4 onwards can be written as the sum of two primes. Goldbach's conjecture is almost certainly true. However, it is possible to concoct similar sorts of conjectures that seem quite plausible but which fail for a surprisingly large counterexample. For instance, consider the claim that every odd number from 3 onwards can be written as the sum of a prime and twice a square.[2] Thus $3 = 3 + 2(0^2)$, $15 = 13 + 2(1^2)$ and $35 = 17 + 2(3^2)$. Write a computer program to disprove this claim. (The smallest counterexample lies between 1000 and 10000.) Then create similar conjectures of your own.

3.7   Existence

As we have just seen, to show that an assertion is false one usually hunts for a counterexample consisting of numbers, a diagram, or some other mathematical object satisfying certain conditions. Thus to disprove the claim "For all positive real numbers x and y it is the case that $\frac{1}{2}(x+y) > \sqrt{xy}$," we need only find a single pair of real numbers x and y for which $\frac{1}{2}(x+y) \le \sqrt{xy}$.

QUICK QUERY   a) Find positive real numbers for which $\frac{1}{2}(x+y) \le \sqrt{xy}$.

Being naturally curious folk, mathematicians are also prone to search for objects with certain properties for the sheer pleasure of discovering whether or not they exist. For example, do there exist integers a, b and c such that $a+b+c = 3$ and $a^3 + b^3 + c^3 = 3$ other than the obvious solution $a = b = c = 1$? Or given two rectangles in the plane, does there necessarily exist a line that simultaneously cuts the areas of both of them in half? The answers to both these questions turns out to be yes, as you will discover in the exercises.

On the surface a question about existence seems more approachable than a proof. After all, one need only come up with a single object satisfying certain properties, as opposed to proving that an assertion is true for all values of the variables. While it is true that a solution to an existence question has a very different flavor than the proofs we have seen in previous sections, they are not necessarily easier to find. For example, Euler made a conjecture centuries ago that implies that it is not possible for the sum of three perfect fourth powers to equal another perfect fourth power. It was not until 1986 (well into the computer age) that Noam Elkies found a counterexample to this claim:

$$2682440^4 + 15365639^4 + 18796760^4 = 20615673^4.$$

The smallest possible counterexample still involves five and six digit numbers.

There are two standard methods for settling an existence question. The most obvious way is to exhibit a certain number or other mathematical object and show that it has the desired properties. This was the technique employed

---

[2]Our thanks to Tom Kilkelly for sharing this entertaining conjecture.

by Elkies, although there was certainly a good deal of insight and deeper mathematics going on behind the scenes. However, it is also possible to argue that something exists even though a precise description is never provided.

To provide a **constructive solution** to an existence problem, carefully describe the sought after mathematical object and demonstrate that it has the desired properties. It is also acceptable to give an **existence proof** by arguing that an object must exist without ever explicitly describing it.

CᴏɴCᴇᴘᴛ b) It is undeniably the fact that there exist two individuals in Los Angeles having the same number of hairs on their head. Which type of proof of this fact is more appropriate, a constructive solution or an existence proof?

To illustrate both approaches, let us prove that there exists a number with the property that adding 287 to this number gives a total of 1000. The most obvious solution would be to point out that 713 has the desired property, since $713 + 287 = 1000$. Believe it or not, one can also convincingly argue for the existence of such a number without actually identifying it! Consider the sums $1 + 287, 2 + 287, 3 + 287$, and so on. The results, of course, are 288, 289, 290 and on up. Eventually we must hit 1000, even if it is not clear at precisely what point we arrive. Hence the number we are seeking does indeed exist.

CᴏɴCᴇᴘᴛ c) Give both an existence proof and a constructive solution showing that there exists a real number satisfying $4x + 4^x = 14$.

Depending on the problem at hand, there are a variety of strategies for obtaining a constructive solution. When searching for a positive integer with certain properties it is often possible to perform a computer search which tests each positive integer in turn for the desired property. This was the approach taken by the author to find the counterexample $n = 26861$ mentioned earlier in this chapter. In geometry problems, a constructive solution generally consists of a step-by-step sequence of geometric operations that yields the sought after point, line, or circle. An existence problem involving numbers might have as its solution an algebraic expression.

To understand what is meant by the latter remark, suppose that we wish to prove that there exists a rational number between any two other rational numbers. Letting $r < s$ be the two given fractions, we claim that the number $\frac{1}{2}(r+s)$ satisfies the statement of the problem. To begin, this quantity is clearly also a rational number: if we write $r = a/b$ and $s = c/d$ for integers a, b, c, d then $\frac{1}{2}(r+s) = (ad+bc)/2bd$, a ratio of integers. And since $\frac{1}{2}(r+s)$ is the average of r and s it lies midway between them. More precisely, we have $r < \frac{1}{2}(r+s)$ since this inequality is equivalent to $\frac{1}{2}r < \frac{1}{2}s$, which reduces to $r < s$, a given fact. In the same way we find that $\frac{1}{2}(r + s) < s$ as well, establishing that $\frac{1}{2}(r + s)$ does lie between r and s.

Solutions to harder existence questions might require a bit of ingenuity to construct. For instance, consider the unexpectedly long list of integers 114, 115, 116, 117, 118, 119, 120, 121, 122, 123, 124, 125, 126, all of which are *not* prime. (We have to wait until 524, 525, ..., 540 to reach a longer string of non-primes.) It is natural to wonder whether there are arbitrarily long strings of consecutive composite numbers; say, one thousand composites in a row. The answer is yes, and the construction of such a sequence is both simple and delightfully clever. Consider the numbers

$$1001! + 2, \; 1001! + 3, \; 1001! + 4, \; \ldots, \; 1001! + 1001,$$

where $1001! = (1001)(1000)(999) \cdots (2)(1)$ as usual. The first number is clearly even, the second number is divisible by 3, and so on, all the way to the final number, which is a multiple of 1001. Voilà, one thousand consecutive numbers, none of which are prime.[†]

CONCEPT CHECK d) Do there exist one thousand consecutive numbers, none of which are perfect squares?

To illustrate an existence proof in another context, we shall convince ourselves that given 101 points in the plane, no three of which lie on the same line, there exists a line through one of the points that neatly divides the remaining points in half, with fifty points on either side. To see why this must always be the case, imagine drawing a line through one of the points (call it P) on the "edge" of the set, so that all the remaining points are to one side of the line. Now steadily rotate the line 180° clockwise, keeping track along the way of how many points the line has crossed. As the line rotates it must cross the other points one at a time, since no three points lie on a single line. Furthermore, after 180° the line will have passed all 100 points. Hence at some point it will have just passed 50 points; this position of the line solves the problem.

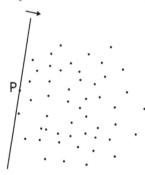

ALL THE ANSWERS a) Choosing $x = y = 5$ results in $\frac{1}{2}(x + y) = 5 = \sqrt{xy}$. This is the best we can do; it is not possible to obtain $\frac{1}{2}(x + y) < \sqrt{xy}$.
b) An existence proof probably springs to mind first. Since every human has less than 200,000 hairs on their head and there are well more than this number of individuals in Los Angeles, it is not possible for everyone to have a different number of hairs on their head. However, a constructive solution is also feasible; just find two completely bald men.
c) Clearly the quantity $4x + 4^x$ grows steadily as x increases. At $x = 1$ we obtain 8, while $x = 2$ gives 24, so at some point in between we must have $4x + 4^x = 14$. (Technically, we are invoking the Intermediate Value Theorem.) However, it is also possible to exhibit a solution. Taking $x = 1.5$ we find that $4(1.5) + 4^{1.5} = 6 + 8 = 14$.
d) There are indeed one thousand consecutive nonsquare numbers. For instance, take the 2000 numbers between 1000^2 and 1001^2.

EXERCISES

50. Show that there are numbers x and y such that $x + y = \pi$ and $x - y = \sqrt{2}$.

51. Disprove the claim that for all positive real numbers x and y it is the case that $x + 2y < \sqrt{8xy}$.

52. Prove that there exist three consecutive integers, one of which is divisible by 3^2, one of which is divisible by 5^2, and one of which is divisible by 7^2.

53. Demonstrate that there exist three integers a, b and c other than the obvious choice $a = b = c = 1$ such that $a + b + c = 3$ and $a^3 + b^3 + c^3 = 3$. (HINT: the solution only involves one-digit numbers, one of which is negative.)

54. Explain why there is a real number x satisfying $8^x + 9x = 10$. Give both an existence proof and a constructive solution.

55. Given a circle in the plane, what must be true of a line that cuts the circle's area in half? Based on your answer, explain how to construct a line that simultaneously cuts the area of two different circles each in half.

56. Use the ideas developed in the previous exercise to show that given any two rectangles in the plane, there exists a line that simultaneously cuts the area of each rectangle in half. In what situations will such a line not be unique?

WRITING

57. Demonstrate that there exist two positive integers which differ by ten whose sum is one million. Give both an existence proof and a constructive solution.

58. Ten children at a party collect a total of 74 pieces of candy from a piñata. Prove that there exists some child who received at least 8 pieces of candy.

59. Show that there exist 1000 consecutive positive integers, each having two or more digits, such that the first number is not even, the next is not a multiple of 3, the third is not a multiple of 4, and so on.

60. Prove that there exists a real number r with $0 < r < 1$ having the property that every possible finite string of digits appears at some place within its decimal expansion. (For example, the string '314159' should occur if we look far enough out in the decimal expansion for r.)

61. Given 102 points in the plane, no three of which lie on the same line, prove that there exists a line passing through two of the points which divides the remaining points in half, with fifty points on each side of the line.

62. Show that for every $n \in \mathbb{N}$, a unique number in the list $n + 1, n + 2, \ldots, 2n$ is a power of 2. (Recall that the powers of 2 are 1, 2, 4, 8, 16, ...)

63. We are give one-hundred points in the plane so that no three are situated along the same line. Fifty of the points are colored red, while the remaining fifty are colored blue. Prove that there exists a line dividing each set of points in half, with twenty-five red points and twenty-five blue points on either side.

3.8   Reference

We give a summary of the various types of proofs that have been presented,
along with a sample paragraph to illustrate how to phrase such a proof.

∗ *Direct Proof* This is the most common type of argument. Each step in such an
argument follows directly from previous steps or from the hypotheses until the
desired conclusion is reached. Along the way the proof may appeal to definitions
or other relevant known facts to move from one step to the next.

∗ *Proof by Contrapositive* This technique is most advantageous when both
the conclusion and hypothesis claim that something does not occur; i.e., are
negative statements. The first task is to carefully state the contrapositive of the
implication $P \Rightarrow Q$, which is written as "If not Q then not P." Then prove the
contrapositive statement instead, using whatever method works best. *Note that
it is not valid to write the contrapositive as* "not P and not Q."

> Begin the proof by saying "We prove the contrapositive, which states that
> [write contrapositive]. This is true because [proof of contrapositive]."

∗ *Proof by Contradiction* This technique is also effective when attempting to
prove that something does *not* occur, such as as an implication of the form
$P \Rightarrow Q$ where Q is a negative statement. The idea is to assume the negative
of the conclusion and then argue to a contradiction. In other words, show that
assuming both P and $\neg Q$ leads to an impossible or absurd situation.

> Begin the proof by saying "Suppose to the contrary that [state negative
> of conclusion here]. Then [main argument leading to absurd statement],
> which is a contradiction. Hence our assumption is false, which means that
> [original conclusion] must be true."

∗ *Biconditional Proofs* Here one wishes to prove a statement of the form "Under
certain conditions, $P \Longleftrightarrow Q$." This is usually signified by the phrase "P if and
only if Q" or "P is necessary and sufficient for Q." To prove a biconditional,
show that each statement implies the other, using any helpful proof techniques.
Present these arguments in separate paragraphs.

> The first paragraph might begin "We first prove that $P \Rightarrow Q$. [Proof of im-
> plication]" An abbreviated form looks like "($\Longrightarrow$) [Proof of implication]"
> The second paragraph could read "Conversely, $Q \Rightarrow P$ because [proof of
> implication]" which can be shortened to "($\Longleftarrow$) [Proof of implication]"

Alternatively, one can prove a biconditional $P \Longleftrightarrow Q$ by showing that $P \Rightarrow Q$
and also $\neg P \Rightarrow \neg Q$. One would again prove each implication separately.

∗ *Characterization* To show that a property characterizes a certain class of
objects, show that an object satisfies has the property if and only if it is a
member of the designated class of objects.

> One could write "To begin, suppose that [x is an object in the class of
> objects]. [Proof that x has the property.] On the other hand, suppose that
> [x has the property]. [Proof that x is a member of the class of objects.]
> This shows that [property] characterizes [class of objects]."

∗ *Vacuous Proof* If while digesting the statement to be proven it comes to light that the premise is never true, one can employ a vacuous proof. (This typically only occurs when dealing with empty sets, special cases of general results, or artificially concocted textbook problems.)

> A proof would look like "We will show that the statement is vacuously true. Observe that [premise] is never true because [include reasons here]. This completes the proof."

∗ *Trivial Proof* If while digesting the statement to be proven it comes to light that the conclusion is always true irregardless of the premise, one can employ a trivial proof. (In actual practice this sort of proof rarely comes up.)

> A proof would look like "We will show that the statement is trivially true. Observe that [conclusion] is always true because [include reasons here]. This completes the proof."

∗ *Disproving an Assertion* A disproof would involve stating and then proving the negation of the assertion. Mathematical claims usually take the form of a universally quantified implication; i.e. a statement of the form "For all values of the variables, $P \Rightarrow Q$." In this situation to supply a disproof it suffices to find a single counterexample: find an instance in which P is true but Q is false. This is essentially an instance of an existence argument.

∗ *Existence* The most common way to demonstrate that a mathematical object having certain properties does indeed exist is to construct an object and then show that it satisfies the stated conditions. At times it may also be possible to convincingly argue for the existence of the object without actually giving an explicit example of such an object.

Sample Proofs

The following proofs provide concise explanations for results discussed within this chapter. They are meant to serve as an illustration for how proofs of similar statements could be phrased. The boldface numbers indicate the section containing each result; the location of that result within the section is marked by a dagger (†).

———◆———

3.4 Prove for any sets A, B and C that if $A - C \not\subseteq A - B$ then $B \not\subseteq C$.

Proof We will prove the contrapositive of the given implication, which states that if $B \subseteq C$ then $A - C \subseteq A - B$. To conclude that $A - C \subseteq A - B$ we must show that if $x \in A - C$ then $x \in A - B$. So suppose that $x \in A - C$. This means that $x \in A$ but $x \notin C$. However, we are given that $B \subseteq C$. Because $x \notin C$, we may deduce that $x \notin B$ either. We now have $x \in A$ but $x \notin B$, which means that $x \in A - B$, as desired. Finally, since the contrapositive is logically equivalent to the original statement, we are done.

———◆———

3.4 Demonstrate that if α is irrational then 3α is also irrational.

Proof Suppose to the contrary that 3α is rational. This would mean that we could write $3\alpha = \frac{m}{n}$ for integers m and n. Dividing by 3 yields $\alpha = \frac{m}{3n}$. But this contradicts the fact that we are told that α is irrational, since we could write α as the ratio $\frac{m}{3n}$ of the integers m and $3n$. Since supposing that 3α is rational leads to a contradiction, we conclude that 3α is irrational, as claimed.

$$\longrightarrow\!\!\!\diamond\!\!\!\longrightarrow$$

3.5 Prove that for sets A and B we have $A \cup B = B$ if and only if $A \subseteq B$.

Proof We first explain why $A \cup B = B$ implies $A \subseteq B$. To deduce that $A \subseteq B$ we will show that if $x \in A$ then $x \in B$. So suppose that $x \in A$. Then clearly $x \in A \cup B$ by definition of union. Since $A \cup B = B$, it follows that $x \in B$.

   We next prove the converse, which states that $A \subseteq B$ implies $A \cup B = B$. To conclude that $A \cup B = B$ we will argue that if $x \in A \cup B$ then $x \in B$ and vice-versa. So suppose that $x \in A \cup B$; then either $x \in A$ or $x \in B$. In the former case, we deduce that $x \in B$ since $A \subseteq B$. Hence $x \in B$ in either case, as desired. It remains to show that if $x \in B$ then $x \in A \cup B$, but this is clear by definition of union. Hence $A \cup B = B$ as claimed, which completes the proof.

$$\longrightarrow\!\!\!\diamond\!\!\!\longrightarrow$$

3.5 Show that $3n + 4$ is a perfect square whenever $n^2 + 5n + 6$ is a prime.

Proof Observe that the expression $n^2 + 5n + 6$ factors as $(n+2)(n+3)$. Since each factor is 3 or more for $n \in \mathbb{N}$, their product cannot be a prime. Hence the premise is always false, meaning that the statement is vacuously true.

$$\longrightarrow\!\!\!\diamond\!\!\!\longrightarrow$$

3.6 Prove or disprove the claim that for all $n \in \mathbb{N}$, if n is prime then $6n + 1$ is also prime.

Disproof We will disprove the statement by showing that its negative is true; namely, that there exists an $n \in \mathbb{N}$ such that n is prime but $6n+1$ is not prime. One such value of n is $n = 19$, since 19 is prime but $6(19)+1 = 115$ is not. This counterexample provides the disproof.

$$\longrightarrow\!\!\!\diamond\!\!\!\longrightarrow$$

3.7 Demonstrate that there exist one thousand consecutive positive integers, none of which are prime.

Proof We claim that the numbers

$$1001! + 2, \ 1001! + 3, \ 1001! + 4, \ \ldots, \ 1001! + 1001$$

satisfy the statement of the problem. Here $1001! = (1001)(1000)(999)\cdots(2)(1)$ as usual. Clearly $1001!$ is a multiple of 2, hence so is $1001! + 2$. Since this number is divisible by 2 it is not prime. In the same manner, for each k in the range $2 \leq k \leq 1001$ we find that $1001!$ is a multiple of k, hence so is $1001! + k$, which means that this number is not prime. In summary, our list contains one thousand consecutive integers, none of which are prime, so we are done.

CHAPTER 4

Number Theory

4.1 Divisibility

Carl Friedrich Gauss, one of the greatest mathematicians the world has ever seen, is quoted as stating that "Mathematics is the queen of the sciences and the theory of numbers is the queen of mathematics." Simply put, number theory is the study of properties of the integers. Therefore its elevation to royal status may seem slightly exaggerated at first—why should we expect deep, beautiful results awaiting us in the list $\{\ldots, -3, -2, -1, 0, 1, 2, 3, \ldots\}$? But the belief that the integers are easily understood is typically based on a view of the integers as an *additive group*; in other words, a set of numbers which can only be combined via addition and subtraction. However, the integers are in fact a *ring*, meaning that they can also be multiplied and (when possible) divided. It is the curious interplay between addition and multiplication that leads to far more exciting mathematics than one would at first imagine.

Let us begin with one of the most basic multiplicative notions.

> Given integers a and b, we say that b is **divisible** by a exactly when b is an integral multiple of a, meaning that we can write $b = ma$ for an integer m. We write $a \mid b$ to indicate that a divides b. This definition does not apply for $a = 0$; in particular, we do not say that 0 is divisible by 0.

Thus -91 is divisible by 7, since we have $-91 = (-13)(7)$. Similarly, it would be correct to write $13 \mid 104$ and $3n^2 \mid 15n^3$ for $n \in \mathbb{N}$. Since 6 does not divide 80, we write $6 \nmid 80$ instead. Observe that 0 is divisible by every nonzero integer, but no integer is divisible by 0.

C⊙NCEPT a) Determine whether the following statements are true or false.
i. $7^2 \mid 2009$ *ii.* $0 \mid 5$ *iii.* $2n \mid n^2$ for $n \in \mathbb{N}$ *iv.* $234 \nmid (-469)$ *v.* $89 \nmid (2^{11} - 1)$

Using only the definition, it is possible to prove quite a few elementary facts involving divisibility. For instance, it stands to reason that if a is even and b is a multiple of 5, then ab will be divisible by 10. We can prove this by using the definition of divisibility to write $a = 2k$ and $b = 5l$ for $k, l \in \mathbb{Z}$, then multiplying to obtain $ab = 10(kl)$. Since kl is an integer, we deduce that ab is divisible by 10 as claimed. Observe that it would have been incorrect to write $a = 2k$ and $b = 5k$ in our proof. To state this would be to require that a and b be the *same* multiple of 2 and 5, which is not necessarily the case. For example, it would be fine to have $a = 34 = 2(17)$ while $b = 35 = 5(7)$.

The concept of divisibility applies to all integers; positive, zero or negative. However, in many situations we are only interested in positive integers.

The synonymous terms **divisor** and **factor** refer to any positive integer dividing a particular natural number. Furthermore, a **proper divisor** is any divisor of a number strictly less than the number.

Thus the divisors (or factors) of 10 are 1, 2, 5 and 10, while the proper divisors of 52 are 1, 2, 4, 13 and 26.

CONCEPT b) What positive integer has proper divisors 1, 3, 7, 9, and 21?

The question of which divisors two numbers have in common plays an important role in certain situations. The next Mathematical Outing illustrates one such instance. For another, consider the economically backward country of Wierdbillia, where currency comes in only two denominations: a $33 bill and a $45 bill. Before reading on, determine the answers to the following questions.

i. How can a Wierdbillian buy a microwave that costs $177?

ii. Describe how a diner in Wierdbillia can buy a $9 meal.

iii. What is the smallest amount for which a transaction can occur?

A little thought reveals that it is possible to make change for any amount that is a multiple of three. In particular, a $3 item may be purchased by handing over three $45 bills and receiving four $33 bills in exchange. (The reader is invited to find similarly efficient means of spending $177 or $9.) The significance of the number 3 is that it is the largest positive integer that divides both 33 and 45.

A **common divisor** of $a, b \in \mathbb{N}$ is a positive integer that divides into both a and b. The largest such divisor is the **greatest common divisor** of a and b, written as $\mathrm{GCD}(a, b)$ or just (a, b) for short. Since 1 is always a common divisor, we know that (a, b) exists for any a and b.

Mathematical Outing ★ ★ ★

Perform the following experiment. Create a rectangle on a sheet of graph paper having width 3 and height 5, enclosing 15 unit squares, as shown. Trace the path of a hypothetical billiard ball that begins in the lower left corner and initially travels upward at a 45° angle. Assuming that the ball bounces off the walls at perfect 45° angles, which corner

does the ball reach first? What fraction of the 15 unit squares does the ball pass through on its way? Repeat this experiment for other rectangles having width a and height b. Come up with a means of predicting the first corner the ball reaches and the fraction of squares visited along the way, based on the values of a and b.

Although the notation (a, b) could potentially be misconstrued as an ordered pair, the context usually makes it clear which concept applies. The most obvious way to compute (a, b) is to list the prime factors of both a and b, then inspect them to find all common prime factors. For instance, since $264 = 2^3 \cdot 3 \cdot 11$ and $308 = 2^2 \cdot 7 \cdot 11$, we compute $(264, 308) = 2^2 \cdot 11 = 44$. (There is a technique known as the *Euclidean algorithm* for finding GCDs that is computationally far superior to inspecting prime factors, but we will not present it here.)

CONCEPT c) Compute the value of $(84, 7000)$ and $(2n, n^2)$ for $n \in \mathbb{N}$.

Most students first encounter greatest common divisors while learning to reduce fractions. We know that to reduce a fraction $\frac{a}{b}$ to lowest terms, we must divide both a and b by their GCD. For instance, we reduce $\frac{18}{30}$ to $\frac{3}{5}$ by dividing both numerator and denominator by $\text{GCD}(18, 30) = 6$. A fraction $\frac{a}{b}$ is already in lowest terms if $\text{GCD}(a, b) = 1$.

When the greatest common divisor of two integers a and b is 1 we say that the integers are **relatively prime**.

On a slightly more sophisticated note, let us demonstrate that the greatest common divisor of $n + 1$ and $2n^2 + 3n + 4$ is 1 or 3 for all natural numbers n.

CONCEPT d) Confirm the above assertion for the values $n = 1, 2, 3, 4$ and 5.

Our strategy will be to suppose that d is a positive integer such that $d \mid (n + 1)$ and $d \mid (2n^2 + 3n + 4)$, then show that we can only have $d = 1$ or $d = 3$. Since $n + 1$ and $2n^2 + 3n + 4$ are both divisible by d, if we subtract a multiple of $n + 1$ from $2n^2 + 3n + 4$, the result will still be a multiple of d. (We will formally establish this fact in the exercises.) In other words, d will divide into

$$(2n^2 + 3n + 4) - 2n(n + 1) = n + 4.$$

Notice that by using $2n$ as the multiplier we eliminated the $2n^2$ term from the quadratic. By the same reasoning, we may further deduce that d must divide evenly into $(n+4) - (n+1) = 3$. Hence $d \mid 3$, which means that we can only have $d = 1$ or $d = 3$, as claimed.[†]

ANSWERS

a) *i.* True *ii.* False *iii.* False (try $n = 1$) *iv.* True *v.* False
b) These are the proper divisors of 63.
c) We find that $(84, 7000) = 28$. Also we have $(2n, n^2) = n$ when n is odd but $(2n, n^2) = 2n$ when n is even.
d) For $n = 1$ through 5 we compute the GCDs as $(2, 9) = 1$, $(3, 18) = 3$, $(4, 31) = 1$, $(5, 48) = 1$, and $(6, 69) = 3$.

In general one should find that the fraction of squares traversed by the billiard ball on its way to a corner is $1/d$, where $d = (a, b)$. Hence the greatest common divisor comes into play. The corner the ball first reaches may be predicted by computing a/d and b/d. (As if one were reducing the fraction a/b.) If both numbers are odd, the ball lands on the upper right corner. If a/d is odd while b/d is even it reaches the upper left corner, and if a/d is even while b/d is odd it lands on the lower right corner. The interested reader may wish to prove these conjectures.

EXERCISES

1. Determine whether the following statements are true or false.
a) $37 \mid 111111$ b) $7 \mid 123456$ c) $-4 \mid (-20)$ d) $-5 \mid 35$
e) $0 \mid 6$ f) $6 \mid 0$ g) $-5 \nmid 6$ h) $2 \nmid (-10)$
i) $-1 \mid 280$ j) $17 \mid 1$ k) $55 \mid 55$ l) $-87 \mid 87$

2. Compile a complete list of integers d such that $d \mid 23$. Now do the same for 24 and -25.

3. Let n be any positive integer. Explain why the following statements are true.
a) $1 \mid n$ b) $(-n) \mid n^3$ c) $n \mid 0$ d) $n \mid (-3n)$ e) $2 \mid n(n+1)$

4. Compute the following greatest common divisors.
a) $(42, 91)$ b) $(-30, -20)$ c) $(105, -64)$ d) $(25, 100)$ e) $(120, 121)$

5. For $n \in \mathbb{N}$, determine the value of $(1, n)$, $(3n, 2n^2)$, and $(n, 7n + 1)$.

6. Name an integer that is relatively prime to every other non-zero integer. How many such integers are there?

7. Find a counterexample to the claim that if a is relatively prime to b, and b is relatively prime to c, then a and c are also relatively prime.

8. Demonstrate that (a, b) is not necessarily equal to $(a, a + 2b)$ for $a, b \in \mathbb{N}$.

9. Suppose instead that Wierdbillia only minted \$22 and \$60 bills. What is the smallest amount for which a transaction is possible? What if the currency consisted only of \$9 and \$14 bills? Demonstrate how the minimal transaction could take place in each case.

Writing

10. Let a, b and c be integers such that $a \mid b$ and $b \mid c$. Prove that $a \mid c$.

11. Suppose that a and b are non-zero integers. Prove that $a \mid b$ and $b \mid a$ if and only if $a = b$ or $a = -b$.

12. For $c, d \in \mathbb{Z}$ with $c \neq 0$, prove that if $c^3 \nmid d^3$ then $c \nmid d$.

13. Disprove the assertion: "There exist distinct positive integers $a, b > 1$ such that for all natural numbers n we have $(a, n) = 1$ or $(b, n) = 1$."

14. Suppose that $d \mid a$ and $d \mid b$. Prove that d also divides the sum of any multiples of a and b; i.e. $d \mid (ak + bl)$ for any $k, l \in \mathbb{Z}$. (This fact justifies the steps used in the final proof of the section.)

15. Prove that the GCD of $n + 2001$ and $n^2 + 1999n - 4000$ is either 1 or 2.

16. Prove that $n + 2$ and $3n^2 + 4n - 5$ are relatively prime for all $n \in \mathbb{N}$.

Further Exploration

17. Which amounts of water may be measured exactly using a seven-cup measure and a ten-cup measure? Obviously seven cups and ten cups. We can also easily obtain three cups, by filling the ten-cup measure, then pouring its contents into the empty seven-cup measure until it is just filled, leaving three cups behind. What other amounts from one to ten cups may be exactly measured? How does the answer change if we replace the seven-cup measure by a six-cup measure? In general, how can one predict the amounts that can be obtained using an a-cup and b-cup measure?

4.2 Divisor Diversions

One of the reasons that number theory appeals to so many students is that delightful, elementary results abound. Therefore we pause to consider two such results in the present section. The first is featured in the next Mathematical Outing, while the second describes a certain Greek ideal, at least where numbers are concerned. Both require an understanding of prime factorization, to which we now turn.

One means of explaining the pattern that appears in the Mathematical Outing relies on a formula for counting the number of divisors of a given natural number. Every $n \geq 2$ is guaranteed to have at least two divisors; namely 1 and n, known as **trivial divisors**. We say that a positive integer $p \geq 2$ is a **prime** if these are its only divisors; i.e. p has no nontrivial divisors. The first ten primes are 2, 3, 5, 7, 11, 13, 17, 19, 23 and 29. Note that 1 is most emphatically *not* a prime; rather, it is more accurately described as "the absence of primes," as you will discover in the exercises.

[CONCEPT] a) Form as long a list of primes as possible, using each of the digits from 1 to 8 exactly once.

Mathematical Outing ★ ★ ★

Imagine that a mischievous group of high school math club students play the following game in a deserted corridor lined with 200 closed but unlocked lockers. One student opens every single locker door, then another closes every second door (lockers 2, 4, 6, ...), then yet another reverses the state of every third locker (closing the open ones and opening the closed ones), then another student reverses the state of every fourth locker, and so on. After the students have collectively made 200 passes down the hall in this manner, how many locker doors will be open?

To answer this question, first perform the experiment with only 20 lockers. Make a conjecture based on your findings and use it to propose an answer for the case of 200 lockers. Finally, explain why your conjecture is valid.

The prime numbers quickly lead to unexpectedly deep mathematical water. We will consider some of the fascinating results and conjectures regarding primes in a later section. At that point we will demonstrate that there are infinitely many primes, although the proof of this fact is far from trivial. Similarly, the following result requires considerably more effort to rigorously prove than most students realize upon first reading it.

> The **Fundamental Theorem of Arithmetic** states that every natural number n can be written uniquely as the product of a finite collection of primes. This unique decomposition of n into a product of primes is known as the **prime factorization** of n.

For instance, the number 123456 is the product of the primes 2, 2, 2, 2, 2, 2, 3, and 643, which we indicate by writing $123456 = 2^6 \cdot 3 \cdot 643$. It is conceivable that we could somehow obtain 123456 by multiplying together a different collection of primes, but the Fundamental Theorem of Arithmetic rules out this possibility.

We are now prepared to develop a shortcut for counting the number of divisors of a given natural number n, a quantity we call $d(n)$. For example, the factors of 15 are 1, 3, 5 and 15, so $d(15) = 4$.

CONCEPT b) What can be said about a natural number n if $d(n) = 2$?

QUERY c) Find an organized method for listing all the divisors of 200 in a rectangular array. Consequently, what is $d(200)$?

We demonstrate the method of counting divisors by computing $d(84)$. To begin, we factor this number as $84 = 2^2 \cdot 3 \cdot 7$. Thus to build a divisor of 84 we start with some 2's (either zero, one, or at most two factors of 2), toss in a 3 if desired, then either multiply in a 7 or leave it out. We have three choices for the number of 2's to include, two choices for the 3, and two choices for the 7, for a total of $3 \cdot 2 \cdot 2 = 12$ ways to build a divisor of 84. By employing the same reasoning we can determine $d(n)$ for any natural number n.

> Given $n \in \mathbb{N}$, let $n = p_1^{e_1} p_2^{e_2} \cdots p_k^{e_k}$ be its prime factorization. Then the number of divisors of n is given by $d(n) = (e_1 + 1)(e_2 + 1) \cdots (e_k + 1)$.

C⅞ℇC⅞ d) How many proper divisors does 1,000,000 have?

In the exercises we will outline how to use this formula to prove the pattern suggested by the Mathematical Outing.

Once one tires of counting divisors, it is natural to add them up instead. It doesn't take long to discover the curious fact that if we sum the proper divisors of 6 we obtain $1 + 2 + 3 = 6$. Similarly, the sum of the proper divisors of 28 is $1 + 2 + 4 + 7 + 14 = 28$. The Greeks were so enamored by this property that they bestowed the title of **perfect number** upon any natural number n which is equal to the sum of its proper divisors. The four perfect numbers known by the Greeks were 6, 28, 496 and 8128. The next largest one is 33550336. Over forty-five perfect numbers are currently known; it is likely that there are infinitely many of them.

C⅞ℇC⅞ e) Confirm that 496 is a perfect number.

Although Euclid is best-known to students today for his systematic treatment of geometry, he made many significant contributions to number theory as well. For instance, Euclid is credited with recognizing that each of the first four perfect numbers has the form $2^{n-1}(2^n - 1)$ and further observing that in each case $(2^n - 1)$ is a prime. He went on to show that whenever $(2^n - 1)$ is prime it follows that $2^{n-1}(2^n - 1)$ is a perfect number. The proof is elementary yet quite satisfying, so we will present it here.

Let us show that if $(2^n - 1)$ is a prime, then $2^{n-1}(2^n - 1)$ is a perfect number. To make our presentation less cluttered, we will write $p = 2^n - 1$ for the prime. We begin by listing all the proper divisors of $2^{n-1}p$.

$$
\begin{array}{cccccc}
1 & 2 & 4 & \cdots & 2^{n-2} & 2^{n-1} \\
p & 2p & 4p & \cdots & 2^{n-2}p &
\end{array}
$$

We left $2^{n-1}p$ off the list since we are including only proper divisors. The sum of the divisors along the top row is $1 + 2 + 4 + \cdots + 2^{n-1}$, which neatly reduces to just $2^n - 1$. (An explanation of this familiar fact is left as an exercise.) Similarly, the sum of the bottom row is

$$p + 2p + 4p + \cdots + 2^{n-2}p = (1 + 2 + 4 + \cdots + 2^{n-2})p = (2^{n-1} - 1)p.$$

The grand total is $2^n - 1 + (2^{n-1} - 1)p$. This doesn't look promising, until we recall that $p = 2^n - 1$, so the sum may be written as $p + (2^{n-1} - 1)p = 2^{n-1}p$.

Sure enough, after summing the proper divisors, we wind up with exactly the same number with which we began.[†]

Centuries after Euclid performed this very computation, the Swiss mathematician Leonhard Euler achieved the somewhat more delicate task of proving that these were the only even perfect numbers; in other words, that all even perfect numbers have the form $2^{n-1}(2^n - 1)$ where $p = 2^n - 1$ is prime. It is almost certainly the case that there are no odd perfect numbers, but this conjecture turns out to be surprisingly difficult to prove. Despite a fair amount of progress, no proof has yet been found to conclusively demonstrate that no odd perfect number exists.

a) No prime ends with 4, 6 or 8 so we can create five primes at most. This can be achieved by taking 2, 5, 41, 67 and 83.

b) The only numbers having just two divisors are the primes.

c) We list 1, 2, 4, 8 as the top row of the array, followed by 5, 10, 20, 40 as the second row and 25, 50, 100, 200 as the third row. (Note that each row is 5 times the previous row.) This is a 3×4 array, hence 200 has exactly 12 divisors.

d) We know that $1,000,000 = 10^6 = 2^6 5^6$, therefore $d(1,000,000) = (6+1)(6+1) = 49$. But we don't count 1,000,000 itself as a proper divisor, so the answer is 48.

e) The divisors of 496 are 1, 2, 4, 8, 16, 31, 62, 124 and 248, which do sum to 496.

🖳 Carefully performing the experiment with twenty lockers results in the doors numbered 1, 4, 9 and 16 being open at the end of the day. These are precisely the square numbers less than 20, so we conjecture that in the case of 200 lockers only doors numbered 1, 4, 9, ..., 169, 196 will be open; a total of 14 doors.

EXERCISES

18. What fraction of the numbers from 1 to 100 are prime?

19. Find the prime factorization of 111111.

20. Without actually listing them all, count the number of divisors of 30. Do the same for 243 and 324.

21. There are five natural numbers less than 100 having exactly twelve divisors. We have seen that 84 is one such number. Find the other four.

22. To help appreciate that factoring numbers is hard, attempt to find the prime factorization of 46903, a zip code in Kokomo, IN, using only a calculator.

23. An alternate way of indicating a prime factorization is to include every prime in the product, but to use an exponent of zero for all but finitely many of the primes. Thus we could write $84 = 2^2 \cdot 3^1 \cdot 5^0 \cdot 7^1 \cdot 11^0 \cdot 13^0 \cdots$. Write the prime factorizations of 1001, 135 and 1 in this manner. Why does it make sense to describe 1 as "the absence of primes"?

24. What can be said about a natural number n if $d(n) = 3$?

25. Multiply out $(1 + 3 + 9)(1 + 7)$. In other words, expand this expression as if you were multiplying two polynomials together. Your answer should look like

$1 + 3 + \cdots + 63$. How does this computation give a shortcut for finding the sum of the divisors of 63?

26. Use the idea from the previous problem to compute the sum of all the divisors of 1000 without actually listing its divisors. Then describe a general method for directly computing the sum of the divisors of a natural number n.

27. Find the sum of all the divisors of 672. In what way does 672 behave like a perfect number?

WRITING

28. Prove that if $n = p_1^{e_1} p_2^{e_2} \cdots p_k^{e_k}$, where $p_1, p_2, \ldots, p_k$ are the prime divisors of n, then $d(n) = (e_1 + 1)(e_2 + 1) \cdots (e_k + 1)$.

29. Prove that $d(n)$ is odd precisely when n is a perfect square.

30. Use the result of the previous problem to show that in the Mathematical Outing for this section, the only locker doors remaining open at the end of the game are those numbered with a perfect square.

31. Find a positive integer having eleven divisors. Then demonstrate that in general there exists a positive integer having exactly t divisors for any $t \in \mathbb{N}$.

32. Prove that if n is odd then $d(2n) = 2d(n)$. Why does this equality not hold when n is even?

33. Suppose that $2^n - 1$ is a prime, so that we can write $p = 2^n - 1$. Show that the sum of the proper divisors of $2^{n-1}p^2$ is equal to $2^{n-1}p^2 + p$. Thus $2^{n-1}p^2$ is not quite a perfect number, but in some respect it comes close.

34. Prove that there exists a positive integer n such that the sum of the divisors of n is more than $3n$.

FURTHER EXPLORATION

35. Using the Fundamental Theorem of Arithmetic it is possible to show that a variety of real numbers are irrational rather than rational. For instance, let us show that $\sqrt{7}$ is irrational. It will come as no surprise to discover that we will employ proof by contradiction. So suppose to the contrary that $\sqrt{7}$ is rational, say $\sqrt{7} = \frac{m}{n}$ for $m, n \in \mathbb{N}$. Squaring both sides and clearing fractions leads to $m^2 = 7n^2$. As we have seen above, in a perfect square every prime factor is raised to an even power. In other words, there are an even number of 7's in the prime factorization of m^2. But m^2 and $7n^2$ are the same number, and there must be an odd number of 7's in the prime factorization of $7n^2$. (Why?) This contradiction forces us to conclude that $\sqrt{7}$ is irrational after all.

This technique of comparing prime factors on two sides of an equality can be applied in several other situations. Try your hand at showing that the following numbers are all irrational:

$$\sqrt{2}, \quad \sqrt{45}, \quad \sqrt[3]{4}, \quad \log_2 3, \quad \log_{10} 20.$$

4.3 Modular Arithmetic

Certain phenomena are *periodic*, meaning that they repeat over and over again. The day of the week or month of the year are both good examples of periodic behavior. Whenever this sort of situation occurs we are naturally led to identify different numbers as having essentially the same meaning. For example, imagine that today is Thursday. Since there are 7 days per week, it will clearly be the same day of the week 16 days from now as it will be 2 days from now; namely, a Saturday. The numbers 16 and 2 are equivalent when it comes to the day of the week, because 16 and 2 differ by a multiple of 7; that is, by a whole number of weeks. We express this observation compactly by writing $16 \equiv 2 \bmod 7$. This statement is read "16 is congruent to 2 mod 7" and simply means that 16 and 2 differ by a multiple of 7. For the same reason it would be correct to write $100 \equiv 2 \bmod 7$ and $-40 \equiv 2 \bmod 7$; it is also a Saturday 100 days from now or -40 days from now. (In other words, 40 days ago.)

CONCEPT CHECK a) Assume for sake of illustration that today is Monday. What day of the week will it be 60 days from now? What about -50 days from now?

Another way of analyzing the above situation is to realize that the numbers -40, 16 and 100 all brought us to a Saturday since they are all 2 more than a multiple of 7. In other words, if we advance the day of the week by any multiple of 7 days, plus 2 more days, then we will always land on a Saturday. We conclude that n days from now will be a Saturday iff n is of the form $7k + 2$, where k is an integer. It is important to understand that the mathematical statements "$n \equiv 2 \bmod 7$" and "$n = 7k + 2$ for some $k \in \mathbb{Z}$" are identical; they provide two different ways of saying that n and 2 differ by a multiple of 7.

CONCEPT CHECK b) Assume once more that today is Monday. Write both a congruence and an algebraic equality that describe the values of n such that n days from now it will be a Friday.

So far we have only considered congruences mod 7. However, we can define congruences in general according to the same principles.

The **congruence** $a \equiv b \bmod m$ means that a and b differ by a multiple of m, where a, b and m are integers with $m \neq 0$. The number m is called the **modulus**, and for most practical purposes we take $m \geq 2$. Declaring that $a \equiv b \bmod m$ is equivalent to saying that $a = km + b$ for some $k \in \mathbb{Z}$, which means that $a - b = km$ for some $k \in \mathbb{Z}$.

Congruences were first used as a mathematical tool by Euler. Not long after, Gauss made a more formal study of the mathematics arising from congruences, notably by developing the theory of quadratic reciprocity. It was Gauss who introduced the $\equiv$ notation that we still use today. Congruences have become an integral part of the language of mathematics for several reasons. Besides leading to elegant ideas and deep results, congruences also provide a convenient notation for many situations. Thus rather than saying "It will be a Saturday any number of days from now for which the number is two more than a multiple of seven," we can more efficiently state "For all $n \equiv 2 \bmod 7$ it will be a Saturday n days from today."

It is not a coincidence that Gauss chose a symbol for congruences that closely resembles an equal sign, for congruences share many properties with equality. For instance, we know that it is valid to square both sides of an equation. The same turns out to be true for congruences. In other words, if $a \equiv b \bmod m$ then we claim that it is also true that $a^2 \equiv b^2 \bmod m$.

CONCEPT CHECK c) Choose any pair of positive integers that are congruent mod 7 and confirm that their squares are also congruent mod 7. Repeat this computation, this time using one positive and one negative integer.

To prove a statement involving congruences, we translate it back into the language of algebra and divisibility, upon which congruences are built. Thus to say that $a \equiv b \bmod m$ means that $a - b = km$ for some $k \in \mathbb{Z}$. Similarly, to claim that $a^2 \equiv b^2 \bmod m$ is equivalent to requiring that $a^2 - b^2$ be a multiple of m. Therefore we must show algebraically that $a^2 - b^2 = (\ \cdots\ )m$, where the expression inside the parentheses is some integer. Keeping this strategy in mind, we focus on the quantity $a^2 - b^2$. Since this expression is a difference of squares, it can be factored:

$$a^2 - b^2 = (a - b)(a + b) = km(a + b) = (ka + kb)m.$$

Since we are given that $a - b = km$ we are able to replace the factor of $(a - b)$ by km above, leading to the discovery that $a^2 - b^2 = (ka + kb)m$. Since $(ka + kb)$ is an integer, we conclude that $a^2 - b^2$ is indeed a multiple of m. Therefore $a^2 \equiv b^2 \bmod m$, as desired. An alternate approach that requires more algebra but avoids the factoring step would be to write $a = km + b$, then substitute in for a in the expression $a^2 - b^2$ and simplify, yielding $(k^2m + 2kb)m$.[†]

Congruences share many other properties with equality. Thus the sums of congruent numbers are again congruent, as are their differences and products. You will develop some of these properties in the exercises. Quotients, however, are another matter. For the time being we will avoid dividing both sides of a congruence by the same number, since the results no longer need be congruent. It is these properties that make congruences such a useful tool for analyzing problems in number theory, as we shall see in the subsequent sections.

a) Since 60 days is 8 weeks plus 4 days, it will be the same day of the week as it will be 4 days from Monday, which is a Friday. Similarly, going back 50 days is the same as going back 7 weeks and one more day, so this time we reach a Sunday.

b) We can express this fact by writing $n \equiv 4 \bmod 7$ or $n = 7k + 4$ or $n - 4 = 7k$.

c) We might try $3 \equiv 10 \bmod 7$, leading to $3^2 \equiv 10^2 \bmod 7$. As predicted, $10^2 - 3^2 = 91 = 7 \cdot 13$ is a multiple of 7. Similarly, $5 \equiv -2 \bmod 7$ leads to $5^2 \equiv (-2)^2 \bmod 7$, which is also true since $5^2 - (-2)^2 = 21$ is a multiple of 7.

EXERCISES

36. Describe an efficient means of reducing 7654321 mod 35 using a calculator. I.e. find the integer r in the range $0 \leq r \leq 34$ for which $7654321 \equiv r$ mod 35.

37. Use the technique developed in the previous exercise to reduce 2468 mod 11, 314159 mod 123, 10^6 mod 17, and 55555 mod 88.

38. Suppose that it is currently 11:00 am and that in n hours it will be 2:00 pm. Write a congruence involving n which summarizes this information.

39. Suppose that it is currently 8:00 pm and that in n hours it will be 3:00 pm. What form must n take, algebraically?

40. Suppose that in the sequence of letters t, o, m, a, t, o, m, a, t, o, m, ... the nth term is an 'o'. What form must n take, algebraically?

41. Suppose that in the sequence of letters above the nth term is an 'm'. Write a congruence involving n which summarizes this information.

42. List the powers of 7 from 7^0 up to 7^9. For which $n \in \mathbb{N}$ is the last digit of 7^n equal to 9? Write your answer using a congruence.

43. Determine whether the following statements are true or false.

   a) $321 \equiv 123$ mod 101   d) $2713 \equiv 2713$ mod 41
   b) $-10 \equiv 10$ mod 6   e) $3 \cdot 16 \equiv 3 \cdot 2$ mod 7
   c) $16^2 \equiv 2^2$ mod 7   f) $91 \equiv 0$ mod 13

44. For which positive integers $m \geq 2$ is it the case that $1^4 \equiv 2^4$ mod m?

45. For how many positive integers $m \geq 2$ is it the case that $-3 \equiv 3^4$ mod m?

46. For how many positive integers $m \geq 2$ do we have $4^5 \equiv 4$ mod m?

47. Find two even numbers a and b such that $a \equiv b$ mod 10, but $\frac{1}{2}a \not\equiv \frac{1}{2}b$ mod 10. (Your example illustrates that division within congruences is not always valid.)

WRITING

48. Prove that a is divisible by m if and only if $a \equiv 0$ mod m.

49. Demonstrate that sums of congruent numbers are again congruent. In other words, show that if $a \equiv b$ mod m and $c \equiv d$ mod m then $a + c \equiv b + d$ mod m.

50. Prove that multiples of congruent numbers are again congruent. Thus show that for any $c \in \mathbb{Z}$, if $a \equiv b$ mod m then $ac \equiv bc$ mod m also.

51. Explain why if $a \not\equiv b$ mod 7 then $4a \not\equiv 4b$ mod 7 either.

52. Prove from first principles that if $a \equiv b$ mod m then $a^2 + 3b \equiv b^2 + 3a$ mod m as well. (I.e. rewrite the given condition as $a - b = km$ and work from there.)

53. Demonstrate that if $a \equiv b$ mod m then $a^3 \equiv b^3$ mod m as well.

54. Establish that if $a \equiv b$ mod m and $c \equiv d$ mod m then $ac \equiv bd$ mod m.

4.4 Complete Residue Systems

Consider the claim that $n^4 + 4$ is a multiple of 5 precisely when $5 \nmid n$. One can easily verify this fact for specific values of n. For example, plugging in $n = 7$ yields $7^4 + 4 = 2405$, which is divisible by 5. But a proof of this fact seems out of reach, at least initially, since there is no way to check the claim for every single integer separately. However, congruences circumvent this difficulty, because where divisibility by 5 is concerned, *there are only five different types of numbers.* More concretely, every integer n falls into exactly one of the following five classes:

$$n \equiv 0 \bmod 5, \quad n \equiv 1 \bmod 5, \quad n \equiv 2 \bmod 5, \quad n \equiv 3 \bmod 5, \quad n \equiv 4 \bmod 5.$$

Equivalently, every integer is either a multiple of 5, one more than a multiple of 5, two more than a multiple of 5, three more than a multiple of 5, or four more than a multiple of 5. Written algebraically, we are saying that either $n = 5k$, $n = 5k + 1$, $n = 5k + 2$, $n = 5k + 3$, or $n = 5k + 4$, for $k \in \mathbb{Z}$. The same distinction may be made for an arbitrary modulus m.

> For a given positive integer $m \geq 2$ the integers may be split into m disjoint subsets according to whether they are congruent to 0, 1, 2, ..., or $m - 1$ mod m. These sets of integers are known as **congruence classes** mod m.

CONCEPT CHECK a) How many congruence classes are there when working mod 7? Describe the various cases using congruences and also via algebraic expressions.

Thus we need only check five cases (rather than infinitely many) in order to prove that $n^4 + 4$ is a multiple of 5 except when $5 \mid n$. Here are the straightforward computations.

$$0^4 + 4 = 4 \not\equiv 0 \bmod 5$$
$$1^4 + 4 = 5 \equiv 0 \bmod 5$$
$$2^4 + 4 = 20 \equiv 0 \bmod 5$$
$$3^4 + 4 = 85 \equiv 0 \bmod 5$$
$$4^4 + 4 = 260 \equiv 0 \bmod 5$$

We find that the result is congruent to 0 mod 5 (meaning that the number is a multiple of 5) precisely when n is not divisible by 5, as claimed. The principle at work here is that if $n \equiv 2 \bmod 5$, for instance, then $n^4 \equiv 2^4 \bmod 5$, hence $n^4 + 4 \equiv 2^4 + 4 \bmod 5$. Therefore our verification that $2^4 + 4 \equiv 0 \bmod 5$ takes care of proving that $5 \mid (n^4 + 4)$ for all n in the class $n \equiv 2 \bmod 5$. This reasoning explains why we need only check five cases to prove that the above statement holds for all integers.[†]

CONCEPT CHECK b) Explain why $n^3 + 3n + 5$ is always odd.

There is a way to simplify our computations even further which will come in handy when dealing with a large modulus m. To illustrate, let us return to the previous example. Observe that every integer n also falls into exactly one of these five congruence classes:

$$n \equiv 0 \bmod 5, \quad n \equiv 1 \bmod 5, \quad n \equiv -1 \bmod 5, \quad n \equiv 2 \bmod 5, \quad n \equiv -2 \bmod 5.$$

In reality, these are precisely the same five congruence classes as before. For instance, $n \equiv 4 \bmod 5$ is the same as $n \equiv -1 \bmod 5$. The advantage in writing the classes in this manner is that they involve smaller numbers. Thus it is far simpler to compute $(-1)^4 + 4 = 5 \equiv 0 \bmod 5$ than to substitute $n = 4$ into $n^4 + 4$. A set of numbers such as $\{0, 1, 2, 3, 4\}$ or $\{-2, -1, 0, 1, 2\}$ which includes exactly one number from each congruence class is such a fundamental concept in modular arithmetic that it is given a special name.

> For a positive integer $m \geq 2$, a **complete residue system** mod m is a set of m integers including exactly one representative from each congruence class mod m. The sets $\{0, 1, 2, \ldots, m - 1\}$ and $\{1, 2, 3, \ldots, m\}$ are both examples of complete residue systems mod m.

As we have just seen, when $m = 2k + 1$ is odd the set

$$\{-k, -(k - 1), \ldots, -1, 0, 1, \ldots, k - 1, k\}$$

can also serve as a convenient complete residue system.

$\boxed{\text{C}^{\text{ON}}_{\text{HE}}\text{C}^{\text{EPT}}_{\text{K}}}$ c) Augment the set $\{6, 7, 42\}$ to get a complete residue system mod 8.

$\boxed{\text{C}^{\text{ON}}_{\text{HE}}\text{C}^{\text{EPT}}_{\text{K}}}$ d) Explain why the set $\{1, 2, 3, 5, 8\}$ is not a complete residue system mod m for any m.

We have demonstrated that $n^4 + 4 \equiv 0 \bmod 5$ whenever $5 \nmid n$ by confirming this congruence for each value of n in a complete residue system mod 5. This principle is an effective means of confirming any polynomial congruence.

> Let $g(n)$ be a polynomial having integer coefficients. To establish that a congruence involving $g(n)$ holds for all values of $n \in \mathbb{Z}$, it suffices to demonstrate that the congruence is valid for each value of n in a complete residue system. This principle rests on the fact that $g(a) \equiv g(b) \bmod m$ whenever $a \equiv b \bmod m$.

Examples of polynomials include $n^3 - 3n^2 + 3n - 1$, n^4, and $n^7 + 3n^2 - 37$. On the other hand $2^n + 5$, $\sqrt{2n + 1}$, and $3^n + n^2 - 5$ are not polynomials.

To illustrate this principle and highlight one other idea, we conclude by showing that $n^6 \equiv 1 \bmod 9$ precisely when $n \equiv 1$ or $2 \bmod 3$. We need only compute the value of n^6 for each n in a complete residue system mod 9, such as $\{0, 1, 2, 3, 4, 5, 6, 7, 8\}$. We find that

$$0^6 = 0 \equiv 0 \bmod 9 \qquad 1^6 = 1 \equiv 1 \bmod 9 \qquad 2^6 = 64 \equiv 1 \bmod 9$$
$$3^6 = 729 \equiv 0 \bmod 9 \qquad 4^6 = 4096 \equiv 1 \bmod 9 \qquad 5^6 = 15625 \equiv 1 \bmod 9$$
$$6^6 = 46656 \equiv 0 \bmod 9 \quad 7^6 = 117649 \equiv 1 \bmod 9 \quad 8^6 = 262144 \equiv 1 \bmod 9.$$

Therefore $n^6 \equiv 1 \bmod 9$ whenever $n \equiv 1, 2, 4, 5, 7, 8 \bmod 9$. The question now becomes, why is this the same as saying that $n \equiv 1$ or $2 \bmod 3$?

The conversion from mod 3 to mod 9 is best understood visually. In the array below all integers congruent to 1 mod 3 appear in the top row, followed by all $n \equiv 2 \bmod 3$, and all $n \equiv 0 \bmod 3$ (the multiples of 3) in the bottom row.

$$
\begin{array}{ccccccccccccc}
& -8 & \boxed{-5} & -2 & 1 & \boxed{4} & 7 & 10 & \boxed{13} & 16 & 19 & \boxed{22} & 25 \\
\cdots & -7 & -4 & -1 & 2 & 5 & 8 & 11 & 14 & 17 & 20 & 23 & 26 & \cdots \\
& -6 & -3 & 0 & 3 & 6 & 9 & 12 & 15 & 18 & 21 & 24 & 27 \\
\end{array}
$$

Now consider those integers congruent to 4 mod 9, such as $-5, 4, 13$ and 22. We have boxed these numbers, which happen to be located in the top row, meaning they are all congruent to 1 mod 3. The same thing occurs for $n \equiv 1$ or $7 \bmod 9$. Together these numbers fill out the entire top row; i.e. comprise the congruence class $n \equiv 1 \bmod 3$. Similarly we find that $n \equiv 2, 5, 8 \bmod 9$ is equivalent to $n \equiv 2 \bmod 3$ and $n \equiv 0, 3, 6 \bmod 9$ means that $n \equiv 0 \bmod 3$. It is now clear that $n \equiv 1, 2, 4, 5, 7, 8 \bmod 9$ is the same as $n \equiv 1$ or $2 \bmod 3$.

It is possible to explain this phenomenon algebraically. Thus, $n \equiv 4 \bmod 9$ means that $n = 9k + 4$ for $k \in \mathbb{Z}$. But this can be rewritten as $n = 3(3k + 1) + 1$, so n is one more than a multiple of 3, giving $n \equiv 1 \bmod 3$. In the same way $n \equiv 1, 7 \bmod 9$ also imply that $n \equiv 1 \bmod 3$. Similar reasoning may applied for the remaining congruence classes mod 9.

$\boxed{\textsf{C}^{\text{ON}}_{\text{HE}}\textsf{C}^{\text{EPT}}_{\text{K}}}$ e) Which congruence classes mod 10 correspond to the congruence classes $n \equiv 1 \bmod 2$ or $n \equiv 3 \bmod 5$?

As a final example, we point out that every integer n satisfies at least one of $n \equiv 1 \bmod 2$, $n \equiv 0 \bmod 3$, or $n \equiv \pm 2 \bmod 6$. This is because these congruence classes correspond to $n \equiv 1, 3, 5 \bmod 6$, $n \equiv 0, 3 \bmod 6$, and $n \equiv 2, 4 \bmod 6$ respectively, as the reader may verify. These possibilities include all congruence classes mod 6, which covers the set of integers.

 a) There are seven congruence classes mod 7. There's $n \equiv 0 \bmod 7$, $n \equiv 1 \bmod 7$, ..., and $n \equiv 6 \bmod 7$. These can be written $n = 7k$, $n = 7k + 1$, ..., and $n = 7k + 6$.

b) We need only show that $n^3 + 3n + 5 \equiv 1 \bmod 2$ for $n \equiv 0 \bmod 2$ and $n \equiv 1 \bmod 2$. Plugging in $n = 0$ and 1 gives 5 and 9, which are both odd, so we are done.

c) There are many possible answers. For instance, we could write $\{0, 1, 3, 4, 5, 6, 7, 42\}$.

d) Since there are five numbers in the set, we could only have $m = 5$. But $3 \equiv 8 \bmod 5$, so there is a repeated number mod 5.

e) We find that the given congruences correspond to $n \equiv 1, 3, 5, 7, 8, 9 \bmod 10$.

EXERCISES

55. Which of the following sets give a complete residue system mod 7? Explain how to modify the incorrect sets so that they become complete residue systems.
  a) $\{0, 1, 2, 3, 4, 5, 6, 7\}$
  b) $\{2, 4, 6, 8, 10, 12, 14\}$
  c) $\{-6, -5, -4, -3, -2, -1\}$
  d) $\{-3, -2, -1, 0, 1, 2, 3\}$

56. Include additional elements in the set $\{-37, -29, -15\}$ to obtain a complete residue system mod 5. Why is the same not possible mod 7?

57. Write down your favorite complete residue system mod 5, then triple each number. Is the result still a complete residue system mod 5? Now repeat this experiment mod 6. Why is the result not the same as before?

58. Let $m = 2k$ be even. Write down a complete residue system mod m in terms of k in which the numbers are as small as possible.

59. For $g(n) = 2^n + 3n$, find $a, b \in \mathbb{N}$ with $a \equiv b \bmod 5$ but $g(a) \not\equiv g(b) \bmod 5$. Why doesn't this example contradict our principle for congruences?

60. For $g(n) = \frac{1}{2}(n^2 + 3n)$, find $a, b \in \mathbb{N}$ with $a \equiv b \bmod 2$ but $g(a) \not\equiv g(b) \bmod 2$. Why doesn't this example contradict our principle for congruences?

61. What single congruence is equivalent to writing $n \equiv 10, 17, 24 \bmod 21$?

62. What single congruence means the same as $n \equiv -4, -9, -14, -19 \bmod 20$?

63. The congruence classes $n \equiv 0 \bmod 2$ or $n \equiv \pm 3 \bmod 7$ correspond to which congruence classes mod 14?

64. Which congruence classes mod 15 give $n \equiv 1 \bmod 3$ and $n \equiv \pm 2 \bmod 5$? (Notice the appearance of 'and' rather than 'or.')

WRITING

65. Demonstrate that $n^2 + 2n + 3$ is never divisible by 5.

66. Prove that $2n^3 + 3n^2 + n$ is always divisible by 6.

67. For $n \in \mathbb{Z}$, prove that exactly one of $n^3 - 1$, n^3 or $n^3 + 1$ is a multiple of 7.

68. Show that the square of any odd integer is one more than a multiple of 8.

69. For $n \in \mathbb{Z}$, prove that $2n^3 + 1 \equiv 2^3 \bmod 9$ exactly when $n \equiv 2 \bmod 3$.

70. Let n be an integer that is not divisible by 10. Establish that $n^4 \equiv 6 \bmod 10$ when $2 \mid n$, that $n^4 \equiv 5 \bmod 10$ when $5 \mid n$, and that $n^4 \equiv 1 \bmod 10$ otherwise.

71. Suppose that $\{a_1, a_2, \ldots, a_{11}\}$ is a complete residue system mod 11. Prove that $\{a_1 + 2, a_2 + 2, \ldots, a_{11} + 2\}$ is also a complete residue system.

72. Explain why every natural number n satisfies exactly one of the congruences $n \equiv 1 \bmod 2$, $n \equiv 0 \bmod 4$, or $n \equiv \pm 2, 6 \bmod 12$.

4.5   Forms of Integers

To illustrate the utility of congruences, we now consider the question of which positive integers can be written as the sum of exactly three perfect squares, i.e. in the form $a^2 + b^2 + c^2$. Thus 9 is such a number, since we have $0^2 + 0^2 + 3^2 = 9$. Furthermore, 99 also falls into this category, since $3^2 + 3^2 + 9^2 = 99$. It seems that a pattern is emerging, so it may come as a surprise to discover that it is impossible to write 999 as a sum of three squares. In fact, we also cannot write 9999 or 99999 or any longer string of 9's as a sum of three squares. Rather than conduct an exhaustive check of all possible cases, we can demonstrate this fact quickly and easily by employing congruences.

QUICK QUERY a) Test all the numbers n in the range $30 \le n \le 50$ to determine which of them may be written as the sum of exactly three perfect squares, where we consider 0 to be a perfect square. Make a conjecture based on your results.

Although it may not be immediately obvious, it will be advantageous to analyze this situation mod 8. (The Concept Check above hints at this fact.) Upon squaring each of the numbers $\{-3, -2, -1, 0, 1, 2, 3, 4\}$ in a complete residue system mod 8, we find that the result always reduces to either 0, 1 or 4 mod 8. In other words, for $n \in \mathbb{Z}$ we have $n^2 \equiv 0, 1$ or 4 mod 8. The fact that only three different values occur when considering squares mod 8 helps to explain why $m = 8$ is a handy modulus to utilize in this investigation.

Let us now demonstrate that 999 cannot be written as the sum of three squares. Suppose that it were possible, so that $a^2 + b^2 + c^2 = 999$. If these two quantities were equal, then they certainly would be the same mod 8. In other words we would have $a^2 + b^2 + c^2 \equiv 999 \equiv 7$ mod 8. We have just seen that each of a^2, b^2 and c^2 will reduce to either 0, 1 or 4 mod 8. But it is impossible to sum three of these numbers and obtain 7 mod 8. Hence our original assumption was false; it is not possible to have $a^2 + b^2 + c^2 = 999$.[†]

QUICK QUERY b) Show that one can add together three of 0, 1, 4 (repeats allowed) to obtain a result congruent to 0, 1, 2, 3, 4, 5 or 6 mod 8, but not 7 mod 8.

A little thought reveals that the same reasoning applies to any positive integer n with $n \equiv 7$ mod 8. For instance, we cannot write 543 as a sum of three perfect squares either. For if we could then we would have $a^2 + b^2 + c^2 = 543$, and reducing mod 8 leads to $a^2 + b^2 + c^2 \equiv 543 \equiv 7$ mod 8, causing the same difficulty as before. Naturally, we might wonder at this point whether or not values of n in the other congruence classes mod 8 can always be written as the sum of three squares. For example, what about 998? A little experimentation reveals that $7^2 + 7^2 + 30^2 = 998$. Moreover, we have $4^2 + 9^2 + 30^2 = 997$, and so on all the way down to 991, which is again impossible since $991 \equiv 7$ mod 8.

It is important to note that while congruences do demonstrate that certain numbers *cannot* be written as a sum of three squares, they do not guarantee that others *can* be so written. Thus just because we have $1 + 1 + 4 \equiv 6$ mod 8 does not immediately mean that every $n \equiv 6$ mod 8 can be written in the form $a^2 + b^2 + c^2$. We still had to verify by hand that $7^2 + 7^2 + 30^2 = 998$ to be sure

Mathematical Outing ★ ★ ★

For which positive integers m does $\sqrt{-1}$ exist mod m? This question may seem preposterous at first, but becomes more feasible once we realize that $\sqrt{-1}$ means "a number which gives -1 when squared." There are no such real numbers, but this result can be achieved with congruences! For instance, we have $5^2 \equiv -1 \bmod 13$, so the number 5 behaves like $\sqrt{-1}$, at least when working mod 13. However, the same phenomenon does not occur mod 7, for if we square all seven types of integers mod 7 (namely $x \equiv 0, \pm 1, \pm 2,$ or $\pm 3 \bmod 7$) then we find that $x^2 \equiv 0, 1, 4,$ or 2 mod 7, but we do not have $x^2 \equiv -1 \bmod 7$ for any x. Thus $\sqrt{-1}$ does not exist mod 7.

Therefore our original question becomes, for which m is there a solution to the congruence $x^2 \equiv -1 \bmod m$? Test all values of m for $2 \leq m \leq 20$, then make some conjectures based on your findings.

in the case of $n = 998$, for instance. Our computations thus far would suggest that every positive integer n other than $n \equiv 7 \bmod 8$ can be written as a sum of three squares, but this conjecture turns out to be false!

QUICK QUERY c) Attempt to express the numbers 20, 24 and 28 as a sum of three squares. Which number cannot be written in this manner?

Upon closer inspection, we find that certain multiples of 4 also fail. Testing a variety of such numbers suggests that if n cannot be written as a sum of three squares, then neither can $4n$. Given the nature of this assertion, we opt to prove the contrapositive instead, which states that if $4n$ can be written as a sum of three squares, then n may be also. So suppose that $a^2 + b^2 + c^2 = 4n$. Reducing mod 4 yields $a^2 + b^2 + c^2 \equiv 0 \bmod 4$. (A proof mod 8 could also work.) It is routine to verify that a square is only congruent to 0 or 1 mod 4; checking the various possibilities reveals that each of a^2, b^2 and c^2 must be 0 mod 4.

QUICK QUERY d) Confirm that if $a^2 + b^2 + c^2 \equiv 0 \bmod 4$ then each of a^2, b^2 and c^2 must be congruent to 0 mod 4.

This implies that a, b and c are even, so we write $a = 2r$, $b = 2s$, and $c = 2t$. Hence our original equation becomes $4r^2 + 4s^2 + 4t^2 = 4n$, or $r^2 + s^2 + t^2 = n$. Therefore n can be written as a sum of three squares, as desired.[†]

Joseph Louis Lagrange, one of the leading mathematicians of his day, studied this and similar problems. He published a proof that *every* positive integer can be expressed as the sum of four perfect squares, a result usually referred to as "Lagrange's Four-Square Theorem." Furthermore, every $n \in \mathbb{N}$ *except* those of the form $4^l(8k + 7)$, for integers $k, l \geq 0$, can actually be written as a sum of three squares. In other words, the only exceptions to the three-square result are the ones we found above: those integers $n \equiv 7 \bmod 8$ and any numbers obtained by multiplying these values by 4 one or more times.

a) We find that all n in the range $30 \leq n \leq 50$ can be written as the sum of three squares except for $n = 31$, 39 and 47. Thus we conjecture that the only exceptions occur when $n \equiv 7 \bmod 8$.

b) We compute $0+0+0 \equiv 0$, $0+0+1 \equiv 1$, $0+1+1 \equiv 2$, $1+1+1 \equiv 3$, $0+0+4 \equiv 4$, $0+1+4 \equiv 5$ and $1+1+4 \equiv 6$. However, there is no way to obtain 7.

c) We have $0^2 + 2^2 + 4^2 = 20$, $2^2 + 2^2 + 4^2 = 24$, but there is no way to obtain 28.

d) The only ways to get 0 or 4 are $0+0+0$, $0+0+4$, $0+4+4$ and $4+4+4$.

📖 We find that $\sqrt{-1}$ exists mod m for $m = 2, 5, 10, 13$, and 17. We observe that no multiples of 3 appear on this list, that only primes $p \equiv 1 \bmod 4$ appear on this list, and that if two primes appear on the list then so does their product.

EXERCISES

73. According to our three-square result it should be possible to write both 1001 and 1002 as a sum of three squares. Exhibit a means of doing so.

74. Compute all values for $a^2 \bmod 9$. Then show that we may obtain every number from 0 to 8 mod 9 by adding three squares. (This fact illustrates that mod 9 would not have been helpful for the discussion in this section.)

75. Find all possible values for $a^3 + b^3 \bmod 7$, where a and b are positive integers.

76. Based on the previous exercise, for which positive integers n in the range $2050 \leq n \leq 2080$ are we sure that n cannot be written as a sum of two cubes?

77. Continuing the above exercises, find two positive integers between 2050 and 2080 which can actually be written as the sum of two perfect cubes.

78. One observation to be made regarding the $\sqrt{-1}$ investigation is that if p is a prime satisfying $p \equiv 1 \bmod 4$ then there is a solution to the congruence $x^2 \equiv -1 \bmod p$. Confirm this observation for $p = 29$, 41 and 53.

WRITING

79. Determine the possible values for $a^2 + b^2 \bmod 4$, for $a, b \in \mathbb{Z}$. Then use your result to prove that it is not possible to write 2011 as a sum of two squares.

80. Demonstrate that it is not possible to write 2345 as the sum of three cubes. (HINT: First show that $n^3 \equiv -1, 0$, or 1 mod 9 for all $n \in \mathbb{Z}$.)

81. Prove that 1600010 cannot be written as a sum of nine perfect fourth powers. (HINT: consider this situation mod 16.)

82. Show that if n can be written as a sum of three squares, then $9n$ can also.

83. Suppose that $11 \nmid a$ or $11 \nmid b$ for $a, b \in \mathbb{Z}$. Explain why it must be the case that $11 \nmid (a^2 + b^2)$ either.

84. Prove that if n cannot be written as a sum of two squares, then $49n$ also cannot be written as a sum of two squares.

85. Let m be a multiple of 3. Show that if $x^2 \equiv -1 \bmod m$ then $x^2 \equiv -1 \bmod 3$ as well. Use this to prove that there are no solutions to $x^2 \equiv -1 \bmod m$.

4.6   Primes

It would not be stretching the truth to say that number theory is fascinating because of the primes. While it is true that there are plenty of nice results which do not rely on a special knowledge of the primes, one cannot progress too far in the subject without being forced to consider them. As the building blocks of the integers (from a multiplicative perspective) they are unavoidable. But they are also irregular—there is no apparent pattern in the gaps between one prime and the next, for example. And there seems to be no simple formula which yields prime numbers. Establishing theorems on the primes typically requires a good deal of care; even proving that there are infinitely many primes (as we shall do momentarily) takes a bit of thought.

Conjectures regarding the primes abound. One of the most attractive ones, at least to this author, concerns a certain observation on the distribution of the primes. Part of its appeal lies in the disparity between the relative simplicity of stating the conjecture and the apparent difficulty in proving it. As of this writing nobody has been able to explain why the following seems to be true. List all the natural numbers in order in a sequence of columns, as follows. The first two columns should each contain one number, followed by a pair of columns with two numbers, then two more columns with three numbers each, and so on.

1	**2**	**3**	**5**	**7**	10	**13**	**17**	21	26	**31**	**37**
		4	6	8	**11**	14	18	22	27	32	38
			9	12	15	**19**	**23**	28	33	39 $\cdots$
				16	20	24	**29**	34	40
					25	30	35	**41**
						36	42

The primes appear in boldface to highlight their location. The conjecture is that there is at least one prime in each column beyond the first.

CHECK CONCEPT   a) Write down the next six columns in the list above and confirm that the conjecture continues to hold.

Our first (and only) substantial proof concerning prime numbers dates back to Euclid, who is the first person on record to have conclusively shown that there are infinitely many primes. The proof we present is based directly upon his argument. In particular, the key idea of adding 1 to a product of primes is due to Euclid. This proof affords an excellent opportunity to utilize lemmas.

> A **lemma** is a smaller, self-contained result which is usually proved in advance of a main theorem so that it may be used as a step within the proof of that theorem.

Lemmas are not presented separately because they are necessarily shorter or simpler—they sometimes are not. Rather, the demonstration of a lemma is separated from the proof of a theorem so that it does not interrupt the flow of the main argument.

The ensuing discussion also provides an excellent illustration of the power of proof by contradiction. This technique is used three times all together; in both lemmas and in the proof. Watch for its appearance and note in each case why it is advantageous to assume the negative of what we wish to prove.

QUERY b) List all the divisors of 99 in increasing order, beginning with 1. Next do the same for the divisors of 64, then for the divisors of 37. Where in any such list do you feel that we are guaranteed to find a prime?

Lemma 1 Every positive integer greater than 1 is divisible by a prime number.

Proof Let $n \geq 2$ be a positive integer and consider the set of divisors of n, which has the form $\{1, \ldots, n\}$. We will show that a prime appears in this set. More precisely, we claim that the smallest number a in the list other than 1 is a prime. To see why, assume to the contrary that a is not prime. Then there is some smaller number d between 1 and a that is a divisor of a. But since $d \mid a$ and $a \mid n$ we may deduce that $d \mid n$. Hence d must also appear on the list of divisors of n. But this contradicts the fact that a was the smallest divisor of n greater than 1. Hence our assumption that a is not prime was faulty, so we conclude that a is in fact prime.

Lemma 2 For all $n \in \mathbb{Z}$, no prime divides evenly into both n and $n + 1$.

Proof Suppose to the contrary that some prime p was a divisor of both n and $n+1$. Then since $p \mid n$ we could write $n = k_1 p$, and because $p \mid (n+1)$ we would have $n+1 = k_2 p$. Subtracting these two equalities yields $(n+1) - n = k_2 p - k_1 p$, which reduces to $1 = (k_2 - k_1)p$. In other words, we could deduce that 1 was a multiple of p. But this is impossible, so our original assumption cannot be true. We conclude that no prime is a divisor of both n and $n + 1$.

With these two facts firmly in hand we can now focus on the beautiful idea at the heart of Euclid's proof of the infinitude of the primes.

Theorem (Euclid) There are infinitely many primes.

Proof Suppose to the contrary that there are only finitely many primes. Then we could write them all down in a (possibly long) list as $p_1, p_2, \ldots, p_k$. Since this list is finite, we may create the positive integer $N = p_1 p_2 \cdots p_k$, which is a multiple of all the primes in our list. Now consider the integer $N + 1$. By Lemma 1, there exists a prime divisor of $N + 1$; call it q. And by Lemma 2, q must be different from any of the primes p_1 through p_k, because no prime can divide evenly into both N and $N + 1$. In other words, we have deduced the existence of a prime not among $p_1, p_2, \ldots, p_k$, contradicting the fact that this list was the complete enumeration of all primes. Hence our original assumption must be false, so we have proved that there are infinitely many primes.

QUERY c) Let $p_1, p_2, \ldots, p_k$ be a list of the first k primes. Show by example that $p_1 p_2 \cdots p_k + 1$ is not always a prime number.

a) Among the next six columns, the first contains the primes 43 and 47, the next has 53, followed by 59 and 61, 67 and 71, 73 and 79, and finally 83 and 89.

b) The divisors of 99 are 1, 3, 9, 11, 33, 99; the divisors of 64 are 1, 2, 4, 8, 16, 32, 64; and the divisors of 37 are 1, 37. The second number in each list must be a prime.

c) The number $p_1 p_2 \cdots p_k + 1$ is a prime number for $k = 1, 2, 3, 4$ and 5. But when $k = 6$ we find that $(2)(3)(5)(7)(11)(13) + 1 = 59 \cdot 509$.

EXERCISES

86. Which odd numbers can be written as the sum of one odd prime plus twice another odd prime? Make a conjecture based on your findings.

87. Compute the values of $n^2 + 3n + 1$ when $n = 1, 2, 3, 4$ and 5. Where do these numbers appear within the table displayed in this section? Make a conjecture suggested by your results and check to see whether or not it is true.

88. Fermat conjectured that the formula $2^{2^n} + 1$ yields a prime for all $n \in \mathbb{N}$. Using a computer, find the smallest value of n for which this statement is false.

89. Give a precise description of all positive integers n such that the set of divisors of n includes exactly one prime.

90. Which primes divide evenly into both N and $N + 21$ for some $N \in \mathbb{N}$?

91. The numbers $N = p_1 p_2 \cdots p_k$ and $N + 1$ in Euclid's proof are not the only expressions that would have worked. Which of the following expressions would also have permitted the proof to go through?
a) $N = 100 p_1 p_2 \cdots p_k$, $N + 1$
b) $N = p_1 + p_2 + \cdots + p_k$, $N + 1$
c) $N = p_1 p_2 \cdots p_k$, $N - 1$
d) $N = p_1 p_2 \cdots p_k$, $N + 100$
e) $N = p_1^2 p_2^2 \cdots p_k^2$, $N + 1$

WRITING

92. Observe that 3, 5, 7 are three consecutive odd numbers, all of which are prime. Explain why it is not possible for any further such instances to occur.

93. Explain why every prime other than 2 and 3 is adjacent to a multiple of 6.

94. Let n be a positive integer that is not a power of 2. Prove that the smallest odd divisor of n (other than 1) must be a prime.

95. Prove that for all $n \in \mathbb{Z}$, no odd prime divides both n and $n + 64$.

96. Prove that for all $n \in \mathbb{Z}$, no prime divides both $n + 1$ and $2n + 1$.

97. Construct an alternate proof that there are infinitely many primes using the quantities $N = 3 p_1 p_2 \cdots p_k$ and $N - 1$.

The next four problems taken together prove that there are infinitely many primes p for which $p \equiv 3 \bmod 4$.

98. (Lemma 1a) Let n be a positive integer such that $n \equiv 3 \bmod 4$. Prove that n has a prime divisor p for which $p \equiv 3 \bmod 4$ as well.

99. (Lemma 2a) Let p be a prime with $p \equiv 3 \bmod 4$. Prove that p cannot divide both N and $N + 2$ for any $N \in \mathbb{N}$.

100. Let $p_1, p_2, \ldots, p_k$ be a list of primes, each of which is congruent to 3 mod 4, and define $N = p_1^2 p_2^2 \cdots p_k^2$. Show that $N \equiv 1 \bmod 4$.

101. Put together these results to prove that there are infinitely many primes p that are congruent to 3 mod 4.

FURTHER EXPLORATION

102. The method of proof outlined in the final four writing problems can be adapted to prove other similar results, but only to a limited degree. For instance, all primes other than 3 either satisfy $p \equiv 1 \bmod 3$ or $p \equiv 2 \bmod 3$. Use the approach suggested above to prove that there are infinitely many of the latter type. Why doesn't the same proof go through to show that there are infinitely many primes satisfying $p \equiv 1 \bmod 3$?

4.7 Reference

A summary of the most important facts and techniques from this chapter is provided below as a reference when studying or working on material from later chapters. We also include a list of the various strategies we have developed for proving statements related to number theory.

- *Vocabulary* divisible, divisor, factor, proper divisor, common divisor, greatest common divisor, relatively prime, trivial divisors, prime, Fundamental Theorem of Arithmetic, prime factorization, perfect number, congruence, modulus, congruence class, complete residue system, lemma

- *Notation*
    $a \mid b$ (a divides b, or b is divisible by a),
    $a \nmid b$ (a does not divide b, or b is not divisible by a),
    (a, b) (the greatest common divisor of a and b, also written $\mathrm{GCD}(a, b)$),
    $2^4 \cdot 3 \cdot 37$ (prime factorization of a number—1776, in this case),
    $p_1^{e_1} p_2^{e_2} \cdots p_k^{e_k}$ (general form of a prime factorization),
    $d(n)$ (the number of divisors of n),
    $a \equiv b \bmod m$ (a is congruent to b mod m),
    $n = mk + r$ (n is r more than a multiple of m; i.e. $n \equiv r \bmod m$),

- *Divisibility* For integers a and b with $a \neq 0$ it is the case that b is divisible by a iff $b = ka$ for some $k \in \mathbb{Z}$. An integer d is a common divisor of a and b if $d \mid a$ and $d \mid b$; the largest such number is the GCD of a and b. When $(a, b) = 1$

we say that a and b are relatively prime. Properties of divisibility include the following facts: 1) If $a \mid b$ and $b \mid c$ then $a \mid c$. 2) If $a \mid c$ and $b \mid d$ then $ab \mid cd$. 3) If $d \mid a$ and $d \mid b$ then d divides any linear combination of a and b; in other words, $d \mid (ak + bl)$ for any $k, l \in \mathbb{Z}$.

• *Divisors* The number of divisors of n can be computed by adding 1 to each exponent in the prime factorization of n and then multiplying the results together. A perfect number has the property that the sum of its proper divisors is equal to the original number. Every even perfect number has the form $2^{n-1}(2^n - 1)$, where $2^n - 1$ is prime. To determine the sum of the divisors of a number such as $2^4 \cdot 3 \cdot 37$, compute the value of the expression $(1 + 2 + 2^2 + 2^3 + 2^4)(1 + 3)(1 + 37)$. Thus the sum of the divisors of 1776 is 4712.

• *Congruences* For $a, b, m \in \mathbb{Z}$ with $m \geq 2$ we write $a \equiv b \bmod m$ to signify that a and b differ by a multiple of m. To numerically reduce a given number mod m, find the remainder when that number is divided by m. Hence 101 reduces to 3 mod 7, since $101 - 14(7) = 3$. One can add, subtract, or multiply two congruences mod m together. It is also valid to square both sides of a congruence. A congruence class refers to all integers congruent to a certain number mod m. A complete residue system consists of one number from each congruence class. For instance, $\{0, 1, 2, 3, 4\}$ is a complete residue system mod 5.

• *Primes* A prime is a positive integer with exactly two divisors; namely, 1 and itself. The first ten primes are 2, 3, 5, 7, 11, 13, 17, 19, 23 and 29. There are infinitely many primes. The Fundamental Theorem of Arithmetic asserts that every positive integer can be written uniquely as the product of a set of primes. In other words, prime factorization is unique.

PROOF STRATEGIES

* *Properties of Divisibility and Congruences* It often helps to write what is given and what must be proved algebraically. Thus $a^2 \mid b^2$ means that $b^2 = ka^2$, $n \equiv 3 \bmod 8$ becomes $n = 8k + 3$, and $ab \equiv b \bmod m$ is equivalent to $ab - b = km$ for some $k \in \mathbb{Z}$. Working from what is given, algebraically manipulate the equalities to obtain the equation to be proved.

* *Using Complete Residue Systems* To prove a statement involving divisibility by m it suffices to verify that the claim is true for each number in a complete residue system mod m. Thus to confirm that $n^2 + 2$ is not divisible by 5 for all $n \in \mathbb{N}$ (or equivalently that $n^2 \equiv -2 \bmod 5$ has no solutions), one need only check that this is the case for $n = -2, -1, 0, 1$ and 2. This principle applies whenever the expression involved is a polynomial with integer coefficients.

* *Forms of Integers* To show that a number cannot be written in a certain form (such as showing that 999 is not the sum of three squares), it is often effective to use proof by contradiction to suppose that the number can be so written, then to reduce mod m for a strategic value of m. (This amounts to replacing $=$ with $\equiv$ mod m.) When dealing with squares, reducing mod 4 or mod 8 is often helpful; when handling cubes, reducing mod 7 or mod 9 can work.

★ TIP ★ *It is often useful to write out an algebraic description of the desired result to help guide the steps employed in a proof.* For instance, suppose we wish to show that if $m \mid (a - b)$ and $m \mid (c - d)$, then $m \mid (ac - bd)$. We would write $a - b = km$ and $c - d = lm$ at the top of a sheet of scrap paper, write $ac - bd = (\cdots)m$ near the bottom, and then attempt to combine the given statements in some manner to obtain the expression $ac - bd$. Since we need the term ac to appear, it now makes sense to try multiplying the two equations together, or perhaps to multiply the first equation by c. In this manner we use the statement to be proved to direct our steps.

GIVEN: $a - b = km$
$c - d = lm$

PROVE: $ac - bd = (\cdots)m$

One should avoid writing down the equation $ac - bd = tm$ at the start of the actual proof, so as not to fall into the trap of inadvertently incorporating the statement to be proven into the argument. This would result in a logical fallacy known as *circular reasoning*. (But it would be OK to write "We must show that $ac - bd$ is a multiple of m," for instance.) The equation $ac - bd = (\cdots)m$ acts only as a destination; it serves to indicate when we have solved the problem. Once we have $ac - bd$ on one side of an equation and a multiple of m on the other, then we know we are done and can begin writing up a proof.

SAMPLE PROOFS

The following proofs provide concise explanations for results discussed within this chapter. They are meant to serve as an illustration for how proofs of similar statements could be phrased. The boldface numbers indicate the section containing each result; the location of that result within the section is marked by a dagger (†).

———◆———

4.1 Prove that the greatest common divisor of $n + 1$ and $2n^2 + 3n + 4$ is either 1 or 3 for all natural numbers n.

Proof For a given $n \in \mathbb{N}$, let d represent $\mathrm{GCD}(n + 1, 2n^2 + 3n + 4)$. Since d divides into both $n + 1$ and $2n^2 + 3n + 4$ we may write

$$n + 1 = ad \qquad \text{and} \qquad 2n^2 + 3n + 4 = bd$$

for some positive integers $a, b \in \mathbb{N}$. It follows that

$$(2n^2 + 3n + 4) - 2n(n + 1) = (bd) - 2n(ad),$$

which reduces to $n + 4 = d(b - 2an)$. Subtracting $n + 1 = ad$ from this equality yields $3 = d(b - 2an - a)$. We deduce that $d \mid 3$, hence $d = 1$ or $d = 3$.

———◆———

4.2 Confirm that if $(2^n - 1)$ is a prime for some $n \in \mathbb{N}$, then $2^{n-1}(2^n - 1)$ is a perfect number.

Proof To begin, we will let p denote the prime, so that $p = 2^n - 1$. The number under consideration can now be written as $2^{n-1}p$, so its proper divisors are

$$
\begin{array}{ccccc}
1 & 2 & 4 & \cdots & 2^{n-2} & 2^{n-1} \\
p & 2p & 4p & \cdots & 2^{n-2}p.
\end{array}
$$

The sum of the divisors along the top row is $1 + 2 + 4 + \cdots + 2^{n-1} = 2^n - 1 = p$. Similarly, the sum of the divisors along the bottom row is

$$p + 2p + 4p + \cdots + 2^{n-2}p = (1 + 2 + 4 + \cdots + 2^{n-2})p = (2^{n-1} - 1)p.$$

The grand total is $p + (2^{n-1} - 1)p = 2^{n-1}p$, the same as our original number. Hence $2^{n-1}(2^n - 1)$ is a perfect number.

———◆———

4.3 Let a and b be integers for which $a \equiv b \bmod m$. Prove that $a^2 \equiv b^2 \bmod m$.

Proof Since $a \equiv b \bmod m$ we may write $a - b = km$ for some $k \in \mathbb{Z}$. Multiplying both sides of this equality by $(a + b)$, we obtain $(a - b)(a + b) = km(a + b)$, which simplifies to $a^2 - b^2 = (ka + kb)m$. In other words, a^2 and b^2 differ by a multiple of m, therefore $a^2 \equiv b^2 \bmod m$.

———◆———

4.4 For $n \in \mathbb{Z}$, demonstrate that $n^4 + 4$ is divisible by 5 precisely when n is not divisible by 5.

Proof By the polynomial congruence principle we need only verify this claim for a complete residue system mod 5. Computing the value of $n^4 + 4$ when $n = 0, 1, 2, 3$ and 4 we find

$$0^4 + 4 = 4 \not\equiv 0 \bmod 5$$
$$1^4 + 4 = 5 \equiv 0 \bmod 5$$
$$2^4 + 4 = 20 \equiv 0 \bmod 5$$
$$3^4 + 4 = 85 \equiv 0 \bmod 5$$
$$4^4 + 4 = 260 \equiv 0 \bmod 5$$

We discover that $n^4 + 4 \equiv 0 \bmod 5$ except when $n = 0$, which corresponds to the congruence class $n \equiv 0 \bmod 5$. Hence $n^4 + 4$ is divisible by 5 except when n is divisible by 5. This proves the statement.

———◆———

4.5 Prove that 999 cannot be written as the sum of three perfect squares.

Proof Suppose to the contrary that it were possible to write $999 = a^2 + b^2 + c^2$ for integers a, b and c. Reducing this equality mod 8, we would have

$$a^2 + b^2 + c^2 \equiv 999 \equiv 7 \bmod 8.$$

We now claim that for any $n \in \mathbb{Z}$ we have $n^2 \equiv 0$, 1, or 4 mod 8. We verify this by checking a complete residue system mod 8, say $n = -3, -2, -1, 0, 1, 2, 3$ and 4. The corresponding values of n^2 are 9, 4, 1, 0, 1, 4, 9 and 16, which reduce to 1, 4, 1, 0, 1, 4, 1 and 0 mod 8, as claimed. Therefore each of a^2, b^2 and c^2 is congruent to one of 0, 1 or 4 mod 8. However, it is impossible to add up three of these numbers to obtain 7 mod 8. The highest possible value is $1 + 1 + 4 \equiv 6$ mod 8; after that we reach $0 + 4 + 4 \equiv 0$ mod 8. Hence our assumption that $a^2 + b^2 + c^2 \equiv 7$ mod 8 is faulty, so we conclude that it is impossible to write $999 = a^2 + b^2 + c^2$.

$$\longrightarrow\!\!\diamond\!\!\longrightarrow$$

4.5 Prove that if n cannot be written as a sum of three squares, then neither can $4n$.

Proof We will prove the contrapositive, which states that if $4n$ can be written as a sum of three squares, then so can n. Therefore suppose that we can write $4n = a^2 + b^2 + c^2$. Reducing this equality mod 4 yields $a^2 + b^2 + c^2 \equiv 0$ mod 4. We now claim that for any $n \in \mathbb{Z}$ we have $n^2 \equiv 0$ or 1 mod 4. We verify this by checking a complete residue system mod 4, say $n = 0, 1, 2$ and 3. The values of n^2 are 0, 1, 4 and 9, which reduce to 0, 1, 0 and 1 mod 4. So $n^2 \equiv 0$ mod 4 if n is even and $n^2 \equiv 1$ mod 4 if n is odd. Hence the sum $a^2 + b^2 + c^2$ will be congruent to either 0, 1, 2 or 3 mod 4, depending upon how many of a, b and c are odd. In particular, $a^2 + b^2 + c^2 \equiv 0$ mod 4 only if all of a, b and c are even, meaning that we can write $a = 2r$, $b = 2s$ and $c = 2t$. Substituting into $4n = a^2 + b^2 + c^2$ and dividing by 4 yields $n = r^2 + s^2 + t^2$. In other words, n can be written as a sum of three squares, which was what we wanted.

CHAPTER **5**

Counting and Induction

5.1 How Many?

Counting is an extraordinarily practical activity. We consider the ways in which various college teams might be paired up in a tournament, then count points scored to determine who wins each game. We count the minutes, count the cost, and count our blessings. Even parents of small children hear the question "How many...," usually around dessert time.

"How many candies can I eat?"

"Two, dear; same as always. Have a red jellybean and a football chocolate."

"But I had a red jellybean and a football chocolate last time!"

"Fine, here's a yellow jellybean and a soccer chocolate instead."

"Can I have three candies tonight?"

Selecting a color of jellybean and a type of chocolate provides a fine example of **independent events**, meaning that the outcome of the first event does not influence or restrict the available outcomes for the second event.

QUERY a) Suppose that these parents have four different colors of jellybean and three different types of chocolate. Determine the number of ways they may give their child one jellybean and one chocolate. What if the kid only eats half his dinner, and so gets to choose either one jellybean or one chocolate?

When two events are independent, we can determine the number of ways to perform both of them based on the number of ways to perform each separately.

The **multiplication principle** states that if there are N_1 ways to perform a certain activity and N_2 ways to perform another independent activity, then there are $N_1 N_2$ ways to perform the first *and* the second activity. Meanwhile, the **addition principle** states that the number of ways to perform *either* the first *or* the second activity is given by $N_1 + N_2$.

The table below illustrates the various ways that a brown, red, yellow, or white jellybean may be paired with a soccer ball, baseball, or football chocolate. For each of the four possible colors of jellybean there are three types of chocolate that could accompany it, for a total of $4 \cdot 3 = 12$ ways to choose one of each.

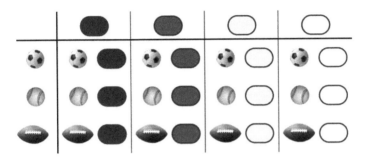

This table is reminiscent of Cartesian products. The equality $|A \times B| = |A| \cdot |B|$ for finite sets is actually just another formulation of the multiplication principle.

CONCEPT b) Now suppose the child has five colors of jellybean, four types of chocolate, and three flavors of ice-cream from which to choose. If he may enjoy a scoop of ice-cream along with either a jellybean or a chocolate, then how many dessert options does he have?

The most elementary counting technique involves listing all possible ways of achieving a particular outcome. Assuming that one makes a reasonably organized list, this approach gives a concrete method of computing an answer and provides an effective means for understanding various counting techniques. On the flip side, a disorganized list usually does not shed light on any underlying patterns and runs the risk of overlooking or duplicating outcomes. Furthermore, answers to counting questions can quickly become unmanageably large.

> The technique of **listing** is best utilized to enumerate small cases with an eye towards discovering patterns, explaining them, and generalizing them to handle larger counting problems.

Let's apply the strategy just described to the task of counting the number of ways that two members of a family may pose for a photograph.

QUERY c) Answer the following questions in order.
i. Alice, Bob and Cathy are having pictures taken. List all possible ways that a photographer can select two of them and arrange them side by side on a couch.
ii. Now do the same for a family of four.
iii. Identify a means of computing these answers without creating lists.
iv. Predict the answer for Snow White and the seven dwarves (family of eight).
v. Finally, create a formula that gives the answer for n people.

When seating people for a picture, not only does the selection of people for the picture matter, but also the order in which they are placed.

A **permutation** is an arrangement of a certain number of objects in which the order of the objects is relevant.

Thus suppose we are interested in lining up five people in a row for a family portrait. We may choose any of the five people to take the leftmost spot, then any of the remaining four to stand next to that person, and so on, for a grand total of $5 \cdot 4 \cdot 3 \cdot 2 \cdot 1 = 120$ possible arrangements. (Not all of these would make for a pleasing photo, of course.) This sort of product occurs so regularly in counting problems that it has been given its own name.

Let n be a positive integer. Then n **factorial**, written as $n!$ in mathematical expressions, is defined to be the product $n! = n(n-1)(n-2)\cdots(2)(1)$. By convention we also define $0! = 1$.

CₒₙCₑₚₜ d) For how many $n \in \mathbb{N}$ does $n!$ not end with a 0?

A permutation need not involve all the available objects. For instance, if we only wished to line up three members from a family of five for a picture we could choose any of the five for the left-hand spot, any of the remaining four for the middle spot, and any of the remaining three for the right-hand spot, for a total of $5 \cdot 4 \cdot 3 = 60$ ways. Similarly, we can set four of ten mugs in front of four guests in $10 \cdot 9 \cdot 8 \cdot 7 = 5040$ ways.

On a slightly more sophisticated note, imagine that three families wish to take a picture of all their children together. One family has five children, the next has four children, and the third has two children. In how many ways can these eleven children line up in a row if siblings must stand in a group? To begin, there are 3! ways to order the three families; perhaps the Lefshetz children on the left, the Mersenne kids in the middle, and the Riemann's on the right. Once this ordering has been settled upon, there are 5! ways to order the group of five siblings, 4! ways to order the set of four siblings, and 2! ways to order the final pair of siblings. Our grand total is

$$(3!)(5! \cdot 4! \cdot 2!) = (6)(120 \cdot 24 \cdot 2) = 34560.$$

On the other hand, if we only wished to photograph the children from one of the three families, we would only have $5! + 4! + 2! = 146$ choices.

CₒₙCₑₚₜ e) In the scenario described above, how many ways are there to choose two siblings from each family and line them up for a photograph if siblings must stand next to one another?

ALL THE
ANSWERS

a) There are $4 \cdot 3 = 12$ ways and $4 + 3 = 7$ ways.

b) There are $3 \cdot (4 + 5) = 27$ dessert options.

c) i. AB, AC, BA, BC, CA, CB (six ways) ii. AB, AC, AD, BA, BC, BD, CA, CB, CD, DA, DB, DC (twelve ways) iii. Multiply the number of ways to choose the first person by the number of ways to choose the second person. iv. There are $8 \cdot 7 = 56$ ways. v. There are $n(n - 1)$ ways.

d) Only for $n = 1$, 2, 3 and 4.

e) A total of $(3!)(5 \cdot 4)(4 \cdot 3)(2 \cdot 1) = 2880$ ways.

EXERCISES

1. How many ways are there to select a vacation destination if one plans to visit a state beginning with the letter 'C' or ending with the letter 'O'?

2. Count the number of ways to plan a New England vacation which visits three states in some order.

3. A parent has jellybeans and chocolates. If she has more jellybean colors than chocolate types and there are 42 ways to choose one of each, then how many jellybean colors and chocolate types are there? (Find all possible answers.)

4. A bowl contains six different jellybeans and seven different chocolates. How many ways are there to line up five of the candies so that no two jellybeans are adjacent and no two chocolates are next to one another either?

5. How many ways are there to list A, B, C and D in a row, if A must not appear between B and D? (Thus both $BADC$ and $DCAB$ are off-limits.)

6. Find the number of ways to write three different rhyming letters in a row. (For example, AJK is a triple of distinct rhyming letters.)

7. In how many ways may five family members be arranged in a line if the shortest person must be located at one end of the line or the other?

8. In how many ways may six family members be arranged in a line if mom and dad plan to stand next to one another?

9. Four children each have three stuffed animals. In how many ways can the stuffed animals be arranged in a row on a shelf if the animals belonging to each child must be grouped together?

10. Three children each have seven stuffed animals. In how many ways can four of the animals be arranged in a row if they must all belong to the same child?

11. Simplify the following expression as much as possible.

a) $\dfrac{n!}{(n - 2)!}$ b) $\dfrac{1}{(n - 1)!} + \dfrac{1}{n!}$ c) $(n + 1)! - n(n!)$

(TIPS: Cancel common factors, find a common denominator, or pull out common factors where appropriate.)

WRITING

12. Prove that there are $n!$ ways to place n dots into an $n \times n$ grid so that no two dots are in the same row or column.

13. Find the number of ways to write 10 as a sum of distinct nonzero digits, if order matters. (Thus $2 + 3 + 5$ and $3 + 5 + 2$ should each be counted.)

14. A certain family contains n members. A photographer wishes to line up k of them in a row for a portrait. Show that there are $n!/(n-k)!$ ways in which this can be accomplished.

15. Prove there exists a positive integer b such that the number $n!$ does not end in exactly b zeros for any $n \in \mathbb{N}$.

FURTHER EXPLORATION

16. In the dialogue at the outset of this section a parent had four colors of jellybean and three types of chocolate, and chose one of each to offer each evening. Find a simple way to create a twelve-day dessert rotation so that all possible pairings occur and no sweet (jellybean or chocolate) is repeated on consecutive evenings. Generalize your strategy to handle m jellybeans and n chocolates for any $m, n \in \mathbb{N}$. Is such a dessert rotation always possible?

5.2 Combinations

Suppose that a math class has decided to send a delegation of three students to petition their professor for less homework. Unlike before, the make-up of the delegation is now all that matters; the order in which the students are named is immaterial. This sort of situation occurs so frequently in counting problems that special notation has been devoted to represent the numbers that arise.

> The number of ways to choose k objects from among a collection of n distinct objects is denoted by $\binom{n}{k}$, read "n choose k," and a particular selection of k objects is called a **combination**.

A few remarks regarding combinations are in order before we proceed to some examples. First, in practice the term 'combination' is not used as often as the term 'permutation,' even though the numbers arising from counting combinations play a much more central role in mathematics. (The term 'choose' is usually employed instead.) Secondly, there is a formula for $\binom{n}{k}$ involving factorials, which we include in the Reference section for sake of completeness. Most calculators will also provide values for $\binom{n}{k}$ if asked properly. However, we will be more interested in the meaning of $\binom{n}{k}$ than its formula. In particular, answers to exercises will often be left in the form $\binom{n}{k}$.

[CONCEPT] a) List the ways to choose a pair of letters from the set $\{a, b, c, d\}$. Consequently, determine the value of $\binom{4}{2}$.

Based solely on its meaning we can deduce the value of $\binom{n}{k}$ for certain special values of k. For instance, we see that $\binom{n}{n} = 1$, because clearly there is only one way to select n out of n objects: we must take all of them.

[CONCEPT] b) Based on the definition, what is the value of $\binom{n}{1}$ in terms of n?

With a modicum of thought it also becomes apparent that $\binom{n}{n-1} = n$, because choosing $n - 1$ out of n objects is equivalent to choosing one object to leave behind, and of course there are n ways to choose one object out of n. The question of what value to assign $\binom{n}{0}$ is more debatable. But choosing zero objects is tantamount to choosing n objects to leave behind, so it makes sense that $\binom{n}{0} = \binom{n}{n} = 1$.

[CONCEPT] c) Why does it make sense to declare that $\binom{n}{k} = 0$ when $k > n$?

Finally, it will be convenient to have a formula for $\binom{n}{2}$ handy. To count $\binom{n}{2}$ combinations, imagine making a list of all ways to choose 2 out of n objects. There are n ways to select the first object, followed by $n - 1$ ways to select the second object. However, in the resulting list each combination is listed twice. (For instance, if we were choosing two of the letters $\{a, b, c, d\}$ we should not count $\{a, b\}$ and $\{b, a\}$ as different combinations.) Hence our list is twice as long as it should be. To account for this we divide by 2, yielding $\binom{n}{2} = \frac{1}{2}n(n - 1)$. This discussion is summarized below.

> For certain values of k the value of $\binom{n}{k}$ may be easily ascertained from its definition. We have
>
> $$\binom{n}{0} = 1, \quad \binom{n}{1} = n, \quad \binom{n}{2} = \frac{n(n - 1)}{2}, \quad \binom{n}{n-1} = n, \quad \binom{n}{n} = 1.$$

Let us return to the hypothetical example involving a delegation of three students. Suppose for sake of illustration that the class size is 31, composed of 10 female and 21 male students. By definition there are $\binom{31}{3}$ delegations that could be formed. However, imagine that the delegation is gender representative in that it contains two males and a female. In that case we have $\binom{21}{2}$ ways to choose the boys and $\binom{10}{1}$ ways to choose the girl, for a total of $\binom{21}{2}\binom{10}{1}$ delegations. Using the above formulas the numerical answer comes to $\frac{1}{2}(21)(20) \cdot 10 = 2100$.

[CONCEPT] d) How many ways are there to form a three-person delegation from this class composed of one male and two female students?

[CONCEPT] e) How many such three-person delegations consist of all male or all female students?

Mathematical Outing ★ ★ ★

Suppose that a child may choose any two items from a bowl containing three colors of jellybeans, even if they are the same color. (This is known as "choosing with repetition.") Make a list of all the possible choices available to the child. Repeat this process for the case of four or five colors of jellybean. What do you notice? Based on your observations, write an expression for the general case of n colors using choose notation.

There is a beautiful explanation for the phenomenon just observed. Imagine that we wish to select two jellybeans (possibly the same color) from among a bowl containing five colors. We will do so by writing a "candy code" which will consist of a row of four arrows ($\rightarrow$) and two circles ($\bigcirc$). The symbols are decoded by beginning with the first color, then interpreting each $\rightarrow$ as "move on to the next color" and letting $\bigcirc$ mean "take a jellybean of the current color." Thus the code $\rightarrow \rightarrow \rightarrow \bigcirc \rightarrow \bigcirc$ amounts to taking one jellybean of color four and one jellybean of color five. Similarly, the code $\rightarrow \bigcirc\bigcirc \rightarrow \rightarrow \rightarrow$ requests two jellybeans, both of the second color. How many different candy codes are there? How does this process explain your previous findings?

The composition of our delegation might be all male, two males and a female, one male and two females, or all female. These can be chosen in $\binom{21}{3}$, $\binom{21}{2}\binom{10}{1}$, $\binom{21}{1}\binom{10}{2}$, and $\binom{10}{3}$ ways, respectively. But this accounts for all possible ways to create a three-person delegation. Therefore we have shown that

$$\binom{21}{3} + \binom{21}{2}\binom{10}{1} + \binom{21}{1}\binom{10}{2} + \binom{10}{3} = \binom{31}{3}.$$

Calculating these values gives $1330 + 2100 + 945 + 120 = 4495$, which checks.[†]

As a nice but decidedly nontrivial application of combinations, we shall determine the probability of obtaining two pairs in a five-card stud poker hand.

Suppose that a certain process could result in N different equally likely outcomes. To compute the probability of obtaining a certain type of outcome, count the number M of outcomes of this type. Then the probability that this type of outcome occurs is $\frac{M}{N}$.

The computation consists chiefly in counting the number of ways to select five cards from a standard deck of fifty-two cards so that some pair of cards share a common value (either 2, 3, 4, ... Q, K or A), another pair of cards has a different common value, and the final card has a third value. There are several valid strategies for completing this computation; we proceed as follows.

i. Choose 3 of the 13 possible values to appear in the hand.

ii. Choose 2 of these 3 values to represent the pairs.

iii. Choose 2 of the 4 suits for the first pair.

iv. Choose 2 of the 4 suits for the second pair.

v. Choose 1 of the 4 suits for the final card.

Using a calculator, our final total comes to

$$\binom{13}{3}\binom{3}{2}\binom{4}{2}\binom{4}{2}\binom{4}{1} = (286)(3)(6)(6)(4) = 123552.$$

Since there are $\binom{52}{5} = 2598960$ poker hands in all, the desired probability comes to $123552/2598960 \approx 0.04754$, or nearly 5% of the time. This probability is surprisingly high for what would seem to be a relatively unusual hand.

a) We could take the subsets $\{a, b\}$, $\{a, c\}$, $\{a, d\}$, $\{b, c\}$, $\{b, d\}$ or $\{c, d\}$. Hence $\binom{4}{2} = 6$.

b) We conclude that $\binom{n}{1} = n$.

c) It is impossible to choose more than n objects from among a collection of n objects.

d) There are $\binom{21}{1}\binom{10}{2}$ ways.

e) There are $\binom{21}{3} + \binom{10}{3}$ ways.

⛏ If the jellybeans have color R, G, B then the 6 possibilities are RR, GG, BB, RG, RB, GB. Including another color Y gives the 10 possibilities RR, GG, BB, YY, RG, RB, RY, GB, GY, BY. Finally, a fifth color leads to 15 choices. (We omit the list.) It appears that there are $\binom{n+1}{2}$ choices with n colors. This is explained by the candy codes, since there $\binom{6}{2} = 15$ ways to choose two of the six spots within the code for the circles. In general, n colors require $n - 1$ arrows and 2 circles, so there will be $\binom{n+1}{2}$ candy codes, verifying our conjecture.

EXERCISES

17. Compute the value of $\binom{5}{2}$ by listing all subsets of $\{a, b, c, d, e\}$ having two elements. Then compare your answer to that given by the formula for $\binom{n}{2}$.

18. How many subsets of $\{b, r, i, d, g, e\}$ have an odd number of elements? (Compute the actual number in this case.) What is unusual about your answer?

19. A class of 21 girls and 10 boys wishes to form a delegation of four students. Which of the possible gender compositions (from all female to all male) allows for the greatest number of delegations?

20. In the class from the previous exercise, how many five-person delegations sport at least one student of each gender?

21. Assuming that Jenny is a member of the class above, how many five-person delegations include Jenny? How many don't include Jenny? How many five-person delegations are there in total?

22. How many ways are there to place sixteen markers onto an 8×8 board so that each row contains two markers, but no two rows have markers on the same pair of squares?

23. An entry at `wikipedia.org` asserts that there are $\binom{13}{2}\binom{4}{2}^2\binom{11}{1}\binom{4}{1}$ ways to obtain two pair in five-card stud. Describe a counting strategy that leads to this expression.

24. How many five-card poker hands contain exactly one pair?

25. Count the number of ways of dealing seven cards from a standard deck and obtaining two three-of-a-kinds.

26. List all the ways to select three jellybeans from a bowl containing four colors of jellybean if it is acceptable to select the same color more than once.

27. Adapt the candy code method from the Mathematical Outing to answer the previous question in the case that there are eight colors of jellybean.

28. Determine a general formula for the number of ways to choose three candies from a bowl containing n colors of candy, assuming that we are permitted to select a given color more than once. Write your answer using choose notation.

WRITING

29. Explain why $\binom{n}{k} = \binom{n}{n-k}$ for all $0 \le k \le n$.

30. Prove that $\binom{n}{3} = \frac{1}{6}n(n-1)(n-2)$.

31. Adapt the exercise above about Jenny to prove that $\binom{n}{4} + \binom{n}{5} = \binom{n+1}{5}$.

32. By tallying the subsets of $\{1, 2, 3, \ldots, n\}$ according to size, prove that

$$\binom{n}{0} + \binom{n}{1} + \binom{n}{2} + \cdots + \binom{n}{n} = 2^n.$$

33. Show that for $n \ge 4$ we have

$$\binom{n}{4}\binom{n}{0} + \binom{n}{3}\binom{n}{1} + \binom{n}{2}\binom{n}{2} + \binom{n}{1}\binom{n}{3} + \binom{n}{0}\binom{n}{4} = \binom{2n}{4}.$$

34. Find, with proof, the probability of being dealt five cards from a standard deck and obtaining a three-of-a-kind. (But not a full house; i.e., the remaining two cards have different values.)

35. Compute, with explanation, the number of ways of being dealt six cards from a standard deck and obtaining precisely two pairs.

36. Determine the probability of being dealt thirteen cards from a standard deck and having four cards of one suit, four cards of another suit, three cards of a third suit, and two cards of the final suit. Justify your steps. (This is the most common suit distribution in a bridge hand.)

5.3   Introduction to Induction

The Principle of Mathematical Induction is one of the most versatile and ubiquitous proof techniques in all of mathematics. Simply put, it provides a method for proving certain statements that involve infinitely many cases. The trick is to show that each case follows from the previous one, thereby disposing of the entire sequence of cases in one fell swoop. The underlying principle is elegant and powerful; however, induction has acquired something of a shady reputation among students because this style of proof is a bit subtle, and the mechanics of a proof by induction have the potential to become confusing.

In order to have a concrete example from which to work, consider a row of n squares as illustrated below and consider the question of how many ways there are to color each square either scarlet or brown so that there are exactly two scarlet squares in the row. Of course, this is equivalent to choosing two out of the n squares to color scarlet, which can be done in $\binom{n}{2} = \frac{1}{2}n(n-1) = \frac{1}{2}(n^2 - n)$ ways. In what follows we will present a means of proving this fact other than using a direct counting argument.

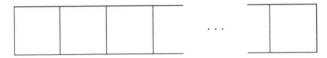

Forgetting about the formula $\frac{1}{2}(n^2 - n)$ for a moment, suppose that it has been revealed to you in a dream that there are precisely 861 ways to color a row of 42 squares either scarlet or brown so that two of the squares are scarlet. With a minimal amount of effort, how can we capitalize on this information to compute the number of ways to color a row of 43 squares? Since we already know something about coloring the first 42 squares, it makes sense to color the 43rd square first, then take stock of the situation. There are two cases to consider: either the final square in the row is brown, or it is scarlet. If it is brown, then we must color the remaining 42 squares so that two of the squares are scarlet. Thanks to the dream, we know that this can be done in 861 ways. On the other hand, if the final square is scarlet, then we must color the remaining squares so that only one of them is scarlet. Clearly this can be done in 42 ways—pick one of the 42 squares to be scarlet and color the rest brown. In total, we conclude that there are $861 + 42 = 903$ ways to perform the task.

The preceding paragraph illustrates the **inductive step**. This reasoning lies at the heart of a proof by induction, since it indicates how we can use the result from one case to help deduce the result for the next case. Granted, we've only shown how to get from case 42 to case 43, but the essence of the argument will not change regardless of which case we are considering. However, when handling the inductive step in general there is substantially more algebra involved, which has the unfortunate effect of obscuring the underlying reasoning. So keep the ideas presented above firmly in mind as we tackle the general case.

Suppose now that we have already confirmed that our formula is correct for the case of k squares. In other words, we know that there are $\frac{1}{2}(k^2 - k)$

ways to color a row of k squares either scarlet or brown with exactly two scarlet squares. This assumption, that our formula is correct for case k, is known as the **induction hypothesis**. We wish to prove that the formula is also valid for the case of $k+1$ squares; i.e. we want to show that there are $\frac{1}{2}((k+1)^2 - (k+1))$ ways to so color a row of $k+1$ squares. (Observe that we just replaced n by $(k+1)$ in our formula.) We can simplify this formula algebraically by writing

$$\tfrac{1}{2}((k+1)^2 - (k+1)) = \tfrac{1}{2}((k^2 + 2k + 1) - (k+1)) = \tfrac{1}{2}(k^2 + k).$$

We apply the same reasoning to get from case k to case $k+1$ as we did to get from case 42 to case 43. Thus given a row of $k+1$ squares, we can either color the final square scarlet or brown. If the final square is brown, then we must color two of the remaining k squares scarlet, which can be done in $\frac{1}{2}(k^2 - k)$ ways according to the induction hypothesis. However, if the final square is scarlet, then we need only color one of the remaining k squares scarlet, which clearly can be done in k ways. This reasoning is summarized in the figure below.

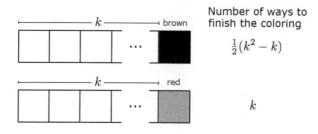

In total we have found that there are

$$\tfrac{1}{2}(k^2 - k) + k = \tfrac{1}{2}k^2 - \tfrac{1}{2}k + k = \tfrac{1}{2}k^2 + \tfrac{1}{2}k = \tfrac{1}{2}(k^2 + k)$$

ways to color a row of $k+1$ squares. Happily, this agrees with the expression predicted by the formula, thus completing our proof of the inductive step.

We have now argued that whenever our formula is true for a certain case, then it is also true for the next case. All that remains is to confirm that the formula actually holds in at least one particular case, for then we will be able to conclude that it holds for all subsequent cases as well. The verification of one or more initial cases is known as checking the **base case(s)**. The point here is to work out the answer "by hand" for several small values of n and confirm that the proposed formula correctly predicts the number of ways the coloring may be achieved. Clearly it is not possible to color a row of $n = 1$ squares and wind up with two scarlet squares, so there are 0 ways in this case. Equally clearly, there is 1 way in the case of $n = 2$ squares; we must color both squares scarlet. Finally, when $n = 3$ we find the colorings RRB, RBR and BRR, for a total of 3 ways. Plugging $n = 1$, 2 and 3 into the formula $\frac{1}{2}(n^2 - n)$ gives

$$\tfrac{1}{2}(1^2 - 1) = 0, \qquad \tfrac{1}{2}(2^2 - 2) = 1, \qquad \tfrac{1}{2}(3^2 - 3) = 3,$$

which agrees with our findings. We are now completely finished with the proof.[†]

Mathematical Outing ★ ★ ★

The game of "Last One Standing" provides an entertaining and concrete introduction to the Principle of Mathematical Induction. Rules for game
play are outlined below.

1. Choose four people to sit in a row. Orient yourselves so that one person
   is in the front and another is in the back. The person in the rear can see
   the other three, while the person in front can't see anyone else.

2. All individuals should be seated initially. The object is to arrange for the
   last person in line to be standing, while all others are seated.

3. The person in front can stand or sit at will.

4. The other three participants can move according to the following rule: a
   person may change state (by standing up or sitting down) if the person
   immediately in front of them is standing, while all others in front of them
   are seated. Otherwise they are locked in position and may not move.
   (The status of people behind them does not matter.)

Once you have solved the puzzle with four people, try it with three people or
with five people. How many moves are required to finish the game? How could
the answer for five people have been figured from the answer for four people?
Predict how many moves it will take for six people to finish the game.

Incidentally, notice that the technique of induction did not help us to find
the formula $\frac{1}{2}(n^2 - n)$ in the first place. Rather, the statement of the problem
obligingly handed us the right formula. Induction just afforded a clever means
of proving that the formula was valid in every case. (In practice one would need
to discover and conjecture this formula by some other means.) Also observe that
when checking the base cases we didn't just substitute $n = 1$, 2 and 3 into the
formula—we also figured out the answer independently, in order to verify that
the formula gave the correct value. To recap, we have introduced the Principle
of Mathematical Induction by using it to confirm a formula for $\binom{n}{2}$ that we had
already established using elementary counting techniques. But as we shall see,
induction applies to a much broader range of problems than just counting.

 You should find that it takes 7, 15 and 31 moves for three, four,
and five people, to finish the game. In each case the total number
of moves is one more than twice the previous number. This makes
sense; to solve the puzzle for six people the front five in line must first complete the
activity, which requires 31 steps. The sixth person is now free to stand, at which point
the front five must again perform all 31 steps in order to seat the fifth person. In total
we needed $31 + 1 + 31 = 63$ moves; twice the previous total plus one.

EXERCISES

37. How is induction like toppling an infinite row of dominoes? Identify the base case and the inductive step in this analogy.

38. List all ways to color a row of n squares so that one is scarlet, one is green, and the rest are brown for $n = 1$, 2 and 3. Verify that the formula $n^2 - n$ correctly predicts this value.

39. Suppose that a computer predicts that there are exactly 1722 ways to color a row of 42 squares so that one is scarlet, one is green, and the rest are brown. Use this information to calculate the number of ways to so color a row of 43 squares. (Do not use the formula $n^2 - n$ anywhere in your calculation.)

40. Show that if there are $k^2 - k$ ways to color a row of k squares so that one is scarlet, one is green, and the rest are brown, then there are $(k + 1)^2 - (k + 1)$ ways to so color a row of $k + 1$ squares.

41. Use a counting argument to show that there are $n^2 - n$ ways to color a row of n squares so that one is scarlet, one is green, and the rest are brown.

WRITING

42. Use induction to prove that there are $2n^2 - 2n$ ways to color a row of n squares so that all but two of the squares are brown and each of the remaining two squares is either scarlet or green.

43. Use induction to prove that there are $\frac{1}{2}(n^2 - 3n + 2)$ ways to color a row of n squares so that two of them are scarlet, the rest are brown, and the two scarlet squares are not adjacent.

44. Use induction to prove that there are $n^2 - 3n + 2$ ways to color a row of n squares so that one is scarlet, one is green, the rest are brown, and the scarlet and green squares are not adjacent.

45. Use induction to prove that there are a total of 2^n ways to color a row of n squares either scarlet or brown, with no restrictions on how many squares of each color there may be.

46. Use induction to prove that there are $n2^{n-1}$ ways to color a row of n squares either scarlet, green or brown so that there is exactly one green square.

5.4 Applications of Induction

Lest the previous section give the impression that induction is used primarily to count the number of ways to color rows of squares, we now present a variety of problems on a range of topics to illustrate the broad applicability of this technique. One standard use of induction involves proving that a proposed formula correctly gives the value of a certain sum. As our first example we will show that combining odd numbers and powers of 3 in the following way leads to an unexpectedly neat result. We shall prove that

$$3(3) + 5(3^2) + 7(3^3) + \cdots + (2n + 1)(3^n) = n3^{n+1}.$$

Keep in mind that this statement represents infinitely many equalities: one for each value of $n \in \mathbb{N}$. We could check that this equality holds for certain values of n, but we could never check them all separately, one by one.

[CONCEPT CHECK] a) Write out the statement above in the cases $n = 3$ and $n = 4$, then confirm that equality does in fact hold.

To establish a result by induction we must first demonstrate that one or more base cases hold. To this end we check that the equality is true for $n = 1$. Indeed, when $n = 1$ the left-hand side is $3(3) = 9$, while the right hand side is $1(3^2) = 9$ as well. For good measure we also check $n = 2$; the left-hand side totals $3(3) + 5(3^2) = 54$, while the right-hand side equals $2(3^3) = 54$.

The inductive step involves proving that if any particular case is true, then the next case is also true. As before, we use the variable k to keep track of our cases. Thus we will show that if the statement is true when $n = k$, then it is also true when $n = k + 1$. One must be careful to distinguish between what is given and what needs to be proved. Therefore we write case k at the top of a sheet of scrap paper and case $k + 1$ near the bottom, like this.

GIVEN: $3(3) + 5(3^2) + \cdots + (2k + 1)(3^k) = k3^{k+1}.$

$$\vdots$$

PROVE: $3(3) + 5(3^2) + \cdots + (2k+1)(3^k) + (2(k+1)+1)3^{k+1} = (k+1)3^{(k+1)+1}.$

Writing these two cases amounts to substituting $n = k$ and $n = k + 1$ into the statement to be proved. A word to the wise—much algebraic anguish can be avoided by replacing n by $(k + 1)$, *parentheses and all*, when writing case $k + 1$. We now simplify the statement to be proved, yielding

PROVE: $3(3) + 5(3^2) + \cdots + (2k + 1)(3^k) + (2k + 3)3^{k+1} = (k + 1)3^{k+2}.$

One enticing thought is to begin manipulating the above equality in some manner. But this approach is logically flawed: it is equivalent to assuming that the result we wish to show is already true. We write the statement to be proved at the bottom of the page for a good reason—it serves as a reference to guide our algebra; but it is a destination only, not a step in the proof.

Our goal is to perform valid algebraic steps beginning with the given statement until we produce the desired equality. With an eye towards reaching the statement to be proved, we see that it makes sense to add $(2k + 3)3^{k+1}$ to both sides of the given equality, giving

$$3(3) + 5(3^2) + \cdots + (2k + 1)(3^k) + (2k + 3)3^{k+1} = k3^{k+1} + (2k + 3)3^{k+1}.$$

But the right-hand side may now be rewritten as

$$\begin{aligned} k3^{k+1} + 2k3^{k+1} + 3(3^{k+1}) &= 3^{k+1}(3k+3) \\ &= 3^{k+1} \cdot 3^1(k+1) \\ &= (k+1)3^{k+2}, \end{aligned}$$

using the fact that $3^{k+1}3^1 = 3^{(k+1)+1} = 3^{k+2}$. Hence we have shown that

$$3(3) + 5(3^2) + \cdots + (2k+1)(3^k) + (2k+3)3^{k+1} = (k+1)3^{k+2},$$

which is exactly the statement we wished to reach. This completes the proof.[†]

We now turn our attention to a curious result involving divisibility. To introduce it, answer the following question before reading on.

QUERY b) Compute the number $4^n - 3n - 1$ for $n = 0, 1, 2, 3$ and 4. What do you notice? Make a conjecture based on your results.

Let us show that the quantity $4^n - 3n - 1$ is divisible by 9 for all integers $n \geq 0$. Our first impulse is to check that $4^n - 3n - 1 \equiv 0 \bmod 9$ for a complete residue system mod 9. Unfortunately this approach is invalid, since $4^n - 3n - 1$ is not a polynomial. So we instead opt for a proof by induction.

The base cases are $n = 0$ and $n = 1$, since these are the smallest two values of n for which the statement to be proved makes sense. We easily find that $4^0 - 3(0) - 1 = 0$ and $4^1 - 3(1) - 1 = 0$, which are both multiples of 9. In order to see a nontrivial case we compute $4^2 - 3(2) - 1 = 9$, also divisible by 9.

Now suppose that the statement is true for the case $n = k$; i.e. suppose we know that $9 \mid 4^k - 3k - 1$. We wish to show that case $(k+1)$ is also true; namely that $9 \mid 4^{(k+1)} - 3(k+1) - 1$, which reduces to $9 \mid 4^{k+1} - 3k - 4$. (Don't forget the parentheses around $(k+1)$.) This leads to the setup shown at left below. As usual, to prove a statement involving divisibility, we rewrite it algebraically. So we are given that $4^k - 3k - 1 = 9m$ for some $m \in \mathbb{Z}$, and we wish to show that $4^{k+1} - 3k - 4 = 9(\underline{\quad})$, where we must fill in the blank with an expression that is an integer. We have arrived at the stage shown on the right.

GIVEN: $9 \mid 4^k - 3k - 1$.

PROVE: $9 \mid 4^{k+1} - 3k - 4$.

GIVEN: $9 \mid 4^k - 3k - 1$.
So $4^k - 3k - 1 = 9m$, for $m \in \mathbb{Z}$.

PROVE: $4^{k+1} - 3k - 4 = 9(\underline{\quad})$,
Thus $9 \mid 4^{k+1} - 3k - 4$.

QUERY c) What arithmetic operation can be applied to $4^k - 3k - 1$ to make it look approximately like $4^{k+1} - 3k - 4$?

Mathematical Outing ★ ★ ★

We saw in an earlier chapter that it is possible, though quite tricky, to dissect a square into a number of smaller squares all of unequal sizes. The task becomes significantly less complicated once we permit some of the squares to be congruent. For instance, the diagram below illustrates how one can dissect a square into eight smaller squares. The

question now becomes, for which positive integers n is it possible to dissect a given square into n smaller squares, some of which may be the same size? Experiment with various configurations of squares until you are certain of the answer. Then attempt to prove your conjecture by induction.

This particular problem clearly illustrates how the statement to be proven informs the steps in our proof. Of all the possible algebraic manipulations that may be performed to the given equality $4^k - 3k - 1 = 9m$, multiplying both sides by 4 is the most promising step given that we wish to obtain an equality of the form $4^{k+1} - 3k - 4 = 9(\underline{\quad})$. Doing so yields

$$4(4^k - 3k - 1) = 4(9m) \quad \Longrightarrow \quad 4^{k+1} - 12k - 4 = 36m.$$

In order to obtain the expression $4^{k+1} - 3k - 4$ (which is what we care about), we next add $9k$ to both sides, resulting in

$$4^{k+1} - 12k - 4 + 9k = 36m + 9k \quad \Longrightarrow \quad 4^{k+1} - 3k - 4 = 9(4m + k).$$

To our delight, the right-hand side resolves as a multiple of 9. Therefore, starting with the fact that $9 \mid 4^k - 3k - 1$, we have shown that $9 \mid 4^{(k+1)} - 3(k+1) - 1$. This completes the proof by induction.[†]

Our final example illustrates that it can be helpful to invoke earlier cases (not just the previous case) when handling the inductive step. Imagine that a professor gives n copies of a practice exam to the most responsible member of her class of n students, along with the following unusual instructions. At any point a student in possession of an even number of papers may give half of them to a single other student. However, a student with

an odd number of papers may only give one paper to another student. We will prove that the students can eventually distribute all the papers so that each member of the class receives a single copy, regardless of the class size.

QUICK QUERY   d) Show that this distribution of papers is possible for $n = 1$ to 10.

The question just posed is not so much meant to establish the base case beyond even an unreasonable doubt, but rather to build up intuition regarding how the distribution works. Trying a number of small cases is often an effective means of developing a strategy for attacking the general case. So the reader is encouraged to return to the above question and work it out before continuing.

The base cases (and beyond) have now been established. So let us assume that such a distribution is possible for class sizes of up to k students and demonstrate that it can also be accomplished for $k+1$ students. Our experimentation with values of n from 1 to 10 show that when k is odd the inductive step is quick—just have the student with all the papers give one paper to a neighbor, who can then stand to the side. There are now $k-1$ papers left to distribute to $k-1$ students, which can be achieved by the inductive hypothesis.

A different strategy is called for when k is even, however. In this case the first student gives half of her papers to a neighbor. The class can now split into two halves containing $k/2$ students each, with one person in each group holding $k/2$ papers. But we know that each group can successfully distribute the papers, again by the inductive hypothesis. (This time we are not appealing to the previous case, but to a much earlier case.) Either way the distribution is possible, so the proof is complete.

We remark in passing that we have employed a slightly different approach here, in that we assumed that not only was case k was true, but so were all earlier cases. This strategy is known as the **Principle of Strong Induction**. It is equivalent to regular induction, so either may be employed depending on what the proof seems to require.

 a) For $n = 3$ we have $3(3) + 5(3^2) + 7(3^3) = 3(3^4)$, which is true since both sides reduce to 243. For $n = 4$ we have $3(3) + 5(3^2) + 7(3^3) + 9(3^4) = 4(3^5)$, which is also true since both sides equal 972.

b) The values are 0, 0, 9, 54, 243. All of these numbers are divisible by 9.

c) Multiply $4^k - 3k - 1$ by 4.

d) We consider $n = 7$ only; label the students as A, B, ..., G. Student A begins with all seven papers, then hands one to G. Student A then hands three papers to D. Next students A and D hand one paper to B and E, respectively. Finally students A and D hand one paper to C and F, respectively.

▦ The dissection is possible for all $n \in \mathbb{N}$ except $n = 2$, 3 and 5. To prove this claim we employ strong induction. We will need three seemingly random base cases: $n = 1$ (just use the whole square), $n = 6$ and $n = 8$ (use the given diagram or a small variation of it). Now observe that if it is possible to obtain k squares, then we can also obtain $k+3$ squares by splitting any of the original squares into four smaller ones using a single horizontal and vertical segment. Starting with $n = 1$, 6 or 8 and repeatedly adding 3 generates all positive integers except $n = 2$, 3 and 5.

❈

EXERCISES

47. Consider the statement $1 + 3 + 9 + \cdots + 3^n = \frac{1}{2}(3^{n+1} - 1)$. Verify that this statement is true for $n = 0$, 1 and 2. This ensures that the base cases hold.

48. Show that if we know $1 + 3 + 9 + \cdots + 3^k = \frac{1}{2}(3^{k+1} - 1)$, then it follows that $1 + 3 + 9 + \cdots + 3^k + 3^{k+1} = \frac{1}{2}(3^{k+2} - 1)$. Mimic the proof in this section; i.e. begin by adding the same expression to both sides of the given equality.

49. For the three starred problems below identify the smallest two values of n which make sense in the statement to be proved. These are the base cases.

50. Set up the proof of the inductive step in each of the three starred problems below. In other words, write out the given statement (case $n = k$) and the statement to be proved (case $n = k+1$). Use parentheses when writing $(k+1)$ and simplify the resulting expression.

WRITING

51.* Prove that $\dfrac{1}{(1)(3)} + \dfrac{1}{(3)(5)} + \cdots + \dfrac{1}{(2n-1)(2n+1)} = \dfrac{n}{2n+1}$.

52. Prove that $2(2) + 3(2^2) + 4(2^3) + \cdots + (n+1)(2^n) = n2^{n+1}$.

53. Compute the value of the sum

$$\frac{1}{(1)(2)} + \frac{1}{(2)(3)} + \cdots + \frac{1}{(n)(n+1)}$$

for $n = 1$, 2 and 3, writing your answer as a fraction in lowest terms. Based on your results, conjecture a formula for this sum in terms of n.

54. Prove your conjecture from the previous problem using induction.

55. Prove that $1(1!) + 2(2!) + 3(3!) + \cdots + n(n!) = (n+1)! - 1$.

56. Prove that $7^n + 3n - 1$ is divisible by 9 for all $n \geq 0$.

57. Prove that $6^n - 5n - 1$ is divisible by 25 for all $n \geq 0$.

58.* Construct a sequence of numbers a_1, a_2, a_3, ... as follows. Begin by setting $a_1 = 5$, then triple each term of the sequence and subtract four to obtain the next term. For instance, $a_2 = 3(5) - 4 = 11$. Compute a_3 and a_4, then prove that the nth term is given by the formula $a_n = 3^n + 2$.

59. Create a sequence of numbers a_1, a_2, a_3, ... by declaring that $a_1 = 2$, $a_2 = 3$, and every term beyond these two is obtained by doubling the previous term and then subtracting the term before that. Compute a_3, a_4 and a_5. Guess a formula for a_n, then prove your conjecture by induction.

60. Suppose that in the distribution problem from this section the instructions are as follows. In the class of $n \geq 3$ students any three students who together hold a number of papers that is divisible by 3 may redistribute their papers among themselves in any manner. If the professor initially hands out one paper to the first student, one paper to the second student, and the remaining $n - 2$ papers to the third student, prove that eventually everyone can get one paper.

61. Prove that for any $n \geq 1$, every positive integer between 1 and 2^{n+1} can be written as a sum of at most n primes. (You may invoke Bertrand's Postulate.)

62.* Given n people in a row, prove that they can completely reverse the order (from left to right) in which they are standing in $\frac{1}{2}n^2 - \frac{1}{2}n$ moves, where a move consists of two adjacent people trading places.

63. Review the "Last One Standing" game described in the Mathematical Outing of Section 5.3 if necessary. Then prove that it is possible for n people to complete the game in $2^n - 1$ moves.

64. In the Towers of Hanoi puzzle a certain number of circular discs of different sizes are stacked from smallest to largest on one of three pegs. The object of the puzzle is to transfer the entire stack of discs to one of the empty pegs by moving one disc at a time so that a larger disc never rests on top of a smaller disc. Prove that it is possible to solve the puzzle with n discs in $2^n - 1$ moves.

FURTHER EXPLORATION

65. The following beautiful problem appeared in *Five Hundred Mathematical Challenges* by Barbeau, Klamkin and Moser. The question concerns which integers one can reach by adding or subtracting together consecutive square numbers, without skipping any. For instance, we have $2 = -1^2 - 2^2 - 3^2 + 4^2$ and $-13 = 1^2 + 2^2 - 3^2 + 4^2 - 5^2$, so both 2 and -13 can be so written. Experiment to see which integers can be expressed in this way, make a conjecture, and then try to prove your conjecture using strong induction. (HINT: note that $7^2 - 8^2 - 9^2 + 10^2 = 4$ and $8^2 - 9^2 - 10^2 + 11^2 = 4$ also. Generalize and prove the pattern suggested by these examples.)

5.5 Fibonacci Numbers

One of the most beloved sequences in all of mathematics begins 1, 1, 2, 3, 5, 8, 13, 21, and so forth. These are the Fibonacci numbers, in which each term is obtained by adding together the two previous terms.

> The **Fibonacci numbers** F_1, F_2, F_3, F_4, ... are defined by setting $F_1 = 1$, $F_2 = 1$, and $F_{n-1} + F_n = F_{n+1}$ for all $n \geq 2$. It is also common to define $F_0 = 0$; this value is chosen so that $F_0 + F_1 = F_2$.

There is such an unending stream of intriguing results involving Fibonacci numbers that an entire mathematical journal, the *Fibonacci Quarterly*, has been devoted to publishing them. The appearance of Fibonacci numbers in both nature and in ancient civilizations has been well-documented.

Mathematical Outing ★ ★ ★

In how many ways is it possible to color a row of n squares either scarlet or brown so that no two scarlet squares are adjacent? (In other words, so that any two scarlet squares are separated by at least one brown square.) Tally the number of ways this can be done for $n = 1$ through $n = 5$. Based on your findings, make a conjecture for the number of ways to color a row of n squares in general. As one might expect, this conjecture may be proved by induction in a manner very similar to the coloring proof described in Section 5.3. The proof is left as an exercise.

Around the year 1200 AD this sequence of numbers was rediscovered in Europe by Leonardo of Pisa, nicknamed Fibonacci ("son of Bonacci"), after whom the sequence is named. He stumbled upon the sequence while modelling the population growth of pairs of bunnies. His approach was slightly complicated and biologically unrealistic, but it did lead to interesting mathematical results. As is often the case, far simpler motivations have since been found. One of them is outlined below, while another appears in the Mathematical Outing above.

Consider tiling a row of n squares with squares and dominoes. More precisely, let us count the number of ways to tile an $n \times 1$ rectangle with 1×1 squares and 2×1 rectangles so that the pieces exactly cover the row without overlapping. There are 5 ways to accomplish this for a row of four squares.

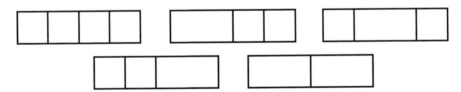

Since it turns out that there are 3 ways to tile a row of three squares and 8 ways to tile a row of 5 squares, we conjecture that in general there are F_{n+1} ways to tile a row of n squares. (We chose $n + 1$ as the subscript because the $n = 4$ case could be done in F_5 ways; i.e. the subscript appears to be 1 more than the value of n we are considering.) We will prove this claim by induction. The base cases are routine, so we turn now to the inductive step.

QUERY a) Count the number of ways to tile a row of $n = 2, 3$ and 4 squares using squares and dominoes. Verify in each case that the total is F_{n+1}.

As we shall see, we will need to rely on *two* previous cases in our argument. (This often occurs in proofs involving Fibonacci numbers; just be sure to confirm at least two base cases.) So suppose that it is possible to tile a row of $(k - 1)$ squares in F_k ways and that it is possible to tile a row of k squares in F_{k+1} ways. We wish to prove that there are F_{k+2} ways to tile a row of $(k + 1)$ squares.

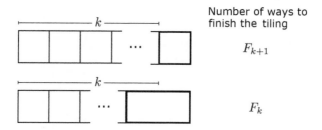

Number of ways to
finish the tiling

F_{k+1}

F_k

Clearly the $(k+1)^{\text{st}}$ square will be covered by either a single square or a domino, as illustrated above, leaving either k squares or $(k-1)$ squares to be tiled. In the former case we know by the inductive hypothesis that there are F_{k+1} ways to finish the tiling, while in the latter case there will be F_k ways to finish the tiling. We conclude that there are $F_{k+1} + F_k$ ways in total. But by definition $F_{k+1} + F_k = F_{k+2}$, so there are F_{k+2} ways to tile a row of $(k+1)$ squares, as desired. This completes the proof.

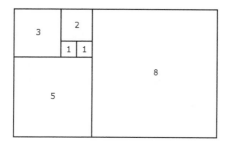

There are many clever mathematical identities involving Fibonacci numbers, one of which is suggested by the diagram above. (The subdivision into squares is almost a perfect square dissection, except for the repeated pair of unit squares.)

C⸗NC⸗PT b) Why are both the length and width of a rectangle constructed in the manner shown above guaranteed to be Fibonacci numbers?

The area of each piece is the square of a Fibonacci number, while the area of the entire rectangle is the product of two consecutive Fibonacci numbers. Of course the sum of the former will equal the latter; in algebraic form this observation may be written as

$$F_1^2 + F_2^2 + F_3^2 + \cdots + F_n^2 = F_n F_{n+1}.$$

In some sense the diagram provides a proof of the statement. Let us supplement that visual demonstration with a more rigorous proof by induction.

We check several base cases, just to be on the safe side. When $n = 1$ we have $1^2 = (1)(1)$, which is true. For $n = 2$ the statement claims that $1^2 + 1^2 = (1)(2)$, which also holds. Finally, when $n = 3$ we have $1^2 + 1^2 + 2^2 = (2)(3)$, which is correct. Now suppose that the statement is valid for the case $n = k$; we will show that it also holds when $n = k + 1$. Thus we are given that

$$F_1^2 + F_2^2 + F_3^2 + \cdots + F_k^2 = F_k F_{k+1}$$

and we wish to show that the sum of the squares of the first $k + 1$ Fibonacci numbers is $F_{k+1} F_{k+2}$. In light of this goal, we add F_{k+1}^2 to both sides, yielding

$$F_1^2 + F_2^2 + F_3^2 + \cdots + F_k^2 + F_{k+1}^2 = F_k F_{k+1} + F_{k+1}^2.$$

But now the right-hand side reduces to

$$F_k F_{k+1} + F_{k+1}^2 = F_{k+1}(F_k + F_{k+1}) = F_{k+1} F_{k+2},$$

which is exactly the expression we were seeking, so we're done.[†]

CONCEPT c) Rewrite the following expressions as a single Fibonacci number or a product of two Fibonacci numbers.

i. $F_{k+2} - F_k$ ii. $F_k + 2F_{k+1}$ iii. $F_{k+1}^2 - F_k^2$

There are enough accessible, fascinating results concerning Fibonacci numbers to fill a book. Several nice results appear as exercises; we will limit ourselves to one more topic in this section. Below we have listed F_1 through F_{16}.

n	1	2	3	4	5	6	7	8	9	10	11	12	13	14	15	16
F_n	1	1	2	3	5	8	13	21	34	55	89	144	233	377	610	987

QUERY d) Examine every fourth term of the sequence, beginning with F_4. Do the same for every fifth term beginning with F_5. What do you notice?

This question illustrates the fact that for any $n \in \mathbb{N}$, every n^{th} Fibonacci number is divisible by F_n. We will demonstrate this property for $n = 4$ by showing that every fourth Fibonacci number is a multiple of $F_4 = 3$. In the language of congruences, we wish to show that $F_{4k} \equiv 0 \bmod 3$ for all $k \in \mathbb{N}$. It will not come as a surprise to learn that we will prove this fact by induction.

We have already provided the base cases by observing that $F_4 = 3$ and $F_8 = 21$ are multiples of 3. So suppose that F_{4k} is divisible by 3. We wish to demonstrate that $F_{4(k+1)} = F_{4k+4}$ is also divisible by 3. In order to relate the value of F_{4k+4} back to F_{4k} we use the Fibonacci recursion to write

$$
\begin{aligned}
F_{4k+4} &= F_{4k+3} + F_{4k+2} \\
&= (F_{4k+2} + F_{4k+1}) + F_{4k+2} \\
&= 2(F_{4k+1} + F_{4k}) + F_{4k+1} \\
&= 3F_{4k+1} + 2F_{4k}.
\end{aligned}
$$

But $3F_{4k+1}$ is clearly a multiple of 3, and $2F_{4k}$ is also by our inductive hypothesis. Hence their sum, which is F_{4k+4}, must be also, and we're done.

a) The totals should come to 2, 3 and 5. We omit the diagrams showing the actual tilings.

b) Because both the length and the width are the sum of two consecutive Fibonacci numbers, which is equal to another Fibonacci number, by definition.

c) i. F_{k+1} ii. F_{k+3} iii. $F_{k-1}F_{k+2}$

d) Every fourth Fibonacci number is divisible by 3, and $F_4 = 3$. Similarly, every fifth Fibonacci number is a multiple of 5, and $F_5 = 5$.

e) Because each term in the sequence is the sum of the previous two terms, and the initial two terms are also 1, 1, the sequence must continue from this point in the same way that it began.

▦ For $n = 1$ to 5 we find that there are 2, 3, 5, 8 and 13 ways to color the row of squares. (For instance, when $n = 3$ we have BBB, RBB, BRB, BBR, RBR.) Hence we conjecture that n squares can be so colored in F_{n+2} ways.

⚙

EXERCISES

66. How should we define F_{-1}, F_{-2}, F_{-3}, F_{-4} and F_{-5} in keeping with the relationship $F_{n-1} + F_n = F_{n+1}$? (For instance, we want $F_{-1} + F_0 = F_1$, or $F_{-1} + 0 = 1$, so we should take $F_{-1} = 1$.)

67. Confirm that there are $F_6 = 8$ ways to tile a row of 5 squares using only squares and dominoes.

68. Calculate $F_n^2 - F_{n-1}F_{n+1}$ for $n = 1$ through $n = 5$. Based on your results, conjecture a formula for the value of $F_n^2 - F_{n-1}F_{n+1}$.

69. Demonstrate that $F_n + 3F_{n+1} + 3F_{n+2} + F_{n+3}$ simplifies to F_{n+6}.

70. There is a three-term recurrence for the squares of the Fibonacci numbers. More precisely, there exist positive integers a, b and c with the property that $F_{n+1}^2 = aF_n^2 + bF_{n-1}^2 - cF_{n-2}^2$ for all $n \geq 2$. Find values of a, b and c for which this recurrence holds.

71. Using the table above, find all positive integers n in the range $2 \leq n \leq 16$ for which n divides evenly into either F_{n+1} or F_{n-1}. Make a conjecture based on your answer, then check it for $n = 17$.

72. The final result outlined in this section indicates that F_{2n} is divisible by F_n for all $n \geq 1$. Compute the value of F_{2n}/F_n for $n = 1$ through $n = 6$. What do you notice about these values? (Other than that they are whole numbers.) Make a conjecture based on your results.

WRITING

73. Prove that there are F_{n+2} ways to color a row of n squares either scarlet or brown so that no two scarlet squares are adjacent.

74. How many ways are there to tile an $n \times 2$ rectangle with 2×1 dominoes? (The dominoes may be oriented horizontally or vertically.) Make a conjecture, writing your answer as a Fibonacci number. Then prove your conjecture.

75. Prove that the sum of the first n Fibonacci numbers is given by the formula

$$F_1 + F_2 + F_3 + \cdots + F_n = F_{n+2} - 1.$$

76. Prove that the sum of every other Fibonacci number is

$$F_1 + F_3 + F_5 + \cdots + F_{2n-1} = F_{2n}.$$

77. Show that $F_{n+5} = 3F_n + 5F_{n+1}$ for all $n \in \mathbb{N}$. Use this fact to prove that F_{5k} is divisible by 5 for all $k \in \mathbb{N}$.

78. Let $C \geq 2$ be a positive integer, and let F_n be the largest Fibonacci number that does not exceed C. Prove that $C - F_n < F_{n-1}$.

79. How many ways are there to tile a row of length n with $n-2$ squares and 1 domino? with $n-4$ squares and 2 dominoes? Use these ideas to prove the identity $\binom{n}{0} + \binom{n-1}{1} + \binom{n-2}{2} + \cdots = F_{n+1}$.

FURTHER EXPLORATION

80. The Lucas numbers, defined as $L_1 = 1$, $L_2 = 3$ and $L_{n+1} = L_n + L_{n-1}$ for $n \geq 2$, are closely related to the Fibonacci numbers. For instance, it is the case that $F_n L_n = F_{2n}$. Compute the first sixteen Lucas numbers and write them beneath the first sixteen Fibonacci numbers. What other patterns and relationships can you find?

5.6   Reference

The purpose of this section is to provide a condensed summary of the most important facts and techniques from this chapter, as a reference when studying or working on material from later chapters. We also include an overview of how to implement a proof by induction.

• *Vocabulary* independent events, addition principle, multiplication principle, listing, permutation, factorial, combination, inductive step, induction hypothesis, base cases, Principle of Strong Induction, Fibonacci numbers

• *Counting* There are several ways to avoid creating an exhaustive list when counting the number of ways to perform a particular task. One rule of thumb involves multiplying for the word 'and' while adding for the word 'or.' There are $n!$ ways to order n objects, where $n!$ (n factorial) equals $n(n-1)\cdots(2)(1)$. Furthermore, there are $n(n-1)\cdots(n-k+1)$ ways to order k of the n objects. These arrangements (in which order matters) are called permutations. The number of ways to choose k objects from a set of n objects is denoted $\binom{n}{k}$ and is given by the formula $\binom{n}{k} = n!/k!(n-k)!$. In particular, we have $\binom{n}{0} = 1$, $\binom{n}{1} = n$, $\binom{n}{2} = \frac{1}{2}n(n-1)$, and $\binom{n}{n} = 1$. These subsets (for which order does not matter) are called combinations.

• *Proof by Induction* The Principle of Mathematical Induction is one of the most powerful, versatile, and ubiquitous proof techniques in all of mathematics. In its most basic guise, one is asked to prove that a certain statement is true for all positive integers n. The statement might involve a formula, or the number of ways to achieve a coloring, or a divisibility argument, or almost anything else.

To prove a result by induction, one must first establish the base cases. This is typically the case $n = 1$, but might be $n = 0$, or $n = 1$ and $n = 2$, depending on the problem. (Establishing the base case is usually routine; just be sure to confirm it "by hand.") Then one must prove the inductive step, which involves showing that if the statement is true for a certain value of n, say $n = k$, then it is also true for $n = k + 1$. (This part is usually *not* routine.) It often helps to work out a few concrete cases by hand, to understand the connection. So solve the problem for $n = 4$ and $n = 5$, or try to show that the $n = 42$ case implies the $n = 43$ case. A standard proof by induction will read something like this.

> "We will prove the result by induction. To begin, the base case states that [base case], which is true because [reasons]. (Or you might just say "which is clearly true," if it applies.) We wish to prove that [statement for $n = k$] implies that [statement for $n = k + 1$]. So suppose that [case $n = k$]. [Main argument goes here, in which one makes the connection between case k and case $k + 1$.] This shows that [statement for $n = k + 1$]."

• *Fibonacci Numbers* This sequence of numbers is defined by setting $F_1 = 1$, $F_2 = 1$, and $F_{n+1} = F_n + F_{n-1}$ for $n \geq 2$. We may also include $F_0 = 0$ if desired. The sequence begins 0, 1, 1, 2, 3, 5, 8, 13, 21, 34, ... and grows exponentially. There are many relationships among the Fibonacci numbers, some of which are listed below.

$$
\begin{aligned}
F_1 + F_2 + F_3 + \cdots + F_n &= F_{n+2} - 1 \\
F_1^2 + F_2^2 + F_3^2 + \cdots + F_n^2 &= F_n F_{n+1} \\
F_m F_n + F_{m+1} F_{n+1} &= F_{m+n+1}
\end{aligned}
$$

Proofs involving Fibonacci numbers often (but not always) involve induction; it is usually necessary to establish at least two base cases for such proofs. It is a fact that every n^{th} Fibonacci number is divisible by F_n; in other words, $F_n \mid F_{an}$ for all $a, n \in \mathbb{N}$.

★ TIP ★ The most tempting logical fallacy to commit when proving statements by induction is to inadvertently use the statement of case $k + 1$ somehow in the midst of your proof. Before working out the details of the inductive step write the statement of case k at the top of a piece of paper, write case $k + 1$ at the bottom, then fill in the middle. This will help to avoid any logical pitfalls.

Another common trap to avoid is to inadvertently use the statement to be proven when verifying the base case. For example, if we wish to show there are $\frac{1}{2}(n^2 - n)$ ways to color a row with exactly two scarlet squares and the rest brown, it would be incorrect to say "By the formula we see there are $\frac{1}{2}3(3 - 1) = 3$ ways to color a row of three squares, which completes the base case." One must actually list all the ways by hand (RRB, RBR, BRR), count them (three ways), and then confirm that the formula gives the correct answer ($\frac{1}{2}3(3 - 1) = 3$). The idea is to verify the formula, not to use it.

SAMPLE PROOFS

The proofs below provide concise explanations for results discussed within this chapter. They are meant to serve as an illustration for how proofs of similar statements could be phrased. The boldface numbers indicate the section containing each result; the location of that result within the section is marked by a dagger (†).

———————◆———————

5.2 Given positive integers $m, n \geq 3$, prove that

$$\binom{m}{3} + \binom{m}{2}\binom{n}{1} + \binom{m}{1}\binom{n}{2} + \binom{n}{3} = \binom{m + n}{3}.$$

Proof Imagine that a certain class consists of m male and n female students. We will count the number of ways to choose a delegation of three students from this class. On the one hand, since there are $m + n$ students in total, there are $\binom{m+n}{3}$ ways to choose three of them. On the other hand, we could break down our count according to the male-female composition of the delegation. There are $\binom{m}{3}$ delegations with three boys, $\binom{m}{2}\binom{n}{1}$ delegations with two boys and a girl, $\binom{m}{1}\binom{n}{2}$ delegations with one boy and two girls, and $\binom{n}{3}$ delegations consisting of three girls. This approach also counts the number of ways to select a group of three students. Since both methods must give the same answer, we conclude that $\binom{m}{3} + \binom{m}{2}\binom{n}{1} + \binom{m}{1}\binom{n}{2} + \binom{n}{3} = \binom{m+n}{3}$.

———————◆———————

5.3 Show there are $\frac{1}{2}(n^2 - n)$ ways to color each square within a row of $n \geq 2$ squares either scarlet or brown so that there are two scarlet squares in all.

Proof We will prove this statement by induction. To begin, when $n = 2$ there is only one coloring, namely to color both squares scarlet. In addition when $n = 3$ there are the three colorings RRB, RBR and BRR. The proposed formula gives $\frac{1}{2}(4 - 2) = 1$ and $\frac{1}{2}(9 - 3) = 3$, which agrees. Therefore the statement is correct for $n = 2$ and 3, which completes the base cases.

Now suppose that the statement is true for a certain value of n, say $n = k$. This means that there are in fact $\frac{1}{2}(k^2 - k)$ ways to color a row of k squares as described above. We will show that the statement is also true for $n = k+1$; i.e. we will show that there are

$$\frac{1}{2}\big((k + 1)^2 - (k + 1)\big) = \frac{1}{2}(k^2 + 2k + 1 - k - 1) = \frac{1}{2}(k^2 + k)$$

ways to color a row of $(k + 1)$ squares.

Given a row of $(k+1)$ squares, we may color the final square either scarlet or brown. In the former case, we need only color one of the remaining k squares scarlet, which clearly can be done in k ways. In the latter case, we must color two of the remaining k squares scarlet, which can be done in $\frac{1}{2}(k^2-k)$ ways by the induction hypothesis. In total there are

$$k + \tfrac{1}{2}(k^2-k) = k + \tfrac{1}{2}k^2 - \tfrac{1}{2}k = \tfrac{1}{2}k^2 + \tfrac{1}{2}k = \tfrac{1}{2}(k^2+k)$$

ways to color a row of $(k+1)$ squares. This is precisely the expression predicted by the formula, which means that the statement is true for $n = k + 1$. This completes the proof.

———◆———

5.4 Prove that $3(3) + 5(3^2) + 7(3^3) + \cdots + (2n+1)(3^n) = n3^{n+1}$ for all $n \in \mathbb{N}$.

Proof We proceed using induction. When $n = 1$ the left-hand side is $3(3) = 9$, while the right hand side is $1(3^2) = 9$ as well. Similarly when $n = 2$ the left-hand side totals $3(3) + 5(3^2) = 54$, while the right-hand side equals $2(3^3) = 54$. Hence the statement is true for the base cases $n = 1$ and 2.

Now suppose that the statement is true when $n = k$, meaning that

$$3(3) + 5(3^2) + \cdots + (2k+1)(3^k) = k3^{k+1}.$$

Adding $(2k+3)3^{k+1}$ to both sides of this equality yields

$$3(3) + 5(3^2) + \cdots + (2k+1)(3^k) + (2k+3)3^{k+1} = k3^{k+1} + (2k+3)3^{k+1}.$$

The right-hand side may now be simplified as

$$\begin{aligned} k3^{k+1} + 2k3^{k+1} + 3(3^{k+1}) &= 3^{k+1}(3k+3) \\ &= 3^{k+1} \cdot 3^1(k+1) \\ &= (k+1)3^{k+2}. \end{aligned}$$

Hence we have shown that

$$3(3) + 5(3^2) + \cdots + (2k+1)(3^k) + (2k+3)3^{k+1} = (k+1)3^{k+2}.$$

But this is exactly the statement for $n = k + 1$, so we're done.

———◆———

5.4 Demonstrate that $4^n - 3n - 1$ is divisible by 9 for all integers $n \geq 0$.

Proof We prove the claim by induction. Computing the value of $4^n - 3n - 1$ for $n = 0$, 1 and 2, gives 0, 0 and 9. In each case we obtain a multiple of 9, thus establishing the base cases. Next suppose that the statement holds for a certain value $n = k$, which means that $4^k - 3k - 1$ is a multiple of 9. Therefore we may write $4^k - 3k - 1 = 9m$ for some $m \in \mathbb{Z}$. Multiplying both sides by 4 yields $4^{k+1} - 12k - 4 = 36m$. Next, adding $9k$ brings us to $4^{k+1} - 3k - 4 = 36m + 9k$. Finally, we rewrite this equality as $4^{k+1} - 3(k+1) - 1 = 9(4m + k)$. In other words, $4^{k+1} - 3(k+1) - 1$ is a multiple of 9, which is exactly what the statement claims in the case $n = k + 1$. Therefore if the statement is true when $n = k$ it is also true when $n = k + 1$, so the proof is complete.

$$\longrightarrow\!\!\!\!\diamond$$

5.5 Show that $F_1^2 + F_2^2 + F_3^2 + \cdots + F_n^2 = F_n F_{n+1}$ for all $n \in \mathbb{N}$.

Proof We employ induction to prove this identity. The sum on the left-hand side is equal to $F_1^2 = 1$ when $n = 1$, comes to $F_1^2 + F_2^2 = 1 + 1 = 2$ for $n = 2$, and totals $F_1^2 + F_2^2 + F_3^2 = 1 + 1 + 4 = 6$ when $n = 3$. The formula on the right-hand side gives $F_1 F_2 = 1 \cdot 1 = 1$, $F_2 F_3 = 1 \cdot 2 = 2$, and $F_3 F_4 = 2 \cdot 3 = 6$ for $n = 1$, 2 and 3. In each case the results agree, which confirms the base cases.

Now suppose that the statement is valid for the case $n = k$, meaning that

$$F_1^2 + F_2^2 + F_3^2 + \cdots + F_k^2 = F_k F_{k+1}.$$

Adding F_{k+1}^2 to both sides we obtain

$$F_1^2 + F_2^2 + F_3^2 + \cdots + F_k^2 + F_{k+1}^2 = F_k F_{k+1} + F_{k+1}^2.$$

But now the right-hand side reduces to

$$F_k F_{k+1} + F_{k+1}^2 = F_{k+1}(F_k + F_{k+1}) = F_{k+1} F_{k+2},$$

by the definition of Fibonacci numbers. Hence the sum of the squares of the first $(k + 1)$ Fibonacci numbers is $F_{k+1} F_{k+2}$, which proves the statement in the case $n = k + 1$. By induction, we conclude that the statement is always true.

CHAPTER 6

Relations and Functions

6.1 Basic Concepts

We have now arrived at one of the most foundational, and consequently also one of the most abstract, concepts that we will consider in this text. Much of mathematics is concerned with identifying and studying the properties of particular relationships between pairs of mathematical objects. For instance, we are familiar with the notion of $a \mid b$ (divisibility), $l_1 \| l_2$ (parallel lines), and $x < y$ (less than). Each of these is an example of a relation: a rule prescribing when one object is related to another.

$\boxed{\text{C}^{\text{ON}}_{\text{HE}}\text{C}^{\text{EPT}}_{\text{K}}}$ a) What is the difference between a relation, such as $a \mid b$, and an operation, such as addition?

Observe that order is often relevant when it comes to a pair of related objects. For instance, in the $<$ relation we have $\pi < 7$, but not $7 < \pi$. Hence it makes sense to list related items as ordered pairs. As a further example, consider the digits 1, 2, ..., 9. Let us say that a digit is related to another digit if its last letter (such as on$\boxed{\text{e}}$) matches the first letter of the other digit (such as $\boxed{\text{e}}$ight). We find that the related digits are given by the ordered pairs

$$(1,8) \quad (2,1) \quad (3,8) \quad (5,8) \quad (7,9) \quad (8,2) \quad (8,3) \quad (9,8).$$

In a very real sense this list of ordered pairs *is* the relation, in its purest, most mathematical form. Of course, the verbal description is rather important for understanding why we care about this particular list of ordered pairs.

Motivated by these ideas, we make the following definition.

A **relation** $\vdash$ from A to B is a subset of the Cartesian product $A \times B$. If (a, b) is an element of our relation $\vdash$, then we say that a is related to b, denoted by $a \vdash b$. We write $a \nvdash b$ to indicate that a is not related to b.

137

Recall that the Cartesian product $A \times B$ is the set of all ordered pairs (a, b) with $a \in A$ and $b \in B$. So we may think of the relation $\vdash$ as a collection of ordered pairs which prescribes exactly which elements of A are related to which elements of B. Many relations, such as divisibility or less than, are referred to so regularly that they have their own dedicated symbol; in these cases $\mid$ and $<$.

CONCEPT CHECK b) We define a "square relation" as follows. For real numbers x and y we say that x is related to y exactly when one of x or y is the square of the other. Find five different ordered pairs (x, y) in this relation.

CONCEPT CHECK c) Write a mathematical description of the ordered pairs that make up the square relation just defined using bar notation.

It is often possible to visually present a relation from A to B by constructing its **graph**. Just as is done for functions, we display the elements of A along a horizontal axis and the elements of B along a vertical axis, then plot the point (a, b) for each ordered pair in the relation. Unlike functions, however, there are no restrictions on where points may appear in the graph of a relation. This is one indication that relations are more general than functions. The graphs of our digit relation and the square relation are shown below.

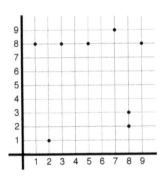
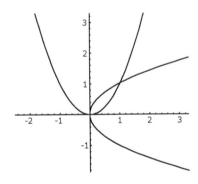

CONCEPT CHECK d) Neither of the graphs above represent functions. Why not?

There are several more general concepts pertaining to relations to examine before we introduce two special types of relations. The domain of a relation from A to B refers to the set of all elements of A that are related to some element of B. Similarly, the range of this relation is the set of all elements of B such that some element of A relates to them.

Let $\vdash$ be a relation from A to B. The **domain** and **range** of $\vdash$ are

$$\mathrm{dom}(\vdash) = \{a \mid a \in A, \ a \vdash b \text{ for some } b \in B\},$$
$$\mathrm{rng}(\vdash) = \{b \mid b \in B, \ a \vdash b \text{ for some } a \in A\}.$$

Note that the domain is a subset of A, while the range is a subset of B.

For example, consider the divisibility relation from $\mathbb{Z}$ to $\mathbb{Z}$, where we write $a \mid b$ to mean that a divides evenly into b. We know that 0 is not in the domain, since by definition 0 does not divide into any number. But every other $a \in \mathbb{Z}$ does divide into another integer, hence the domain is the set of all nonzero integers. On the other hand, the range consists of all integers b, because every $b \in \mathbb{Z}$ (even $b = 0$) is divisible some other integer; for instance, by 1.

CONCEPT CHECK e) Determine the domain and range for the digit relation.

Finally, we briefly discuss the inverse of a relation $\vdash$, which we write as $\dashv$. (Inverses will play a more important role when we discuss functions.) Loosely speaking, we say that b is related to a in the inverse relation exactly when a was related to b in the original relation. In other words, $b \dashv a$ if and only if $a \vdash b$.

The **inverse** $\dashv$ of a relation $\vdash$ consists of precisely those ordered pairs $(b, a) \in B \times A$ for which (a, b) was an element of the relation $\vdash$.

Thus the inverse of our digit relation consists of the ordered pairs

$$(1, 2) \quad (2, 8) \quad (3, 8) \quad (8, 1) \quad (8, 3) \quad (8, 5) \quad (8, 9) \quad (9, 7).$$

CONCEPT CHECK f) Give a verbal description for the inverse of the digit relation.

CONCEPT CHECK g) What is the inverse of the $<$ relation?

As an aside, we mention that many authors use the letter R to represent a relation, and write $a \, R \, b$ (and $a \, \cancel{R} \, b$) to indicate that a is related (or not related) to b. We prefer the alternate symbol $\vdash$, in part because it resembles the standard symbol $\mapsto$ that we will introduce shortly when we discuss functions.

It is also worth noting that we usually talk about a **relation on a set** A, meaning that the objects that are being related to one another are all part of the same set A rather than two different sets A and B. (This has been the case in all the examples presented thus far.) In the subsequent sections we will focus more or less exclusively on these sorts of relations. We chose to introduce relations using two sets A and B partly to emphasize their connection with functions, and partly because it is easier to understand the introductory concepts when the domain and range have distinct names.

 a) A relation links two different objects, while an operation combines two objects to produce a third.

b) Some ordered pairs in the square relation include $(0, 0)$, $(1, 1)$, $(1, -1)$, $(-1, 1)$, $(-2, 4)$, $(4, -2)$, $(\sqrt{2}, 2)$, $(3, -\sqrt{3})$, among other possible answers.

c) The relation can be written in bar notation as $\{(x, y) \mid x, y \in \mathbb{R}, \ y = x^2 \text{ or } x = y^2\}$.

d) Both graphs fail the "vertical line test," meaning that there is some "input value" which is related to two different "output values." (Take $a = 8$ for the digit relation and $x = 2$ for the square relation.)

e) The domain is the set $\{1, 2, 3, 5, 7, 8, 9\}$ while the range is the set $\{1, 2, 3, 8, 9\}$.

f) In the inverse, one digit is related to another if the first letter of the one digit is the same as the last letter of the other digit.

g) The inverse is the $>$ relation. (Not the $\geq$ relation.) This is because $x < y$ precisely when $y > x$.

❋

EXERCISES

1. Determine whether the following statements are true or false.
a) Multiplication is an example of a relation from $\mathbb{R}$ to $\mathbb{R}$.
b) If $\dashv$ is the inverse of a relation $\vdash$, then the inverse of $\dashv$ is $\vdash$.
c) If $\vdash$ is a relation on a set A and $a \in A$, then $a \vdash a$.

2. Construct a relation $\vdash$ from $A = \{a, b, c, d\}$ to $B = \{1, 2, 3, 4, 5\}$ such that $\text{dom}(\vdash) = \{c, d\}$ and $\text{rng}(\vdash) = B$.

3. For the sets in the previous exercise, how many relations are there from A to B such that $\text{dom}(\vdash) = \{a, b\}$ and $\text{rng}(\vdash) = \{2, 3\}$? List the ordered pairs in each such relation.

4. We define a relation $\vdash$ on the set of digits $\{1, 2, 3, 4, 5\}$ by writing $a \vdash b$ when the two-digit number ab is divisible by 3. (Do not interpret 'ab' as multiplication in this question.) List the ordered pairs in this relation, and create its graph.

5. In the previous exercise, find $\text{dom}(\vdash)$ and $\text{rng}(\vdash)$. How does $\vdash$ compare to its inverse $\dashv$? How is this indicated by the graph of $\vdash$?

6. The graph of a relation $\vdash$ is shown at right.
a) Which of the following is correct: $4 \vdash 3$, $4 \dashv 3$, $1 \nvdash 5$?
b) For which $a \in \mathbb{R}$ do we have $a \vdash a$?
c) Determine $\text{dom}(\vdash)$ and $\text{rng}(\vdash)$.

7. Sketch the graph of the $<$ relation.

8. Define a relation $\vdash$ on $\mathbb{N}$ by saying that $a \vdash b$ when ab is a multiple of 9. Find numbers a, b and c such that $a \vdash b$ and $b \vdash c$, but $a \nvdash c$.

9. We define a relation as $\vdash = \{(x, y) \mid x, y \in \mathbb{R},\ y^2 - x^2 = 9\}$. Sketch the graph of this relation, then determine $\text{dom}(\vdash)$ and $\text{rng}(\vdash)$.

10. We define a relation as $\vdash = \{(x, y) \mid x, y \in \mathbb{R},\ |2x| + |y| = 4\}$. Sketch the graph of this relation, then determine $\text{dom}(\vdash)$ and $\text{rng}(\vdash)$.

11. We define a relation as $\vdash = \{(m, n) \mid m, n \in \mathbb{Z},\ m^2 + 2n^2 = 9\}$. Sketch the graph of this relation and use it to determine $\text{dom}(\vdash)$ and $\text{rng}(\vdash)$.

12. How does the graph of an inverse relation compare to the original graph?

13. Let $\dashv$ be the inverse of a relation $\vdash$. How do the domain and range of $\vdash$ compare to the domain and range of $\dashv$?

14. Given sets A and B with $|A| = 3$ and $|B| = 4$, how many relations are there from A to B?

6.2 Order Relations

The relations which play a significant role in mathematics tend to fall into two broad categories—order relations and equivalence relations. We shall briefly consider each in turn. On the one hand, we have those relations which indicate instances in which one object is "smaller" or "larger" than another. Common examples of order relations include $x < y$ (we can order real numbers by value), $A \subseteq B$ (we can order sets via inclusion) and $a \mid b$ (we can order natural numbers via divisibility). Let us now isolate the properties of these relations that causes them to have the effect of ordering the objects which they relate. To see how these properties naturally arise, the reader is strongly encouraged to try out the Mathematical Outing on the following page before proceeding further.

CONCEPT CHECK a) How are the $<$ and $\subseteq$ relations similar? How are they different?

There are two essential characteristics that a relation $\vdash$ must possess to order the elements of a set. It makes sense that we should not allow both $x \vdash y$ and $y \vdash x$; two different elements cannot each be smaller (or larger) than the other. Furthermore, we ought to require that if $x \vdash y$ and $y \vdash z$, then $x \vdash z$ as well. Finally, we must distinguish between relations such as $<$ in which no element is related to itself (it is not true that $3 < 3$, for example) and relations such as $\mid$ in which every element is related to itself (it is true that $3 \mid 3$). Both situations lead to valid order relations, but our strategy for proving the antisymmetric property will differ slightly in each case, so we will consider them separately.

Let $\vdash$ be a relation on a set A. We say that

- *i.* $\vdash$ is **nonreflexive** if $x \nvdash x$ for all $x \in A$, while
  $\vdash$ is **reflexive** if $x \vdash x$ for all $x \in A$,

- *ii.* $\vdash$ is **antisymmetric** if we do not have both $x \vdash y$ and $y \vdash x$ for any pair of distinct elements $x, y \in A$,

- *iii.* $\vdash$ is **transitive** if $x \vdash y$ and $y \vdash z$ imply that $x \vdash z$.

A relation that is nonreflexive, antisymmetric, and transitive is called a **strict partial order**, while a relation that is reflexive, antisymmetric, and transitive is called a **partial order**.

For the time being we will focus on strict partial orders. Notice that all the graphs in the Mathematical Outing are candidates for strict partial orders, since all of them are nonreflexive.

CONCEPT CHECK b) Explain why each graph in the Mathematical Outing represents a nonreflexive relation.

As an illustration, let us define a relation $\vdash$ on the set of all words by declaring that $\alpha \vdash \beta$ whenever word α is a proper substring of word β, meaning that the

Mathematical Outing ★ ★ ★

Consider the graphs of the following four relations on the set $\{a, b, c, d, e\}$. In each case determine the ordering of $\{a, b, c, d, e\}$ induced by the relation or identify the aspect of the relation that prevents it from being a good candidate for ordering the elements of the set. Thus we could interpret the pairs (b, c) and (c, e) in the first graph to mean that b is less than c, which is less than e.

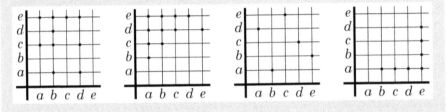

letters of word α appear within word β in order and adjacent to one another, and word β includes one or more additional letters. Thus bridge $\vdash$ hybridgerbil, but throb $\nvdash$ broth and cape $\nvdash$ carpet.

CONCEPT CHECK c) Find words α, β_1, β_2, and γ such that $\alpha \vdash \beta_1 \vdash \gamma$ and $\alpha \vdash \beta_2 \vdash \gamma$, but β_1 and β_2 are not related to one another in either order.

We will now verify that $\vdash$ possesses each of the properties necessary for a strict partial order.

- To begin we must explain why no word can be related to itself. We know that $\alpha \nvdash \alpha$ because the second word is required to be longer than the first. This prevents a word from being a proper substring of itself. (Just as a set A is not a proper subset of itself.)

- We next argue that if α and β are different words then we cannot have both $\alpha \vdash \beta$ and $\beta \vdash \alpha$. But this is clear, since the two words cannot each be longer than the other.

- Finally, we will show that if $\alpha \vdash \beta$ and $\beta \vdash \gamma$ then $\alpha \vdash \gamma$. This property holds because if a copy of α is contained within β and a copy of β is contained within γ, then a copy of α is guaranteed to appear within γ; it's inside the copy of β. (Such as with rid $\vdash$ bridge $\vdash$ hybridgerbil.)[†]

Another interesting example of a strict partial order arises through family trees, by saying that $a \vdash b$ whenever person a is a direct descendent of person b.

CONCEPT CHECK d) Confirm that the family tree relation just described is in fact an example of a strict partial order.

We now turn our attention to partial orders. There are two main differences between strict partial orders and partial orders, at least where establishing the properties is concerned. The first is obvious—we must show that $x \vdash x$ (rather than $x \nvdash x$) for all $x \in A$, since partial orders are reflexive instead of nonreflexive. The second is more subtle, but just as important.

> To prove that a relation is antisymmetric, argue that if $x \vdash y$ and $y \vdash x$ then it follows that $x = y$.

This formulation of the antisymmetric property is equivalent to the one given earlier, since it ensures that we can only have $x \vdash y$ and $y \vdash x$ when $x = y$, never when x and y are distinct elements of A. The motivation for using this version is that it is often easier to implement in a partial order proof.

CON**C**EPT **C**HE**C**K   e) The divisibility relation on $\mathbb{Z}$ is not antisymmetric. Demonstrate this fact by finding two integers a and b such that $a \mid b$ and $b \mid a$ but $a \neq b$.

To showcase this proof strategy in action, consider the relation $\vdash$ on $\mathbb{R}$ in which $x \vdash y$ whenever $x - y \in \mathbb{Z}_{\geq 0}$, where $\mathbb{Z}_{\geq 0} = \{0, 1, 2, 3, \ldots\}$ is the set of nonnegative integers. We will show that $\vdash$ is a partial order.

- To conclude that $\vdash$ is reflexive we must show that $x \vdash x$ for all $x \in \mathbb{R}$. So we must confirm that $x - x \in \mathbb{Z}_{\geq 0}$. But $x - x = 0$, which is certainly a nonnegative integer.

- We next show that $\vdash$ is antisymmetric. So suppose that $x \vdash y$ and $y \vdash x$. This means that $x - y$ and $y - x$ are both nonnegative integers, so we know that $x - y \geq 0$ and $y - x \geq 0$. In other words $x \geq y$ and $y \geq x$, which only occurs when $x = y$. According to the above proof strategy, we may now deduce that $\vdash$ is antisymmetric.

- Finally we will explain why $\vdash$ is transitive. Suppose that $x \vdash y$ and $y \vdash z$. This means that $x - y = a$ and $y - z = b$ for $a, b \in \mathbb{Z}_{\geq 0}$. Adding these equations together yields $x - z = a + b$. But clearly $a + b$ is also a nonnegative integer, hence $x \vdash z$, thus proving transitivity.[†]

Be aware that our definitions do not require that a relation compare every possible pair of elements to qualify as a partial order or strict partial order. (Hence the use of the modifier 'partial.') Thus the fourth example in the Mathematical Outing is a strict partial order, even though we are not able to tell whether $b < c$ or $c < b$. The order induced by that particular relation is best illustrated in a tree, with larger elements above smaller ones, as shown at right. When an order does provide a comparison between every pair of distinct elements we call it a **total order**. For example, the $\leq$ relation on the real numbers is a total order since given any $x, y \in \mathbb{R}$ we have $x \leq y$ or $y \leq x$.

a) Both relations do provide a comparison by identifying some objects as "smaller" than others. There are two important differences. We can have $A \subseteq A$, but it is not true that $x < x$. Furthermore, the $<$ relation can be used to compare any two unequal numbers, but we cannot compare every pair of unequal sets with $\subseteq$.

b) None of the points (a, a), (b, b), etc. are plotted on any graph. Therefore $a \nless a$, $b \nless b$, ..., $e \nless e$, meaning that each relation is nonreflexive.

c) The words $\alpha = $ is, $\beta_1 = $ wish, $\beta_2 = $ list, and $\gamma = $ wishlist will work, for example.

d) No person is their own descendant, two people cannot simultaneously be descendants of one another, and if a is a descendant of b who is a descendant of c, then a is a descendant of c. Hence this relation is nonreflexive, antisymmetric, and transitive.

e) For instance, $7 \mid (-7)$ and $(-7) \mid 7$, but $-7 \neq 7$.

▦ The first relation does provide a means of arranging the elements in order as $b < d < a < c < e$. The second does not, since then we would have $d < e$ and $e < d$ simultaneously. The third graph is problematic for two reasons. First, if $b < a$ and $a < d$ then we should have $b < d$, but the point (b, d) does not appear. Also, this relation gives $a < d < c < e < b < a$, which suggests that $a < a$. Finally, the fourth does give a legitimate strict partial order, but it does not compare every pair of elements, which may not be desirable.

EXERCISES

15. Draw the graph of a relation on the set $\{a, b, c, d, e\}$ which induces the strict partial order $e < b < c < d < a$.

16. Draw the graph of a relation on the set $\{a, b, c, d, e, f\}$ giving the strict partial order suggested by the tree diagram at right.

17. Draw a tree diagram for the strict partial order given by the ordered pairs (a, c), (a, e), (b, c), (b, e), (d, b), (d, c), (d, e), (e, c).

18. How can one modify a strict partial order to obtain a partial order?

19. Given a partial order $\vdash$ on a set A, we call w a **maximal element** if there is no $a \in A$ with $w \vdash a$. (Other than $a = w$). Identify all maximal elements in the tree diagram above.

20. Let S be the set of proper subsets of $\{b, r, i, d, g, e\}$. Determine all maximal elements of S with respect to the partial order induced by the $\subseteq$ relation.

21. Let $B = \{n \in \mathbb{N} \mid 1 \leq n \leq 10\}$, ordered via the divisibility relation. Draw a tree diagram for this ordering of B and describe the maximal elements.

22. It is a fact that the divisibility relation is a partial order on the set $\mathbb{Z}_{\geq 0}$ of nonnegative integers. What is the unique maximal element with respect to this order? Explain your answer.

23. For a given set A, define the **identity relation** on A as the relation $\vdash$ consisting of only the pairs $\{(a, a) \mid a \in A\}$. Is $\vdash$ a total order, a partial order, a strict partial order, or not an order relation at all?

24. Define a relation $\vdash$ on the set of points in the plane by saying that $P_1 \vdash P_2$ if $x_1 + y_1 \le x_2 + y_2$, where (x_1, y_1) and (x_2, y_2) are the coordinates of P_1 and P_2. Which properties does $\vdash$ possess? (Briefly explain your answers.)

25. We define a relation $\vdash$ on the set of five-digit numbers by declaring that $m \vdash n$ precisely when each digit of m is less than the corresponding digit of n. Thus $48613 \vdash 79825$. Which properties does $\vdash$ possess? (Explain your answers.)

26. How many strict partial orders are there on the set $\{a, b, c\}$ for which $a < b$? Draw tree diagrams to illustrate each possibility.

27. How many total orders are there on the set $\{a, b, c, d, e\}$ for which $d < e$?

28. Show that $\subseteq$ is not a total order on the collection of subsets of $\{1, 2, \ldots, 9\}$.

29. Give an example of a total order on the set of all words. (Recall that for our purposes, a 'word' is a finite string of letters.)

WRITING

30. Consider the relation $\vdash$ on $\mathbb{N}$ in which $m \vdash n$ means that n can be obtained from m by appending one or more digits to the end of m. Thus $3 \vdash 385$ but $29 \nvdash 219$, for example. Prove that $\vdash$ is a strict partial order.

31. We define a relation $\vdash$ on the set of points in the plane by saying that $P_1 \vdash P_2$ if $2x_1 + 3y_1 < 2x_2 + 3y_2$, where (x_1, y_1) and (x_2, y_2) are the coordinates of P_1 and P_2. Demonstrate that $\vdash$ is a strict partial order.

32. Let $\mathcal{S}$ consist of all subsets of $\{a, b, c, \ldots, z\}$. Explain why the relation $\subset$ on $\mathcal{S}$ is a strict partial order. (Recall that $\subset$ means proper subset.)

33. Consider the set $\mathcal{F}$ of all linear functions; that is, functions f of the form $f(x) = ax + b$. Let us say that $f_1 \vdash f_2$ if the graph of $f_1(x) - f_2(x)$ has positive slope. Show that $\vdash$ is a strict partial order.

34. Show that the divisibility relation $|$ on $\mathbb{N}$ is a partial order but not a total order. Give a complete algebraic argument for each property.

35. Let $\mathbb{Q}^*$ be the set of nonzero rational numbers. Define a relation $\vdash$ on $\mathbb{Q}^*$ by declaring that $r \vdash s$ whenever $\frac{s}{r}$ is a positive integer. (For instance we would have $-\frac{3}{8} \vdash -\frac{15}{4}$, but $2 \nvdash 3$.) Prove that $\vdash$ is a partial order.

36. Define a relation $\vdash$ on the set of points in the plane by saying that $P_1 \vdash P_2$ whenever $x_1 + 2y_1 \le x_2 + 2y_2$ and $2x_1 + y_1 \le 2x_2 + y_2$, where (x_1, y_1) and (x_2, y_2) are the coordinates of P_1 and P_2. Demonstrate that $\vdash$ is a partial order.

37. We create a relation on the set of all words by declaring that $\alpha \vdash \beta$ whenever all the letters of α also appear in β in the same order, but not necessarily adjacent to one another. Thus cape $\vdash$ carpet and lunch $\vdash$ lunch, but fool $\nvdash$ folly. Prove that $\vdash$ is a partial order but not a total order.

38. Carefully describe a relation that provides a total order on the points in the Cartesian plane. Prove that your relation is a total order.

6.3   Equivalence Relations

Aside from ordering the elements of a set, a relation can also have the effect of splitting the elements of a set into several classes. We have already seen one example of such a relation; namely, congruence mod m. Recall that we defined a "congruence mod 5" relation by saying that $a \equiv b$ mod 5 exactly when $5|(a-b)$. If we group together those integers that are congruent to one another mod 5 we create five **congruence classes**:

$$\{\ldots, -5, 0, 5, 10, \ldots\} \qquad \{\ldots, -4, 1, 6, 11, \ldots\} \qquad \{\ldots, -3, 2, 7, 12, \ldots\}$$
$$\{\ldots, -2, 3, 8, 13, \ldots\} \quad \text{and} \quad \{\ldots, -1, 4, 9, 14, \ldots\}.$$

C⌁N⌁C⌁PT a) Which congruence class contains the number 999?

As was the case for order relations, a relation must possess certain properties to have the effect of splitting the elements of a given set into classes. These properties will look rather familiar, but if you skipped over the previous section then try the Mathematical Outing to discover them. (Otherwise just read on.) Traditionally, the symbol $\sim$ is used to denote an equivalence relation, so we will employ this symbol from here onwards.

There are three properties that a relation $\sim$ on a set A must possess in order to effectively split the elements of A into one or more classes so that the elements within each class are all related to one another. For starters, if we have $x \sim y$ then we should also have $y \sim x$; being in the same class is by nature a reciprocal relationship. It is also clear that if x and y are in the same class, and y and z are in the same class, then x and z must also be in the same class. Finally, an element is obviously in the same class as itself, so we should have $x \sim x$. These conditions are summarized below.

Let $\sim$ be a relation on a set A. We say that

    i. $\sim$ is **reflexive** if $x \sim x$ for all $x \in A$,

    ii. $\sim$ is **symmetric** if $x \sim y$ implies that $y \sim x$,

    iii. $\sim$ is **transitive** if $x \sim y$ and $y \sim z$ imply that $x \sim z$.

A relation having all three properties is called an **equivalence relation**.

This definition is remarkably similar to that of a partial order—we only replaced the antisymmetric property by a symmetry condition—so it is curious that equivalence relations and partial orders behave in quite different ways.

C⌁N⌁C⌁PT b) Determine whether or not the parallel relation $l_1 \| l_2$ on lines in the plane is an equivalence relation.

C⌁N⌁C⌁PT c) Say that two individuals are siblings when they have at least one common biological parent. Explain why this is not an equivalence relation.

Mathematical Outing ★ ★ ★

Consider the four relations on $A = \{a, b, c, d, e\}$ defined by the graphs below and decide whether or not these relations can be used to sort the elements into several classes. In each instance list the subsets of elements that are related to one another, or explain why the relation is not a viable candidate for splitting the elements of A into several classes of related elements.

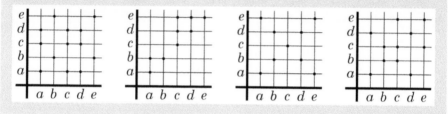

We claim that the following relation $\sim$ on the nonzero rational numbers $\mathbb{Q}^*$ is an equivalence relation. For $a, b \in \mathbb{Q}^*$ let $a \sim b$ mean that $\frac{a}{b} = 2^k$ for some $k \in \mathbb{Z}$. In other words, $a \sim b$ is equivalent to $\frac{a}{b} \in \{\ldots, \frac{1}{4}, \frac{1}{2}, 1, 2, 4, 8, \ldots\}$.

- We first check that we have $a \sim a$ for all $a \in \mathbb{Q}^*$. This is clearly true, since $\frac{a}{a} = 1 = 2^0$ is a power of 2. Hence $\sim$ is reflexive.

- Next suppose that $a \sim b$; we wish to show that this implies $b \sim a$. According to the definition of $\sim$, we know that $\frac{a}{b} = 2^k$ for some $k \in \mathbb{Z}$. But this means that $\frac{b}{a} = \frac{1}{2^k} = 2^{-k}$. Because $-k$ is an integer we find that $\frac{b}{a}$ is an integer power of 2, thus establishing that $b \sim a$. Therefore $\sim$ is symmetric.

- Finally, suppose that $a \sim b$ and $b \sim c$ for $a, b, c \in \mathbb{Q}^*$. This means that $\frac{a}{b} = 2^k$ and $\frac{b}{c} = 2^l$ for $k, l \in \mathbb{Z}$. We are interested in the ratio $\frac{a}{c}$, so we multiply these equalities to obtain $\frac{a}{c} = 2^k 2^l = 2^{k+l}$. Since $k + l \in \mathbb{Z}$ this shows that $a \sim c$, so we conclude that $\sim$ is transitive.

An equivalence relation $\sim$ on a set A splits the set into a collection of disjoint subsets by grouping together elements of A which are related to one another. Such a collection of subsets is known as a partition of A.

Given a set A, a **partition** of A is collection of nonempty subsets A_i, where $i \in I$ for some index set I, satisfying the conditions

i. The sets A_i are pairwise disjoint, so that $A_i \cap A_j = \emptyset$ for $i \neq j$.

ii. The sets A_i together comprise all of A, so that $\bigcup_{i \in I} A_i = A$.

We all know how to partition the integers into even and odd numbers. Another familiar partition is given by the quadrants in the Cartesian plane. Points are either in quadrant I, II, III, IV, or on one of the coordinate axes, giving a partition of the plane into five subsets.

CONCEPT d) Create a partition of the real numbers involving three sets.

Suppose that $\sim$ is an equivalence relation on a set A. Given any particular $a \in A$, the collection of all elements of A that are related to a will form one of the subsets in the partition of A determined by $\sim$. These subsets have a special name and a particular notation.

Let $\sim$ be an equivalence relation on A. Then $\sim$ partitions A into various **equivalence classes**. Given any $a \in A$, the equivalence class containing a is denoted by $[a]$, and consists of all elements of A related to a:

$$[a] = \{x \in A \mid x \sim a\}.$$

We say that a is a **representative** for the class $[a]$.

For instance, consider the equivalence relation defined by the first graph in the Mathematical Outing above. We see that $[a] = \{a, c, d\}$ since $a \sim a$, $a \sim c$, and $a \sim d$. The other equivalence class is $[b]$.

CONCEPT e) Suppose that $a \sim b$ for an equivalence relation $\sim$ on A. What can be said of the equivalence classes $[a]$ and $[b]$?

Returning to the equivalence relation on $\mathbb{Q}^*$ defined above, in which $a \sim b$ iff $\frac{a}{b} = 2^k$ for some $k \in \mathbb{Z}$, we see that $\sim$ partitions $\mathbb{Q}^*$ into infinitely many equivalence classes, each of which has infinitely many elements. For instance, the class $[3]$ consists of all $r \in \mathbb{Q}^*$ such that $r \sim 3$, which means that $\frac{r}{3} = 2^k$ for some $k \in \mathbb{Z}$. In other words $r = 3(2^k)$, so

$$[3] = \{\ldots, \frac{3}{8}, \frac{3}{4}, \frac{3}{2}, 3, 6, 12, 24, \ldots\}.$$

Clearly 5 does not belong to this equivalence class, so $[5]$ is a different equivalence class from $[3]$.

CONCEPT f) Describe the equivalence class $[1]$. Then name an equivalence class for $\sim$ that is distinct from the classes $[1]$, $[3]$ and $[5]$.

We conclude this section with an example involving equivalence classes with a nice geometric interpretation. Given points P_1 and P_2 in the Euclidean plane, we say that $P_1 \sim P_2$ if $x_1 - x_2 = 3(y_1 - y_2)$, where (x_1, y_1) and (x_2, y_2) are the coordinates of P_1 and P_2, respectively. We first show that $\sim$ is in fact an equivalence relation.

- Clearly $P_1 \sim P_1$ for all points P_1, since the quantities $x_1 - x_1$ and $3(y_1 - y_1)$ are both equal to 0 in this case.

- Next suppose that $P_1 \sim P_2$, which means that $x_1 - x_2 = 3(y_1 - y_2)$. We wish to prove that $P_2 \sim P_1$, so we must demonstrate that $x_2 - x_1 = 3(y_2 - y_1)$. But the latter equation may be obtained from the former by negating both sides of that equation, so $P_1 \sim P_2$ does imply that $P_2 \sim P_1$.

- Finally, suppose that $P_1 \sim P_2$ and $P_2 \sim P_3$, so that we have

$$x_1 - x_2 = 3(y_1 - y_2) \quad \text{and} \quad x_2 - x_3 = 3(y_2 - y_3).$$

We would like to deduce that $P_1 \sim P_3$; i.e. that $x_1 - x_3 = 3(y_1 - y_3)$. Comparing the given equations to the one we would like to prove, we realize that we should add the given equations. This immediately yields the desired equality, so we're done.[†]

$\boxed{\text{C{\scriptsize ON}C{\scriptsize EPT}}}$ g) Why do we not obtain an equivalence relation when we define $\sim$ via $x_1 + x_2 = 3(y_1 + y_2)$?

It will be illuminating to describe the set of all points in the equivalence class of $(5, 2)$ in a geometric fashion. If (x, y) is a point related to $(5, 2)$ then we have $x - 5 = 3(y - 2)$. Rearranging this equation gives $3y = x + 1$, or $y = \frac{1}{3}x + \frac{1}{3}$. Observe that this line passes through the point $(5, 2)$, so the equivalence class consists of all points on the line through $(5, 2)$ having a slope of $\frac{1}{3}$. This occurs in general—the equivalence class $[P]$ consists of all points on the line through P having slope $\frac{1}{3}$.

$\boxed{\text{A{\scriptsize LL THE} N{\scriptsize SWERS}}}$ a) Based on its last digit, $999 \in \{\ldots, -1, 4, 9, 14, \ldots\}$.
b) We will propose that a line should be considered to be parallel to itself. It is clear that if $l_1 \| l_2$ then $l_2 \| l_1$; it is just as obvious that parallelism is transitive, so this is an equivalence relation.
c) The sibling relation is reflexive and symmetric, but not necessarily transitive. Imagine that A has parents P and Q, and B has parents Q and R, while C has parents R and S. Then A is a sibling of B, who is a sibling of C, but A and C are not siblings.
d) One natural choice is to place all positive real numbers in one set, all negative real numbers in another set, and 0 by itself in the third set.
e) If $a \sim b$ then the equivalence classes $[a]$ and $[b]$ are the same.
f) The equivalence class $[1]$ is the set $\{\ldots, \frac{1}{4}, \frac{1}{2}, 1, 2, 4, 8, \ldots\}$. Since 7 does not appear in any of the classes $[1]$, $[3]$ or $[5]$ we know that $[7]$ is distinct from those three classes.
g) The resulting relation would be symmetric, but neither reflexive nor transitive. For example, given a point P_1, we would need to have $x_1 + x_1 = 3(y_1 + y_1)$, or $x_1 = 3y_1$, in order to have $P_1 \sim P_1$, and clearly this will not occur for all points P_1.
🏛 The first relation splits set A into the two subsets $\{a, c, d\}$ and $\{b, e\}$, while the third splits A into the sets $\{a, e\}$, $\{b, d\}$ and $\{c\}$. The second relation is not a feasible candidate since $a \vdash b$ but $b \nvdash a$, so it is not clear whether or not a and b are in the same group. The fourth relation is also problematic in that $b \vdash c$ and $c \vdash e$, but $b \nvdash e$, so it is not clear whether or not b and e should be placed in the same group.

EXERCISES

39. For natural numbers m and n we write $m \vdash n$ to mean that $GCD(m, n) > 1$. Is $\vdash$ an equivalence relation? Why or why not?

40. We define a relation on the real numbers by saying that $x \vdash y$ when $xy \geq 0$. Is $\vdash$ an equivalence relation? Why or why not?

41. Define a relation $\vdash$ on the set of all lines in the plane by declaring that $l_1 \vdash l_2$ whenever l_1 and l_2 are either parallel or perpendicular. Is $\vdash$ an equivalence relation? Why or why not?

42. We define a relation on the set of words by saying that $\alpha \vdash \beta$ if β contains some letter appearing in α. (Recall that a word consists of any finite sequence of letters.) Is $\vdash$ an equivalence relation? Why or why not?

43. An equivalence relation $\sim$ on the set $\{a, b, c, d, e\}$ gives rise to the equivalence classes $\{a, c, e\}$, $\{b\}$ and $\{d\}$. Draw the graph of this relation.

44. How many partitions of the set $\{a, b, c\}$ are there? List the subsets of the partition in each case.

45. How many partitions of the set $\{a, b, c, d\}$ are there for which the elements a and b are in different subsets? List the subsets of each such partition.

46. Consider the equivalence relation $\sim$ on the set of points in the Cartesian plane defined by $P_1 \sim P_2$ whenever $x_1 y_1 = x_2 y_2$, where P_1 and P_2 have coordinates (x_1, y_1) and (x_2, y_2). Describe the equivalence classes of the points $(1, 4)$, $(-2, 3)$ and $(0, 5)$.

47. An equivalence relation on the integers gives rise to the equivalence classes

$$\ldots, \ \{-4, -3, -2, -1\}, \ \{0, 1, 2, 3\}, \ \{4, 5, 6, 7\}, \ \{8, 9, 10, 11\}, \ \ldots$$

List the elements in the equivalence classes $[101]$ and $[-101]$. Then find a convenient way to list one representative from each equivalence class.

48. Recall that congruence mod m is an equivalence relation. How many equivalence classes arise? What do we call a set containing exactly one representative from each equivalence class?

49. We define an equivalence relation $\sim$ on the set of all words by saying that $\alpha \sim \beta$ whenever the words α and β contain the same letters, counting repeated letters. (Thus silent $\sim$ listen but moose $\nsim$ some.) How many words are in [stop]? List all the elements of [ddee].

50. The equivalence classes $[1]$, $[-1]$, $[3]$, $[-3]$, $[5]$, $[-5]$, $\ldots$ are all distinct for the equivalence relation $\sim$ on $\mathbb{Q}^*$ defined above, in which $a \sim b$ iff $\frac{a}{b} = 2^k$ for some $k \in \mathbb{Z}$. Are there any other equivalence classes aside from these?

51. Suppose that a relation $\sim$ is symmetric and transitive, and furthermore that every element is related to at least one other element. Briefly explain why $\sim$ must be reflexive also.

WRITING

52. For $m, n \in \mathbb{Z}$ let us say that $m \sim n$ whenever $m + 2n$ is a multiple of 3. Show that $\sim$ is an equivalence relation.

53. Prove that congruence mod 7 is an equivalence relation. (Recall $a \equiv b \bmod 7$ means that $a - b = 7k$ for some integer k.)

54. Let $\mathbb{Q}^*$ represent the set of nonzero rational numbers. For $u, v \in \mathbb{Q}^*$ we say that $u \sim v$ exactly when uv is a rational square, meaning that $uv = r^2$ for some $r \in \mathbb{Q}^*$. Prove that $\sim$ is an equivalence relation.

55. For positive real numbers x and y let us say that $x \sim y$ whenever $\frac{x}{y}$ is a rational number. Prove that $\sim$ is an equivalence relation.

56. We define a relation on the points in the Cartesian plane by declaring that $P_1 \sim P_2$ whenever $4x_1 + y_2 = 4x_2 + y_1$, where P_1 and P_2 have coordinates (x_1, y_1) and (x_2, y_2). Prove that $\sim$ is an equivalence relation.

57. Consider the set E^* of all points in the Euclidean plane except for the origin. Define a relation on E^* by declaring that $P_1 \sim P_2$ whenever $x_1 y_2 = x_2 y_1$. Prove that $\sim$ is an equivalence relation, and describe its equivalence classes.

58. Let $U = \{a, b, c, \ldots, z\}$ be the universal set. For sets $A, B \subseteq U$ let us say that $A \sim B$ as long as the number of elements that are in either A or B, but not both, is even. Prove that $\sim$ is an equivalence relation, and describe the equivalence classes that arise.

6.4 Definition of Function

Of all the topics covered in this text, functions are likely to sound the most familiar. Our purpose here is to properly place the common understanding of function within the more general, abstract framework of relations and make precise the abundance of terms such as domain, range, inverse, and composition that accompany this important topic.

When functions are first introduced in a standard mathematics curriculum they are usually presented via a formula, a graph, or a table of values. However, the emphasis on functions given by formulas predominates most discussions of functions, particularly in calculus. This perspective on functions is perfectly adequate and appropriate for the pre-calculus and calculus setting. Indeed, when European mathematicians such as Leibniz, Bernoulli and Euler first attempted to formally express what should be encompassed by the concept of function they came up with a very similar sort of definition. Incidentally, it was Euler who invented the $f(x)$ notation still in use today.

Over the intervening years the understanding of what constitutes a function has gradually broadened. Our modern definition brings into focus the underlying feature common to all functions; namely, that a function assigns to each input value a unique corresponding output value. It also reflects the conviction that, just as with relations, the "essence" of a function is captured by the complete collection of ordered pairs (a, b) for which the output b is assigned to the input a.

For sets A and B, a **function** f from A to B is a subset of $A \times B$ with the property that for each $a \in A$ there exists a unique $b \in B$ such that (a, b) is an ordered pair in the function. We write $f(a) = b$ to indicate that b is the element of B associated with a. The set A is called the **domain** of f, while B is called the **codomain**. A function f is also known as a **mapping** from A to B, denoted by $f : A \rightarrow B$. If $f(a) = b$ we say that f **maps** a to b, which may be shortened to $a \mapsto b$. In this case b is referred to as the **image** of a, while a is a **preimage** of b.

In light of this definition, we see that a function can be thought of as a special type of a relation. For a relation from A to B to qualify as a function, its domain must be all of A. (Because *every* $a \in A$ is given an output value.) Furthermore, the graph of the relation must pass the "vertical line test," meaning that a vertical line may not pass through two or more points of the graph. (Because only one output value b is assigned to any particular $a \in A$.) A relation with these two properties is a function. For instance, the set of ordered pairs $\{(x, y) \mid x, y \in \mathbb{R}, \ y^2 = 4x^2\}$ does not define a function $f : \mathbb{R} \rightarrow \mathbb{R}$, because the pairs $(1, 2)$ and $(1, -2)$ are both ordered pairs in the given set. Hence the value of $f(1)$ is not well-defined.

CONCEPT a) Does the formula $f(x) = \frac{1}{x}$ define a function $f : \mathbb{R} \rightarrow \mathbb{R}$?

CONCEPT b) For the function $g : \mathbb{Z} \rightarrow \mathbb{Z}$ which maps $n \mapsto n^2 + n$, what is the image of 9? What are the two preimages of 20?

Observe that, according to our definition, it is not necessary for every element of the codomain B to appear as the image of an element of A. The set of those elements of B that are image points has a familiar name, as does the set of all pairs (a, b) comprising the function.

Given a function $f : A \rightarrow B$, set A is the **domain** of f, abbreviated to $\mathrm{dom}(f)$. The **range** of f, denoted by $\mathrm{rng}(f)$, consists of all $b \in B$ such that $a \mapsto b$ for some $a \in A$. Therefore $\mathrm{dom}(f) = A$, while $\mathrm{rng}(f) \subseteq B$. The **graph** of f is obtained by plotting all pairs (a, b) for which $f(a) = b$.

CONCEPT c) For the function $f : \mathbb{R} \rightarrow \mathbb{R}$ given by $f(x) = |x - 2| + 3$ determine the domain, codomain, and range of f.

CONCEPT d) Draw the graphs of the functions $f : \mathbb{R} \rightarrow \mathbb{R}$ mapping $x \mapsto x^2 + x$ and $g : \mathbb{N} \rightarrow \mathbb{N}$ mapping $n \mapsto n^2 + n$.

When A and B are small finite sets there is a more natural way to illustrate the mapping $h : A \to B$ than via a graph. Instead, we list the elements in each set and draw arrows to indicate which elements of B are the images of the elements of A. We call such an illustration an **arrow diagram**. The function on the left consists of the pairs $(1, 4)$, $(2, 2)$, $(3, 3)$, $(4, 1)$ and $(5, 4)$. The center graph defines a **constant function**, since the output value remains constant for any input value; in this case $a \mapsto 2$ for all $a \in A$.

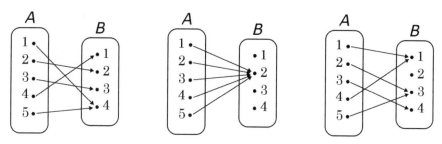

e) For the function $h : A \to B$ shown on the right, what ordered pairs define h? What are the preimages of 1 and 2? Determine $\mathrm{rng}(h)$.

The arrow diagrams above illustrate only a few of all the possible functions $h : A \to B$. However, we can easily determine the number of such functions. There are four possible choices for the value of $h(1)$, followed by four choices for $h(2)$, and so on. In total there are $4^5 = 1024$ functions $h : A \to B$.

Certain functions play such an important role in the natural sciences that they are given names. For instance, most readers know about the cosine function, the natural logarithm, and so on. But there are other less familiar functions that are nonetheless part of every mathematician's repertoire. We introduce several of these now.

The **identity function** $I_A : A \to A$ maps each element of A to itself, so that $a \mapsto a$ for all $a \in A$. The codomain must equal the domain for I_A.

The identity is fundamental among the set of all functions $f : A \to A$. It plays a role analogous to the number 1, as we shall see in the next section.

Another standard function that occurs in many branches of mathematics has the effect of picking out whether or not an element of the domain belongs to a certain subset of the domain.

Given a subset $C \subseteq A$, the **characteristic function** $\chi_C : A \to \{0, 1\}$ is defined as

$$\chi_C(a) = \begin{cases} 1 & a \in C \\ 0 & a \notin C \end{cases} .$$

CONCEPT
CHECK   f) For subsets $C \subseteq A$ and $D \subseteq A$, the product $\chi_C(a)\,\chi_D(a)$ behaves like the characteristic function for what subset of A?

We conclude by mentioning one other function that is commonly encountered in number theory and analysis, among other places.

> The **greatest integer function** assigns to each real number x the largest integer not exceeding x. We denote this function by $\lfloor x \rfloor$; its domain is $\mathbb{R}$ while its codomain is $\mathbb{Z}$.

Thus we have $\lfloor \pi \rfloor = 3$, $\lfloor 7 \rfloor = 7$, $\lfloor \frac{4}{5} \rfloor = 0$ and $\lfloor -5.38 \rfloor = -6$. Note that the latter answer is not -5, because -5 is greater than -5.38. (So the greatest integer function does not simply delete all digits past the decimal point for negative input values.) The greatest integer function is also sometimes written as $[x]$, and also goes by the name "floor function."

There is more to the greatest integer function than meets the eye, as the following question demonstrates.

QUERY   g) Two of the functions $\lfloor 2x \rfloor$, $2\lfloor x \rfloor$, and $\lfloor x \rfloor + \lfloor x + \frac{1}{2} \rfloor$ are identical. Which pair of functions are the same?

In order to clarify some of the steps in the upcoming proof, we next consider the question of when $\lfloor x \rfloor = 5$. By definition, this occurs when $5 \leq x < 6$. Now consider the related equation $\lfloor 2x \rfloor = 10$. Observe that the solution is no longer $5 \leq x < 6$; for instance, when $x = 5.7$ we have $\lfloor 2(5.7) \rfloor = \lfloor 11.4 \rfloor = 11$. Intuitively we see that the cutoff takes place at $x = 5.5$. More formally, we know that $\lfloor 2x \rfloor = 10$ is equivalent to $10 \leq 2x < 11$. Dividing by 2 we obtain the solution $5 \leq x < 5.5$.

We are now prepared to prove that $\lfloor x \rfloor + \lfloor x + \frac{1}{2} \rfloor = \lfloor 2x \rfloor$ for all $x \in \mathbb{R}$. Motivated by the observations in the previous paragraph, our strategy will be to split the real number line into the collection of intervals

$$\ldots, \quad -\tfrac{1}{2} \leq x < 0, \quad 0 \leq x < \tfrac{1}{2}, \quad \tfrac{1}{2} \leq x < 1, \quad 1 \leq x < 1\tfrac{1}{2}, \quad \ldots$$

We will then show that the proposed identity holds for each interval separately.

There are two types of intervals in our list; those of the form $n \leq x < n + \frac{1}{2}$ and those of the form $n + \frac{1}{2} \leq x < n + 1$, where n is an integer. We begin with the first type. So suppose that $n \leq x < n + \frac{1}{2}$ for some $n \in \mathbb{Z}$. Then clearly $\lfloor x \rfloor = n$, but it is also true that $\lfloor x + \frac{1}{2} \rfloor = n$, because $x + \frac{1}{2}$ is still less than $n+1$. Therefore $\lfloor x \rfloor + \lfloor x + \frac{1}{2} \rfloor = 2n$ in this case. On the other hand, multiplying the inequality $n \leq x < n + \frac{1}{2}$ by 2 yields $2n \leq 2x < 2n + 1$, which means that $\lfloor 2x \rfloor = 2n$. In summary, we conclude that for $n \leq x < n + \frac{1}{2}$ we have

$$\lfloor x \rfloor + \lfloor x + \tfrac{1}{2} \rfloor = 2n = \lfloor 2x \rfloor,$$

so the two expressions are equal.[†] The remaining case is left as an exercise.

a) No, because the domain of $f(x)$ is not all of $\mathbb{R}$. Since $f(x)$ is not defined at $x = 0$ we must write $f : \mathbb{R} - \{0\} \to \mathbb{R}$.

b) The image of 9 is $9^2 + 9 = 90$. The preimages of 20 satisfy $n^2 + n = 20$, which occurs for $n = 4$ and $n = -5$.

c) The domain is $\mathbb{R}$, the codomain is $\mathbb{R}$, and the range is $\{y \in \mathbb{R} \mid y \geq 3\}$ since absolute value is zero or positive.

d) The graph of f will be a parabola having vertex at $(-\frac{1}{2}, -\frac{1}{4})$ and opening upward. The graph of g contains the points $(1, 2)$, $(2, 6)$, $(3, 12)$, ... which lie along this parabola. Note the dramatic effect of altering the domain and codomain.

e) The function h consists of the pairs $\{(1, 1)\ (2, 3)\ (3, 4)\ (4, 1)\ (5, 3)\}$. The preimages of 1 are 1 and 4, while there is no preimage of 2. Finally, $\mathrm{rng}(h) = \{1, 3, 4\}$.

f) Observe that $\chi_C(a)\chi_D(a) = 0$ unless $a \in C$ and $a \in D$, where $\chi_C(a)\chi_D(a) = 1$. Therefore this product behaves like the characteristic function of $C \cap D$.

g) The functions $\lfloor x \rfloor + \lfloor x + \frac{1}{2} \rfloor$ and $\lfloor 2x \rfloor$ are equal. The three functions can be compared by graphing them or by plugging in values of x to determine where they disagree.

EXERCISES

59. A function is defined by letting $f(x) = \sqrt{2x - 6}$.
a) What are the domain and range of f?
b) What are the images of 5 and 10 under this mapping?
c) What are the preimages of 6 and 7?

60. A function is defined by letting $f(x) = \ln(5 - x^2)$.
a) What are the domain and codomain of f?
b) What are the images of 2 and -1 under this mapping?
c) What are the preimages of 0 and -3?

61. Explain why the set of ordered pairs given by $\{(x, y) \mid x, y \in \mathbb{R}, |3x| + |y| = 6\}$ does not define a function.

62. Show that the set of ordered pairs $\{(x, y) \mid x, y \in \mathbb{R}, xy - 3x - y + 6\}$ defines a function. What are the domain and range of this function?

63. Let $g : \mathbb{N}_{\geq 2} \to \mathbb{N}$ map a value n to the smallest prime divisor of n. Here $\mathbb{N}_{\geq 2}$ refers to the set $\{2, 3, 4, \ldots\}$.
a) Why did we specify the domain as $\mathbb{N}_{\geq 2}$ rather than $\mathbb{N}$?
b) Find a positive integer $n > 50$ for which $n \mapsto 7$.
c) How many preimages does the value 3 have?

64. Let $g : \mathbb{N} \to \mathbb{N}$ be defined as $g(n) = \lfloor \sqrt{n} \rfloor$.
a) Find a value of n in the range $100 \leq n \leq 200$ with $g(n) \neq g(n + 1)$.
b) Determine $\mathrm{rng}(g)$.
c) How many preimages does the value 3 have?

65. Draw the graph of a function $f : \mathbb{R} \to \mathbb{R}$ such that 1 has infinitely many preimages, but all other real numbers have exactly one preimage.

66. Let $\mathbb{R}^2$ be the set of all points in the Cartesian plane, and define a function $f : \mathbb{R}^2 \to \mathbb{R}^2$ which maps $(x, y) \mapsto (x, -y)$. Describe this function geometrically.

67. Let $A = \{1, 2, 3, 4, 5\}$ and $B = \{1, 2, 3, 4\}$. Find a function $h : A \to B$ such that 2 has three preimages while 3 and 4 each have one preimage. Illustrate your function using an arrow diagram. Then draw the graph of your function.

68. What can be said about a function $f : A \to B$ if we have $|\text{rng}(f)| = 1$?

69. Suppose that $|A| = 5$ and $|B| = 2$. How many functions $h : A \to B$ are there? How many of these are not constant functions?

70. Suppose that $|A| = 4$ and $|B| = 3$. Are there more functions $h_1 : A \to B$ or $h_2 : B \to A$?

71. If a characteristic function $\chi_C : A \to \{0, 1\}$ is a constant function, then what can we conclude about set C?

72. Compute the value of $\lfloor -13.8 \rfloor$, $\lfloor \sqrt{55} \rfloor$, $\lfloor -10 \rfloor$, $\lfloor e \rfloor$ and $\lfloor \frac{20}{3} \rfloor$.

73. Find all values of x for which $\lfloor 3x + 2 \rfloor = 10$.

74. Find all values of x for which $\lfloor x + \frac{1}{3} \rfloor = -4$.

WRITING

75. Let C and D be subsets of a set A, and let χ_C and χ_D be their characteristic functions. Prove that $\chi_{C \cup D}(a) = \chi_C(a) + \chi_D(a) - \chi_C(a)\chi_D(a)$.

76. Prove that there exists a function $g : \mathbb{N} \to \mathbb{N}$ such that $g(n) > 1$ for all input values and $g(m)g(n) = g(m + n)$ for all $m, n \in \mathbb{N}$.

77. Suppose that x is a real number in the interval $n + \frac{1}{2} \le x < n + 1$ for some $n \in \mathbb{Z}$. Show that in this case $\lfloor x \rfloor + \lfloor x + \frac{1}{2} \rfloor = 2n + 1$ and that $\lfloor 2x \rfloor = 2n + 1$ also, thus completing the proof begun in this section.

78. Prove that $\lfloor x \rfloor + \lfloor x + \frac{1}{3} \rfloor + \lfloor x + \frac{2}{3} \rfloor = \lfloor 3x \rfloor$ for all $x \in \mathbb{R}$.

6.5   Inverse Functions

We all know that there is something special about a triangle with sides of length 3, 4 and 5. Since $3^2 + 4^2 = 5^2$ the Pythagorean Theorem guarantees that the largest angle of such a triangle measures $90°$. However, relatively fewer people are aware that there is a feature of a triangle having sides of length 3, 5 and 7 that is almost as special. To discover this feature, let us compute the measure of the largest angle of this triangle.

     A standard result from Euclidean geometry tells us that the largest angle is opposite the longest side, so we let θ be the measure of the angle across from the side of length 7, as shown here. According to the Law of Cosines, we know that

$$7^2 = 3^2 + 5^2 - 2(3)(5) \cos \theta.$$

Rearranging then leads to $\cos \theta = -\frac{1}{2}$. So we are looking for an angle whose cosine is $-\frac{1}{2}$.

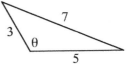

Mathematical Outing ★ ★ ★

The arrow diagrams below illustrate three functions $f : A \to B$. In each case decide whether an inverse function $f^{-1} : B \to A$ exists that assigns to each $b \in B$ the element $a \in A$ which maps to it. When such a function exists, list the ordered pairs defining the inverse function. Otherwise, describe the aspect of the function that prevents the construction of an inverse.

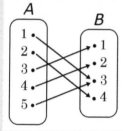
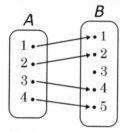
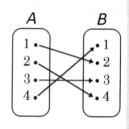

It is important at this juncture to appreciate the difference between taking the cosine of an angle (such as computing $\cos 40°$) and trying to find an angle when we know its cosine (such as finding $\cos \theta = -\frac{1}{2}$). The need for functions that accomplish the latter sort of task arises so frequently in mathematics, particularly when solving equations, that they have been given a name; they are known as **inverse functions**.

Fortunately, scientific calculators are equipped with an inverse cosine button. Upon typing $\text{Cos}^{-1}(-1/2)$ (in degree mode) we are rewarded with the answer to our original question: a 3–5–7 triangle contains a 120° angle, which is a very nifty fact. This concludes our digression into geometry, but only begins to broach the subject of inverse functions. For example, there are actually infinitely many angles whose cosine is equal to $-\frac{1}{2}$. Examining the graph of the cosine function below suggests that $\pm 240°$, $\pm 480°$ and many other angles all have cosine equal to $-\frac{1}{2}$. How did our calculator know which angle to choose?

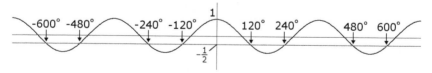

Before attempting to formally define inverse functions, we will first identify the two properties that a function must possess in order to permit an inverse to exist. For the time being we will just mention that the inverse of a function $f : A \to B$ is denoted f^{-1} and say that for $b \in B$ we compute $f^{-1}(b)$ by finding the element $a \in A$ for which $a \mapsto b$ and then declare that $f^{-1}(b) = a$. With this in mind, now consider the Mathematical Outing above.

Suppose that for a function $f : A \to B$ there exist values $a_1, a_2 \in A$ such that $f(a_1) = b$ and $f(a_2) = b$ as well. Then it would not be possible to determine the value of $f^{-1}(b)$, since we cannot have both $f^{-1}(b) = a_1$ and $f^{-1}(b) = a_2$. All functions, including inverse functions, are only allowed one output value for each input value. The difficulty, of course, is that the original function f maps two different values in A to the same value in B. A function must avoid this behavior in order to have an inverse.

A function $f : A \to B$ is called **injective** (or **one-to-one**) if distinct elements of A are mapped to distinct elements of B. Equivalently, we may conclude that f is injective by verifying that the equality $f(a_1) = f(a_2)$ necessarily implies that $a_1 = a_2$.

$\boxed{\text{CONCEPT}}$ a) Explain why $g : \mathbb{Z} \to \mathbb{Z}$ given by $n \mapsto n^2 + n$ is not injective.

When a function is presented via a formula, the second condition described in our definition is typically more useful for proving that a function is injective. For instance, let us prove that $f(x) = (2x + 1)/(x - 3)$ is an injective function. So suppose that $f(x_1) = f(x_2)$; this means that

$$\frac{2x_1 + 1}{x_1 - 3} = \frac{2x_2 + 1}{x_2 - 3}$$
$$(2x_1 + 1)(x_2 - 3) = (2x_2 + 1)(x_1 - 3)$$
$$2x_1 x_2 - 6x_1 + x_2 - 3 = 2x_1 x_2 + x_1 - 6x_2 - 3$$
$$-7x_1 = -7x_2$$
$$x_1 = x_2.$$

Since $f(x_1) = f(x_2)$ implies that $x_1 = x_2$, we deduce that $f(x)$ is injective.[†]
We can visually confirm that a function is injective by checking that its graph passes the "horizontal line test," meaning that no two points of the graph lie on a horizontal line. For if two points (x_1, y_1) and (x_2, y_2) on the graph of a function f lie on the same horizontal line then they have the same y-coordinates. But this means that $f(x_1) = f(x_2)$, so that f is not injective. Unlike the graph of the cosine function, in which the horizontal line $y = -\frac{1}{2}$ intersected the graph in more than one place, every horizontal line in the graph of $f(x) = (2x + 1)/(x - 3)$, shown at right, intersects the graph at most once, indicating that it is one-to-one.

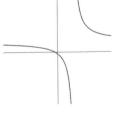

However, injectivity is not enough to guarantee that a function has an inverse. Suppose for a function $f : A \to B$ there exists $b \in B$ such that $f(a) \neq b$ for all $a \in A$. In this case there is no way to assign a value to $f^{-1}(b)$ because no element of A maps to b. Clearly every element of the codomain must occur as an output value in order for the function to have an inverse.

> A function $f : A \to B$ is called **surjective** (or **onto**) if every element $b \in B$ has a preimage in A. Thus f is surjective if for every $b \in B$ there exists an $a \in A$ such that $a \mapsto b$. Equivalently, we have $\operatorname{rng}(f) = B$.

CONCEPT b) Is the function $f : \mathbb{R} \to \mathbb{R}$ given by $f(x) = 2x - 1$ surjective? What about the function $g : \mathbb{N} \to \mathbb{N}$ that maps $n \mapsto 2n - 1$?

As the definition suggests, proving that a given function is onto amounts to an existence proof. For instance, suppose that $g : \mathbb{N}_{\geq 2} \to \mathbb{N}$ is defined for $n \geq 2$ by letting $g(n)$ be the largest proper divisor of n. Given any positive integer b, how can we be sure that there exists an $n \in \mathbb{N}$ such that $g(n) = b$?

QUICK QUERY c) Find a positive integer whose largest proper divisor is 7. Do the same for 30 and 123.

This question suggests the key to a proof that g is surjective. Given any $b \in \mathbb{N}$, we claim that $g(2b) = b$. Clearly b is a proper divisor of $2b$. Furthermore, there are no more divisors of $2b$ larger than b, because any such number would be over half the size of $2b$. Hence b is the largest proper divisor, and we have shown that g is surjective.[†]

Although proving that a function is onto requires some thought, the proof itself can be relatively brief. Thus to prove that the function $f : \mathbb{R} \to \mathbb{R}$ given by $f(x) = 2x - 1$ is onto, we need to show that for any possible output value $w \in \mathbb{R}$, there is some $x \in \mathbb{R}$ for which $f(x) = w$. We claim that $x = \frac{1}{2}(w + 1)$ does the job. Indeed, we find that

$$f(\tfrac{1}{2}(w + 1)) = 2(\tfrac{1}{2}(w + 1)) - 1 = (w + 1) - 1 = w.$$

Therefore f is onto, and the proof is complete. Of course, we didn't just pull the expression $x = \frac{1}{2}(w + 1)$ out of a hat. We reasoned that in order to have $f(x) = w$ we must have $2x - 1 = w$. Solving for x gives $x = \frac{1}{2}(w + 1)$.

As we have now seen, a necessary condition for a function $f : A \to B$ to have an inverse is that f be both one-to-one and onto. This condition is also sufficient, for in this case we are guaranteed that for every $b \in B$ there exists (since f is onto) a unique (since f is one-to-one) $a \in A$ such that $a \mapsto b$. We then know that f^{-1} should map b to a.

> Let $f : A \to B$ be a function that is both injective and surjective. Then the **inverse function** $f^{-1} : B \to A$ exists, and consists of exactly those ordered pairs (b, a) such that (a, b) is an ordered pair of the function f. Thus f^{-1} is defined for each $b \in B$ by setting $f^{-1}(b) = a$, where $a \in A$ is the unique element for which $a \mapsto b$.

CONCEPT d) Suppose a function f has an inverse. What is the inverse of f^{-1}?

If f is presented via an arrow diagram, then f^{-1} is obtained by swapping the two sets and also reversing the directions of all the arrows. Given the ordered pairs that make up f, we just exchange the two elements of each pair to obtain the ordered pairs comprising f^{-1}. In light of this, for $f : \mathbb{R} \to \mathbb{R}$ the graph of f^{-1} is obtained from the graph of f by reflecting it over the line $y = x$, since this has the effect of exchanging the x and y-coordinates. All of these perspectives on the inverse function stem directly from the same underlying principle.

A function $f : A \to B$ that is both one-to-one and onto is called a **bijection**. Aside from having an inverse, such a function provides a **one-to-one correspondence** between the elements of A and the elements of B. This correspondence is illustrated most vividly by an arrow diagram, such as the right-hand example in the Mathematical Outing. Bijections will play a central role when we discuss cardinality in the next chapter.

a) Since $4 \mapsto 20$ and $-5 \mapsto 20$ also this function is not one-to-one.
b) The function $f : \mathbb{R} \to \mathbb{R}$ is surjective, as proved in the text. However, $g : \mathbb{N} \to \mathbb{N}$ with the same formula is not surjective. Since $2n - 1$ is always odd no even numbers can be obtained as output values.
c) The first integer that comes to mind is 14, since 7 is clearly the largest proper divisor of 14. Similarly, 60 and 246 have 30 and 123 as their largest proper divisors.
d) The inverse of f^{-1} is just the original function f, because reversing the ordered pairs twice gives back the original set of ordered pairs defining f.
🏛 The function on the left does not have an inverse, because there is no way to define $f^{-1}(3)$; we can't have both $f^{-1}(3) = 1$ and $f^{-1}(3) = 5$. The middle function does not have an inverse either, since there is no way to define $f^{-1}(3)$. However, the function on the right does have an inverse, given by the pairs $(2, 1)$, $(4, 2)$, $(3, 3)$ and $(1, 4)$.

EXERCISES

79. Which of the functions in the Mathematical Outing are one-to-one? onto?

80. Let $A = \{1, 2, 3, 4, 5\}$ and define a function $f : A \to A$ via the ordered pairs $\{(1, 4)\ (2, 5)\ (3, 1)\ (4, 4)\ (5, 3)\}$. Draw the arrow diagram for f, and explain why f is neither one-to-one nor onto. How can we modify just one of the ordered pairs to obtain a function that is both one-to-one and onto?

81. How many injective functions $h : A \to B$ are there in each case?
a) $A = \{a, b, c\}$ and $B = \{1, 2, 3, 4, 5, 6\}$
b) $A = \{a, b, c, d\}$ and $B = \{1, 2, 3, 4\}$
c) $A = \{a, b, c, d, e\}$ and $B = \{1, 2, 3, 4\}$

82. Define $g : \mathbb{N} \to \mathbb{N}$ by declaring that $g(n)$ is equal to n plus the sum of the digits of n. For instance, $g(7) = 7 + 7 = 14$ while $g(142) = 142 + 1 + 4 + 2 = 149$. Demonstrate that g is not one-to-one.

83. For a function $f : A \to B$, explain why the statements below are equivalent.
i. If a_1 and a_2 are distinct, then $f(a_1)$ and $f(a_2)$ are also distinct.
ii. If $f(a_1) = f(a_2)$ then $a_1 = a_2$.

84. How many surjective functions $h : A \to B$ are there in each case?
a) $A = \{a, b, c\}$ and $B = \{1, 2, 3, 4, 5, 6\}$
b) $A = \{a, b, c, d\}$ and $B = \{1, 2, 3, 4\}$
c) $A = \{a, b, c, d, e\}$ and $B = \{1, 2, 3, 4\}$

85. Let $\mathbb{N}_{\geq 10}$ represent the set of all positive integers which are 10 or greater; i.e. having two or more digits. Define a function $g : \mathbb{N}_{\geq 10} \to \mathbb{N}$ by letting $g(n)$ be the number obtained by deleting the final digit of n. Show that g is onto.

86. Let $h : A \to B$ be the function given by the right-hand arrow diagram in the Mathematical Outing in this section. Draw the arrow diagram for h^{-1}.

87. Sketch the graph of the function $f : \mathbb{R} \to \mathbb{R}$ defined by $f(x) = -x$ for $x < 0$ while $f(x) = -x^2$ when $x \geq 0$. Explain visually how we know that f is both one-to-one and onto, then sketch the graph of f^{-1}.

88. Using the technique described in the final writing problem below, determine a formula for the inverse of the following functions.
a) $f(x) = 4x + 7$
b) $f(x) = \sqrt[3]{5x + 1}$
c) $f(x) = (3x + 2)/(x - 1)$

89. Find a formula for a bijection $f : [0, 1] \to [10, 15]$.

90. Let $\cos : \mathbb{R} \to \mathbb{R}$ be the usual cosine function. By appealing to the graph, explain why cosine is neither one-to-one nor onto.

91. Let $I = \{x \mid 0 \leq x \leq \pi\}$ and define $J = \{y \mid -1 \leq y \leq 1\}$. Draw the graph of the portion of the cosine function where $0 \leq x \leq \pi$. This is known as **restricting the domain** of a function. In this way we obtain the closely related function $\text{Cos} : I \to J$, defined on a smaller domain. Show graphically that this function is one-to-one and onto. Hence it has an inverse, Cos^{-1}.

WRITING

92. Prove that the function f given by $f(x) = (3x + 2)/(x - 1)$ is one-to-one.

93. Define $g : \mathbb{N} \to \mathbb{N}$ as follows. For $a \in \mathbb{N}$ let $d_1, d_2, \ldots, d_k$ be the digits of a from right to left. Then define $g(a) = p_1^{d_1} p_2^{d_2} \cdots p_k^{d_k}$, where $p_1, p_2, \ldots, p_k$ are the first k primes. Prove that g is injective but not surjective.

94. Prove that $f : \mathbb{R} \to \mathbb{R}$ given by $f(x) = \sqrt[3]{5x + 1}$ is onto.

95. Define $g : \mathbb{R}^2 \to \mathbb{R}$ by defining $g(x, y) = 2^x - y$. Prove that g is surjective but not injective. (Think of $\mathbb{R}^2$ as the plane and (x, y) as coordinates.)

96. Suppose that a function $f(x) = ax + b$ is its own inverse, meaning that $f^{-1}(x) = ax + b$ also. Prove that we must have either $a = -1$ or $a = 1$, $b = 0$.

97. Precalculus textbooks often suggest the following recipe for constructing the inverse of a function. Given a formula for $f(x)$, write out the equation $x = f(y)$ and then solve for y. The resulting expression gives the formula for $f^{-1}(x)$. Explain why this technique works.

6.6   Composition of Functions

When the codomain of one function is the same as the domain of another function, there is a natural way to combine the two functions to obtain a new function. This process is almost intuitively obvious when given arrow diagrams. For instance, consider the two functions $f : A \to B$ and $g : B \to C$ below.

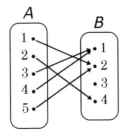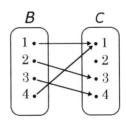

QUICK ERY a) How can we combine these two functions to obtain a third function? What are the domain, codomain and range of the new function? What is the image of 2, and what are the preimages of 3?

We now formally define the operation of applying two functions to a given input value, one after the other.

> Given functions $f : A \to B$ and $g : B \to C$, the **composition** of f with g is the function $g \circ f : A \to C$ which maps $a \mapsto g(f(a))$. Thus $g \circ f$ may be thought of as the function obtained by first applying f to an element of A, then applying g to the result.

CONCEPT CHECK b) Given $f : A \to B$ and $g : B \to C$, which of f, g and $g \circ f$ have the same domain? Which two have the same codomain?

Given arrow diagrams for $f : A \to B$ and $g : B \to C$, composing f with g amounts to just following the arrows from A to B to C. For instance, in the diagram above we see that f maps $1 \mapsto 2$, then g maps $2 \mapsto 3$, so we conclude that $g \circ f(1) = g(f(1)) = g(2) = 3$. Be aware that "$f$ composed with g" is written as $g \circ f$, rather than $f \circ g$. This order is counterintuitive in the context of arrow diagrams, where we apply f and then g. However, it does make sense when we think of "plugging f into g," as occurs when writing $g(f(a))$.

When we have formulas for f and g, their composition may be found via the familiar process of substituting one formula into the other. For example, if $f(x) = \sqrt{x}$ and $g(x) = 2x - 8$, then

$$f \circ g(x) = f(g(x)) = \sqrt{2x - 8}, \qquad g \circ f(x) = g(f(x)) = 2\sqrt{x} - 8.$$

A subtle restriction of domain takes place behind the scenes in one of these examples, though, which needs to be elucidated. Observe that the domain of f

is the set $\mathbb{R}_{\geq 0}$ of nonnegative real numbers. Since $f : \mathbb{R}_{\geq 0} \to \mathbb{R}$ and $g : \mathbb{R} \to \mathbb{R}$, the codomain of f matches the domain of g so there is no obstacle to forming the composition $g \circ f : \mathbb{R}_{\geq 0} \to \mathbb{R}$ given by $g \circ f(x) = 2\sqrt{x} - 8$.

But the same is not true when composing $g : \mathbb{R} \to \mathbb{R}$ with $f : \mathbb{R}_{\geq 0} \to \mathbb{R}$, since the codomain of g does not match the domain of f. In theory this leads to trouble—we have $g(1) = -6$ but $f \circ g(1) = \sqrt{-6}$ is not defined. In practice we just restrict the domain of g to avoid this situation. In other words, we automatically limit ourselves to the domain $\{x \in \mathbb{R} \mid x \geq 4\}$ for g, so that its range will be contained within $\mathbb{R}_{\geq 0}$, at which point it is safe to apply f. We typically adopt this convention when composing real-valued functions.

Let f and g be functions whose domain and range are subsets of the real numbers. Then by convention the domain of $g \circ f$ consists of all real numbers x in the domain of f for which $f(x)$ is also in the domain of g, so that $g(f(x))$ is defined.

CONCEPT CHECK c) Let $f(x) = 3x + 2$ and $g(x) = 1/x$. What is the domain of $g \circ f$? What is the domain of $f \circ g$?

The concept of composition provides an excellent means of deepening our understanding of some of the properties of functions presented previously.

QUICK QUERY d) Let $A = \{a, b, c\}$, $B = \{1, 2, 3, 4\}$ and $C = \{a, b, c, d, e\}$. Now draw arrow diagrams for injective functions $f : A \to B$ and $g : B \to C$. Must $g \circ f$ always be injective? Why or why not?

Some experimentation suggests that if $f : A \to B$ and $g : B \to C$ are both injective functions then their composition $g \circ f : A \to C$ will also be injective. To prove this, we must show that if $a_1, a_2 \in A$ are distinct then the elements $g(f(a_1)), g(f(a_2)) \in C$ are also distinct. So suppose that $a_1 \neq a_2$. Since f is injective, we deduce that $f(a_1) \neq f(a_2)$. But now since g is also injective, when we apply g to the unequal elements $f(a_1), f(a_2) \in B$ we obtain different elements of C, so that $g(f(a_1)) \neq g(f(a_2))$. This completes the proof.[†]

It is natural to conjecture at this point that if f and g are both surjective, then $g \circ f$ will be also. This turns out to be the case; a proof of this fact is relegated to the exercises. But suppose instead that only g is surjective. Is this enough to conclude that $g \circ f$ must also be surjective?

QUICK QUERY e) Change one arrow in the arrow diagram for $g : B \to C$ above so that g will be surjective, but the composition $g \circ f$ will not be surjective.

Recall that the identity function $I_A : A \to A$ is the map sending each element of A to itself. Thus $I_A(a) = a$ for all $a \in A$. Within the context of composing functions, the identity function I_A is analogous to the multiplicative identity 1 in that $I_A \circ f = f$ and $f \circ I_A = f$ for any function $f : A \to A$. (Hence the name "identity" function.) To see that $f \circ I_A = f$ we will show that these two functions give the same output value for every element $a \in A$. This is easily shown, since $f \circ I_A(a) = f(I_A(a)) = f(a)$, as desired.

CONCEPT CHECK f) Suppose that $f : A \to B$ has an inverse $f^{-1} : B \to A$. Describe the net effect of the function $f^{-1} \circ f : A \to A$.

From our experience at solving equations we are familiar with the effect of inverse functions "canceling each other out." Thus to solve $e^x = 7$ we take the natural log of both sides, yielding $\ln(e^x) = \ln 7$, which reduces to just $x = \ln 7$, the answer. This property is shared by all inverse functions—if a function $f : A \to B$ has an inverse $f^{-1} : B \to A$, then $f^{-1} \circ f : A \to A$ is the same as the identity function I_A and $f \circ f^{-1} : B \to B$ is equal to I_B. Let us establish the former equality by showing that $f^{-1} \circ f(a) = I_A(a)$ for all $a \in A$. Of course $I_A(a) = a$. Suppose that f maps $a \mapsto b$. Then by definition, f^{-1} maps $b \mapsto a$. Hence $f^{-1}(f(a)) = f^{-1}(b) = a$, which completes the proof.

As a concluding remark, we note that the most abstract definition of inverse function is based on this fundamental property. In other words, a more modern treatment of functions would begin by defining the identity function I_A on a set A, then declaring that two functions $f : A \to B$ and $g : B \to A$ are inverses of one another if and only if $g \circ f = I_A$ and $f \circ g = I_B$. Our definition could then be deduced as a consequence of this one. We chose to present inverse functions from a slightly more intuitive, concrete perspective; either approach is valid.

a) We can combine f and g by applying f and then g in succession. The domain of this new function is A, the codomain is C, and the range is the set $\{1,3\}$. This new function maps $2 \mapsto 1$, while the preimages of 3 are 1 and 5.

b) The domain of f and $g \circ f$ are both A; the codomain of g and $g \circ f$ are both C.

c) The domain of $g \circ f$ is $\mathbb{R} - \{-\frac{2}{3}\}$. We delete $-\frac{2}{3}$ from the domain of f since f maps $-\frac{2}{3} \mapsto 0$, which is not in the domain of $g(x) = \frac{1}{x}$. Similarly, $\mathrm{dom}(f \circ g) = \mathbb{R} - \{0\}$.

d) Yes, $g \circ f$ will always be injective, as explained in the subsequent paragraphs.

e) Define $1 \mapsto 2$ instead of $1 \mapsto 1$ in the arrow diagram for $g : B \to C$.

f) The composition $f^{-1} \circ f$ leaves every element of A unchanged in the end.

Exercises

98. Let $A = \{a,b,c,d\}$, $B = \{1,2,3,4\}$ and $C = \{a,b,c,d,e\}$. Draw arrow diagrams of functions $f : A \to B$ and $g : B \to C$ such that $\mathrm{rng}(f) = \{2,3,4\}$, $\mathrm{rng}(g \circ f) = \{a,c,e\}$ and $g(1) = b$.

99. Let $A = \{a,b,c,d\}$, $B = \{1,2,3,4,5\}$ and $C = \{a,b,c,d\}$. Draw arrow diagrams of functions $f : A \to B$ and $g : B \to C$ such that f is one-to-one, g is onto, but $g \circ f$ is not onto.

100. Let $A = \{1,2,3,4\}$ and $B = \{1,2,3,4,5\}$. Draw arrow diagrams of functions $f : A \to B$ and $g : B \to A$ such that $g \circ f(x) = x$ for all $x \in A$. Is g the inverse of f? Why or why not?

101. Suppose that $f : A \to B$ and $g : B \to A$ are functions. Determine the domain and codomain of $f \circ g$.

102. Find a formula for the function $g \circ f$ and state its domain in each case.
a) $f(x) = 4x - 2$, $g(x) = \ln x$
b) $f(x) = \sqrt{x + 3}$, $g(x) = \frac{1}{x-2}$
c) $f(x) = \cos x$, $g(x) = \frac{1}{x-1}$
d) $f(x) = x^2 + 4x$, $g(x) = \sqrt{x - 5}$
e) $f(x) = \pi x$, $g(x) = \tan x$

103. Suppose that $f(x) = \frac{x+1}{x-1}$ and $g(x) = x + 3$. Find all values of x for which $f \circ g(x) = g \circ f(x)$.

104. Let $f(x) = \frac{5x-8}{x-1}$ and $g(x) = \frac{x-8}{x-5}$. What is the domain of $g \circ f$? Verify that $g \circ f(x) = x$ for all x in this domain.

105. The function $f(x) = \frac{1}{1-x}$ has a very curious property. Show that $f \circ f \circ f$ is the identity function. (So in a sense $f(x)$ is a "cube root" of the identity.)

106. Given the function $f(x) = 2x + 3$, explain how to find a linear function $g(x) = ax + b$ such that $g(1) = 0$ and $f \circ g$ and $g \circ f$ have the same formula.

107. Draw the graph of a function $g : \mathbb{R} \to \mathbb{R}$ such that g is an injective function and $g(g(20)) = 13$.

108. Let E be the set of points in the plane. We define $f, g : E \to E$ by declaring that f maps each point 4 units upward, while g rotates a point $90°$ clockwise about the origin. Find the unique point P in the plane such that $g \circ f(P) = P$. Also find the unique point Q for which $f \circ g(Q) = Q$.

WRITING

109. Suppose that $f : A \to B$ and $g : B \to C$ are injective functions. Provide another proof that $g \circ f$ is also injective by proving that if $g(f(a_1)) = g(f(a_2))$ then $a_1 = a_2$.

110. Let $f : A \to B$ and $g : B \to C$ be surjective functions. Prove that their composition $g \circ f : A \to C$ is also surjective.

111. Recall that a function $f : \mathbb{R} \to \mathbb{R}$ is *increasing* if $f(a) < f(b)$ whenever $a < b$, while f is *decreasing* if $f(b) < f(a)$ whenever $a < b$. Suppose that functions f and g are both decreasing. Determine, with proof, whether $g \circ f$ is increasing or decreasing.

112. Define $g(x) = (x - 1)(x - 2)(x - 3)$ and set $h(x) = g(g(x) + x)$. Without finding a formula for $h(x)$, explain how we know $h(x) = 0$ when $x = 1$, 2 and 3.

113. Let $f : \mathbb{N} \to \mathbb{N}$ be a function such that $f(1) = 2$ and $f(f(n)) = n + 3$ for all $n \in \mathbb{N}$. Using induction, prove that $f(3n - 1) = 3n + 1$ for all $n \in \mathbb{N}$.

114. Suppose that $f : A \to A$ is a function satisfying $f(f(a)) = a$ for all $a \in A$. Prove that f is both injective and surjective.

6.7   Reference

The purpose of this section is to provide a condensed summary of the most important facts and techniques from this chapter, as a reference when studying or working on material from later chapters. We also include an overview of strategies for proving that relations or functions possess certain properties.

• *Vocabulary (relations)* relation, graph, domain, range, inverse, relation on a set A, reflexive, nonreflexive, symmetric, antisymmetric, transitive, partial order, strict partial order, total order, identity relation, maximal element, congruence class, equivalence relation, equivalence class, representative, partition

• *Vocabulary (functions)* function, domain, codomain, range, mapping, image, preimage, graph, arrow diagram, constant function, identity function, characteristic function, greatest integer function, inverse function, injective, one-to-one, surjective, onto, inverse function, bijection, one-to-one correspondence, restricting the domain, composition

• *Relations* A relation $\vdash$ on a set A is a subset of $A \times A$; the ordered pairs of the relation indicate which elements of A are related to which other elements of A. Certain relations are important enough to warrant their own symbol, such as $<, \leq, >, \geq, \subset, \subseteq, \mid$ (divisibility), $\parallel$ (parallel), $\perp$ (perpendicular), and $\equiv$ (congruence). Note that operations such as addition, multiplication, or union are *not* relations—they involve combining two numbers or sets to obtain a third rather than indicating when one object is related to another.

• *Order Relations* A strict partial order is a relation that is nonreflexive, antisymmetric, and transitive. To prove that a relation $\vdash$ on a set A is a strict partial order one must show that $x \nvdash x$ for all $x \in A$, that we never have both $x \vdash y$ and $y \vdash x$ for distinct $x, y \in A$, and that $x \vdash y$ and $y \vdash z$ together imply that $x \vdash z$. When A is finite a tree diagram is handy way to visualize the order.
  A partial order is a relation that is reflexive, antisymmetric, and transitive. To prove that a relation $\vdash$ on a set A is a partial order one must show that $x \vdash x$ for all $x \in A$, that $x \vdash y$ and $y \vdash x$ imply that $x = y$, and that $x \vdash y$ and $y \vdash z$ imply that $x \vdash z$. A partial order need not compare every two elements of A, but when it does (such as for $\leq$, but not $\subseteq$) it is called a total order.

• *Equivalence Relations* An equivalence relation is a relation that is reflexive, symmetric, and transitive. To prove that a relation $\sim$ on a set A is an equivalence relation one must show that $x \sim x$ for all $x \in A$, that $x \sim y$ implies that $y \sim x$, and that $x \sim y$ and $y \sim z$ imply that $x \sim z$. An equivalence relation partitions the elements of A into equivalence classes; we write $[a]$ to indicate the equivalence class containing a. Congruence mod m is one of the most important and frequently used equivalence relations.

• *Functions* A function $f : A \to B$ is a collection of ordered pairs in $A \times B$ such that each $a \in A$ is associated with exactly one element of B. One may think of f mapping each element of A to an element of B, written as $a \mapsto b$. Functions are often given by formulas, but may also be presented via a graph, arrow diagram or verbal description. Set A is the domain and set B is the codomain of f. The latter is not necessarily the same as the range of f, the set of all "output values" for f.

Mathematics is pervaded by functions, including polynomial, trigonometric and exponential functions. Other less familiar functions that still play an important role in many branches of mathematics include the identity function I_A, the characteristic function χ_C, and the greatest integer function $\lfloor x \rfloor$. When proving statements involving the greatest integer function it is usually helpful to rewrite the equation $\lfloor x \rfloor = n$ for $n \in \mathbb{Z}$ as an inequality $n \leq x < n + 1$, then perform algebra on the inequality.

• *Properties of Functions* A function $f : A \to B$ is injective, or one-to-one, if distinct elements of A are mapped to distinct elements of B. Given a formula for f, we prove that f is injective by showing that $f(a_1) = f(a_2)$ implies that $a_1 = a_2$. To show that a function is not injective, it suffices to find a single instance of elements $a_1 \neq a_2$ for which $f(a_1) = f(a_2)$. The graph of an injective function passes the "horizontal line test," meaning that no two points of the graph lie on the same horizontal line.

A function $f : A \to B$ is called a surjective, or onto, function if every element of B is the image of some element of A. Given a formula for f, we may prove that f is surjective by solving $f(x) = w$ for x, thereby writing x in terms of w. This shows that given any $w \in B$, there is always an $x \in A$ such that $f(x) = w$. To show that a function f is not surjective, we need only find a single $w \in B$ such that $f(x) \neq w$ for all $x \in A$.

A function $f : A \to B$ that is both surjective and injective is called a bijection and has the effect of creating a one-to-one correspondence between the elements of A and the elements of B. If f is a bijection then it possesses an inverse $f^{-1} : B \to A$ defined by setting $f^{-1}(b) = a$ whenever $f(a) = b$.

• *Composition* The composition of two functions $f : A \to B$ and $g : B \to C$ is obtained by applying f and g in succession. Thus if f maps $a \mapsto b$ and g maps $b \mapsto c$, then $g \circ f$ maps $a \mapsto c$, because $g \circ f(a) = g(f(a)) = g(b) = c$. When f and g are given by formulas then we may "plug $f(x)$ into $g(x)$" as usual, taking care to restrict the domain of $f(x)$ where necessary to ensure that $g(f(x))$ is always defined. If f and g are both injective then so is $g \circ f$, and if f and g are both surjective then $g \circ f$ is also surjective. The composition of a bijective function with its inverse is the identity function.

$\boxed{\bigstar \ \text{TIP} \ \bigstar}$ Take care to avoid the following common pitfall when proving that a given relation $\sim$ is an equivalence relation. It is quite enticing to begin the proof of the symmetric property by writing "To prove that $\sim$ is symmetric we need to show that $x \sim y$ and $y \sim x$." (This statement has an appealing symmetry to it, after all.) But this approach is logically invalid. *To establish the symmetric property one must prove an implication.* The correct way to begin the proof is "To prove that $\sim$ is symmetric we need to show that if $x \sim y$ then $y \sim x$." Keep this pitfall in mind when working on equivalence relation proofs.

Sample Proofs

The following proofs provide concise explanations for results discussed within this chapter. They are meant to serve as an illustration for how proofs of similar statements could be phrased. The boldface numbers indicate the section containing each result; the location of that result within the section is marked by a dagger (†).

6.2 Let $\vdash$ be the relation on the set of all words defined by $\alpha \vdash \beta$ whenever word α is a proper substring of word β. Prove that $\vdash$ is a strict partial order.

Proof We begin by explaining why $\vdash$ is nonreflexive. In order for α to be a proper substring of β, clearly β must have more letters than α. For this reason no word can be a proper substring of itself, so $\alpha \nvdash \alpha$ for all words α. Similarly we cannot have both $\alpha \vdash \beta$ and $\beta \vdash \alpha$, since α cannot have simultaneously fewer and more letters than β.

   Finally we must show that $\vdash$ is transitive. So suppose that $\alpha \vdash \beta$ and $\beta \vdash \gamma$ for words α, β and γ. This means that a copy of α appears within β, which itself appears within γ. It follows that a copy of α appears within γ; more precisely, it appears within the copy of β inside γ. Hence $\vdash$ is nonreflexive, antisymmetric and transitive, so it is a strict partial order.

6.2 Consider the relation $\vdash$ on $\mathbb{R}$ in which $x \vdash y$ whenever $x - y \in \mathbb{Z}_{\geq 0}$, where $\mathbb{Z}_{\geq 0} = \{0, 1, 2, 3, \ldots\}$ are nonnegative integers. Prove that $\vdash$ is a partial order.

Proof To show that $\vdash$ is reflexive we must explain why $x \vdash x$ for all $x \in \mathbb{R}$. But $x - x = 0$, which is a nonnegative integer, so $x \vdash x$ according to the definition of $\vdash$. We next demonstrate that $\vdash$ is antisymmetric. Thus suppose that $x \vdash y$ and $y \vdash x$. This means that $x - y$ and $y - x$ are both nonnegative integers; in particular, we would have $x \geq y$ and $y \geq x$. But this can only occur if $x = y$. Hence $\vdash$ is antisymmetric.

   Finally, suppose that $x \vdash y$ and $y \vdash z$. Then we would have $x - y = a$ and $y - z = b$ for $a, b \in \mathbb{Z}_{\geq 0}$. Adding these two equations yields $x - z = a + b$. Since a and b are both nonnegative integers, $a + b$ is as well, implying that $x \vdash z$. Hence $\vdash$ is also transitive, so $\vdash$ is a partial order.

6.3 Given points P_1 and P_2 in the plane, let us say that $P_1 \sim P_2$ whenever $x_1 - x_2 = 3(y_1 - y_2)$, where (x_1, y_1) and (x_2, y_2) are the coordinates of P_1 and P_2, respectively. Prove that $\sim$ is an equivalence relation.

Proof To begin we confirm that $P_1 \sim P_1$ for all points P_1. We must verify that $x_1 - x_1 = 3(y_1 - y_1)$, which is clearly true since both sides equal 0. Therefore $\sim$ is reflexive. Next suppose that $P_1 \sim P_2$, meaning that $x_1 - x_2 = 3(y_1 - y_2)$. Negating both sides leads to $x_2 - x_1 = 3(y_2 - y_1)$, which is equivalent to $P_2 \sim P_1$, hence $\sim$ is symmetric as well.

   Finally, suppose that $P_1 \sim P_2$ and $P_2 \sim P_3$, so that we have

$$x_1 - x_2 = 3(y_1 - y_2) \quad \text{and} \quad x_2 - x_3 = 3(y_2 - y_3).$$

Adding these two equations yields $x_1 - x_3 = 3(y_1 - y_3)$. But this implies that $P_1 \sim P_3$, so $\sim$ is transitive. Since $\sim$ is reflexive, symmetric and transitive it is an equivalence relation.

———◆———

6.4 Prove that $\lfloor x \rfloor + \lfloor x + \frac{1}{2} \rfloor = \lfloor 2x \rfloor$ if x is at most $\frac{1}{2}$ more than an integer; that is, whenever x lies in an interval of the form $n \leq x < n + \frac{1}{2}$ for some $n \in \mathbb{Z}$.

Proof Suppose that $n \leq x < n + \frac{1}{2}$ for some $n \in \mathbb{Z}$. Then clearly $\lfloor x \rfloor = n$, but it is also true that $\lfloor x + \frac{1}{2} \rfloor = n$, because $x + \frac{1}{2}$ is still less than $n + 1$. Therefore $\lfloor x \rfloor + \lfloor x + \frac{1}{2} \rfloor = 2n$. On the other hand, multiplying the inequality $n \leq x < n + \frac{1}{2}$ by 2 yields $2n \leq 2x < 2n + 1$, which means that $\lfloor 2x \rfloor = 2n$. In summary, we conclude that for $n \leq x < n + \frac{1}{2}$ we have

$$\lfloor x \rfloor + \lfloor x + \tfrac{1}{2} \rfloor = 2n = \lfloor 2x \rfloor,$$

so the two expressions are equal.

———◆———

6.5 Demonstrate that $f(x) = (2x + 1)/(x - 3)$ is an injective function.

Proof Suppose that $f(x_1) = f(x_2)$; this means that

$$\frac{2x_1 + 1}{x_1 - 3} = \frac{2x_2 + 1}{x_2 - 3}.$$

Cross-multiplying gives $(2x_1+1)(x_2-3) = (2x_2+1)(x_1-3)$, and then expanding each side yields $2x_1x_2 - 6x_1 + x_2 - 3 = 2x_1x_2 + x_1 - 6x_2 - 3$. Cancelling and combining like terms gives $-7x_1 = -7x_2$, from which we get $x_1 = x_2$. Since $f(x_1) = f(x_2)$ implies that $x_1 = x_2$, we deduce that $f(x)$ is injective.

———◆———

6.5 We define a function $g : \mathbb{N}_{\geq 2} \to \mathbb{N}$ by letting $g(n)$ be the largest proper divisor of n for $n \geq 2$. Prove that g is onto.

Proof Given any natural number $b \in \mathbb{N}$, we will show that there exists some natural number $n \geq 2$ such that $g(n) = b$. We claim that taking $n = 2b$ does the job. The divisors of $2b$ are $1, 2, \ldots, b, 2b$. There is no other divisor of $2b$ between b and $2b$, because any such number would divide into $2b$ between 1 and 2 times, so would not divide evenly into $2b$. Therefore the largest proper divisor of $2b$ is b, meaning that $g(2b) = b$. Hence g is onto.

———◆———

6.6 Let $f : A \to B$ and $g : B \to C$ be injective functions. Show that their composition $g \circ f : A \to C$ is also injective.

Proof We must show that if $a_1, a_2 \in A$ are distinct then the elements $g(f(a_1))$ and $g(f(a_2))$ in C are also distinct. So suppose that $a_1 \neq a_2$. Since f is injective, we deduce that $f(a_1) \neq f(a_2)$. But now since g is also injective, when we apply g to the unequal elements $f(a_1), f(a_2) \in B$ we obtain different elements of C, so that $g(f(a_1)) \neq g(f(a_2))$, and we're done.

CHAPTER 7

Cardinality

7.1 Comparing Sets

The present chapter addresses the matter of comparing the relative sizes of sets. At the outset it may be hard to imagine how such a discussion could fill more than a page, let alone an entire chapter. After all, we already know how to measure the size of a set, right? Simply count up its elements—and if there happen to be infinitely many, just say so. However, it turns out that there is a lot more to determining the size of a given set than meets the eye, particularly when dealing with infinite sets.

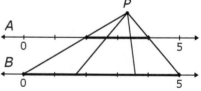

Part of the reason that our intuition so often leads us astray when dealing with infinite sets is that we have become accustomed to measuring the size of a set via a number of some sort. Thus the set of black keys on a piano has size 36, while the set of points within a circle of radius 5 has "size" (area) 25π. These quantities may then presumably be used as a means for comparing sets. For example, consider the closed intervals $A = [2, 4]$ and $B = [0, 5]$ shown above along with an auxiliary point P to help us gain perspective.

QUᴵᶜᴷᴱᴿʸ a) Why does it make sense to say that set B contains more points? On the other hand, how could we argue that the two sets have the same number of points? Which viewpoint is correct?

Suppose we wish to ascertain whether or not there are enough chocolates left in a bowl to distribute among a large group of trick-or-treaters. When faced with this dilemma, most people would count both the chocolates and the kids, then mentally compare the two numbers to figure out whether the remaining candy is sufficient.

However, there is an alternate approach that does not involve counting—simply hand out one chocolate per trick-or-treater until either the bowl is empty or every child has received a treat (or both). Of course, this method does have its drawbacks, especially in the case where it turns out that there is not enough chocolate to go around!

CᴏɴCᴇᴘᴛ b) Without counting, determine which row below has more objects.

The technique of pairing up the elements of two sets in order to determine their relative size would seem to be less sophisticated than counting the elements of each set. In actuality, the former approach turns out to be the more powerful method for deciding whether or not two sets have the same size. While counting elements is sufficient for finite sets, it is clearly of little use when dealing with infinite sets. This would be a moot point if all infinite sets were the same size. But as we shall discover shortly, they are not! Therefore it is necessary to establish a more effective means for comparing the relative sizes of sets.

> Given sets A and B, we say that A has the same **cardinality** as B if and only if there exists a bijection $f : A \to B$. In this case we write $|A| = |B|$, where $|A|$ and $|B|$ refer to the cardinality of sets A and B.

Recall that a bijection from A to B has the effect of creating a one-to-one correspondence between the elements of A and B.

Observe that our definition is one-sided in that it only requires a bijection from A to B. Clearly we would run into trouble with this concept if there were sets A and B for which there existed a bijection $f : A \to B$ but such that there did *not* exist a bijection $g : B \to A$. Fortunately the notion of having the same cardinality is an equivalence relation on sets, so our definition is consistent.

QUᴇʀʏ c) Why must there exist a bijection $g : B \to A$?

We remark that sets having the same cardinality are also known as "equivalent sets," or "numerically equivalent sets," or "sets in one-to-one correspondence."

Let us employ this definition to demonstrate that various pairs of sets have the same cardinality. For instance, we can show that the sets $A = \{a, b, \ldots, x, y\}$ and $B = \{b, c, \ldots, y, z\}$ have the same cardinality. Let $f : A \to B$ be the "successor function," in the sense that for any letter α we define $f(\alpha)$ to be the next letter in the alphabet. Then clearly $f : A \to B$ is a bijection.

On a slightly more interesting note, let us show that the closed intervals $A = [2, 4]$ and $B = [0, 5]$ are sets having the same cardinality. We claim that the function $g(x) = \frac{5}{2}x - 5$ provides a bijection $g : A \to B$. (This is the algebraic incarnation of the bijection suggested by the diagram on the previous page.) We must first check that g has the correct codomain; i.e. that if we compute

Mathematical Outing ★ ★ ★

Five pairs of sets A_1, A_2 through E_1, E_2 are described below. Based on your intuitive understanding of how to compare their size, decide in each case whether the first set is larger than the second, is smaller than the second, or has the same cardinality as the second.

- Set A_1 consists of the lowercase letters in the English alphabet.
- Set $A_2 = \{x \in \mathbb{R} \mid \sin x = \frac{x}{42}\}$, with x in radians.

- Let B_1 contain the names of all states in the USA starting with the letter B.
- Let $B_2 = \{n \in \mathbb{N} \mid 4n^2 + 4n - 3 = 0\}$.

- Set C_1 consists of the positive integers that are perfect squares.
- Set $C_2 = \{x \in \mathbb{R} \mid \cos x = \frac{42}{x}\}$, with x in radians.

- Define D_1 as the set of all real numbers x with $-3 \le x \le 3$.
- Define D_2 as the set of all real numbers x with $5 \le x \le 9$.

- Let E_1 be the set of all possible functions $f : \mathbb{N} \to \{a, b\}$.
- Let E_2 be the set of all possible functions $g : \{a, b\} \to \mathbb{N}$.

$g(x)$ for a number $x \in A$ the output is actually in B. We find that if $2 \le x \le 4$ then $5 \le \frac{5}{2}x \le 10$, hence $0 \le \frac{5}{2}x - 5 \le 5$. In other words, $g(x) \in B$, as desired.

We now show that g is one-to-one and onto. Suppose that $g(x_1) = g(x_2)$. This means that $\frac{5}{2}x_1 - 5 = \frac{5}{2}x_2 - 5$, which quickly yields $x_1 = x_2$, showing that g is one-to-one. Furthermore, given any $w \in B$ we will show that $\frac{2}{5}w + 2$ maps to w. We first check that $\frac{2}{5}w + 2 \in A$. This follows since $0 \le w \le 5$ gives $0 \le \frac{2}{5}w \le 2$, thus $2 \le \frac{2}{5}w + 2 \le 4$. Finally, we compute

$$f\left(\frac{2}{5}w + 2\right) = \frac{5}{2}\left(\frac{2}{5}w + 2\right) - 5 = (w + 5) - 5 = w.$$

Therefore g is also onto, completing the proof that $g : A \to B$ is a bijection.[†]

It has probably not escaped your attention that the set $A = [2, 4]$ is a proper subset of $B = [0, 5]$. So how can A and B have the same size? According to the history books, this sort of example bothered Galileo, who pondered such paradoxical behavior on the part of infinite sets. For instance, he was aware that it is possible to create a one-to-one correspondence between $\mathbb{N}$ and the set of perfect squares $\{1, 4, 9, 16, \ldots\}$ via the bijection $n \mapsto n^2$, even though the squares are a proper subset of $\mathbb{N}$. However, Galileo apparently was never able to fully reconcile in his mind the fact that it is possible for sets A and B to satisfy both $A \subset B$ and $|A| = |B|$.

a) Since A is a proper subset of B, it stands to reason that B has more points. But by drawing lines emanating from P we can pair up each point of A with each point of B, suggesting that $|A| = |B|$.
b) The top row has one more object than the bottom row.
c) If $f : A \to B$ is a bijection, then $f^{-1} : B \to A$ is also a bijection, so take $g = f^{-1}$.

First, A_1 is smaller than A_2 since A_1 has 26 elements while A_2 has 27 elements. Next, sets B_1 and B_2 are the same size since they are both the empty set. It is harder to compare C_1 and C_2, but it turns out that they both have the same size. Sets D_1 and D_2 also have the same size, as we shall see in the exercises. However, E_1 is demonstrably larger than E_2, despite the fact that they are both infinite sets.

EXERCISES

1. Find creative examples of sets D and E such that $|D| = 101$ and $|E| = 12$.

2. Construct a bijection from $\mathbb{N}$ to the set B of all positive rational numbers, such as $\frac{4}{3}$, whose numerator is one greater than their denominator.

3. Let $A = \{\dots, -7, -3, 1, 5, 9, 13, \dots\}$ and let $B = \{\dots, -6, -3, 0, 3, 6, 9, \dots\}$. Find a formula for a bijection $f : A \to B$, then give a bijection $g : B \to A$.

4. Find two different bijections $f : [1, 2] \to [1, 4]$. (Recall that $[1, 2]$ is a closed interval, consisting of all real numbers x satisfying $1 \le x \le 2$.)

5. Suppose that $A = \{x \in \mathbb{R} \mid 0 < x < 2\}$ and $B = \{x \in \mathbb{R} \mid x > 2\}$. Find a formula for a bijection $f : A \to B$.

6. Find a bijection between the points in quadrant I and quadrant II.

7. Describe a bijection between the set of all horizontal lines and the set of all vertical lines in the plane.

8. Why is it important for the notion of "having the same cardinality" to be a transitive relation on sets in order for the definition of $|A| = |B|$ to be consistent?

WRITING

9. Given sets A and B, we say that $A \sim B$ if and only if there exists a bijection $f : A \to B$. Prove that $\sim$ is an equivalence relation on sets. (This shows that the notion of "having the same cardinality" is well-defined.)

10. We define A as the set of all integers congruent to 3 mod 5. Prove that $\mathbb{Z}$ and A have the same cardinality.

11. Suppose that B is the set of all perfect squares having three or more digits. Find, with proof, a bijection $f : \mathbb{N} \to B$.

12. Let L be the set of lines in the plane having slope -1 which pass through a lattice point in the first quadrant; i.e. a point having coordinates (m, n) for some $m, n \in \mathbb{N}$. Prove that $|\mathbb{N}| = |L|$.

13. Let C be the set of all circles in the plane centered at the origin, and let H be the set of all horizontal lines above the x-axis. Prove that $|C| = |H|$.

14. Prove that the closed intervals $[-3, 3]$ and $[5, 9]$ have the same cardinality. (Model your proof after the one detailed in this section.)

15. Find, with proof, a bijection between the set of all real numbers and the set of positive real numbers.

16. Let P_1 be the collection of all subsets of $\{a, b, c, \ldots, y\}$, and let P_2 be the collection of those subsets of $\{a, b, c, \ldots, y, z\}$ having an even number of elements. Find, with proof, a bijection $h : P_1 \to P_2$ in order to show that $|P_1| = |P_2|$.

7.2 Finite and Infinite Sets

Before going further, we should formally define what we mean by finite and infinite sets. To do so we return to the familiar idea that if a set is finite, then its elements can be tallied by counting from 1 up to some natural number. So let $C_n = \{1, 2, 3, \ldots, n\}$ be the set consisting of the first n counting numbers. We will use this family of sets as a "yardstick" for officially determining when a given set is finite.

If there exists a bijection $f : C_n \to A$ for $n \in \mathbb{N}$ then A is a **finite set** and we have $|A| = n$. Also, if $A = \emptyset$ then A is again a finite set with $|A| = 0$. Any other set which does not satisfy these conditions is an **infinite set**.

Establishing a bijection between a set (such as a group of trick-or-treaters) and one of our counting sets (such as C_{13}) amounts to pairing up each of the numbers $\{1, 2, 3, \ldots, 13\}$ with one of the trick-or-treaters. Of course this is exactly what occurs when we count them. In fact, one rite of passage for youngsters is learning that they must not miss any objects while counting them (surjection) and they must not count any object twice (injection).

CONCEPT a) What can we conclude about sets A and B if their Cartesian product $A \times B$ is an infinite set?

Although this definition provides a perfectly reasonable way to check that a given set is finite (just count its elements), it is not entirely straight-forward to employ in proving that a given set is infinite. For instance, consider the set B of all positive rational numbers whose numerator and denominator differ by 3 or less when written in lowest terms. To rigorously prove that B is an infinite set we must show that B is not the empty set (which is clear) and that there does not exist a bijection $f : C_n \to B$ for any $n \in \mathbb{N}$.

QUICK QUERY b) Which proof technique is most appropriate for showing that there does not exist a bijection $f : C_n \to B$ for any $n \in \mathbb{N}$?

Suppose to the contrary that there does exist a bijection $f : C_n \to B$ for some $n \in \mathbb{N}$. This amounts to numbering the elements in B from 1 to n; in other words, we can label our fractions as $r_1, r_2, \ldots, r_n$. We will now reach a contradiction by showing that despite the fact that we ostensibly included all elements of B in our list, we actually must have missed at least one element. Of all the numerators appearing among the fractions $r_1, r_2, \ldots, r_n$, let N be the largest. Now consider the fraction $(N+1)/(N+2)$. This fraction is clearly an element of B, but by construction it is not equal to any of $r_1, r_2, \ldots, r_n$, since its numerator is too large. This contradicts the fact that $f : C_n \to B$ was a bijection, so we have shown that B is actually an infinite set after all.[†]

C‌ON‌CEPT c) What would go wrong with this proof if we had instead claimed that the fraction $(N+1)/(N+3)$ was not equal to any of $r_1, r_2, \ldots, r_n$?

Since directly applying our definition of infinite sets can be unwieldy, we provide an alternate characterization of infinite sets. The proof that this criterion is equivalent to the above definition is well within reach. However, supplying all the details runs the risk of carefully proving a result that feels intuitively obvious, which can be unsatisfying. Therefore we outline its proof in the exercises.

A given set A is an infinite set if and only if there exists an injective function $g : \mathbb{N} \to A$.

This characterization essentially says that a set is infinite if it contains a copy of the natural numbers as a subset. Equivalently, we can create an infinite list of distinct elements of A. This latter perspective provides a practical means for constructing an injection $g : \mathbb{N} \to A$. *Write down a sequence of elements of A that follows a predictable pattern, then find a formula for the nth term in the sequence.* This formula is the desired injection.

For instance, we can demonstrate that the set B of rational numbers between 2 and 3 is infinite by first writing down the sequence $2\frac{1}{2}, 2\frac{2}{3}, 2\frac{3}{4}, 2\frac{4}{5}, \ldots$, then recognizing that the nth term is given by the formula $2 + \frac{n}{n+1}$. We can now assert that this set is infinite because there exists an injective function $g : \mathbb{N} \to B$ given by $n \mapsto 2 + \frac{n}{n+1}$. The proof that g is injective is straight-forward.[†]

C‌ON‌CEPT d) Find a different injection $g : \mathbb{N} \to B$ than the one above.

We mention in passing that there is a second characterization of infinite sets, based on the property that Galileo found so disturbing. It states that a given set A is infinite if and only if there exists a mapping $h : A \to A$ that is one-to-one but not onto. In other words, a set A is infinite if A has the same cardinality as one of its proper subsets. On a slightly unrelated note, we also mention that an infinite set has "infinitely many" elements, not an "infinite number" of elements. Infinity is a concept, not a number, so avoid using the phrase "infinite number" when discussing how many elements are present in an infinite set.

a) We conclude that either A is infinite or B is infinite (or both).

b) Proof by contradiction is the best proof strategy.

c) If N were odd then the fraction $(N+1)/(N+3)$ would reduce, so the numerator would not be greater than N when written in lowest in terms, and hence it might actually appear in the list $r_1, r_2, \ldots, r_n$.

d) There are many possible answers; for example, $g(n) = 2 + 1/(n+1)$.

Exercises

17. Show by example that it is possible to have infinite sets A and B such that their intersection $A \cap B$ is a nonempty finite set.

18. Given sets A and B such that $B - A$ is an infinite set, what can we conclude (if anything) about the cardinalities of sets A and B?

19. Suppose that $r_1, r_2, \ldots, r_n$ is a finite list of positive rational numbers written in lowest terms such that the numerator and denominator of each fraction have the same number of digits. Describe how to construct a rational number of this form that is not on our list.

20. Let $S_1, S_2, \ldots, S_n$ be a collection of finite sets of positive integers whose largest element is 3 more than its cardinality. (Sets such as $\{4,5\}$ or $\{1,3,5,7\}$.) Explain how to construct another such set which is not already listed.

21. Define set A as $A = \{x \in \mathbb{R} \mid x > 4,\ x \notin \mathbb{Q}\}$. Find a formula for an injective function $g : \mathbb{N} \to A$.

22. Let B be the set of rational numbers whose denominators are even when written in lowest terms. Find a formula for an injective function $g : \mathbb{N} \to B$.

23. Let W be the set of all finite words containing exactly one 'l'. (Such as 'doodle' or 'bahbahblacksheep'.) Define an injective function $g : \mathbb{N} \to W$.

24. For the set W of words from the previous exercise, describe a function $h : W \to W$ that is one-to-one but not onto.

Writing

25. We define B as the set of positive rational numbers whose numerator has one digit and whose denominator is a power of 7 when written in lowest terms. Prove that there does not exist a bijection $f : C_n \to B$ for any $n \in \mathbb{N}$.

26. Let A be the set of rectangles in the plane having one vertex at the origin and having area equal to 42. Show that A is infinite by finding, with proof, an injective function $g : \mathbb{N} \to A$.

27. Suppose that $I = \{x \in \mathbb{R} \mid 6 < x < 12\}$. Demonstrate that I is infinite by finding a function $h : I \to I$ that is one-to-one but not onto. Prove that your function maps I into I and has the desired properties.

28. Let S be the collection of all sets of positive integers having exactly 7 elements. Prove that S is infinite.

29. Prove that the set B of rational numbers between 7 and 7.1 is infinite.

30. Let W be the set consisting of all words whose first and last letters are the same. Prove that W is infinite.

31. Prove that A is an infinite set if and only if $\mathcal{P}(A)$ is an infinite set.

The next two exercises prove our first characterization for infinite sets.

32. To begin, we will show that if there is an injective function $g : \mathbb{N} \to A$ then A is infinite by proving the contrapositive, which states that if A is finite then every function $g : \mathbb{N} \to A$ is not injective. Observe that if $A = \emptyset$ then there are no functions $g : \mathbb{N} \to A$ at all, so the claim is vacuously true. Now suppose that A is a nonempty finite set, meaning there is a bijection $f : C_n \to A$ for some $n \in \mathbb{N}$, and let $g : \mathbb{N} \to A$ be any function. Prove that g is not injective.

33. Next we prove the converse, which states that if A is infinite then there exists an injective function $g : \mathbb{N} \to A$. We define g inductively. For the base case, explain why it is possible to define $g(1)$. Now suppose that we have defined $g(1), g(2), \ldots, g(k)$ so that no two values are the same. Prove that it is possible to define $g(k + 1)$ so that its value is not equal to any of the previous values.

7.3   Denumerable Sets

The discussion thus far might give the impression that the set $\mathbb{N}$ of natural numbers is not that much larger than the really big finite sets. But this conception of infinity is hopelessly distorted by our physical intuition, which tends to lump together all sets beyond a certain size in the same "large beyond imagining" category. In fact, the set $\mathbb{N}$ is incredibly roomy. If we were to number all the atoms in the known universe we would not begin to put a dent in the natural numbers available to us. There are enough natural numbers to fill infinitely many sets with infinitely many elements each and still have infinitely many natural numbers left over.

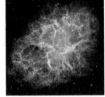

Our first characterization of infinite sets given in the previous section shows that the set $\mathbb{N}$ is the "smallest" infinite set, in the sense that if a set A is not finite, then it must contain a copy of $\mathbb{N}$ embedded within it via an injection $g : \mathbb{N} \to A$. Sets having the same size as $\mathbb{N}$ occur frequently enough that they are given a special name.

A set D is **denumerable** if there exists a bijection $f : \mathbb{N} \to D$. Therefore all denumerable sets have the same cardinality as $\mathbb{N}$. We write $|D| = \aleph_0$ (read "aleph nought") to indicate this cardinality.

In practice this definition says that if it is possible to number all the elements of an infinite set as element number one, element number two, element number three, and so on without missing any elements, then the set is denumerable. To gain a sense of what sorts of sets can be numbered in this manner, try out the Mathematical Outing on the next page.

[CONCEPT CHECK] a) The collections of ducks pictured on the next page correspond to the following sets, in some order. Determine which picture goes with which set.

$$\mathbb{N} \times \mathbb{N} \qquad \mathbb{N} \times \{1, 2\} \qquad \mathbb{Z} \qquad \mathbb{Z} \times \mathbb{Z} \qquad \mathbb{Z} \times \{1, 2, 3\}$$

Since all of the elements in each of the above sets may be numbered (which is equivalent to finding an bijection from $\mathbb{N}$ to each of the sets), it follows that they are all denumerable.

It is often helpful to create a visual representation of a set when attempting to come up with a numbering scheme in order to prove that the set is denumerable. For instance, imagine that we are confronted with a sequence of bottomless boxes, each capable of holding infinitely many index cards. The first box contains cards with 1, 2, 3, ... dots; the second has cards sporting 2, 3, 4, ... dots; the third box holds cards with 3, 4, 5, ... dots; and so on. Although each of the infinitely many boxes holds infinitely many index cards, we shall show that the collection of all index cards is still denumerable.

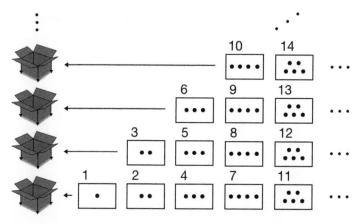

By arranging the cards in a triangular array and then numbering them as shown, it becomes clear that it is possible to label every card with a distinct natural number. In more formal terms, we have exhibited a bijection $f : \mathbb{N} \to D$, where D is the set of index cards contained in all the boxes. Note that it would have been a mistake to begin numbering to the right along the bottom row, because we never would have made it back to number the cards in the second row. However, we shouldn't declare that our set is not denumerable just because some numbering fails to include all the elements; we can only conclude that this particular numbering scheme did not settle the matter.

[CONCEPT CHECK] b) Explain why the set of all dots appearing on all the index cards contained within the sequence of bottomless boxes above is a denumerable set.

Mathematical Outing ★ ★ ★

Show that in each of the illustrations below it is possible to put all the ducks in a row. In other words, find a way to number the ducks 1, 2, 3, 4, 5, 6, 7, 8 ... so that every duck is assigned a positive integer via a clearly discernible numbering pattern. A trio of dots means infinitely many ducks in the indicated direction.

LEVEL ONE

LEVEL TWO

LEVEL THREE

LEVEL FOUR

LEVEL FIVE

The ducks in level five extend infinitely in all directions.

Just as with infinite sets, there are at least two other methods for showing that a given set is denumerable aside from appealing directly to the definition.

> To show that a given set A is denumerable, prove that there exists a bijection $f : D \to A$ with a set D that is known to be denumerable.

For example, we can show that the set of all functions $g : \{a, b\} \to \mathbb{N}$ is denumerable. Upon reflection, we realize that defining such a function involves selecting one value for $g(a)$ and another value for $g(b)$; say $g(a) = 17$ and $g(b) = 100$. In other words, a function $g : \{a, b\} \to \mathbb{N}$ is completely determined by a pair of natural numbers. Hence the set of all such functions is in one-to-one correspondence with $\mathbb{N} \times \mathbb{N}$. We already know that the latter set is denumerable, so the set of functions $g : \{a, b\} \to \mathbb{N}$ must be also.[†]

CONCEPT CHECK c) Let S be a set containing two copies of the natural numbers, say with a red 1 and a blue 1, a red 2 and a blue 2, a red 3 and a blue 3, and so on. Explain why S is denumerable.

Our second strategy is well-suited for sets which are irregular, meaning that they cannot easily be arranged in a manner which permits us to number them. We outline a proof of this characterization in the exercises.

> To show that a given set A is denumerable, prove that A is an infinite set and also that A is a subset of a known denumerable set.

For instance, we can immediately conclude that the set of primes is denumerable, since we proved earlier that there are infinitely many primes, and clearly the set of primes is a subset of $\mathbb{N}$, which is denumerable.

One of the most celebrated theorems on the cardinality of sets is the fact that the set $\mathbb{Q}$ of rational numbers is denumerable. At first glance this seems preposterous, since the natural numbers appear at regular intervals along the positive half of the real number line, while the rationals are virtually everywhere. (There are infinitely many rationals just between 7 and 7.1, for instance.)

positive integers   rational numbers

Nonetheless, $\mathbb{Q}$ and $\mathbb{N}$ have the same cardinality. Recall that a rational $\frac{m}{n}$ is constructed from two integers m and n which are relatively prime, with $n > 0$. Hence a rational number corresponds to a pair (m, n) of integers. To illustrate,

$$\frac{3}{5} \leftrightarrow (3, 5) \qquad -6\frac{7}{8} \leftrightarrow (-55, 8) \qquad -13 \leftrightarrow (-13, 1) \qquad 0 \leftrightarrow (0, 1).$$

Note that not every ordered pair of integers arises in this manner. (The reader may verify that $(4, 10)$, $(13, -1)$ and $(1, 0)$ do not, among others.) This fact makes directly numbering the rationals slightly tricky. But we can sidestep the issue by observing that $\mathbb{Q}$ is an infinite set which is in one-to-one correspondence with a subset of $\mathbb{Z} \times \mathbb{Z}$. Therefore $\mathbb{Q}$ is denumerable, as claimed.[†]

[CONCEPT] d) Show that the set of positive rational numbers whose numerator and denominator differ by 3 or less when written in lowest terms is denumerable.

We have seen two ways of combining sets to produce larger sets: the union and the Cartesian product. For the record, the union of two denumerable sets is again denumerable. Without much additional effort it can be shown that if A_1, A_2, ..., A_n are each denumerable then so is $A_1 \cup A_2 \cup \cdots \cup A_n$. In fact, an infinite union of denumerable sets of the form $\bigcup_{k=1}^{\infty} A_k$ is still denumerable. Furthermore, the Cartesian product $A_1 \times A_2 \times \cdots \times A_n$ is also denumerable.

Finite and denumerable sets are collectively dubbed **countable** sets, because their elements can be listed (i.e. counted) as a_1, a_2, ..., a_n for finite sets or as a_1, a_2, a_3, ... for denumerable sets. All "larger" sets are called **uncountable** sets. The diagram below organizes the cardinalities discussed thus far.

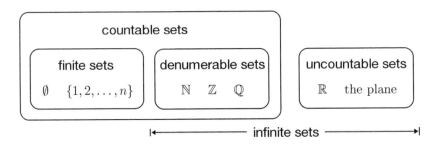

Although it may not be immediately obvious that uncountable sets exist at all, we have already encountered three such sets, namely the set of real numbers, the set of points in the plane, and the set of all functions $f : \mathbb{N} \to \{a, b\}$. In the upcoming sections we will prove that these sets are indeed uncountable and describe a means of constructing even larger sets than these.

[ALL THE ANSWERS] a) Levels one through five correspond to $\mathbb{N} \times \{1, 2\}$, $\mathbb{Z}$, $\mathbb{Z} \times \{1, 2, 3\}$, $\mathbb{N} \times \mathbb{N}$ and $\mathbb{Z} \times \mathbb{Z}$, respectively.
   b) They can be numbered by progressing through the cards in the order shown and numbering all the dots on each card before moving on to the next.
c) We can match the elements of S with the ducks in level one of the Mathematical Outing. In other words, there is a bijection between S and the set $\mathbb{N} \times \{1, 2\}$.
d) Call this set B. We already saw that B is infinite, and $B \subset \mathbb{Q}$, which is denumerable. We omit full answers to this Mathematical Outing, on the grounds that a verbal description of the numbering schemes would not do justice to the elegant solutions that the reader undoubtedly found. As a hint for level four, try starting in the upper left corner, then proceed from the left side to the top side and back along successive diagonals. For level five begin in the middle and spiral outward.

EXERCISES

34. Draw a picture to represent $\mathbb{N} \times \mathbb{Z}$ and illustrate a means of numbering all the elements in this set.

35. We define $A = \{(m, n) \mid m, n \in \mathbb{N}, \ m + n \equiv 2 \bmod 3\}$. Plot these points in the Cartesian plane, then demonstrate a way to number all the points.

36. Suppose that B is the set of points in the plane whose y-coordinate is a positive integer and whose distance from the origin is also a positive integer. Find an organized method of numbering all such points.

37. Set C consists of all positive rationals whose denominator is a multiple of 5. Briefly explain why C is a denumerable set.

38. Let D be the set of all integers (such as 438 or -2003) which include a 3 among their digits. Briefly explain why D is a denumerable set.

39. Imagine in the example involving the sequence of bottomless boxes that each of the index cards contained infinitely many dots (a denumerable set of dots, to be precise). Do you suppose that the set of all dots on all the index cards in all the boxes is countable or uncountable?

40. An infinite stairway is a path constructed by starting at the origin and then repeatedly drawing segments, either up one unit or to the right one unit. (One such path is shown.)
Do you suppose that the set of all infinite stairways is countable or uncountable?

WRITING

41. Define D as the set of all pairs (m, n) of positive integers such that $m + n$ includes the digit 7. Demonstrate that D is a denumerable set.

42. Let A, B and C be disjoint denumerable sets. Prove that $A \cup B \cup C$ is also denumerable. (TIP: write $A = \{a_1, a_2, a_3, \ldots\}$ and similarly for B and C.)

43. A *lattice point* is a point (m, n) in the plane with $m, n \in \mathbb{Z}$. Let us say that a sneaky segment has one endpoint at a lattice point along the x-axis, its other endpoint at a lattice point along the y-axis, but doesn't pass through any other lattice points. Prove that the set of sneaky segments is denumerable.

44. Prove that the set of all words is a denumerable set. (Recall that a word is a finite string of lower case letters, such as 'frabjous' or 'abracadabra'.)

45. An infinite stairway of height h is an infinite stairway (defined above) which eventually reaches a level h units above the x-axis and remains there. Equivalently, the infinite stairway includes exactly h vertical segments. Prove that the set of infinite stairways of height 1 is denumerable.

46. Continuing the previous problem, prove that the set of infinite stairways of height 2 is a denumerable set.

47. Continuing the previous problems, prove that the set of stairways of height h is denumerable set for all $h \in \mathbb{N}$.

48. Given denumerable sets $C = \{c_1, c_2, c_3, \ldots\}$ and $D = \{d_1, d_2, d_3, \ldots\}$, provide a diagram that presents all the elements of $C \times D$ in an organized fashion. Then use your diagram to prove that $C \times D$ is also denumerable.

49. Let D_1, D_2, $\ldots$, D_n be denumerable sets. Prove that $D_1 \times D_2 \times \cdots \times D_n$ is also a denumerable set. (Use the result from the previous exercise.)

50. Show that the set of all functions $g : \{a, b, c\} \to \mathbb{N}$ is a denumerable set by proving that there exists a bijection with a known denumerable set.

51. Suppose that A is an infinite set and that $A \subseteq D$ for some denumerable set D. Prove that A is also a denumerable set. (HINT: since D is denumerable we may list its elements as $D = \{d_1, d_2, d_3, \ldots\}$. How can we use this ordering to create a numbered list of all the elements of A?)

7.4   Uncountable Sets

The chart below shows an infinite rubber ducky family tree, with the grand matriarch duck appearing on the far left. The first generation beyond her has two ducks, the second generation consists of four ducks, and in general the nth generation will contain 2^n rubber duckies.

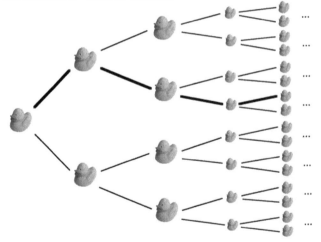

It is clear that the set of all ducks can be numbered, beginning with the duck on the left and working our way through successive generations of the family tree. Therefore the set of ducks is denumerable.

Let us now turn our attention to the set of all infinite paths through the family tree, one of which is highlighted above. Of course, there are only finitely many paths up to any particular generation. For instance, there are sixteen different paths in the portion of the family tree depicted above, one for each duck in the fourth generation.

QUICK QUERY   a) If we were to extend the family tree to include n generations of rubber duckies, would there be more ducks or paths up to this point?

It is an undisputable fact that within the first n generations of the family tree there are 2^n paths and $2^{n+1}-1$ ducks; nearly twice as many ducks as paths. Therefore it comes as a complete shock to learn that the set of all infinite paths through the family tree is larger (in a rigorous sense) than the set of all ducks. We now present our first proof that a certain set is uncountable.

> To prove that an infinite set is uncountable one must show that there does not exist a bijection from $\mathbb{N}$ to this set. In practical terms, one must demonstrate that any infinite list of elements of the given set will always be incomplete, meaning that some element is left out.

Let $\mathcal{P}$ be the set of all infinite paths through the family tree. We indicate a particular path via an infinite string of a's and b's, which stand for 'above' and 'below'. Thus the highlighted path is represented by $abba\cdots$; the nth letter tells us whether to branch up or down going into the nth generation.

To show that $\mathcal{P}$ is uncountable we employ proof by contradiction. Suppose to the contrary that $\mathcal{P}$ is countable, meaning that we can include all the paths in a list, say $p_1, p_2, p_3, \ldots$, where each p_k is a path, i.e. an infinite string of a's and b's. We will now find a path that was omitted using a clever construction due to Georg Cantor. This technique has found a wide range of applications and is usually referred to as **Cantor's diagonal argument**.

Arrange our sequence of infinite paths one above the other; a possible listing is shown below to help illustrate the technique.

$$
\begin{aligned}
p_1 &= a \quad a \quad a \quad a \quad a \quad a \quad a \quad a \quad a \ \cdots \\
p_2 &= b \quad b \quad b \quad b \quad b \quad b \quad b \quad b \quad b \ \cdots \\
p_3 &= a \quad b \quad a \quad b \quad a \quad b \quad a \quad b \quad a \ \cdots \\
p_4 &= b \quad a \quad b \quad a \quad b \quad a \quad b \quad a \quad b \ \cdots \\
p_5 &= a \quad b \quad b \quad a \quad b \quad b \quad b \quad a \quad a \ \cdots \\
p_6 &= b \quad a \quad a \quad b \quad a \quad a \quad a \quad a \quad b \ \cdots \\
&\quad\ \ \vdots \qquad\qquad \vdots \qquad\qquad \vdots
\end{aligned}
$$

$$? \ = \ b \quad a \quad b \quad b \quad a \quad b \ \cdots$$

We create a new infinite string of a's and b's underneath the list by replacing each a along the main diagonal with a b and vice versa. More precisely, we construct this path by determining the nth letter of the nth path and using the *other* letter as the nth letter of the new path. Clearly this string of a's and b's cannot match any path appearing on the list. For it differs from the first path at the first branching, it differs from the second path at the second branching, and so on. Therefore our list does not include all possible paths, and we're done.[†]

QUERY b) Suppose we include the omitted path $babbab\cdots$ at the top of the list. Why does this not remedy the problem?

Armed with one uncountable set, we are now able to quickly illustrate several others. We will employ the same sorts of techniques that we did when dealing with infinite and denumerable sets.

> To demonstrate that a given set is uncountable, prove that there exists a bijection between the given set and a set that is known to be uncountable.

For instance, we may at long last settle the question as to whether the set of functions $f : \{a, b\} \to \mathbb{N}$ or the set of functions $g : \mathbb{N} \to \{a, b\}$ has the greater cardinality. We have already seen that the former set is denumerable. Now consider what is involved in defining a function $g : \mathbb{N} \to \{a, b\}$. We must decide whether to let $g(1) = a$ or $g(1) = b$, then select either $g(2) = a$ or $g(2) = b$, then pick between $g(3) = a$ or $g(3) = b$, and so on. In other words, a function $g : \mathbb{N} \to \{a, b\}$ is equivalent to an infinite string of a's and b's, which catalog the values we choose for $g(1)$, $g(2)$, $g(3)$, etc. But we already know that the set of infinite strings of a's and b's is uncountable. Hence the set of functions $g : \mathbb{N} \to \{a, b\}$ is also uncountable, so has the greater cardinality.

CONCEPT CHECK c) Why is the set of all infinite strings of 3's and 7's uncountable?

Just as the set $\mathbb{N}$ serves as a yardstick for denumerable sets, the set of all infinite strings of a's and b's serves as a basis for showing that certain sets are uncountable. The open interval $(0, 1)$ may also be used for this purpose.

> To show that a given set E is uncountable, prove that E contains a known uncountable set as a subset. In particular, it suffices to show that E contains a copy of the set of all infinite strings of a's and b's. It would also suffice to exhibit an injective function $g : (0, 1) \to E$.

Of course, we need to show that the open interval $(0, 1)$ is an uncountable set before the second half of this proof strategy will make sense. To do so, convert each infinite sequence of a's and b's into a real number by replacing each a by a 3 and each b by a 7, then insert a decimal point at the front. For example,

$$baababbba \cdots \mapsto .733737773 \cdots, \quad aaaaaaaaa \cdots \mapsto \frac{1}{3}.$$

Hence the real numbers between 0 and 1 contain a copy of the set of all infinite strings of a's and b's, so the open interval $(0, 1)$ must contain uncountably many real numbers. We can immediately conclude that $\mathbb{R}$ itself is also uncountable, since $(0, 1)$ is a subset. Furthermore, every open interval is uncountable. For instance, the bijection $g : (0, 1) \to (7, 7.1)$ given by $g(x) = \frac{1}{10}x + 7$ shows that the open interval $(7, 7.1)$ is an uncountable set.

CONCEPT CHECK d) Explain why the set of all circles in the plane is uncountable.

a) There would be more ducks.

b) We would wind up with another infinite list of paths, so we could construct a missing path in the same manner as before.

c) There is a bijection between sequences of 3's or 7's and sequences of a's or b's obtained by replacing each a by a 3 and each b by a 7.

d) Map each real number $r \in (0, 1)$ to the circle with radius r and center at the origin. This gives an injection from $(0, 1)$ to the set of all circles in the plane.

EXERCISES

52. Find a formula for a bijection $g : (0, 1) \to (4.6, 4.7)$, thereby showing that this open interval contains uncountably many real numbers.

53. Describe an injection from the open interval $(0, 1)$ to the set of all rectangles in the plane having perimeter 8.

54. Draw the graph of a bijection between $(0, 1)$ and $\mathbb{R}$. This shows that not only is $\mathbb{R}$ uncountable, but it has the same cardinality as $(0, 1)$.

55. Briefly explain why the set of all circles in the plane tangent to both the x-axis and the y-axis is an uncountable set.

56. Let S be the set of all infinite sequences using the letters x, y and z. Briefly explain why S is uncountable by showing that S contains a copy of a known uncountable set as a subset.

57. Let S be the set of all infinite sequences using the letters x, y and z. Suppose that s_1, s_2, s_3, ... is a list of such sequences. Describe how to construct a sequence in S that does not appear in the list.

58. Briefly explain why there are uncountably many paths through the duck family tree that begin by following the route highlighted in the diagram.

59. Describe a bijection between the set of all infinite strings using the letters w, x, y and z and the set of all infinite strings of a's and b's.

WRITING

60. Consider the set of all functions $h : \mathbb{N} \to \{a, b, c, d\}$. Prove directly that this set is uncountable by arguing that every list h_1, h_2, h_3, ... of such functions must omit at least one of them.

61. Prove directly that the set of real numbers between 4 and 5 is uncountable by arguing that no list x_1, x_2, x_3, ... could contain them all.

62. An infinite stairway is a path constructed by starting at the origin and then repeatedly drawing segments, either up one unit or to the right one unit. (One such path is shown to the right.) Prove that the set of infinite stairways is uncountable.

63. Let S be the set of permutations of the sequence 1, 2, 3, 4, 5, ... in which no number moves more than one spot from its original location. For example, 1, 3, 2, 4, 6, 5, 7, 8, 9, ... is one such sequence. Prove that S is uncountable.

64. We know that the set of real numbers is uncountable, while the set of rational numbers is countable. Use these facts to prove that the set of irrational numbers is uncountable.

65. Prove that there are uncountably many segments in the plane having the point $(3,0)$ as their midpoint.

66. Prove that there are uncountably many quadratic functions having $x = 2$ as one of their roots.

67. Find, with proof, a bijection between $\mathcal{P}(\mathbb{N})$, the collection of all subsets of the natural numbers, and the set of infinite sequences of a's and b's. (Thereby showing that $\mathcal{P}(\mathbb{N})$ is an uncountable set.)

7.5   Cantor's Theorem

The inquisitive reader will realize that our discussion of uncountable sets in the previous section actually raises more questions than it answers. For instance, using Cantor's diagonal argument we have seen that the set of real numbers is an example of an uncountable set; i.e. it has larger cardinality than the set of positive integers. It is natural to wonder at this stage whether there also exist sets whose cardinality is larger than the real numbers. For that matter, how do we formally define "larger cardinality" anyway?

Let us begin by explaining how we compare the sizes of two sets.

> Suppose there exists an injective function $f : A \to B$ for sets A and B. Then we say that the cardinality of A is no greater than the cardinality of B, indicated by writing $|A| \le |B|$.

This makes sense on an intuitive level, for an injective function $f : A \to B$ has the effect of showing that B contains a copy of A as a subset, hence B ought to contain at least as many elements as A.

CONCEPT a) Let $A = \{1, 2, 3, \ldots, 999\}$ and let B be the set of rational numbers from 0 to 1, inclusive. Use the above definition to show that $|A| \le |B|$.

CONCEPT b) We know that the open intervals $(0, 10)$ and $(2, 5)$ have the same cardinality. Find an injection $f : (0, 10) \to (2, 5)$ that is not also a surjection.

The above question points out that when working with infinite sets, it would be erroneous to jump to the conclusion that $|A| < |B|$ just because some injective function $f : A \to B$ doesn't include every element of B in its range. For example, the function $f : \mathbb{N} \to \mathbb{Z}$ mapping $n \mapsto (n - 1000)$ is clearly one-to-one,

Mathematical Outing ★ ★ ★

Suppose that a volunteer were to list, in order, five different subsets of the set $\{1, 2, 3, 4, 5\}$, by numbering them as subsets 1 through 5. For instance, this person might select

#1 $\{2, 4, 5\}$ #2 $\{2, 3\}$ #3 $\{1, 2, 3, 4, 5\}$ #4 $\{1\}$ #5 $\{3, 5\}$

Without looking at these subsets, you then ask the volunteer whether the number 1 is in the first set, whether 2 is an element of the second set, and so on. In the example above the responses would be NO, YES, YES, NO, YES. To the amazement of all onlookers, you are then able to correctly predict a subset that is *not* on the list. How is this "trick" performed?

Thanks to Jim Tanton for suggesting this activity, which is based on the article "A Game-Like Activity for Learning Cantor's Theorem" by Shay Gueron appearing in the *College Mathematics Journal*.

but doesn't come close to being onto, since no integer below -1000 is part of the range. Nonetheless, $\mathbb{N}$ and $\mathbb{Z}$ do have the same cardinality.

Of course, it would be nice to have a means of ascertaining when one set is truly larger than another. Given sets A and B, to argue that $|A| < |B|$ we would need to show that $|A| \leq |B|$ and $|A| \neq |B|$. In practical terms, this means that there is an injection from A to B, but no bijection.

> To prove that $|A| < |B|$, first show that there exists an injective function $f : A \to B$. Then demonstrate that every such injective function fails to provide a bijection, meaning that there is always some element of B that is not the image of any element of A.

This is the approach we took to show that the set of infinite sequences of a's and b's is larger than the set $\mathbb{N}$ of natural numbers—we argued that regardless of the manner in which we attempted to pair up natural numbers to sequences of a's and b's, we always missed some sequence.

We are now in a position to settle the other question raised at the outset of this section by presenting a set whose cardinality is greater than the cardinality of the set of real numbers. The Mathematical Outing above features a puzzle which helps to illustrate the central idea in the following construction, so the reader is encouraged to try it out first.

CONNECT c) Would you guess that the set $\mathbb{R} \times \mathbb{R}$ of all points in the Cartesian plane has the same cardinality as $\mathbb{R}$ or is strictly larger?

We claim that the collection of all subsets of the real numbers has larger cardinality than the set of real numbers; in other words, that $|\mathbb{R}| < |\mathcal{P}(\mathbb{R})|$. The proof is deceptively simple. To begin, there is certainly an injective function $f : \mathbb{R} \to \mathcal{P}(\mathbb{R})$ mapping each real number x to the subset $\{x\}$ of $\mathbb{R}$ containing the single element x. (Of course, there are many other subsets of $\mathbb{R}$, such as $\{3, \pi\}$ or the set of all positive reals.) We now claim that no such injection can also be a surjection. So consider any such $f : \mathbb{R} \to \mathcal{P}(\mathbb{R})$, meaning that for each $x \in \mathbb{R}$, $f(x)$ is some subset of $\mathbb{R}$. (Perhaps $f(7) = \{x \mid 10 \le x \le 20\}$, for sake of illustration.) In the spirit of Cantor's diagonal argument, we will now construct a subset C of $\mathbb{R}$ that is not equal to any of the sets $f(x)$.

For each real number x, include x in our set C precisely when x is *not* an element of $f(x)$. (So we would include $7 \in C$ since $7 \notin \{x \mid 10 \le x \le 20\}$.) We will show that $C \ne f(x)$ for any $x \in \mathbb{R}$. For instance, let us show that C and $f(2)$ are different sets. We consider two cases. If $2 \in C$ then it must have been the case that $2 \notin f(2)$, by our rules for constructing set C. Since 2 is an element of one set but not the other, then clearly $C \ne f(2)$.[†]

QUERY   d) Explain why C and $f(2)$ must be different sets in the case $2 \notin C$.

The above discussion and query show that $C \ne f(2)$ regardless of whether or not $2 \in C$. The same reasoning applies for any other real number, so we conclude that $C \ne f(x)$ for any $x \in \mathbb{R}$, proving that f is not a surjection.

The argument just presented is equally valid when applied to any set S. This more general result was first stated and proved by Georg Cantor in 1891 (although in a slightly different form), at the same time that he presented his diagonal argument to prove that the set of real numbers is uncountable.

Cantor's Theorem states that for any set S the power set of S has a strictly greater cardinality than S. In other words, $|S| < |\mathcal{P}(S)|$ for all S.

The proposition that infinite sets can have different sizes is hard to swallow, even today. But when it was first advanced in the late 1800's, at a time when even the notion of infinity was still relatively murky, it raised a veritable storm of controversy, at least within mathematical circles. Several influential mathematicians of the day, notably Kronecker, rejected Cantor's arguments and had a hand in preventing him from securing more prestigious positions than he held at the time. It was only later that the endorsement of Cantor's ideas by well-respected figures such as Hilbert led to the widespread acceptance that these results now enjoy.

a) One possible injection is $f(n) = 1/n$; another is $f(n) = (n-1)/n$.
b) The function $f(x) = x/5 + 2$ maps the open interval $(0, 10)$ to $(2, 4)$. Since the range of f is not all of $(2, 5)$, f is not onto.
c) The sets $\mathbb{R}$ and $\mathbb{R} \times \mathbb{R}$ have the same cardinality, as we shall see in the next section.
d) If $2 \notin C$ then according to our construction of set C we must have had $2 \in f(2)$. Since 2 is in one set but not the other, they must be different sets.

EXERCISES

68. Let $A = \{1000, 1001, 1002, \ldots, 2000\}$ and let B be the set of powers of 2. Find an injective function $f : A \rightarrow B$.

69. Suppose that A and B are finite sets and there exists an injective function $f : A \rightarrow B$ that is not surjective. How does $|A|$ compare to $|B|$? How does your answer change if A and B are infinite sets?

70. Is there a set that is strictly larger than the set $\mathcal{P}(\mathbb{R})$ of all subsets of the real numbers? Why or why not?

71. Find an injective function $f : \mathbb{Z} \rightarrow \mathbb{Z}$ that is almost a surjection, by arranging for rng(f) to include every integer except 0.

72. Find an injection $f : \mathbb{Z} \rightarrow \mathbb{N}$. Use an arrow diagram to define your function.

73. In the proof that $|\mathbb{R}| < |\mathcal{P}(\mathbb{R})|$, give an example of a set $f(2)$ that would result in having $2 \notin C$.

74. In the Mathematical Outing, suppose that the volunteer responds NO, NO, NO, YES, NO. What set is guaranteed not to appear on their list?

75. In the Mathematical Outing, suppose that all five answers are YES. In this case what set is guaranteed not to appear on the volunteer's list?

76. Let $A = \{x \in \mathbb{R} \mid x > 1\}$ and let $B = \{x \in \mathbb{R} \mid x \geq 2\}$. Explain why it is not trivial to find a bijection between sets A and B.

WRITING

77. Prove by induction that $n < 2^n$ for all integers $n \geq 0$. Then explain how this gives a direct confirmation of Cantor's Theorem for finite sets.

78. Prove Cantor's theorem for infinite sets. In other words, show that if S is any infinite set then there is an injective function $f : S \rightarrow \mathcal{P}(S)$, but that any such injection fails to be a surjection.

79. In the Mathematical Outing, suppose that all five answers are NO. Explain why the set $\{1, 2, 3, 4, 5\}$ is the *only* set that is guaranteed not to appear on the volunteer's list.

80. Let $A = \{x \in \mathbb{R} \mid x > 1\}$ and let $B = \{x \in \mathbb{R} \mid x \geq 2\}$. Prove that $|A| \leq |B|$ and that $|B| \leq |A|$.

81. Given sets $A = \{r \in \mathbb{Q} \mid 0 \leq r \leq 6\}$ and $B = \{r \in \mathbb{Q} \mid 1 < r < 4\}$, prove that $|A| \leq |B|$ and that $|B| \leq |A|$.

82. Show that the set of all functions $f : \mathbb{N} \rightarrow \{a, b\}$ has cardinality no greater than the set of all functions $g : \mathbb{N} \rightarrow \{a, b, c\}$ and vice-versa.

83. Let A contain all sets of natural numbers with four elements, and let B consist of all sets of five natural numbers. Prove that $|A| \leq |B|$ and $|B| \leq |A|$.

84. Let S be the set containing all infinite sequences of positive integers. Prove that we have $|S| \leq |\mathbb{R}|$.

7.6   Ordering Cardinal Numbers

Given any set S we know, thanks to Cantor's Theorem, that there exists another set with strictly larger cardinality. In fact, beginning with the natural numbers (the "smallest" infinite set), we can construct an entire sequence of infinite sets, each of which has strictly greater cardinality than the one before it:

$$\mathbb{N}, \ \mathcal{P}(\mathbb{N}), \ \mathcal{P}(\mathcal{P}(\mathbb{N})), \ \mathcal{P}(\mathcal{P}(\mathcal{P}(\mathbb{N}))), \ \mathcal{P}(\mathcal{P}(\mathcal{P}(\mathcal{P}(\mathbb{N})))), \ \ldots$$

But writing out such a list immediately raises several thorny issues. For starters, is the above list complete, or does there exist an infinite set whose cardinality is not equal to the cardinality of any of these sets? In particular, where does the set of real numbers fit into the picture? More generally, is it even possible to order sets according to their cardinality in the first place?

Let us pause to review the cardinalities that we have encountered thus far. Earlier we introduced the symbol $\aleph_0$ to represent the size of the set of natural numbers. The set of real numbers is often referred to as the **continuum**, and the letter c is commonly used to represent the size of this set. Of course, we use the numbers 0, 1, 2, 3, ... to indicate the various sizes of finite sets.

> A quantity used to indicate the size of a set is called a **cardinal number**. For finite sets we have $|\emptyset| = 0$ and $|C_n| = n$, where $C_n = \{1, 2, \ldots, n\}$. We have also defined $|\mathbb{N}| = \aleph_0$ and $|\mathbb{R}| = c$.

Although we have nowhere explicitly stated so, the tacit assumption is that the $\leq$ relation provides a total order on the collection of all cardinal numbers. (Just by using the $\leq$ symbol we are practically implying that this is the case, since $\leq$ is already a total order in the more familiar setting of real numbers.) Recall that we write $|A| \leq |B|$ when there exists an injective function $f : A \to B$. Here is precisely what it means for $\leq$ to be a total order on cardinal numbers.

i. (*Reflexivity*) For any set A, we have $|A| \leq |A|$, meaning that there exists an injective function $f : A \to A$.

ii. (*Antisymmetry*) Given any sets A and B with $|A| \leq |B|$ and $|B| \leq |A|$ it follows that $|A| = |B|$. In other words, given injections $f : A \to B$ and $g : B \to A$ there must be a bijection between A and B.

iii. (*Transitivity*) For sets A, B and C, if $|A| \leq |B|$ and $|B| \leq |C|$, then we have $|A| \leq |C|$.

iv. (*Total order*) Given any two sets A and B, either $|A| \leq |B|$ or $|B| \leq |A|$.

QUICK ERY   a) Demonstrate that statement *i.* above is true.

QUICK ERY   b) Explain how to show that statement *iii.* is also true.

Mathematical Outing	⋆ ⋆ ⋆

Consider the two sets $A = \{x \in \mathbb{R} \mid x \geq 1\}$ and $B = \{x \in \mathbb{R} \mid x > 1\}$, which differ by a single point. Clearly there are injections from A to B and vice-versa (for instance, $f(x) = x+1$ suffices for both directions), so it is a fact that $|A| \leq |B|$ and $|B| \leq |A|$. The puzzle is to figure out how to show directly that $|A| = |B|$. Can you construct a bijection from A to B? (TIP: try an arrow diagram approach rather than a formula.)

For a tougher task, take the closed interval $A = [1, 2]$ and the open interval $B = (1, 2)$. As before it is routine to demonstrate that $|A| \leq |B|$ and $|B| \leq |A|$. The challenge is to construct a bijection between these two sets.

Although the reflexive and transitive properties of $\leq$ for cardinal numbers are relatively clear, the antisymmetric property is far from trivial. (To appreciate this fact, spend a few moments contemplating the Mathematical Outing above.) The antisymmetric property for $\leq$, which was originally formulated and proven by Cantor, represents one of the most beloved results in set theory.

> Suppose we are given sets A and B for which there are injective functions $f : A \to B$ and $g : B \to A$. Then the **Schroeder-Bernstein Theorem** asserts that there exists a bijection from A to B.

The proof of this theorem involves one elegant idea coupled with some careful bookkeeping. We outline the argument in the writing problems below.

Let us now employ this powerful result to establish where c, the cardinality of the continuum, fits into the list $|\mathbb{N}|, |\mathcal{P}(\mathbb{N})|, |\mathcal{P}(\mathcal{P}(\mathbb{N}))|, \ldots$ of cardinal numbers by showing that $\mathbb{R}$ and $\mathcal{P}(\mathbb{N})$ have the same cardinality. According to the Schroeder-Bernstein Theorem, it suffices to show that each set contains a copy of the other embedded within it; i.e. we need only exhibit injective functions from each set to the other.

To begin, let $S \in \mathcal{P}(\mathbb{N})$, meaning that S is a subset of $\mathbb{N}$. Such a subset is equivalent to an infinite string of O's and I's, where an O in the nth position indicates that n is *O*mitted from the subset, while an I means that n is *I*ncluded in the subset. For example, the subset $S = \{1, 4, 5, 7, 10 \ldots\}$ corresponds to the string $IOOIIOIOOI \cdots$. Next convert such a string into a real number by changing O's to 0's and I's to 1's, then inserting a decimal point in front. Thus our set S from before would become $.1001101001 \cdots$. In this way each subset $S \subseteq \mathbb{N}$ is mapped to a real number; in fact, to a real number in the closed interval $[0, \frac{1}{9}]$. Clearly different subsets give rise to different strings of O's and I's, which yield different decimals, so this function is injective.

CON**C**EPT**C**HE**C**K c) What real number does the set $S = \{2, 3, 4, 5, \ldots\}$ correspond to?

To create an injection going the other way, let $x \in \mathbb{R}$ be any real number. First map x to another real number in the open interval $(0, 1)$ via the function $x \mapsto e^x/(e^x + 1)$. Then write the resulting real number in binary, rather than in base ten. Such a binary number consists of a decimal point followed by an infinite string of 0's and 1's. Now build a subset $S \subseteq \mathbb{N}$ by interpreting a 0 (or 1) in the nth position as an instruction to omit (or include) n from the subset. To illustrate this process, take the real number $x = \ln 2$. This number maps to $\frac{2}{3}$, which has binary decimal expansion $.10101010 \cdots$. Hence the element $S \in \mathcal{P}(\mathbb{N})$ corresponding to $\ln 2$ is the set $\{1, 3, 5, 7, \ldots\}$ of odd numbers.

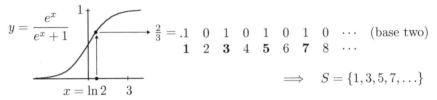

$$y = \frac{e^x}{e^x + 1}$$

$$\frac{2}{3} = .1 \quad 0 \quad 1 \quad 0 \quad 1 \quad 0 \quad 1 \quad 0 \quad \cdots \quad \text{(base two)}$$

$$\phantom{\frac{2}{3} = .} 1 \quad 2 \quad 3 \quad 4 \quad 5 \quad 6 \quad 7 \quad 8 \quad \cdots$$

$$\Longrightarrow \quad S = \{1, 3, 5, 7, \ldots\}$$

Just as before, each step in this process is one-to-one, so the resulting function is injective. We conclude that $|\mathbb{R}| = |\mathcal{P}(\mathbb{N})|$, by the Schroeder-Bernstein Theorem.

CONCEPT CHECK d) Which set S does the real number $x = \ln 3$ correspond to?

It is interesting to note that the correspondence described in the second half of the above proof is very nearly a bijection from $\mathbb{R}$ to $\mathcal{P}(\mathbb{N})$ in and of itself. However, not quite every subset arises in the manner described, due to a peculiarity of decimal expansions. For instance, no real number maps to $\{4, 5, 6, 7, \ldots\}$. This set should correspond to the binary decimal $.00011111 \cdots$, which is equal to $\frac{1}{8}$. But $\frac{1}{8}$ has a more standard binary expansion, namely $.001000 \cdots$, giving the set $\{3\}$. It is the fact that some real numbers have two possible binary decimals (one standard terminating decimal and one non-standard representation involving repeating 1's at the end) that causes the trouble. We mention that Cantor managed to find a patch for this difficulty, so he was able to prove that $|\mathbb{R}| = |\mathcal{P}(\mathbb{N})|$ directly by exhibiting a bijection between these two sets.

To provide one more illustration of the Schroeder-Bernstein Theorem in action, we will demonstrate that there are just as many points on the x-axis as there are above the x-axis. In other words, we will prove that $|\mathbb{R}| = |\mathcal{H}|$, where $\mathcal{H}$ is the upper half plane. It is a simple matter to obtain an injection in one direction; just map the real number x to the point $(x, 1)$. The more delicate task is to turn a point $(x, y) \in \mathcal{H}$ into a single real number. The clever means of doing so involves weaving together the digits of each number. We illustrate this process on the point $(-1234.56, \pi)$.

$$\left. \begin{array}{ccccccccc} -1 & 2 & 3 & 4 & . & 5 & 6 & 0 & 0 & 0 & \cdots \\ 0 & 0 & 0 & 3 & . & 1 & 4 & 1 & 5 & 9 & \cdots \end{array} \right\} \mapsto -10203043.5164010509 \cdots$$

Changing either of the coordinates of the point (x, y) results in a different decimal number when we alternate their digits, so this process defines an injection. Hence $|\mathbb{R}| = |\mathcal{H}|$ by the Schroeder-Bernstein Theorem.[†] A modification of this argument can be used to show that $|\mathbb{R}| = |\mathbb{R} \times \mathbb{R}|$ as well.

a) The identity, mapping $a \mapsto a$ for all $a \in A$, is an injection.

b) If $f : A \to B$ and $g : B \to C$ are both injections, then so is $g \circ f : A \to C$, thereby showing that $|A| \leq |C|$.

c) The set $S = \{2, 3, 4, 5, \ldots\}$ is described by the string $OIIII \cdots$, which corresponds to the decimal expansion $.01111\cdots = 1/90$.

d) The real number $x = \ln 3$ maps to $3/4$, which has binary representation $.110000\cdots$. Hence $\ln 3$ corresponds to the subset of $\{1, 2\}$ of $\mathbb{N}$.

The trick is to handle the positive integer values in A separately from the rest. So for any $x \in A$ which happens to be a positive integer, we declare that $x \mapsto x + 1$. For all other values of x we let $x \mapsto x$. This gives a bijection from A to B.

For the second puzzle it seems that we do not have enough room within the interval $(1, 2)$ to make the same trick work. But there is plenty of room within infinite sets. Consider the two sequences of numbers 1, 1.3, 1.33, 1.333, 1.3333, ... and 2, 1.6, 1.66, 1.666, 1.6666, etc. By mapping each number within these sequences to the next, and mapping all other numbers to themselves, the endpoints of the interval magically disappear and we have a bijection from $[1, 2]$ to $(1, 2)$

EXERCISES

85. Are there finitely many or infinitely many cardinal numbers beyond $\aleph_0$?

86. In the list $\mathbb{N}$, $\mathcal{P}(\mathbb{N})$, $\mathcal{P}(\mathcal{P}(\mathbb{N}))$, $\mathcal{P}(\mathcal{P}(\mathcal{P}(\mathbb{N})))$, ..., which set has the same cardinality as the set of irrational numbers?

87. In the list $\mathbb{N}$, $\mathcal{P}(\mathbb{N})$, $\mathcal{P}(\mathcal{P}(\mathbb{N}))$, $\mathcal{P}(\mathcal{P}(\mathcal{P}(\mathbb{N})))$, ..., which set has the same cardinality as the collection of all subsets of the plane?

88. Construct a bijection between the open interval $(1, 3)$ and the union of open intervals $(1, 2) \cup (2, 3)$.

89. Explain how to create a bijection between $\mathbb{R}$ and the set $\{x \in \mathbb{R} \mid x \geq 0\}$.

90. Describe how to turn an infinite string of a's, b's and c's into a real number.

91. Let A be the set of all infinite sequences using the letters a, b and c. Create an injective function $f : \mathbb{R} \to A$.

92. In the proof that $|\mathbb{R}| = |\mathcal{P}(\mathbb{N})|$ we mapped $x \mapsto e^x/(e^x + 1)$, then converted the result to a binary decimal. Why didn't we convert x to binary right away?

93. In the proof that $|\mathbb{R}| = |\mathcal{P}(\mathbb{N})|$, which real number maps to the set of positive even integers?

94. In the proof that $|\mathbb{R}| = |\mathcal{H}|$, show that $(\sqrt{2}, \sqrt{3})$ and $(\sqrt{3}, \sqrt{2})$ map to different real numbers.

95. In the proof that $|\mathbb{R}| = |\mathcal{H}|$, which point in the plane maps to $25\frac{14}{33}$?

96. The map $g : \mathcal{H} \to \mathbb{R}$ described above comes close to being a bijection. Show that it is not onto by explaining why there is no $(x, y) \in \mathcal{H}$ which maps to $\frac{13}{33}$.

WRITING

97. Use the Schroeder-Bernstein Theorem to prove that the closed interval $[1, 4]$ and the union of open intervals $(0, 1) \cup (2, 3)$ have the same cardinality.

98. Prove that the closed interval $[0, 1]$ has the same cardinality as $\mathbb{R}$.

99. Use the Schroeder-Bernstein Theorem to demonstrate that the set of positive integers which contain the digit 7 has the same cardinality as $\mathbb{N}$.

100. Let D be the set of all infinite sequences using the letters a, b, c and d. Prove that $|D| = |\mathbb{R}|$ via the Schroeder-Bernstein Theorem.

101. Prove that the set of positive real numbers $\{w \in \mathbb{R} \mid w > 0\}$ has the same cardinality as all triples of positive real numbers $\{(x, y, z) \mid x, y, z > 0\}$.

102. Suppose that A is the set of all functions from $(0, 2)$ to $\mathbb{R}$, while B consists of all functions from $\mathbb{R}$ to $\mathbb{R}$. Prove that $|A| = |B|$.

103. Let C be the set of all points in the plane and let D be the set of all lines in the plane. Establish that sets C and D have the same cardinality.

The remaining exercises outline a proof of the Schroeder-Bernstein Theorem.

Suppose that we are given sets A and B along with injective functions $f : A \to B$ and $g : B \to A$. For any $a_0 \in A$ create an infinite sequence as follows. First extend the sequence to the right by letting $b_0 = f(a_0)$, $a_1 = g(b_0)$, $b_1 = f(a_1)$, $a_2 = g(b_1)$, and so on. Then extend the sequence to the left by letting b_{-1} be the element of B for which $g(b_{-1}) = a_0$, if such an element exists. Then define a_{-1} as the element of A for which $g(a_{-1}) = b_{-1}$, if there is such an element. Continue in this manner as far left as possible.

$$\cdots \overset{f}{\longmapsto} b_{-2} \overset{g}{\longmapsto} a_{-1} \overset{f}{\longmapsto} b_{-1} \overset{g}{\longmapsto} a_0 \overset{f}{\longmapsto} b_0 \overset{g}{\longmapsto} a_1 \overset{f}{\longmapsto} b_1 \overset{g}{\longmapsto} a_2 \overset{f}{\longmapsto} \cdots$$

We will use such sequences to create a bijection between A and B.

104. Assuming that it exists, explain why b_{-1} is uniquely determined by a_0. Then argue that all terms to the left of a_0 are uniquely determined by a_0.

105. Prove that if we choose some $\tilde{a}_0$ that does not appear in the sequence above to serve as our initial value, then the resulting sequence $\dots, \tilde{b}_{-2}, \tilde{a}_{-1}, \tilde{b}_{-1}, \tilde{a}_0$, $\tilde{b}_0, \tilde{a}_1, \tilde{b}_1, \dots$ will be completely disjoint from the one above.

106. Explain how these sequences may be used to partition A and B into subsets.

107. Suppose that our sequence terminates to the left at b_{-2} (i.e. no $a_{-2} \mapsto b_{-2}$ exists) and all the terms of the sequence are distinct. Describe how to pair up all the a_k and b_k terms within this sequence.

108. Suppose that our sequence does *not* terminate to the left and all the terms of the sequence are distinct. Describe how to pair up all the a_k and b_k terms.

109. What sort of sequence would result if it so happened that $a_5 = a_0$? How could we pair up all the a_k and b_k terms in this case?

110. Combine all these ideas to construct a bijection between sets A and B.

7.7 Choosing Axioms Carefully

We conclude our foray into the realm of cardinality by addressing the questions raised at the outset of the previous section that have yet to be resolved. To place these questions in the proper context, it will be illuminating to briefly relate a bit more of the story behind the development of modern set theory.

Recall that in the closing decades of the nineteenth century Frege attempted to construct a set theoretic foundation for mathematics, only to have Russell point out an unavoidable paradox inherent in his approach at the turn of the century. In subsequent years a fair amount of effort was directed towards placing set theory on a logically consistent basis. By the late 1920's this program was more or less successfully completed, due to the work of Zermelo and later Fraenkel. The system of axioms they developed has come to be known as Zermelo-Fraenkel set theory (ZF). It was a success in that it provided an internally consistent basis from which arithmetic could be developed and met with widespread acceptance from the mathematical community.

However, it soon became clear that although ZF was consistent, it was not complete. To explain what we mean by this, let us return to the matter of whether or not the list $\mathbb{N}$, $\mathcal{P}(\mathbb{N})$, $\mathcal{P}(\mathcal{P}(\mathbb{N}))$, $\mathcal{P}(\mathcal{P}(\mathcal{P}(\mathbb{N})))$, ... represents every possible cardinal number. We have seen that $\mathbb{N}$ is the "smallest" infinite set in the sense that every infinite set must contain a copy of $\mathbb{N}$ within it. Equivalently, there is no set which is larger than every finite set but smaller than $\mathbb{N}$. It seems as though it ought to follow that there is also no set S that falls strictly between $\mathbb{N}$ and $\mathbb{R}$ in size, thus satisfying $\aleph_0 < |S| < c$. It turns out that the existence of such a set can neither be proven nor disproven using the axioms of ZF! In other words, mathematicians are free to decide whether or not such a set exists, without building an inherent contradiction into set theory. Cantor hypothesized that no such set exists.

The **Continuum Hypothesis** states that there does not exist a set S for which $|\mathbb{N}| < |S| < |\mathbb{R}|$. In other words, there is no cardinal number between $\aleph_0$ and c, the cardinality of the continuum.

Logicians remain divided over whether or not to accept the Continuum Hypothesis, which seems to be as much a philosophical as a mathematical issue.

While we are on the subject, let us clear up one other nagging matter. The alert reader has probably been wondering why we write $|\mathbb{N}| = \aleph_0$, when no mention has been made of $\aleph_1$ or $\aleph_2$, for instance. The official definition of $\aleph_1$ states that it is the next cardinal number after $\aleph_0$. Given the debate over the Continuum Hypothesis, it is unclear whether or not the real numbers should be assigned cardinality $\aleph_1$, rendering this symbol relatively useless for practical purposes. Some mathematicians are in favor of declaring that $|\mathcal{P}(\mathbb{N})| = \aleph_1$, $|\mathcal{P}(\mathcal{P}(\mathbb{N}))| = \aleph_2$, and so on, but there is not sufficient evidence that this is the way that mathematics "ought" to be formulated to sway the verdict.

There is one final loose end to tie off. In the previous section we claimed that the $\leq$ relation on cardinal numbers is a total order. However, we only proved the first three properties that $\leq$ must have in order to qualify as a total order. The fourth condition in that list is better known by the following name.

The **Comparability Theorem** states that given any two sets A and B, either $|A| \leq |B|$ or $|B| \leq |A|$.

While it seems inconceivable that there could exist two infinite sets, neither of which is larger than the other, the Comparability Theorem (like the Continuum Hypothesis) cannot be proven using Zermelo-Fraenkel set theory by itself. The proof requires an independent postulate, known as the **Axiom of Choice**. Zermelo formulated this statement in the midst of his development of set theory; however, it was initially regarded with skepticism and consequently was not packaged into ZF along with the other axioms.

By now the Axiom of Choice (AC) is widely accepted within the mathematical community, in part because it is required to rigorously establish a number of results whose validity is highly desirable. We have just indicated that the Comparability Theorem is one such result. The Axiom of Choice is also necessary to guarantee that an infinite dimensional vector space has a basis. You may have even invoked AC earlier in this chapter without realizing it while working on the Section 7.2 problems—it is needed to prove that if a set A is infinite then there exists an injection $g : \mathbb{N} \to A$.

Dewdney once quipped that the Axiom of Choice is so named *not* because mathematicians prefer it to other axioms. Rather, it refers to the process of making infinitely many arbitrary choices. To illustrate, consider how one might go about constructing an injective function $g : \mathbb{N} \to A$ when A is infinite. We begin by defining $g(1) = a_1$, where a_1 is any element of A. Next we let $g(2) = a_2$, where a_2 is some element of A other than a_1. Continuing, we choose a third element $a_3 \in A$ distinct from a_1 and a_2 and let $g(3) = a_3$, and so forth. Since A is infinite we never exhaust our supply of elements to choose from, hence we can be certain that no output is duplicated as we define g.

This process of defining g feels so natural that it is easy to overlook the fact that no tenant of Zermelo-Fraenkel set theory ensures that such a process is permissible, technically speaking. The catch is that we are making infinitely many *arbitrary* choices as we build our function. We don't know anything about A other than the fact that it contains infinitely many elements, so the best we can do is to declare that a_1 is "some element of A"—we can't actually specify a particular value for $g(1)$, though. The same is true for each of the choices we made when defining $g(2)$, $g(3)$, and so on. The situation is entirely different when we define an injection $g : \mathbb{N} \to (0,2)$ by declaring that $g(n) = \frac{1}{n}$, for instance. In this case we are specifying exactly what value $g(n)$ should take for each $n \in \mathbb{N}$: we want $g(1) = 1$, $g(2) = \frac{1}{2}$, $g(3) = \frac{1}{3}$, etc. Hence there is no need to call upon the Axiom of Choice.

However, the Axiom of Choice does lead to some rather paradoxical results. Perhaps the best known among these is the Banach-Tarski paradox. The paradox, which is actually a theorem that relies on AC, demonstrates that it is possible to partition the points within a solid unit sphere into a finite number of subsets which can then be moved through space using only rigid motions (rotations and translations) and reassembled into two unit spheres without any of the pieces overlapping and without either of the resulting spheres lacking even a single point. Obviously the sets of points utilized in such a trick are rather fantastical; they could not be physically realized. But from an ideal mathematical viewpoint such sets of points do exist, if we accept the Axiom of Choice.

Naturally there is more to say about AC than was mentioned in this section. The interested reader should also consider learning about the Well-ordering Theorem and Zorn's Lemma, each of which is equivalent to the Axiom of Choice. In fact, most of the mathematics contained within these chapters represents only the barest of introductions to the subjects which they introduced. The student who pursues them in more depth will discover many beautiful and compelling results along the way. Good luck, and enjoy the mathematics!

7.8 Reference

• *Vocabulary* cardinality, finite set, infinite set, denumerable, countable, uncountable, Cantor's diagonal argument, Cantor's Theorem, continuum, cardinal number, Schroeder-Bernstein Theorem, Continuum Hypothesis, Comparability Theorem, Axiom of Choice

• *Comparing Sets* Two sets A and B have the same cardinality precisely when there exists a bijection $f : A \to B$, in which case we write $|A| = |B|$. When there is an injective function $g : A \to B$ then the cardinality of B is at least as large as that of A, denoted by $|A| \le |B|$. If there exists an injection from A to B but no bijection, then we have $|A| < |B|$.

• *Terminology and Notation* A given set A is finite if either A is the empty set, in which case $|A| = 0$, or if there is a bijection $f : C_n \to A$, in which case $|A| = n$. (Recall that $C_n = \{1, 2, \ldots, n\}$.) A set which is not finite is called an infinite set. We say that A is denumerable if there is a bijection $f : \mathbb{N} \to A$ and write $|A| = \aleph_0$. The finite and denumerable sets together make up the countable sets; denumerable sets are also referred to as countably infinite sets. Any set that is not countable, such as the set of real numbers (the continuum), is called uncountable. A set A the size of the continuum is indicated by writing $|A| = c$.

• *Cardinalities of Common Sets* Denumerable sets include $\mathbb{N}$, $\mathbb{Z}$, $\mathbb{Q}$, and the set of primes. If A and B are denumerable sets then so are $A \cup B$, $A \times B$, but *not* $\mathcal{P}(A)$. Sets having the cardinality of the continuum include $\mathbb{R}$, $\mathbb{R} \times \mathbb{R}$, the set of irrational numbers, the open interval $(0, 1)$, $\mathcal{P}(\mathbb{N})$, and all infinite sequences of a's and b's. Sets with strictly larger cardinality than the continuum include $\mathcal{P}(\mathbb{R})$ and the set of all functions $f : \mathbb{R} \to \mathbb{R}$.

• *Theorems on Cardinality* Cantor's Theorem states that for any set S the power set of S has a strictly greater cardinality than S. In other words, $|S| < |\mathcal{P}(S)|$ for all sets S. The relation $\leq$ provides a total order on the collection of all cardinal numbers. The fact that $\leq$ is antisymmetric is the Schroeder-Bernstein Theorem, which states that if there exist injections $f : A \to B$ and $g : B \to A$ for sets A and B, then it follows that $|A| = |B|$. The Comparability Theorem, which states that $|A| \leq |B|$ or $|B| \leq |A|$ for any two sets, relies on the Axiom of Choice. This axiom, which is independent of the other axioms of Zermelo-Fraenkel set theory (ZF), allows us to make infinitely many arbitrary choices in the course of a proof. The Continuum Hypothesis claims that there does not exist a set S for which $\aleph_0 < |S| < c$; this statement is also independent of ZF.

PROOF STRATEGIES

* *Equal Cardinality* The most direct approach for showing that sets A and B have the same cardinality is to define a function $f : A \to B$, then prove that it is a bijection by showing that it is both one-to-one and onto. Another method is to determine the size of each set separately. For instance, one could conclude that $|A| = |B|$ if one could show that both A and B were denumerable sets. A third approach is to construct functions $f : A \to B$ and $g : B \to A$ and then prove that both f and g are injections, for then the Schroeder-Bernstein Theorem would imply that $|A| = |B|$.

* *Infinite Sets* To prove that a set A is infinite using the definition, suppose to the contrary that A is finite, meaning that its elements can be listed as $A = \{a_1, a_2, \ldots, a_n\}$. Then demonstrate how to construct some element of A that was overlooked, usually by finding a "largest" element (by some measure) in the list and then exhibiting an even larger one. One can also construct an injective function $g : \mathbb{N} \to A$ to show that A is infinite. This amounts to writing down an infinite sequence of distinct terms $a_1, a_2, a_3, \ldots$ of elements of A which follow some simple pattern, so that it is possible to create a formula for the nth term. This formula is the desired injection g.

* *Denumerable Sets* To prove that a set A is denumerable using the definition, illustrate a means of numbering the elements of A using all the natural numbers. This is equivalent to listing all the elements $a_1, a_2, a_3, \ldots$ of A in an infinite sequence. For sets A that are more irregular, prove that A is infinite using a technique from the previous paragraph and also show that A is a subset of a known denumerable set. Finally, one could construct a bijection $f : D \to A$ with a known denumerable set D.

* *Uncountable Sets* To show directly that a given set A is uncountable, suppose to the contrary that A is countable, meaning that the elements of A may be listed as $a_1, a_2, a_3, \ldots$ in a sequence. Then prove that some element of A must have been omitted, usually by employing Cantor's diagonal argument. It would also suffice to exhibit an injective function $g : E \to A$ for some set E known to be uncountable, such as the open interval $(0, 1)$ or the set of infinite sequences of a's and b's.

SAMPLE PROOFS

The following proofs provide concise explanations for results discussed within this chapter. They are meant to serve as an illustration for how proofs of similar statements could be phrased. The boldface numbers indicate the section containing each result; the location of that result within the section is marked by a dagger (†).

$\longleftrightarrow$

7.1 Show that the closed intervals $A = [2, 4]$ and $B = [0, 5]$ are sets having the same cardinality.

Proof We claim that the function $g(x) = \frac{5}{2}x - 5$ provides a bijection $g : A \to B$. We must first confirm that g has the correct codomain; i.e. that if we compute $g(x)$ for a number $x \in A$ the output is actually in B. We find that if $2 \le x \le 4$ then $5 \le \frac{5}{2}x \le 10$, hence $0 \le \frac{5}{2}x - 5 \le 5$. In other words, $g(x) \in B$, as desired.

We now show that g is one-to-one and onto. Suppose that $g(x_1) = g(x_2)$. This means that $\frac{5}{2}x_1 - 5 = \frac{5}{2}x_2 - 5$, which quickly yields $x_1 = x_2$, showing that g is one-to-one. Furthermore, given any $w \in B$ we will show that $\frac{2}{5}w + 2$ maps to w. We first check that $\frac{2}{5}w + 2 \in A$. This follows since $0 \le w \le 5$ gives $0 \le \frac{2}{5}w \le 2$, thus $2 \le \frac{2}{5}w + 2 \le 4$. Finally, we compute

$$g\left(\frac{2}{5}w + 2\right) = \frac{5}{2}\left(\frac{2}{5}w + 2\right) - 5 = (w + 5) - 5 = w.$$

Therefore g is also onto, which completes the proof that $g : A \to B$ is a bijection.

$\longleftrightarrow$

7.2 Let set B consist of all positive rational numbers whose numerator and denominator differ by 3 or less when written in lowest terms. Prove that B is an infinite set.

Proof Suppose to the contrary that B were only a finite set, meaning that we could we could label the fractions in B as $r_1, r_2, \ldots, r_n$. Of all the numerators appearing among these fractions let N be the largest. Now consider the fraction $(N + 1)/(N + 2)$. This fraction is an element of B, since it is in lowest terms and its numerator and denominator differ by 1. But by construction it is not equal to any of $r_1, r_2, \ldots, r_n$, since its numerator is too large. This contradicts the fact that the list $r_1, r_2, \ldots, r_n$ supposedly included all the elements of B. Therefore we have shown that B is an infinite set.

$\longleftrightarrow$

7.2 Explain why the set B of rational numbers between 2 and 3 is infinite.

Proof We will show that the function $g : \mathbb{N} \to B$ given by $g(n) = 2 + \frac{n}{n+1}$ is an injection. First note that this formula can be written in several different ways:

$$g(n) = 2 + \frac{n}{n + 1} = 3 - \frac{1}{n + 1} = \frac{3n + 2}{n + 1}.$$

It is clear that $g(n)$ is a rational number since n is an integer. It is also clear from the first two expressions above that $g(n)$ falls between 2 and 3 for all n.

Furthermore, g is injective because if $g(n_1) = g(n_2)$ then

$$3 - \frac{1}{n_1 + 1} = 3 - \frac{1}{n_2 + 1} \quad \Longrightarrow \quad \frac{1}{n_2 + 1} = \frac{1}{n_1 + 1},$$

from which we quickly find that $n_1 + 1 = n_2 + 1$ giving $n_1 = n_2$. Since we have found an injection $g : \mathbb{N} \to B$, we conclude that B is infinite.

———◆———

7.3 Demonstrate that the set of all functions $g : \{a, b\} \to \mathbb{N}$ is denumerable.

Proof   A function $g : \{a, b\} \to \mathbb{N}$ is determined by choosing a value for $g(a)$ and a value for $g(b)$. Hence each such function corresponds to a pair of natural numbers, which means that the set of all such functions is in one-to-one correspondence with $\mathbb{N} \times \mathbb{N}$. But the latter set is known to be denumerable, so the set of functions $g : \{a, b\} \to \mathbb{N}$ must be also.

———◆———

7.3 Prove that the set $\mathbb{Q}$ of rational numbers is denumerable.

Proof   We will show that $\mathbb{Q}$ is an infinite set and that the rational numbers can be viewed as a subset of $\mathbb{Z} \times \mathbb{Z}$, which is a known denumerable set. To begin, $\mathbb{Q}$ is clearly infinite since it contains a copy of $\mathbb{N}$ embedded within it. Now take any rational number and write it in lowest terms in the form p/q, with $p \in \mathbb{Z}$ and $q \in \mathbb{N}$. (For instance, we would write $-2\frac{3}{4}$ as $-11/4$, with $p = -11$ and $q = 4$.) Hence each rational gives rise to an order pair (p, q) of integers. Since different rationals correspond to different ordered pairs of integers, $\mathbb{Q}$ can be viewed as a subset of $\mathbb{Z} \times \mathbb{Z}$, completing the proof.

———◆———

7.4 Prove that the set $\mathcal{P}$ of all infinite strings of a's and b's is uncountable.

Proof   Suppose to the contrary that $\mathcal{P}$ is countable, meaning that we can include all the infinite strings in a list, say p_1, p_2, p_3, $\ldots$, where each p_n represents an infinite string of a's and b's. We now create a new infinite string by determining the nth letter of p_n and using the other letter as the nth letter of our new string. Clearly this string of a's and b's cannot match any one appearing on the list. For it differs from p_1 at the first letter, it differs from p_2 at the second letter, and so on. Hence our list does not include all possible infinite strings, contradicting our assumption that it did. Therefore the set $\mathcal{P}$ is indeed uncountable.

———◆———

7.5 Prove that $|\mathbb{R}| < |\mathcal{P}(\mathbb{R})|$, where the power set $\mathcal{P}(\mathbb{R})$ denotes the collection of all subsets of the real numbers, as usual.

Proof   To show that $|\mathbb{R}| < |\mathcal{P}(\mathbb{R})|$, we will first exhibit an injective function $f : \mathbb{R} \to \mathcal{P}(\mathbb{R})$, then show that there does not exist a bijection between these two sets. To begin, consider the function $f : \mathbb{R} \to \mathcal{P}(\mathbb{R})$ mapping each real number x to the subset $\{x\}$ of $\mathbb{R}$ containing the single element x. This mapping is clearly one-to-one, thus so far we may conclude that $|\mathbb{R}| \le |\mathcal{P}(\mathbb{R})|$.

However, we claim that no function $f : \mathbb{R} \to \mathcal{P}(\mathbb{R})$ can be a surjection. To see why, consider any $f : \mathbb{R} \to \mathcal{P}(\mathbb{R})$, meaning that $f(x)$ is some subset of $\mathbb{R}$. Based on this particular function we will now construct a set $C \subseteq \mathbb{R}$ that is not the image of any $x \in \mathbb{R}$, which will imply that f is not onto. For each real number x, include x in our set C precisely when x is *not* an element of $f(x)$. We claim that $C \neq f(x)$ for any $x \in \mathbb{R}$. This follows because for each $x \in \mathbb{R}$, if $x \in f(x)$ then $x \notin C$, and vice-versa, by our construction of C. Since x will always be in one set and not the other for each $x \in \mathbb{R}$, set C differs from every set $f(x)$, which means that it is not in the image of $f : \mathbb{R} \to \mathcal{P}(\mathbb{R})$. Therefore f is not a bijection, and we deduce that $|\mathbb{R}| < |\mathcal{P}(\mathbb{R})|$.

———————◆———————

7.6 Demonstrate that the sets $\mathbb{R}$ and $\mathcal{H}$ have the same cardinality, where $\mathcal{H}$ is the upper half plane; i.e. the set of all points (x, y) with $y > 0$.

Proof By Schroeder-Bernstein, we need only furnish injective functions from each set into the other. It is a simple matter to exhibit an injection from $\mathbb{R}$ to $\mathcal{H}$; just map the real number x to the point $(x, 1)$. To obtain an injective function in the other direction, we take a point $(x, y) \in \mathcal{H}$ and weave together the digits in the decimal expansions of x and y to create a single real number. We illustrate this process on the point $(-1234.56, \pi)$.

$$
\left.
\begin{array}{cccccccccc}
-1 & 2 & 3 & 4 & . & 5 & 6 & 0 & 0 & 0 & \cdots \\
0 & 0 & 0 & 3 & . & 1 & 4 & 1 & 5 & 9 & \cdots
\end{array}
\right\} \mapsto -10203043.5164010509\cdots
$$

Changing either of the coordinates of the point (x, y) results in a different decimal number when we alternate their digits, so this process defines an injection. (Note that there is no ambiguity regarding the negative sign, since y is always positive.) Hence $|\mathbb{R}| = |\mathcal{H}|$ by the Schroeder-Bernstein Theorem.

CHAPTER 8

Answers and Hints

These pages contain answers to every exercise appearing in the book. Before getting overly excited, though, keep in mind that a thorough understanding of an exercise encompasses much more than just the correct answer. It will include a mastery of notation and vocabulary, a working knowledge of the material on which the exercise is based, discussions with classmates that reveal alternate methods of solution, and so on. That being said, having an answer key at one's disposal does have its advantages. At the very least an answer serves as a blaze on a trail; it provides an indication that one is (or isn't, as the case may be) headed in the right direction.

Hints to all of the writing problems are also included below. They should be used sparingly, of course, and certainly never consulted before a sincere effort has been made to first solve a problem independently. Each hint will hopefully guide the solver in a fruitful direction, perhaps even past an obstacle or two. But good math problems will typically yield to several different approaches, only one of which is indicated by a hint. So don't become worried if you have found a solution that seems to strike out in a different direction than the one suggested by the hint. Just be sure that your solution addresses any issues that may be raised by the hint. Good luck with the problems, and enjoy the math!

Chapter 1: Logical Foundations

1.1 Statements and Open Sentences

EXERCISES

1. a) False b) True c) True d) True e) False
2. The open sentence is true for $n = 2$ and false for $n = 11$
3. The set of even numbers
4. $x = 40$ is the only solution
5. n is an integer, k is a positive integer, and x is a real number
6. The equation is satisfied if $x + 3 = 0$ OR $x^2 - 9 = 0$
7. a) True b) False c) True d) False e) False f) True g) True
8. $n = 9$ and $n = 15$ also serve as counterexamples

WRITING

9. Consider the latest arrival time and the earliest departure time. Why must the latter occur later than the former?

10. Group the twenty students into ten pairs of adjacent students. (But don't argue along the lines that if the first student can recite π then the second one can't, so the third one must know π, etc. This approach doesn't consider all possible arrangements.)

11. If all the students received the same grade on the first quiz then we are done. Otherwise, two students got different grades on the first quiz; call them A and B. Hence we know that A and B got the same grade on the second quiz. Now show that any other student C must have gotten the same grade as A and B on the second quiz.

1.2 Logical Equivalence

EXERCISES

13. a) $\neg P \wedge \neg Q \wedge \neg R$ b) $P \wedge \neg R$ c) $(P \vee Q) \wedge R$ d) $\neg(Q \wedge R)$ e) $(P \wedge \neg Q) \vee (\neg P \wedge Q)$

14. The truth tables will not match; for instance, when P and Q are both false then $\neg(P \wedge Q)$ is true while $\neg P \wedge Q$ is false.

15. Both statements indicate that neither action will be taken. Letting P be "I will run for president," and Q be "I will stage a military coup," the two statements may be written as $\neg(P \vee Q)$ and $\neg P \wedge \neg Q$.

16. The truth tables match; they will contain three F's and a T in that order.

17. a) Triangle ABC doesn't have a perimeter of 12 or doesn't have an area of 6.

b) The number k is an integer such that k is odd and $k > 10$.

c) I am younger than Al or older than Betty.

d) It is the case that $2x < y$ and $2y < x$.

e) Jack will not answer this question nor the next one.

f) There is not a new car behind any of the doors.

18. b) is correct; the truth tables for $P \wedge (Q \vee R)$ and $(P \wedge Q) \vee (P \wedge R)$ are identical.

19. The statement P EOR Q is true when P is true and Q is false, and also when P is false and Q is true. The statement is false in the other two cases.

20. One possibility is $(P \wedge \neg Q) \vee (\neg P \wedge Q)$.

21. The truth tables for $(P \wedge Q) \vee R$ and $P \wedge (Q \vee R)$ do not match. For instance, when P is false and R is true (and Q is either true or false) the former statement is true while the latter statement is false.

22. The statement $P \vee Q \vee R$ is true whenever at least one of P, Q or R is true. But the statement $P \wedge Q \wedge R$ is true only if all three of P, Q and R are true.

23. The truth table should contain all T's.

24. The truth table should contain all F's.

25. Create a truth table with two rows, where P is always false but Q can be either true or false. The outcome should be false in both cases.

WRITING

26. The oldest son only needs to buy a vote from two of his younger brothers (by giving them a better deal than dad would) in order to ensure that his plan is voted in.

27. This situation is considerably more intricate. The oldest son's best strategy is to allocate the dollar bills in a manner that will cause the second brother to increase the oldest son's share in order to buy his vote, say by proposing a 6–0–7–7–0 distribution.

28. There are relatively few products that Mr. Strump could have had in mind. For example, if he told Abby that the product was 14, Abby would know that his digits were 2 and 7, since this is the only pair of digits which multiply to give 14. Begin by finding all five products that can be obtained in more than one way.

1.3 The Implication

EXERCISES

29. a) If it rains, then it pours. b) If I try escargot then Al must eat some first. c) If $7a$ is even then a is even. d) If a fire was started then a match was lit. e) If $\angle A \cong \angle B$ then $\triangle ABC$ is isosceles. f) If the discriminant is positive then the quadratic has two distinct solutions.

30. We would need to find a prime p for which $2^p - 1$ is not prime.

31. The implication $P \Rightarrow Q$ is logically equivalent to $\neg P \vee Q$.

32. Both truth tables should read F, T, F, F in that order.

33. a) Cinderella married the prince but I didn't eat my hat. b) The number a^2 is divisible by 12 but a is odd and a is not a multiple of 3. c) Quadrilateral $ABCD$ has four congruent sides but is not a square. d) One can make bread and omit at least one of flour, water or yeast.

34. a) $n = 9$ b) $n = 3$ c) $n = 73$ d) $n = 4$ (Other answers are possible.)

35. The only such value is $x = 2$.

36. The implication is true exactly when $y > -2$. For all $y \leq -2$ the premise $y < 2$ is true but the conclusion $y^2 < 4$ is false.

37. The statement may be interpreted to say that if both P and $P \Rightarrow Q$ are true, then it follows that Q is true. The truth table reveals that the statement is a tautology, which validates it as a rule of inference.

38. The statement can be translated to mean that if P implies Q and Q implies R, then it follows that P implies R. Now finish as before.

WRITING

39. Pick any student, whom we shall call A. Now explain why among the remaining students A either knows at least three of them or is unacquainted with at least three of them. Suppose A knows B, C and D. What happens if any of these three know each other? What happens if none of them are acquainted?

40. Notice that n handshakes involve $2n$ hands, which is an even number.

41. How many handshakes could a particular guest make? What is forced to occur if all eight guests shake hands a different number of times, and why is this a problem?

1.4 The Biconditional

EXERCISES

42. a) True b) False c) False d) False e) True

43. It would be a value of x for which one of P or Q is true while the other is false.

44. The truth tables should agree.

45. They are not logically equivalent. For example, when P is true but Q and R are false we find that $(P \vee Q) \Longleftrightarrow R$ is false while $(P \Longleftrightarrow R) \vee (Q \Longleftrightarrow R)$ is true.

46. a) For integers n, if $n^2 + 5$ is a multiple of 3, then n is not a multiple of 3.
b) If two rectangles have the same area then they are congruent.
c) For positive real numbers, if $1/x \leq 1/y$ then $x \geq y$.
d) If R is in quadrant I and L is in quadrant II, then line RL has positive y-intercept.
e) For positive integers a and b, if the number $a + b$ involves the digit 0, then both a and b have the digit 0.

47. a) True, true, equivalent b) True, false, not equivalent c) True, true, equivalent
d) False, true, not equivalent e) False, false, not equivalent

48. The only way for $P \Rightarrow Q$ to be false is for P to be true but for Q to be false. However, in this case $Q \Rightarrow P$ would be true.

49. The truth tables for $Q \Rightarrow P$ and $\neg P \Rightarrow \neg Q$ are identical.

50. a) Let k be a positive integer. If $3^k + 1$ is a multiple of 4 then k is odd.

b) If $ABCD$ does not have four congruent sides then it is not a square.

c) For a real number a, if a is positive then $2^x = a$ has a solution.

WRITING

51. Clearly we have a winning position when $n \leq 4$, since the player about to move can win by taking all the pennies. However, $n = 5$ represents a losing position. (Why?) Use this fact to explain how to guarantee a win when $n = 6, 7, 8$ or 9.

52. Carefully examine each value of n, beginning with $n = 1$ and working your way upwards. You should find that of the first seven values, only $n = 2$ and $n = 7$ are losing positions. For instance, $n = 6$ is a winning position, since it is possible to take four pennies, thereby handing a losing position to the other player.

1.5 Quantifiers

EXERCISES

54. a) There exists an integer n such that n contains every odd digit.

b) There does not exist a real number x for which $x^2 + 4x + 5 = 0$.

c) There exists a unique point C on the lines $y = x$ and $y = 3x - 5$.

d) There exists a unique real number t such that $|t - 4| \leq 3$ and $|t + 5| \leq 6$.

e) For all integers k the number $6k + 5$ is odd.

f) There exists a point U such that the distance from U to the origin is positive.

55. For all real numbers x we have $\cos x \neq 3x$.

56. There exists a positive integer n such that n is prime but $2^n - 1$ is not prime. This is the case for $n = 11$, for instance, since $2^{11} - 1 = 2047 = 23 \cdot 89$.

57. There is a linear function $f(x)$ for which $f(1) + f(2) \neq f(3)$. When $f(x) = 2x + 5$ we have $f(1) = 7$, $f(2) = 9$ and $f(3) = 11$, and sure enough $7 + 9 \neq 11$.

58. The square is not unique—there are three such squares. Can you find them all?

59. Quadratic equations usually have two solutions or no solutions. But when $a = -16$ the equation has exactly one solution. Try applying the quadratic formula to see why.

60. There exists a rectangle in the plane such that no circle is tangent to all four sides. (Literally, "such that every circle is not tangent to all four sides.")

61. The claim is true, as it asserts that given any real number, there is a larger one.

62. This claim is false, as there is no real number larger than every other real number.

63. For every positive integer N there is some integer $n > N$ with $\cos n \geq 0.99$.

64. The assertion is false; we could choose $x = 7$ and $y = 7$, for instance.

65. One can take $m = 3$ and $n = 5$, for example. Other answers are possible.

66. The statement does not necessarily follow. It might be the case that sometimes P is true and Q is false, while at other times P is false and Q is true. This occurs for the statements "m is odd" and "m is even," for example.

WRITING

67. Find values of b that work for $a = 1, 2, 3$ and 4. Do you notice a pattern?

68. Choose the length of the rectangle to guarantee that the perimeter is at least $4r$.

69. Such a path will need to meander into every part of the plane and always pass relatively close to itself. What sort of curve will accomplish this?

70. Choose a polynomial that factors to guarantee that $f(n)$ also factors.

71. The desired triangle will need to be small. What quantity can we use to measure the size of a triangle? Now examine the triangle for which this quantity is the smallest.

Chapter 2: Set Theory

2.1 Presenting Sets

EXERCISES

1. The empty set, since the Jamaican flag is yellow, green and black.
2. The numbers appearing in this set are powers of positive integers; i.e. the perfect squares, cubes, fourth powers, and so on.
3. This set consists of those months having 31 days.
4. One answer could be $\{-2x + 6, 4x^2 - 12x - 100, 6x^3 + 8x^2 + 10\}$.
5. We could take $C = \{\{a, b, c, d\}, \{a, c, e, g\}\}$, for instance.
6. We have $D = \{2, 6, 12, 20, 30, 42, \ldots\}$ or $D = \{n(n+1) \mid n \in \mathbb{N}\}$. The second option is probably better as it clarifies the method by which the elements of D are generated.
7. a) False b) True c) False d) False e) Depends f) True
8. There are six such sets, for instance {NH, ME, MA, RI, CT}.
9. a) $A = \{7k \mid k \in \mathbb{Z}\}$ b) $B = \{2^n + 1 \mid n \in \mathbb{N}\}$ c) $C = \{x \mid x \in \mathbb{R}, \sqrt{2} < x < \pi\}$
d) $D = \{1/(m + 1) \mid m \in \mathbb{N}\}$
10. The first set is $\{m/n \mid m, n \in \mathbb{N}$ and $m < n\}$. The second set may be described as $\{m/2^k \mid m, k \in \mathbb{Z}$ and $m \geq 1, k \geq 0\}$.
11. These objects are equations of non-vertical lines passing through the point $(1, 0)$. (Note that the objects are *equations*, not actually lines.)
12. We have $10 \notin B$ but $13 \in B$.

WRITING

13. Given any three integers, why must two of them have the same parity? (I.e. be both even or both odd.)
14. What would go wrong if every letter of the alphabet were either in all three sets or else in none of them?
15. Suppose that 1 and 2 are in the same set, say $1, 2 \in A$. Then we must have $3 \in B$. Now explain why there must be some other number $n \geq 6$ also in A, then argue that $n-2, n-1, n+1$, and $n+2$ must all be in B. Why is this a problem? Finally, handle the case where 1 and 2 are in different sets.
16. First subdivide the points in C into four smaller 3×3 squares, then explain why it is not possible for all five chosen points to occupy different squares.

2.2 Combining Sets

EXERCISES

17. The set is $A \cup \overline{B}$.
18. One possibility is $A = \{a, b, c, d, e\}$ and $B = \{d, e, f, g\}$. Regardless of your choice, you should find that $|\overline{A} \cap \overline{B}| = 1$.
19. The first statement requires that $u \in A$ and $u \in B$. So must have $u \in A \cup B$.
20. a) True b) True c) False d) True e) False f) False g) False
21. $A \cup C = \{x \mid 1 < x < 6\}$, $(A \cup B) \cap C = \{x \mid 2 < x < 3$ or $5 \leq x < 6\}$ and finally $B \cap \overline{C} = \{x \mid 6 \leq x \leq 7\}$
22. We have $x \in A$ and $x \in B$ (region II), $x \in A$ and $x \notin B$ (region I), $x \notin A$ and $x \in B$ (region III), $x \notin A$ and $x \notin B$ (region IV)
23. The Venn diagram for either set consists solely of the region outside of all three circles. (Diagram omitted.)
24. The Venn diagram for either set consists of that portion of circle A which overlaps with the other two circles. (Diagram omitted.)

WRITING

25. The only way two sets can fail to be equal is if some object belongs to one of the sets but not the other. Explain why this cannot occur.

26. According to our strategy, we should first show that if $x \in \overline{A \cup B}$ then $x \in \overline{A} \cap \overline{B}$. Begin by noting that $x \in \overline{A \cup B}$ means that $x \notin A \cup B$, so x can be in neither A nor B, since it is not in their union.

27. Suppose that $x \in A \cup (B \cap C)$. This means that either $x \in A$ or $x \in B \cap C$. Now argue that in either case x is an element of both $A \cup B$ and $A \cup C$.

28. Adapt the proof given in the text so that it applies to four sets instead of just two.

29. We need to count how many letters are in neither of the sets A nor B. Why can't we just subtract off the number of elements of A and B from the total number of letters in the alphabet to get the correct answer?

30. Let x_1 through x_8 represent the number of elements within each of the eight regions in a Venn diagram for three sets. Now rewrite each side of the inequality in terms of x_1 through x_8.

2.3 Subsets and Power Sets

EXERCISES

32. We should write $A - \{l\}$.

33. We would have $\overline{B} \subseteq \overline{A}$.

34. The set $B - A$ would be nonempty.

35. Both are valid. Since the elements of $\mathcal{P}(A)$ are subsets of A, in $\emptyset \subseteq \mathcal{P}(A)$ the empty set means "the set containing no subsets of A." On the other hand, in $\emptyset \in \mathcal{P}(A)$ the empty set here plays the role of a subset of A, and hence an element in $\mathcal{P}(A)$.

36. a) False b) True c) True d) False e) False

37. We might have $B = \{d, e, l, i, g, h, t\}$ and $A = \{v, a, l, i, d\}$, for instance.

38. We must have $|A - B| = 44$.

39. The empty set.

40. There are 15 nonempty subsets of B that are disjoint from the set $\{s, t, r, e, a, m\}$.

41. There are 10 subsets of $\{s, a, t, i, n\}$ having exactly two elements.

42. Exactly 64 subsets of A contain the element m.

43. There are 48 subsets in $\mathcal{P}(B) - \mathcal{P}(A)$.

WRITING

44. Suppose that $x \in A \cap B$, so that $x \in A$ and $x \in B$. Figure out why $x \notin B - A$.

45. If we have $x \in \overline{B \cup C}$ then $x \notin B \cup C$, which only occurs when $x \notin B$ and $x \notin C$. Now use these facts to argue that $x \notin (A \cap B) \cup C$.

46. Begin your proof "We must show that if $x \in (A \cup B) \cap C$ then $x \in A \cup (B \cap C)$." But if $x \in (A \cup B) \cap C$ we know that $x \in A \cup B$ and $x \in C$. Now consider two cases; either $x \in A$ and $x \in C$ or $x \in B$ and $x \in C$. Show that $x \in A \cup (B \cap C)$ regardless.

47. Begin your proof by writing "We must show that if $x \in (A - B) - C$ then $x \in A - (B - C)$." Figure out why $x \in (A - B) - C$ leads to $x \in A$, $x \notin B$ and $x \notin C$, then employ these facts to show that $x \in A - (B - C)$.

48. We need to prove that $A \cup \overline{C} \subseteq A \cup \overline{B}$, i.e. we need to show that if $x \in A \cup \overline{C}$ then it follows that $x \in A \cup \overline{B}$. So suppose that $x \in A \cup \overline{C}$. This means that $x \in A$ or $x \in \overline{C}$. Now consider each case separately and show that $x \in A \cup \overline{B}$ regardless.

49. We need to prove that $\overline{C} \subseteq \overline{A} \cup B$, so begin by supposing that $x \in \overline{C}$. This means that $x \notin C$, so deduce that $x \notin A - B$ either. The trickiest step in this argument is to figure out how to deal with $x \notin A - B$. This could occur in two ways—either $x \notin A$ at all, or else $x \in A$ but $x \in B$ also.

50. We need to show that if X is an element of $\mathcal{P}(A)$ (which means that $X \subseteq A$) or if X is an element of $\mathcal{P}(B)$, then X is in $\mathcal{P}(A \cup B)$. Consider each case separately.

51. Note that we have a set equality to prove here, which involves two separate arguments. Begin by explaining why it is the case that if $X \in \mathcal{P}(A)$ and $X \in \mathcal{P}(B)$ (i.e. that $X \subseteq A$ and $X \subseteq B$) then it follows that $X \in \mathcal{P}(A \cap B)$.

52. One could prove that each set is a subset of the other, but there is an alternate approach available. Show that the only subsets removed from $\mathcal{P}(B)$ when subtracting subsets in $\mathcal{P}(A)$ are those subsets all of whose elements are contained in $A \cap B$.

53. Consider the fate of each piece of candy separately, just as we did in the process of building a subset earlier in the section.

2.4 Cartesian Products

EXERCISES

54. It must be the case that $A = \emptyset$ or $B = \emptyset$.

55. We define $A \times B = \{(a, b) \mid a \in A \text{ and } b \in B\}$.

56. The set of cards is the Cartesian product of the suits ($\spadesuit$, $\heartsuit$, $\diamondsuit$, $\clubsuit$) with the possible card values (A, 2, 3, ..., Q, K).

57. a) 81 b) 15 c) 24 d) 66 e) 12 f) 9

58. The two sets cannot be equal, since they have a different number of elements.

59. An ellipse, or more precisely, the graph of an equation of an ellipse.

60. a) The region is a rectangle in the first quadrant having width 2 and height 3. b) This region is also a rectangle, but with width 3 and height 2. c) The intersection will be the square with vertices $(2, 2)$, $(2, 3)$, $(3, 3)$ and $(3, 2)$.

61. The intersection will be the Cartesian product $\{c, a, p, e, r\} \times \{2, 3, 5\}$, a set consisting of 15 ordered pairs.

62. The set $A \times B \times C$ is all ordered triples (a, b, c) with $a \in A$, $b \in B$ and $c \in C$.

63. We have $|A \times B \times C| = |A| \cdot |B| \cdot |C| = 5 \cdot 6 \cdot 3 = 90$.

WRITING

64. Suppose that $(x, y) \in \overline{A} \times \overline{B}$. This means that $x \in \overline{A}$ and $y \in \overline{B}$. In particular, we may conclude that $x \notin A$. Consequently, is $(x, y) \in A \times B$?

65. We must show that each set is a subset of the other. To begin, suppose that $(x, y) \in A \times (B \cup C)$. This means that $x \in A$ and $y \in B \cup C$; that is, $y \in B$ or $y \in C$. Now consider the case $y \in B$ and show that $(x, y) \in (A \times B) \cup (A \times C)$, etc.

66. One conjectures that the two sets are equal. To prove this, we show that each set is a subset of the other. For instance, if $(x, y) \in (A \times B) - (A \times C)$, then $(x, y) \in A \times B$ but $(x, y) \notin A \times C$. The former statement means that $x \in A$ and $y \in B$, while the latter means that we have $x \notin A$ or $y \notin C$. (Why?) And so on.

67. As usual, we show that each set is a subset of the other. For the first half of the proof, argue that if $(x, y) \in (A \times C) \cap (B \times D)$ then $(x, y) \in (A \times C)$ and $(x, y) \in (B \times D)$, which means that $x \in A$, $x \in B$, $y \in C$, and $y \in D$. We may now deduce that (x, y) is an element of the right-hand set.

68. Consider what it would mean for (x, y) to be an ordered pair in $(A \times B) \cap (B \times A)$. For starters, we must have $(x, y) \in A \times B$, meaning that $x \in A$ and $y \in B$. What else must be true about (x, y)?

69. Suppose we group all the ordered pairs in $A \times A$ according to the sum of their coordinates. How many different groups will result? How does this help?

70. The first move introduces two characters into the list; one letter and one number. How many new characters are included in the list of plays on each subsequent move? How does this limit the length of the game?

2.5 Index Sets

EXERCISES

71. The sets are circles, so we could call such a set C_r. We are told that $r \geq 2$, so the index set is $J = \{r \in \mathbb{R} \mid r \geq 2\}$.

72. We could write $\bigcup_{r \in J'} C_r$, where $J' = [3, 5]$. (Other answers are possible.) This set of points looks like a solid ring, with inner radius 3 and outer radius 5.

73. $\bigcup_{k \in I} A_k = \{x \mid x \in A_k \text{ for some } k \in I\}$

74. a) sixtytwo b) vivacious c) mississippi d) boldface

75. All words that contain at least one of the letters a, b, c, d, e, f.

76. a) $\bigcup_{n=8}^{12} A_n$ b) $\bigcap_{n=1}^{\infty} B_{3n}$ c) $\bigcup_{n=2}^{\infty} C_n$ d) $\bigcap_{n=5}^{8} D_n$

77. a) $\{1, 2, 3, 4, 5, 7, 8, 14, 15, 16\}$ b) $\{4, 20, 100\}$ c) $\{1, 2, 3, \ldots, 99, 100\}$ d) $\{1\}$

78. We omit the sketch of the intervals. One finds that $\bigcap_{k=4}^{6} C_k = \{x \in \mathbb{R} \mid 6 \leq x \leq 8\}$ and similarly that $\bigcup_{k=4}^{6} C_k = \{x \in \mathbb{R} \mid 4 \leq x \leq 12\}$.

79. We have $\bigcap_{r \in J} C_r = \emptyset$ and $\bigcup_{r \in J} C_r = \{x \mid x \geq 1\}$.

80. In this case $\bigcap_{r \in J'} C_r = [4.5, 6]$ and $\bigcup_{r \in J} C_r = [3, 9]$.

81. We find that $M_3 \cap M_5 = M_{15}$, $M_4 \cap M_6 = M_{12}$, and $M_{10} \cap M_{15} \cap M_{20} = M_{60}$.

82. We have $M_a \cap M_b = M_c$, where c is the least common multiple of a and b. We also find that $\bigcap_{n \in \mathbb{N}} M_n = \{0\}$.

83. The intersection is the set $\{x \mid 4 \leq x < 10\}$.

84. One possible method is to write $\bigcap_{r \in J} B_r$, where $J = [3, 6]$. (The 3 could be replaced by any other number less than 6.)

WRITING

85. The same reasoning that was used to show that $\overline{A \cap B} = \overline{A} \cup \overline{B}$ applies here. Thus suppose that x is an element of the left-hand side. Then x is not in the intersection of this family of sets, which can only happen if x fails to be in at least one of the sets, say $x \notin A_k$ for some $k \in I$. Continue in this manner.

86. Let $x > 8$ be a real number. Explain why x is not in the intersection by showing that we can always choose r small enough so that $x \notin (5 + r, 8 + r)$. Use the same argument for any $x < 6$ by choosing r close enough to 1. Finally, demonstrate that any x in the range $6 \leq x \leq 8$ is in all of the sets B_r.

87. You should be able to guess the answer by figuring out the ten smallest elements of $M_3 \cup M_5 \cup M_7 \cup M_9 \cup M_{11} \cup M_{13}$ and noticing a pattern among the integers that are missing from this set. To explain your answer, argue that if $n \in \mathbb{Z}$ has any odd divisor, then it is excluded when we subtract the set $\bigcup_{n=1}^{\infty} M_{2n+1}$ from the set of all integers. What sorts of numbers remain?

2.6 Reference

Show that $A - B = \emptyset$ means that $A \subseteq B$. (This is a whole separate little proof in and of itself.) How does this help to finish the main proof?

Chapter 3: Proof Techniques

3.2 Mathematical Writing

EXERCISES

1. a) The sum of two 3's and four 5's is 26.

b) Let x be a real number satisfying $x \geq 0$ or $x \leq -1$.

c) We use a truth table to show that $\neg(P \wedge Q \wedge R) \equiv \neg P \vee \neg Q \vee \neg R$.

d) There are three kinds of people: those who can count and those who can't.

e) The set relation $A \supseteq B$ can also be written as $B \subseteq A$.

f) To solve the equation $x^2 = 36$ one may take the square root of both sides.

g) If $f(x) = x^2$ and $g(x) = 3x + 4$, then $f(x) = g(x)$ when $x = 4$.

h) The set $A \cup B$ contains more elements than B as long as $B \not\subseteq A$.

i) It comes as a surprise to learn that

$$\sqrt{\frac{6}{1^2} + \frac{6}{2^2} + \frac{6}{3^2} + \frac{6}{4^2} + \cdots} = \pi.$$

3.3 Sudoku Interlude

EXERCISES

2.

1	4	2	3	5
4	3	5	2	1
5	2	1	4	3
2	5	3	1	4
3	1	4	5	2

3. There are a variety of possible answers. Check that every row, column and pentomino contains every digit from 1 to 5, and verify that squares c, l, i, p, y do not all contain the same digit.

WRITING

4. The solution might continue in this manner. "The only squares in the second column that may contain a 2 are b and l. But we know b $\neq$ 2, thus l = 2, and now c is the only location for the remaining 2." The last sentence can be as short as "Now by process of elimination we deduce that e = 5, j = 1, o = 3, and t = 4."

5. First convince yourself that swapping any two particular digits in the grid will produce another solution. (For instance, replacing all 4's by 5's and vice-versa.) What does this fact have to do with the question?

3.4 Indirect Proofs

EXERCISES

7. Each truth table should contain all T's except for when P is true and Q is false.

8. a) For positive integers m and n, if m is divisible by n then m^3 is divisible by n^3.

b) For a real number x, if $3^x \leq 3x$ then $x \leq 1$.

c) For finite sets A and B, if $|A| = 0$ then $A \subseteq B$.

d) If a triangle has two congruent angles, then it has two congruent sides.

A proof by contrapositive is preferable for parts a), c) and d).

9. a) Suppose to the contrary that $\sqrt{7}$ is rational. Then $\sqrt{7} = p/q$ for integers p and q.

b) Suppose to the contrary that there are only finitely many primes.

c) Suppose to the contrary that each sister has less than 400 grams of chocolate.

d) Suppose to the contrary that every angle formed by three of the points is acute.

10. a) Contradiction b) Contrapositive c) Direct proof d) Contrapositive e) Direct proof f) Contradiction

WRITING

11. Prove the contrapositive. You should be able to argue that there are elements $x \in A$ and $y \in B$. How does this help prove that $A \times B$ is nonempty?

12. First state the contrapositive of the given implication. To show that $A \subseteq B \cup C$ suppose that $x \in A$. Then handle the cases $x \in B$ and $x \notin B$ separately, and show that $x \in B \cup C$ regardless.

13. To prove that $\overline{B \cup C} \subseteq \overline{A}$ you need to show that if $x \in \overline{B \cup C}$ then $x \in \overline{A}$. Show the contrapositive of this implication to complete the proof.

14. We are given that $A - C \not\subseteq A - B$, which means there is some element x satisfying $x \in A - C$ but $x \notin A - B$. Now $x \in A - C$ means that $x \in A$ but $x \notin C$. And so on.

15. Suppose to the contrary that $x \geq 3$. What can we say about the value of x^3? What about the value of $5x$? Combine these results to reach a statement that contradicts the fact that $x^3 + 5x = 40$.

16. Prove the contrapositive instead. When you simplify the equality $\frac{x}{2x-1} = \frac{y}{2y-1}$ several terms should conveniently cancel.

17. Suppose to the contrary that $\frac{x}{x+2y} < \frac{1}{3}$ and $\frac{y}{y+2x} < \frac{1}{3}$. Simplifying both inequalities should lead to an impossible situation.

18. The contrapositive states that if $\beta - 4$ is rational then β is also rational. Prove this statement instead.

19. Suppose to the contrary that $\sqrt{\beta}$ is actually rational, so that we can write $\sqrt{\beta} = m/n$. How does this lead to a contradiction with the fact that we are given that β is irrational?

20. Suppose to the contrary that m/n is the smallest positive rational number. Obtain a contradiction by demonstrating how to use m/n to create a smaller positive rational.

21. Begin by noting that since $A \in \mathcal{P}(A)$ we can deduce that $A \in \mathcal{P}(C)$, which means that $A \subseteq C$. Similarly we find that $B \subseteq C$. Now suppose that A and B are both proper subsets of C and reach a contradiction.

3.5 Biconditional, Vacuous and Trivial Proofs

EXERCISES

23. Because $Q \Rightarrow P$ and $\neg P \Rightarrow \neg Q$ are logically equivalent statements. (The latter is the contrapositive of the former.)

24. a) False b) True c) True d) False

25. The set of odd integers.

26. The set of rational numbers.

27. We must show that if $f(x)$ is a linear function, then $f(x - a) + f(x + a) = 2f(x)$ for all $a, x \in \mathbb{R}$. Conversely we must also show that if $f(x - a) + f(x + a) = 2f(x)$ for all $a, x \in \mathbb{R}$ then $f(x)$ is a linear function.

28. This set of points is characterized by the property that they are the same distance from the x-axis as the y-axis. (Other answers are possible.)

29. a) Trivially true b) Vacuously true c) Vacuously true d) Trivially true
e) Vacuously true f) Trivially true g) Trivially true h) Vacuously true

WRITING

30. We omit the outline here. The example given in the text gives a good indication of how to frame the outline.

31. We must prove that if $A \subseteq B$ then $A \cap B = A$ and also that if $A \cap B = A$ then $A \subseteq B$. To establish the latter implication, suppose that $x \in A$. We wish to show that $x \in B$ also. Now use the fact that $A = A \cap B$ to your advantage.

32. Let the circles have radii R_1 and R_2, respectively. We must show that if $\pi R_1^2 = \pi R_2^2$ then $2\pi R_1 = 2\pi R_2$ and conversely. To prove the stated implication, begin by dividing by π and taking square roots. Continue in this manner to reach the desired conclusion.

33. Transform each equation into the other. For instance, multiply both sides of $\frac{2}{x} + \frac{3}{y} = 1$ by xy, move all terms to one side, then add 6 to both sides.

34. For this argument it is best to adopt our alternate approach to biconditional proofs. In other words, show that if a is even then a^2 ends with 0, 4 or 6; while if a is not even (i.e. a is odd) then a^2 does not end with one of these digits.

35. We must prove that if $A \subseteq B$ then $A \cap \overline{B} = \emptyset$ and also that if $A \cap \overline{B} = \emptyset$ then $A \subseteq B$. In the latter case we must show that if $x \in A$ then $x \in B$. So suppose that $x \in A$. Since $A \cap \overline{B} = \emptyset$, it must be the case that $x \notin \overline{B}$, which is equivalent to $x \in B$.

36. We must prove that if $-1 \le x \le 1$ then x^2 is at least as close to 0 as x is, and conversely. It helps to rephrase the problem in terms of absolute values. So we must show that $|x| \le 1$ if and only if $|x^2| \le |x|$.

37. We provide a proof of the first part to illustrate how a proof may be phrased. We will show that the statement is trivially true. Since we may rewrite $n^2 + 2n + 1$ as $(n+1)^2$, it is clear that this expression is a perfect square for all values of n. Hence the conclusion is always true, so the claim is trivially true.

3.6 Conjecture and Disproof

EXERCISES

38. Pairs satisfying $3m^2 = n^2 \pm 1$ are $(1, 2)$, $(4, 7)$ and $(15, 26)$.

39. Perhaps the most noticeable observations include the fact that the minus sign is always used, the sum $2m + n$ gives the next m value, and the sum $3m + 2n$ gives the next n value. (Several other conjectures are possible.) The next two pairs are $(56, 97)$ and $(209, 362)$.

40. One should find that in each case $x + y + z \ge 3\sqrt[3]{xyz}$. It is possible for the two values to be equal, but only when $x = y = z$.

41. We find that $11 \to 34 \to 17$, at which point we are done because we have already seen that the sequence beginning with 17 eventually reaches 1. We omit the verification of the remaining numbers.

42. Of all the positive integers from 1 to 20 the numbers 2, 6, 10, 14 and 18 cannot be written as a difference of two squares. This list consists of every fourth natural number beginning with 2. Equivalently (and more relevantly), these are the natural numbers with exactly one factor of 2.

43. One should find that $AG = 2(GL)$ and $BG = 2(GM)$ for any triangle ABC. Furthermore, segment $\overline{CN}$ passes through G.

WRITING

44. Substitute the values $m = k^2 - 1$ for $k = 1, 2, 3, \ldots$ into $5m + 1$. You should find another perfect square fairly soon.

45. Try drawing a long skinny kite-shaped quadrilateral to find a counterexample.

46. First write down the negative of the given statement. Next take $x = 1$ and find a value of y other than 1 which satisfies the equation.

47. We are looking for a prime p and a perfect square n^2 such that $p = n^2 - 1$. Now use the fact that the right-hand side factors.

48. We know that three points equidistant from one another must form an equilateral triangle. Now consider where the fourth point might be located.

3.7 Existence

Exercises

50. The numbers $x = \frac{1}{2}(\pi + \sqrt{2})$ and $y = \frac{1}{2}(\pi - \sqrt{2})$ fill the bill.

51. If we take $x = 10$ and $y = 5$ then $x + 2y = 20 = \sqrt{8xy}$. (Other pairs can work.)

52. The smallest such trio of positive integers is 98, 99 and 100.

53. The only other solution is to use the numbers 4, 4 and -5.

54. As x increases from 0 to 1 the quantity $8^x + 9x$ increases from 1 to 17, so at some point it must equal 10. In fact, this occurs at $x = \frac{2}{3}$.

55. The line must pass through the center of the circle. Thus we should take the line passing through the center of both circles.

56. Take the line passing through the center of both rectangles. If these centers happen to coincide, then such a line will not be unique.

Writing

57. Consider the sums $10 + 0$, $11 + 1$, $12 + 2$ and so on.

58. What would go wrong if every child received less than eight pieces of candy?

59. Slightly modify the proof that there are 1000 consecutive composite numbers.

60. Construct the decimal expansion of r in a way that guarantees that every finite string of digits appear. For instance, if we start $r = 0.123456789\ldots$ then so far r contains every possible one-digit string.

61. Adapt the proof given in the text. At what point should we stop rotating the line to solve the problem?

62. Let 2^k be the largest power of 2 that is less than all the numbers on the list. (Why does such a power of 2 exist?) What can be said of the number s 2^{k+1} and 2^{k+2}?

63. First show that for almost any direction there is a line parallel to that direction which divides all the blue points in half. Now rotate this line $180°$, all the while evenly splitting the blue points, and keep track of how the line divides the red points throughout the process.

Chapter 4: Number Theory

4.1 Divisibility

Exercises

1. a) True b) False c) True d) True e) False f) True g) True h) False i) True j) False k) True l) True

2. We have $d \mid 23$ for $d = -23, -1, 1$ and 23. Next, $d \mid 24$ iff $d = \pm 1, \pm 2, \pm 3, \pm 4, \pm 6, \pm 8, \pm 12$, or ± 24. Finally, $d \mid (-25)$ for $d = \pm 1, \pm 5$, and ± 25.

3. a) $n = (n)(1)$ b) $n^3 = (-n^2)(-n)$ c) $0 = (0)(n)$ d) $-3n = (-3)(n)$ e) either n or $n + 1$ will be even, hence $n(n + 1)$ is divisible by 2

4. a) 7 b) 10 c) 1 d) 25 e) 1

5. We find that $(1, n) = 1$, $(3n, 2n^2) = n$ if $3 \nmid n$ while $(3n, 2n^2) = 3n$ if $3 \mid n$, and $(n, 7n + 1) = 1$.

6. There are two such integers, 1 and -1.

7. For instance, take $a = 4$, $b = 5$ and $c = 6$.

8. One possibility is to use $a = 4$ and $b = 5$.

9. With \$22 and \$60 bills one can buy any item costing an even number of dollars. And with \$9 and \$14 bills one can spend any whole number of dollars. We have $11(\$22) - 4(\$60) = \$2$ and $2(\$14) - 3(\$9) = \$1$.

WRITING

10. Write down equations that mean the same thing as $a \mid b$ and $b \mid c$, then substitute one into the other to obtain an equation of the form $c = (\cdots)a$.

11. To prove one implication, combine $a = mb$ and $b = na$ to obtain $mn = 1$, for $m, n \in \mathbb{Z}$. What does this reveal? Don't forget to prove the other implication as well, since this is a biconditional proof.

12. First determine the correct proof strategy. Cubing both sides of an equation should come in handy at some point.

13. Try finding the smallest such counterexample when $a = 2$ and $b = 5$. How does this suggest that we construct a counterexample in general?

14. Translate $d \mid a$ and $d \mid b$ into algebraic equalities, then substitute in for a and b in the expression $ak + bl$.

15. Suppose that d divides evenly into both of $n + 2001$ and $n^2 + 1999n - 4000$. Next argue that $(n^2 + 1999n - 4000) - n(n + 2001)$ is a multiple of d, and ultimately show that $d \mid 2$. This will yield the desired result.

16. Suppose that d divides evenly into both of $n + 2$ and $3n^2 + 4n - 5$. Explain how we know that $3n(n + 2) - (3n^2 + 4n - 5)$ must also be a multiple of d, and eventually show that $d \mid 1$. Use this to complete the proof.

4.2 Divisor Diversions

EXERCISES

18. There are 25 primes among the first 100 numbers, so $1/4$ of them are prime.

19. We find that $111111 = 3 \cdot 7 \cdot 11 \cdot 13 \cdot 37$.

20. Since $30 = 2^1 3^1 5^1$ we have $d(30) = 2 \cdot 2 \cdot 2 = 8$. Similarly, $243 = 3^5$ means that $d(243) = 6$ and $324 = 2^2 3^4$ gives $d(324) = 15$.

21. The five numbers are 60, 72, 84, 90 and 96.

22. One finds that $46903 = 17 \cdot 31 \cdot 89$.

23. We find $1001 = 2^0 3^0 5^0 7^1 11^1 13^1 17^0 \cdots$ and $135 = 2^0 3^3 5^1 7^0 11^0 \cdots$. We also have $1 = 2^0 3^0 5^0 7^0 \cdots$; in other words, no primes are used in the prime factorization of 1.

24. We must have $n = p^2$ for a prime p.

25. The product is $(1 + 3 + 9)(1 + 7) = 1 + 3 + 9 + 7 + 21 + 63$, which is exactly the sum of the divisors of 63. Hence this sum equals $(1 + 3 + 9)(1 + 7) = 13 \cdot 8 = 104$.

26. The sum of the divisors of 1000 is $(1 + 2 + 4 + 8)(1 + 5 + 25 + 125) = 15 \cdot 156 = 2340$. In general, if $n = p_1^{e_1} p_2^{e_2} \cdots p_k^{e_k}$ then the sum of the divisors of n is given by

$$(1 + p_1 + \cdots + p_1^{e_1})(1 + p_2 + \cdots + p_2^{e_2}) \cdots (1 + p_k + \cdots + p_k^{e_k}).$$

27. Since $672 = 2^5 \cdot 3 \cdot 7$ the sum of its divisors is $(1 + 2 + 4 + 8 + 16 + 32)(1 + 3)(1 + 7) = (63)(4)(8) = 3(672)$. Note that when n is a perfect number the sum of the divisors is exactly twice n; for 672 the sum of divisors is exactly three times as large.

WRITING

28. Imagine "building" a divisor of n. How many options are there for the power of p_1 to include? For p_2 through p_k? Now put these values together in the right way.

29. This is a biconditional statement; we must prove that if $d(n)$ is odd then n is a square and conversely. In the former case, argue that if $d(n)$ is odd then each factor in the product $(e_1 + 1)(e_2 + 1) \cdots (e_k + 1)$ must be odd. What does this tell you about the values of e_1 through e_k?

30. Argue that the state of locker door n is reversed $d(n)$ times. What must be true of $d(n)$ if the door is open at the end?

31. Observe that we can have $d(n) = 11$ if $n = p^{10}$ for some prime p.

32. Write $n = p_1^{e_1} p_2^{e_2} \cdots p_k^{e_k}$, where none of the primes equal 2. How does the formula for $d(n)$ change if we include a factor of 2^1 in the factorization of n?

33. List the proper divisors of $2^{n-1} p^2$ in an array with three rows:

$$
\begin{array}{cccccc}
1 & 2 & 4 & \cdots & 2^{n-2} & 2^{n-1} \\
p & 2p & 4p & \cdots & 2^{n-2}p & 2^{n-1}p \\
p^2 & 2p^2 & 4p^2 & \cdots & 2^{n-2}p^2 &
\end{array}
$$

Now add them together as done in the text.

34. It will help to include three or four primes in the factorization of n, each raised to a relatively high power. (A fourth or fifth power should suffice.)

4.3 Modular Arithmetic

EXERCISES

36. Observe that the desired number r will be the remainder upon dividing 7654321 by 35, since we subtract a whole number of 35's to get from 7654321 to r. One efficient way to calculate this value of r would be to divide 7654321 by 35 on a calculator, subtract off the integer part (which is 218694 in this case), then multiply the decimal by 35 to obtain the answer of 31.

37. The reduced numbers are 4 mod 11, 17 mod 123, 9 mod 17, and 27 mod 88.

38. We must have $n \equiv 3 \bmod 24$.

39. We may write $n = 24k - 5$ (or $n + 5 = 24k$) for some $k \in \mathbb{Z}$.

40. We write $n = 4k + 2$.

41. We must have $n \equiv 3 \bmod 4$.

42. The final digits of the powers of 7 are 1, 7, 9, 3, 1, 7, 9, 3, 1, 7, ... Therefore the last digit is a 9 when $n \equiv 2 \bmod 4$.

43. a) False b) False c) True d) True e) True f) True

44. The congruence holds for $m = 3$, 5 or 15.

45. This congruence is true for all divisors m of 84 besides $m = 1$, of which there are $d(84) - 1 = 11$ of them.

46. There are $d(1020) - 1 = 23$ such values of m.

47. The numbers $a = 32$ and $b = 42$ are one pair among many valid choices.

WRITING

48. This is a biconditional statement, so first prove that $m \mid a$ implies $a \equiv 0 \bmod m$, then show that if $a \equiv 0 \bmod m$ then $m \mid a$. For the first part, argue that $m \mid a$ is equivalent to $a = mk$, which can be rewritten as $a - 0 = mk$. Now take it from there.

49. We are given that $a - b = k_1 m$ and $c - d = k_2 m$. How should we combine these equalities? (And why couldn't we just write km in both cases?)

50. What algebraic step is required to transform $a - b = km$ into an equation of the form $ac - bc = (\cdots)m$?

51. What indirect proof technique will be most helpful here? It will also be advantageous at one point to multiply both sides of an equation by 2.

52. Rewrite $(a^2 + 3b) - (b^2 + 3a)$ as $(a - b)(a + b) - 3(a - b)$.

53. Recall that $a^3 - b^3$ factors as $(a - b)(a^2 + ab + b^2)$.

54. Try interpreting the congruences as $a = km + b$ and $c = lm + d$, then computing $ac - bd$ by substituting in for a and c. (Other approaches will work too.)

4.4 Complete Residue Systems

EXERCISES

55. a) Not a CRS; delete the 0 or 7 to obtain a CRS. b) This is a CRS c) Not a CRS; include 0 or -7, for instance, to obtain a CRS. d) This is a CRS.

56. One answer is $\{-37, -29, -15, -11, -3\}$. Since $-29 \equiv -15 \bmod 7$ we cannot create a complete residue system mod 7.

57. We might take $\{0, 1, 2, 3, 4\}$, which becomes $\{0, 3, 6, 9, 12\}$, which is still a CRS mod 5. However, mod 6 if we start with $\{0, 1, 2, 3, 4, 5\}$ we obtain $\{0, 3, 6, 9, 12, 15\}$, which is not a CRS since 0, 6 and 12 are congruent mod 6. The difference is that 3 is a factor of 6 but not of 5.

58. We could write $\{-(k-1), -(k-2), \ldots, -1, 0, 1, \ldots, k-1, k\}$.

59. Take $a = 1$ and $b = 6$, for instance. Our principle does not apply to exponential functions, so this example does not provide a contradiction.

60. Take $a = 1$ and $b = 3$, for instance. In this case $g(n)$ is a polynomial, but it does not have integer coefficients, so we still do not contradict our principle.

61. This is equivalent to $n \equiv 3 \bmod 7$.

62. This is the same as $n \equiv 1 \bmod 5$.

63. Those congruence classes correspond to $n \equiv 0, 2, 3, 4, 6, 8, 10, 11, 12 \bmod 14$.

64. Only the congruence classes $n \equiv 7, 13 \bmod 15$ satisfy the given condition.

WRITING

65. Substitute in $n = -2, -1, 0, 1, 2$ and show that $n^2 + 2n + 3 \not\equiv 0 \bmod 5$.

66. Show that $n(n+1)(2n+1) \equiv 0 \bmod 6$ for $n \in \{-2, -1, 0, 1, 2, 3\}$.

67. Check that the assertion holds for $n \in \{-3, -2, \ldots, 3\}$.

68. Confirm that $n^2 \equiv 1 \bmod 8$ for $n \equiv 1, 3, 5, 7 \bmod 8$, which exactly corresponds to $n \equiv 1 \bmod 2$.

69. Check that $2n^3 + 1 \equiv 8 \bmod 9$ when $n \equiv 2, 5, 8 \bmod 9$.

70. Find the values of n^4 for a complete residue system mod 10, then check that the possible outputs occur in the correct places. For instance, show that $n^4 \equiv 6 \bmod 10$ for $n \equiv 2, 4, 6, 8 \bmod 10$, then explain why these values of n correspond to $2 \mid n$.

71. There are already eleven numbers in the proposed set, so we need only show that no two are congruent mod 11. What would go wrong if $a_j + 2 \equiv a_k + 2 \bmod 11$?

72. Show that the given congruences correspond to each of the congruence classes mod 12 exactly once.

4.5 Forms of Integers

EXERCISES

73. One finds that $30^2 + 10^2 + 1^2 = 1001$ and $25^2 + 19^2 + 4^2 = 1002$.

74. We have $a^2 \equiv 0, 1, 4, 7 \bmod 9$. This allows us to obtain all values from 0 to 8 as a sum of three squares. For instance, one should find that $0 + 1 + 4 \equiv 5$, $1 + 1 + 4 \equiv 6$ and $0 + 0 + 7 \equiv 7$.

75. We find that $a^3 \equiv 0, \pm 1 \bmod 7$, and similarly for b^3. Hence $a^3 + b^3$ can only be congruent to $\equiv 0, \pm 1, \pm 2 \bmod 7$.

76. We have just seen that $a^3 + b^3 \not\equiv \pm 3 \bmod 7$. Therefore we can rule out 2054, 2055, 2061, 2062, 2068, 2069, 2075 and 2076 as sums of two cubes.

77. Using positive cubes one can only obtain $2060 = 9^3 + 11^3$ and $2071 = 7^3 + 12^3$ as the sum of two cubes.

78. We have $12^2 \equiv -1 \bmod 29$, $9^2 \equiv -1 \bmod 41$, and $23^2 \equiv -1 \bmod 53$.

WRITING

79. You should discover that $a^2 + b^2 \equiv 0, 1,$ or 2 mod 4, while $2011 \equiv 3$ mod 4.

80. Argue that $a^3 + b^3 + c^3 \equiv 0, \pm 1 \pm 2, \pm 3$ mod 9. Then reduce 2345 mod 9.

81. First show that all fourth powers reduce to either 0 or 1 mod 16. Consequently, what values can a sum of nine fourth powers reduce to mod 16?

82. Try tripling the values of a, b and c used to obtain n.

83. Prove the contrapositive, which states that if $a^2 + b^2 \equiv 0$ mod 11 then $a \equiv 0$ and $b \equiv 0$. Now find all possible values for a^2 and b^2 mod 11, and show that there is only one way to have $a^2 + b^2 \equiv 0$ mod 11.

84. Prove the contrapositive, which states that if $a^2 + b^2 = 49n$ then n can be written as a sum of two squares. Reduce the former equation mod 7, then show that the resulting congruence is only possible if $a \equiv 0$ mod 7 and $b \equiv 0$ mod 7.

85. Rewrite the given congruence as $a - b = 3k$. For the next part use proof by contradiction: if we did have $x^2 \equiv -1$ mod m then we would have $x^2 \equiv -1$ mod 3 as well, but show the latter congruence is impossible.

4.6 Primes

EXERCISES

86. It appears that every odd number above 10 can be obtained in this manner, except for 15. (Note that writing $15 = 5 + 2(5)$ is not valid, since the primes must be distinct.)

87. The values are 5, 11, 19, 29, 41. They are located along a diagonal of the table and appear to all be prime. But the next such value is 55, so the conjecture is false.

88. The smallest counterexample to Fermat's conjecture is $n = 5$, since $2^{32} + 1 = (641)(6700417)$.

89. The divisors of n include exactly one prime if and only if n is a power of a prime, such as $n = 64, 27$ or 13.

90. The prime p must be a divisor of 21; i.e. we could only have $p = 3$ or $p = 7$.

91. a) Yes b) No c) Yes d) No (or Yes, with a few modifications) e) Yes

WRITING

92. Argue that for any $n \in \mathbb{N}$ one of n, $n + 2$ and $n + 4$ is a multiple of 3.

93. Every number is of the form $6k$, $6k + 1$, $6k + 2$, $6k + 3$, $6k + 4$ or $6k + 5$. Show that four of these types are automatically divisible by a smaller factor when $k \geq 1$. (Consider $k = 0$ separately.)

94. Mimic the proof of Lemma 1 to show that if smallest odd divisor of n is not prime then we can find a smaller odd divisor of n, leading to a contradiction.

95. Suppose that p were an odd prime for which $p \,|\, n$ and $p \,|\, n + 64$. Show that $p \,|\, 64$, and derive a contradiction.

96. Consider the quantity $2(n + 1) - (2n + 1)$.

97. Find a prime factor q of $N - 1$, then explain why q must be different from any of $p_1, p_2, \ldots p_k$.

98. First argue that n is odd and hence has only odd prime factors. Then show that it is not possible for all prime divisors of n to satisfy $p \equiv 1$ mod 4.

99. Otherwise p would divide $(N + 2) - (N)$.

100. Note that if $p \equiv 3$ mod 4 then $p^2 \equiv 1$ mod 4.

101. Suppose that there were only finitely many such primes, and let $p_1, p_2, \ldots, p_k$ be a complete list. Let $N = p_1^2 p_2^2 \cdots p_k^2$ and argue that we can find a new prime q with $q \equiv 3$ mod 4 by considering $N + 2$.

Chapter 5: Counting and Induction

5.1 How Many?

EXERCISES

1. There are six such states. (Don't count Colorado twice.)

2. There are six New England states, so the answer is $6 \cdot 5 \cdot 4 = 120$.

3. Either 7 and 6, 14 and 3, 21 and 2, or 42 and 1 jellybeans and chocolates.

4. The row must alternate candies, beginning with either a jellybean or a chocolate, so there are $(6 \cdot 5 \cdot 4)(7 \cdot 6) + (7 \cdot 6 \cdot 5)(6 \cdot 5) = 11{,}340$ ways.

5. Using an organized list we count 16 valid rows of letters.

6. There are $(9 \cdot 8 \cdot 7) + 3! + 3! = 516$ rhyming triples. (Don't forget about QUW.)

7. We find $4! + 4! = 48$ possible arrangements.

8. There are $2(5!) = 240$ ways to line up.

9. We count $4!(3! \cdot 3! \cdot 3! \cdot 3!) = 31104$ arrangements.

10. We find a total of $7 \cdot 6 \cdot 5 \cdot 4 + 7 \cdot 6 \cdot 5 \cdot 4 + 7 \cdot 6 \cdot 5 \cdot 4 = 2520$ ways.

11. a) $n(n-1)$ b) $(n+1)/n!$ c) $n!$

WRITING

12. Place the dots one row at a time. The first dot can occupy any of the n squares in the top row. How many options are there for placing the next dot in the second row?

13. First list all the ways to write 10 as a sum of distinct digits, such as $2+3+5 = 10$. (You should find that there are nine ways.) Then count the permutations of each sum separately. (For instance, there are six permutations of the sum $2+3+5$.)

14. We have a permutation to compute. Explain why the resulting product is equal to $n(n-1)\cdots(n-k+1)$ rather than $n(n-1)\cdots(n-k)$. Then simplify $n!/(n-k)!$ by cancelling common factors.

15. Think about the difference in the number of zeros at the end of 99! and 100!.

5.2 Combinations

EXERCISES

17. There are ten subsets: $\{a,b\}$, $\{a,c\}$, $\{a,d\}$, $\{a,e\}$, $\{b,c\}$, $\{b,d\}$, $\{b,e\}$, $\{c,d\}$, $\{c,e\}$, $\{d,e\}$. This agrees with the formula $\frac{1}{2}(5)(4) = 10$.

18. There are $\binom{6}{1} + \binom{6}{3} + \binom{6}{5} = 6 + 20 + 6 = 32$ such subsets. Note that $32 = 2^5$.

19. A delegation with three females and one male allows for 13300 combinations.

20. Either $\binom{21}{4}\binom{10}{1} + \binom{21}{3}\binom{10}{2} + \binom{21}{2}\binom{10}{3} + \binom{21}{1}\binom{10}{4}$ or $\binom{31}{5} - \binom{10}{5} - \binom{21}{5}$ are correct.

21. We have $\binom{30}{4}$ delegations with Jenny, $\binom{30}{5}$ without Jenny, and $\binom{31}{5}$ in total. Observe that we may deduce that $\binom{30}{4} + \binom{30}{5} = \binom{31}{5}$.

22. There are $\binom{8}{2} = 28$ ways to choose two squares within the first row for a pair of markers. We have only 27 choices for the second row, though, to avoid duplicating the first row. In total, there are $(28)(27)\cdots(21) = 125318793600$ arrangements.

23. First choose 2 of 13 values for the pairs, then choose 2 of 4 suits for each pair. Next choose 1 of 11 values for the final card, then choose 1 of 4 suits for that card.

24. There are $\binom{13}{1}\binom{4}{2}\binom{12}{3}\binom{4}{1}^3$ such hands. (Other forms of this answer are possible.)

25. We count $\binom{13}{3}\binom{3}{2}\binom{4}{3}^2\binom{4}{1}$ ways. (Other forms of this answer are possible.)

26. Let the jellybean colors be R, G, B, Y. Then the list of 20 choices is RRR, GGG, BBB, YYY, RRG, RGG, RRB, RBB, RRY, RYY, GGB, GBB, GGY, GYY, BBY, BYY, RGB, RGY, RBY, GBY.

27. A candy code would consist of seven arrows and three circles, for a total of $\binom{10}{3}$ ways to select the jellybeans.

28. A candy code would consist of $n-1$ arrows and three circles, for a total of $\binom{n+2}{3}$ ways to select the jellybeans.

WRITING

29. Think of choosing k objects as leaving $n-k$ objects behind.

30. First imagine listing any three objects in order. Then explain why each possible combination has been included six times on such a list.

31. Suppose we have a class consisting of Jenny along with n other students. Count how many ways there are to form a five-person delegation from this class. Then consider two cases, based on whether or not Jenny is a member of the delegation.

32. Observe that there are $\binom{n}{0}$ subsets with no elements, $\binom{n}{1}$ subsets with one element, $\binom{n}{2}$ subsets with two elements, and so on.

33. Count the number of ways that a class of n boys and n girls may create a four-person delegation based on the boy-girl composition of the delegation.

34. First explain why there are $\binom{13}{3}\binom{3}{1}\binom{4}{3}\binom{4}{1}^2$ three-of-a-kind hands.

35. Choose the four values that appear in the hand, then choose which two will be pairs. Continue along these lines.

36. Begin by selecting 2 of the 4 suits that will have four cards each, then select which 4 of the 13 values will appear for each suit. Continue in this manner.

5.3 Introduction to Induction

EXERCISES

37. Knocking over the first domino is akin to the base case; the fact that each subsequent domino knocks down the next is analogous to the induction step.

38. The list is empty for $n=1$, we have R, G for $n=1$, and we have RGB, RBG, BRG, BGR, GRB, GBR when $n=2$. The formula gives $1^2-1=0$ ways, $2^2-2=2$ ways, and $3^2-3=6$ ways, which agrees with our list sizes.

39. Consider a row of 43 squares. If the final one is brown then there are 1722 ways to color the first 42 squares. However if the final square is scarlet then we need only pick one of the other squares to be green, which can be done in 42 ways, and similarly if the final square is green. This gives a total of $1722+42+42=1806$ ways.

40. Consider a row of $k+1$ squares. If the final one is brown then there are k^2-k ways to color the first 42 squares. However if the final square is scarlet then we need only pick one of the other squares to be green, which can be done in k ways, and similarly if the final square is green. This gives a total of $(k^2-k)+k+k=k^2+k$ ways. This agrees with the given expression, since $(k+1)^2-(k+1)=(k^2+2k+1)-(k+1)=k^2+k$.

41. There are n ways to choose which square to color scarlet, then $n-1$ ways to choose which of the remaining squares to color green. (The rest of the squares will be brown.) This gives a total of $n(n-1)=n^2-n$ ways to perform the coloring.

WRITING

42. After confirming the base cases (try $n=1,2,3$), you will need to consider a row of $k+1$ squares. There are three possibilities: the final square is either brown, scarlet, or green. The induction hypothesis applies in the first case to give $2k^2-2k$ ways to finish the coloring. In the other cases we must choose one of the first k squares, then color it either scarlet or green. This can be done in $2k$ ways in each case.

43. This proof is almost identical to the one presented in the section. (Try $n = 1, 2,$ 3, 4 as base cases.) At some point it will be helpful to show that if the final square in a row of $k + 1$ squares is colored scarlet, then there are only $k - 1$ ways (rather than k) to complete the coloring.

44. Along the way it will help to show that in a row of $k + 1$ squares, if the last one is colored scarlet then there are $(k - 1)$ ways to finish the coloring.

45. You should find that in a row of $k + 1$ squares there are 2^k ways to color the first k squares regardless of whether the final square is scarlet or brown. It will also help to note that $2^k + 2^k = 2(2^k) = 2^1 \cdot 2^k = 2^{k+1}$.

46. At some point you will need to deal with the expression $k2^{k-1} + k2^{k-1} + 2^k$. Use ideas from the previous hint to combine the first two terms.

5.4 Applications of Induction

EXERCISES

47. For $n = 0$ the two sides of the equality are 1 and $\frac{1}{2}(3 - 1) = 1$. When $n = 1$ we obtain $1 + 3 = 4$ and $\frac{1}{2}(9 - 1) = 4$, and for $n = 2$ we have $1 + 3 + 9 = 13$ and $\frac{1}{2}(27 - 1) = 13$ as well.

48. Adding 3^{k+1} to both sides yields $1 + 3 + 9 + \cdots + 3^k + 3^{k+1} = \frac{1}{2}(3^{k+1} - 1) + 3^{k+1}$. The right-hand side may be rewritten as $\frac{1}{2}(3^{k+1} - 1 + 2(3^{k+1})) = \frac{1}{2}(3(3^{k+1}) - 1) = \frac{1}{2}(3^{k+2} - 1)$, as desired.

49. In order we have $n = 1, 2$; then $n = 0, 1$; then $n = 1, 2$.

50. In the first problem we are given that $\frac{1}{(1)(3)} + \frac{1}{(3)(5)} + \cdots + \frac{1}{(2k-1)(2k+1)} = \frac{k}{2k+1}$ and wish to prove that $\frac{1}{(1)(3)} + \frac{1}{(3)(5)} + \cdots + \frac{1}{(2k+1)(2k+3)} = \frac{k+1}{2k+3}$. In the next problem we are given that $a_k = 3^k + 2$ and wish to prove that $a_{k+1} = 3^{k+1} + 2$. In the third problem we are given that k people can reverse order in $\frac{1}{2}k^2 - \frac{1}{2}k$ swaps, and wish to demonstrate that $k + 1$ people can reverse order in $\frac{1}{2}(k + 1)^2 - \frac{1}{2}(k + 1)$ swaps.

WRITING

51. When simplifying $\frac{k}{2k+1} + \frac{1}{(2k+1)(2k+3)}$ find a common denominator, combine the fractions, factor the numerator, then simplify the result.

52. It will help to recall that $2k2^{k+1} = k2^{k+2}$ by laws of exponents.

53. You should find that the sum is equal to $\frac{n}{n+1}$.

54. Employ the same steps as suggested for the first writing problem above.

55. When simplifying $(k + 1)! + (k + 1)(k + 1)! - 1$ begin by pulling out a factor of $(k + 1)!$ from the first two terms.

56. It will help to multiply both sides of $7^k + 3k - 1 = 9m$ by 7.

57. It will help to multiply both sides of $6^k - 5k - 1 = 25m$ by 6.

58. By the induction hypothesis we know that $a_k = 3^k + 2$. Now compute $3a_k - 4$ and show that we obtain the value predicted by the formula for a_{k+1}.

59. One computes that $a_3 = 4$, $a_4 = 5$ and $a_5 = 6$ so it appears that $a_n = n + 1$. Now suppose that $a_{k-1} = k$ and $a_k = k + 1$ and show that $2a_k - a_{k-1}$ agrees with our formula for a_{k+1}.

60. Work out a distribution by hand for $n = 3$ through $n = 10$ if you haven't already. When handling the inductive step, be careful to recreate the exact same conditions as occur at the start of the distribution, meaning that two students have one paper each and a third student has the rest of the papers. For instance, suppose that for case $n = k + 1$ it happens that $k = 3t$ is a multiple of 3. At the start three students have 1, 1, and $3t - 1$ papers, while the rest have no papers. Group three students with 0,

1, and $3t - 1$ papers together, and redistribute as 1, 1, and $3t - 2$ papers. Now there are three students with 1 paper, so one of them can stand aside and we know by the inductive hypothesis that the rest can finish the distribution.

61. For the inductive step, let m be an even number with $m < 2^{k+2}$. By Bertrand's Postulate, there is a prime p satisfying $\frac{1}{2}m \le p \le m$. Now show that $m - p < 2^{k+1}$, so $m - p$ can be written as a sum of at most k primes by the inductive hypothesis. How does this help? Now handle the case of m odd.

62. First reverse the order of the first k people in line, which will take less than $\frac{1}{2}k^2$ moves. How many more swaps will it take for the $(k + 1)$st person to move to the other end of the line to finish the job? Then show that the total is less than $\frac{1}{2}(k+1)^2$.

63. Note that in order for $k + 1$ people to finish the game, the first k people have to finish the task ($2^k - 1$ moves), then the final person can stand (1 move), then the first k people must once again perform the task ($2^k - 1$ moves) to seat the kth person. Add these amounts to find the total for $k + 1$ people.

64. The process is very similar to the Last One Standing game. (See previous hint.) Just replace "first k people perform the task" with "move the top k disks in the stack."

5.5 Fibonacci Numbers

EXERCISES

66. We should define $F_{-1} = 1$, $F_{-2} = -1$, $F_{-3} = 2$, $F_{-4} = -3$, and $F_{-5} = 5$.

67. Write D and S for domino and square. The eight tilings are DDS, DSD, SDD, $DSSS$, $SDSS$, $SSDS$, $SSSD$, and $SSSSS$.

68. For $n = 1$ to 5 the values are $1, -1, 1, -1, 1$. Hence we conjecture the formula $(-1)^{n+1}$. (Or $(-1)^{n-1}$ works also.)

69. Use the fact that $F_n + F_{n+1} = F_{n+2}$ to turn the given expression into $2F_{n+1} + 4F_{n+2} + F_{n+3}$. Continue in this fashion.

70. We find that $F_{n+1}^2 = 2F_n^2 + 2F_{n-1}^2 - F_{n-2}^2$ for all $n \ge 3$.

71. It appears that $n \mid F_{n-1}$ or $n \mid F_{n+1}$ precisely when n is prime.

72. The most striking property of these quotients is that the sum of any two of them gives the next; the same recurrence that governs the Fibonacci numbers.

WRITING

73. Consider two cases in your inductive step, depending on the color of the $(k + 1)$st square. If that square is brown, any valid coloring of the first k squares will work. What must be true of the kth square if the $(k + 1)$st square is scarlet?

74. One should conjecture that there are F_{n+1} tilings. For the inductive step, consider two cases based upon whether the end of the tiling consists of one vertical domino or a pair of horizontal dominoes.

75. Adding F_{k+1} to both sides is useful in the inductive step. Check $n = 1$, 2 and 3 for the base cases.

76. Adding F_{2k+1} to both sides of case $n = k$ is useful in the inductive step.

77. Use the technique presented in the text to simplify $3F_n + 5F_{n+1}$. Check base cases $n = 1$ and $n = 2$, then mimic the proof at the end of the section to complete the inductive step.

78. Suppose to the contrary that $C - F_n \ge F_{n-1}$, which leads to $C \ge F_{n+1}$. Why is this a contradiction?

79. When using $n - 4$ squares and 2 dominoes we have a total of $n - 2$ tiles in a row, two of which are dominoes, so there are $\binom{n-2}{2}$ ways to place the dominoes in the row. Now combine this reasoning with the result presented at the start of the section.

Chapter 6: Relations and Functions

6.1 Basic Concepts

EXERCISES

1. a) False b) True c) False (consider the $<$ relation, for instance)
2. One possibility is $(c, 1)$, $(c, 2)$, $(c, 3)$, $(d, 4)$, $(d, 5)$.
3. There are seven such relations. For instance, one of them is $(a, 2)$, $(a, 3)$, $(b, 2)$.
4. The relation consists of the ordered pairs $(1, 2)$, $(1, 5)$, $(2, 1)$, $(2, 4)$, $(3, 3)$, $(4, 2)$, $(4, 5)$, $(5, 1)$ and $(5, 4)$. (We omit the graph.)
5. We find that $\text{dom}(\vdash) = \text{rng}(\vdash) = \{1, 2, 3, 4, 5\}$. The inverse is identical to the original relation. This is indicated by the fact that the graph of the relation is unchanged when reflected over the line $y = x$.
6. a) No, Yes, No b) Only for $a = 5$ is $a \vdash a$ c) $\text{dom}(\vdash) = \{x \mid 1 \le x \le 4 \text{ or } x = 5\}$, $\text{rng}(\vdash) = \{y \mid y = 1 \text{ or } 2 \le y \le 5\}$.
7. The graph in the xy-plane consists of all points above the line $y = x$.
8. For instance $a = 17$, $b = 18$ and $c = 19$.
9. The graph is a vertical hyperbola with vertices at $(0, 3)$ and $(0, -3)$. It passes through the points $(\pm 5, \pm 4)$ and approaches the asymptotes $y = \pm x$. We find that $\text{dom}(\vdash) = \mathbb{R}$, $\text{rng}(\vdash) = \{y \mid y \ge 3 \text{ or } y \le -3\}$.
10. The graph is a diamond having vertices at $(2, 0)$, $(0, 4)$, $(-2, 0)$ and $(0, -4)$. We find that $\text{dom}(\vdash) = \{x \mid -2 \le x \le 2\}$, $\text{rng}(\vdash) = \{y \mid -4 \le y \le 4\}$.
11. The graph consists of the six points $(-3, 0)$, $(3, 0)$, $(1, 2)$, $(-1, 2)$, $(1, -2)$, $(-1, -2)$. Hence $\text{dom}(\vdash) = \{-3, -1, 1, 3\}$ while $\text{rng}(\vdash) = \{-2, 0, 2\}$.
12. The graph of the inverse relation is obtained by reflecting the graph of the original relation over the line $y = x$.
13. We have $\text{dom}(\vdash) = \text{rng}(\dashv)$ and $\text{rng}(\vdash) = \text{dom}(\dashv)$.
14. There are $3 \cdot 4 = 12$ ordered pairs which might be part of a relation from A to B. We may either include or exclude each ordered pair, for a total of 2^{12} relations.

6.2 Order Relations

EXERCISES

15. The graph should include the points (b, a), (b, c), (b, d), (c, a), (c, d), (d, a), (e, a), (e, b), (e, c), (e, d). (Diagram omitted.)
16. The graph should include the points (b, a),(c, a), (e, a), (e, c), (e, d), (f, a), (f, b), (f, c). (Diagram omitted.)
17. Element c will be at the top of the tree, with e directly beneath, then both a and b under e (side by side), and finally d beneath b.
18. Given a strict partial order on a set A, include all ordered pairs of the form (a, a) for $a \in A$ to obtain a partial order.
19. Elements a and d are maximal elements.
20. The subsets having five elements, such as $\{r, i, d, g, e\}$, are the maximal elements.
21. The maximal elements are the numbers 6, 7, 8, 9 and 10. (Tree diagram omitted.)
22. The unique maximal element is 0. Because $n \mid 0$ for all $n \in \mathbb{N}$ we know that no other positive integer can be a maximal element.
23. The identity relation is a partial order.
24. The relation $\vdash$ is reflexive and transitive. It is not antisymmetric, since we have both $(1, 4) \vdash (2, 3)$ and $(2, 3) \vdash (1, 4)$, for example.
25. The relation $\vdash$ is nonreflexive, antisymmetric, and transitive, hence it is a strict partial order.

26. There are six order relations. (It is possible for c to be unrelated to either a or b.)

27. There are $\frac{1}{2}5! = 60$ such total orders.

28. There exist sets A and B, neither of which are a subset of the other, such as $A = \{1, 2, 3\}$ and $B = \{3, 4, 5, 6\}$.

29. Alphabetical order is perhaps the most natural example.

WRITING

30. First explain why $\vdash$ is nonreflexive. Now observe that we can't have both $m \vdash n$ and $n \vdash m$, since this would imply that each number had more digits than the other. Finish by explaining why $\vdash$ is transitive.

31. To handle the transitive property, we must show that if $P_1 \vdash P_2$ and $P_2 \vdash P_3$ then $P_1 \vdash P_3$. So we may suppose that $2x_1 + 3y_1 < 2x_2 + 3y_2$ and that $2x_2 + 3y_2 < 2x_3 + 3y_3$. But since $2x_1 + 3y_1$ is less than $2x_2 + 3y_2$, which is less than $2x_3 + 3y_3$, we deduce that $2x_1 + 3y_1 < 2x_3 + 3y_3$, hence $P_1 \vdash P_3$.

32. By definition we know that a set A is never a proper subset of itself, showing nonreflexivity. Why do we know that if $A \subseteq B$ and $B \subseteq A$ then $A = B$? Now provide a short set theory proof to establish transitivity.

33. One means of proving the antisymmetric property is to write $f_1(x) = a_1 x + b_1$ and $f_2(x) = a_2 x + b_2$, then examine $f_1(x) - f_2(x) = (a_1 - a_2)x + (b_1 - b_2)$ and $f_2(x) - f_1(x) = (a_2 - a_1)x + (b_2 - b_1)$. Why is it not possible for both of these linear functions to have positive slope?

34. To prove transitivity we must show that if $a \mid b$ and $b \mid c$ then $a \mid c$. Begin by writing $b = ka$ and $c = lb$, then make a suitable substitution. To show that $\mid$ is not a total order, exhibit positive integers a and b such that $a \nmid b$ and $b \nmid a$.

35. To show antisymmetry suppose that $r \vdash s$ and $s \vdash r$. This means that $r/s = a$ and $s/r = b$ for $a, b \in \mathbb{N}$. Now multiply these equalities and argue that $a = b = 1$. For the transitive property, try multiplying the equalities that arise from $r \vdash s$ and $s \vdash t$.

36. The antisymmetric property is the trickiest to establish. Suppose that $P_1 \vdash P_2$ and $P_2 \vdash P_1$. Show that this leads to $x_1 + 2y_1 = x_2 + 2y_2$ and $2x_1 + y_1 = 2x_2 + y_2$. Then argue that this implies that $x_1 = x_2$ and $y_1 = y_2$. (Try subtracting the first equation from twice the second, for instance.)

37. The proof of the transitive property can be modeled fairly closely on the substring example appearing in the text.

38. A total order is obtained by saying that $(x_1, y_1) \vdash (x_2, y_2)$ when $y_1 < y_2$, and also in the case that $y_1 = y_2$ and $x_1 \leq x_2$. Thus points are "read" from smaller to larger by moving upwards through the set of horizontal lines and reading from left to right within each horizontal line. A proof that this gives a total order is left to the reader.

6.3 Equivalence Relations

EXERCISES

39. This relation is not an equivalence relation, since $\vdash$ is not reflexive for all $n \in \mathbb{N}$. In particular, note that $1 \nvdash 1$.

40. This relation is not an equivalence relation, since $\vdash$ is not transitive. For instance, $-3 \vdash 0$ and $0 \vdash 2$, but $-3 \nvdash 2$.

41. This is an equivalence relation, since it is reflexive, symmetric and transitive.

42. This relation is not an equivalence relation, since $\vdash$ is not transitive. For instance, half $\vdash$ back and back $\vdash$ bone, but half $\nvdash$ bone.

43. The graph should include the points (a, a), (a, c), (a, e), (b, b), (c, a), (c, c), (c, e), (d, d), (e, a), (e, c), (e, e). (Diagram omitted.)

44. There are five partitions: $\{a,b,c\}$, $\{a,b\}$ $\{c\}$, $\{a,c\}$ $\{b\}$, $\{b,c\}$ $\{a\}$, $\{a\}$ $\{b\}$ $\{c\}$.

45. There are ten such partitions. (Subset lists are omitted.)

46. The first two equivalence classes consist of all points on the hyperbolas $xy = 4$ and $xy = -6$. The third equivalence class consists of the x and y-axes together.

47. We have $[101] = \{100, 101, 102, 103\}$ while $[-101] = \{-104, -103, -102, -101\}$. A complete list of representatives would be $\ldots$, -8, -4, 0, 4, 8, $\ldots$

48. There are m equivalence classes; the set described is a complete residue system.

49. There are 24 words in the equivalence class [stop]. There are six words in [ddee]; namely ddee, dede, deed, eded, edde, eedd.

50. Notice that $\frac{1}{3}$ is not an element of any of the equivalence classes listed. Therefore $\left[\frac{1}{3}\right]$ is another equivalence class.

51. We need only prove the reflexive property. So given any $a \in A$, we need to show that $a \sim a$. We know that we can write $a \sim b$ for some $b \in A$. Furthermore, $\sim$ is symmetric, so we also have $b \sim a$. Now applying transitivity we deduce that $a \sim a$.

WRITING

52. To prove the symmetric property, we must show that if $m + 2n$ is a multiple of 3 then $n + 2m$ is also a multiple of 3. Since $3 \mid (m + 2n)$ we can write $m + 2n = 3k$, from which it follows that $2m + 4n = 6k$. Subtracting $3n$ gives $2m + n = 6k - 3n = 3(2k - n)$, so $2m + n$ is a multiple of 3, as desired.

53. Proving the transitive property involves showing that if $a - b = 7k$ and $b - c = 7l$ for $k, l \in \mathbb{Z}$ then $a - c$ is also a multiple of 7. Try adding the previous two equalities to complete the argument.

54. Proving the transitive property involves showing that if $uv = r^2$ and $vw = s^2$ for $r, s \in \mathbb{Q}$ then uw is also a perfect square. Multiplying these equalities and then dividing by v^2 will demonstrate this fact.

55. To show the symmetric property we must show that if $x/y = r$ for some positive $r \in \mathbb{Q}$ then y/x is also a rational number. But we have $y/x = 1/r$, and if r is a positive fraction then so is $1/r$.

56. The proof will be very similar to the one appearing in the section.

57. The reflexive and symmetric properties are relatively routine to verify. Transitivity takes some care, though, because some of the values may equal 0, meaning that we can't necessarily divide where we would like to. So suppose that $P_1 \sim P_2$ and $P_2 \sim P_3$, meaning that $x_1y_2 = x_2y_1$ and $x_2y_3 = x_3y_2$. We know that x_1 and y_1 are not both zero; assume without loss of generality that $x_1 \neq 0$. Next argue that $x_2 \neq 0$ either. (What goes wrong with $x_1y_2 = x_2y_1$ if $x_1 \neq 0$ but $x_2 = 0$?) Now solve for y_2 in the first equation and substitute into the second equation, then finish from there.

58. Suppose that $A \sim B$ and $B \sim C$. Draw a Venn diagram for all three sets and let x_1 through x_8 represent the number of elements in the various regions. Write an equality that expresses the fact that the number of elements in either A or B, but not both, is even. Do the same for B and C, then add them to help show that $A \sim C$.

6.4 Definition of Function

EXERCISES

59. a) $\text{dom}(f) = \{x \in \mathbb{R} \mid x \geq 3\}$, $\text{rng}(f) = \{y \in \mathbb{R} \mid y \geq 0\}$ b) $5 \mapsto 2$, $10 \mapsto \sqrt{14}$
c) $21 \mapsto 6$, $27.5 \mapsto 7$

60. $\text{dom}(f) = \{x \mid -\sqrt{5} < x < \sqrt{5}\}$, $\text{cod}(f) = \mathbb{R}$ b) $2 \mapsto 0$, $-1 \mapsto \ln 4$ c) $\pm 2 \mapsto 0$, $\pm\sqrt{5 - e^{-3}} \mapsto -3$

61. This set of ordered pairs does not define a function, since a single input value is associated with more than one output value, such as $(1, 3)$ and $(1, -3)$.

62. We can solve for y to obtain $y = (3x - 6)/(x - 1)$. The domain is $\mathbb{R} - \{1\}$ while the range is $\mathbb{R} - \{3\}$.

63. a) Because 1 has no prime divisors b) For instance, $77 \mapsto 7$ c) Infinitely many

64. a) $n = 120$ is the smallest such value b) $\text{rng}(g) = \mathbb{N}$ c) 3 has seven preimages

65. One possibility is to draw the line $y = x$ for $x \le 1$, draw a horizontal segment at $y = 1$ for $1 \le x \le 2$, and draw the line $y = x - 1$ for $x \ge 2$.

66. The function f reflects a given point over the x-axis.

67. One possibility consists of the ordered pairs $(1, 2)$, $(2, 2)$, $(3, 2)$, $(4, 3)$, $(5, 4)$. Arrow diagram and graph are omitted.

68. The function f must be a constant function.

69. There are $2^5 = 32$ such functions, of which $32 - 2 = 30$ are not constant functions.

70. There are $3^4 = 81$ of the former functions but only $4^3 = 64$ of the latter.

71. Either $C = A$ or C is the empty set.

72. We have $\lfloor -13.8 \rfloor = -14$, $\lfloor \sqrt{55} \rfloor = 7$, $\lfloor -10 \rfloor = -10$, $\lfloor e \rfloor = 2$, and $\lfloor 20/3 \rfloor = 6$.

73. The solution set is $\frac{8}{3} \le x < 3$.

74. The solution set is $-4\frac{1}{3} \le x < -3\frac{1}{3}$.

WRITING

75. Consider the cases $a \in C$ and $a \in D$, $a \in C$ and $a \notin D$, $a \notin C$ and $a \in D$, and $a \notin C$ and $a \notin D$ each separately.

76. Try an exponential function, such as $g(n) = 3^n$.

77. Explain why $\lfloor x \rfloor = n$ but $\lfloor x + \frac{1}{2} \rfloor = n + 1$ to conclude that $\lfloor x \rfloor + \lfloor x + \frac{1}{2} \rfloor = 2n + 1$. Next show that $\lfloor 2x \rfloor = 2n + 1$.

78. Mimic the proof from the section, but divide the real number line up into smaller intervals, namely $0 \le x < \frac{1}{3}$, $\frac{1}{3} \le x < \frac{2}{3}$, $\frac{2}{3} \le x < 1$, and so on. Now show that for x in an interval of the form $n + \frac{1}{3} \le x < n + \frac{2}{3}$ we have $\lfloor x \rfloor = n$, $\lfloor x + \frac{1}{3} \rfloor = n$, $\lfloor x + \frac{2}{3} \rfloor = n + 1$, and $\lfloor 3x \rfloor = 3n + 1$. Use similar reasoning for the other two cases.

6.5 Inverse Functions

EXERCISES

79. The second and third are one-to-one; the first and third are onto.

80. Changing $(4, 4)$ to $(4, 2)$ would do the job, as would changing $(1, 4)$ to $(1, 2)$.

81. a) 120 injective functions b) 24 injective functions c) no injective functions

82. For instance, $g(91) = 91 + 9 + 1 = 101$ and $g(100) = 100 + 1 + 0 + 0 = 101$ as well.

83. The second statement is simply the contrapositive of the first.

84. a) no surjective functions b) 24 surjective functions e) 240 surjective functions

85. Observe that given any $N \in \mathbb{N}$ we have $g(10N) = N$.

86. The arrow diagram should map $1 \mapsto 4$, $2 \mapsto 1$, $3 \mapsto 3$, and $4 \mapsto 2$.

87. We omit the sketch, but every horizontal and vertical line should cross the graph exactly once.

88. a) $f^{-1}(x) = \frac{1}{4}(x - 7)$ b) $f^{-1}(x) = \frac{1}{5}(x^3 - 1)$ c) $f^{-1}(x) = (x + 2)/(x - 3)$

89. One possibility is to let $f(x) = 5x + 10$.

90. The graph fails the horizontal line test, so it is not one-to-one. Furthermore, $\cos x \ne 2$ for any $x \in \mathbb{R}$, so cosine is not onto either.

91. The graph is omitted; just check that every horizontal and vertical line crosses the graph exactly once.

WRITING

92. Follow the example detailed in the section.

93. Distinct natural numbers a_1 and a_2 will differ in at least one digit, which will result in some prime being raised to different powers when computing $g(a_1)$ and $g(a_2)$. Since prime factorization is unique, we conclude that $g(a_1)$ and $g(a_2)$ will be distinct also. Now explain why $g(a) \neq 1024$ for any $a \in \mathbb{N}$.

94. Solve $\sqrt[3]{5x+1} = w$ for x and then plug this value into $f(x)$ to show that any output value w may be obtained.

95. Given any value $w \in \mathbb{R}$, find a suitable value for y so that $(1, y) \mapsto w$. To show f is not injective, find two different pairs (x, y) which both map to 3, for example.

96. Since f maps $x \mapsto ax + b$, it must be the case that f^{-1} maps $ax + b \mapsto x$ for all x. In other words, $a(ax + b) + b$ is the same formula as x. Now solve for a and b.

97. Explain that if (x, y) is an ordered pair defining the function f, then (y, x) is an ordered pair of the new function created by following the process described.

6.6 Composition of Functions

EXERCISES

98. The reader may check that their arrow diagrams satisfy the given conditions.

99. One possibility is to let f map $a \mapsto 1$, $b \mapsto 2$, $c \mapsto 3$ and $d \mapsto 4$; then let g map $1 \mapsto a$, $2 \mapsto a$, $3 \mapsto b$, $4 \mapsto c$, and $5 \mapsto d$.

100. Let both f and g map each of 1, 2, 3, 4 to itself and also define $g(5) = 4$. Then $g(f(x)) = x$ for all $x \in A$. However, g is not the inverse of f because f does not have an inverse, since it is not onto.

101. Both the domain and codomain of $f \circ g$ are set B.

102. a) $g \circ f(x) = \ln(4x - 2)$, with domain $x > \frac{1}{2}$.

b) $g \circ f(x) = 1/(\sqrt{x+3} - 2)$, with domain $x \geq -3$ and $x \neq 1$.

c) $g \circ f(x) = 1/(\cos x - 1)$, with domain all $x \in \mathbb{R}$ except $x = 2\pi k$ for $k \in \mathbb{Z}$.

d) $g \circ f(x) = \sqrt{x^2 + 4x - 5}$, with domain $x \leq -5$ or $x \geq 1$.

e) $g \circ f(x) = \tan \pi x$, with domain all $x \in \mathbb{R}$ except $x = k + \frac{1}{2}$ for $k \in \mathbb{Z}$.

103. Solving the equation $\frac{(x+3)+1}{(x+3)-1} = \frac{x+1}{x-1} + 3$ yields $x = 0$ or $x = -1$.

104. We have $\text{dom}(g \circ f) = \mathbb{R} - \{1\}$. One should find that algebraically simplifying the expression for $g(f(x))$ yields just x. (TIP: multiply both numerator and denominator of the resulting fraction by $(x - 1)$.) Next, $\text{dom}(f \circ g) = \mathbb{R} - \{5\}$ and $f(g(x))$ also reduces to just x after multiplying top and bottom by $(x - 5)$.

105. To get started, show that $f(f(x)) = \frac{x-1}{x}$. Then plug this expression into $f(x)$ to confirm that $f(f(f(x))) = x$, as desired.

106. Since $g(1) = 0$ we know that $a + b = 0$. Furthermore, $f(g(x)) = 2(ax + b) + 3 = 2ax + 2b + 3$ while $g(f(x)) = a(2x + 3) + b = 2ax + 3a + b$. In order for these formulas to match we would need $2b + 3 = 3a + b$. Hence $a = 3/4$ and $b = -3/4$.

107. Choose some value b between 13 and 20, then create an injective function g (such as a line) for which $g(20) = b$ and $g(b) = 13$.

108. The points $P(2, -2)$ and $Q(2, 2)$ satisfy the given equations.

WRITING

109. Suppose that $g(f(a_1)) = g(f(a_2))$. Since g is injective, what can we deduce about $f(a_1)$ and $f(a_2)$? Now finish from here.

110. Given any $c \in C$ we must show there exists an $a \in A$ such that $g(f(a)) = c$. Work backwards one step at a time by first finding $b \in B$ such that $g(b) = c$.

111. For any a and b with $a < b$ we know that $f(b) < f(a)$. Since g is decreasing, how do $g(f(a))$ and $g(f(b))$ compare, given that $f(b) < f(a)$?

112. We may compute $h(1)$ by substituting $x = 1$ into $g(g(x)+x)$, yielding $g(g(1)+1)$. Now use the fact that $g(1) = 0$.

113. Substituting $n = 1$ into the equation $f(f(n)) = n + 3$ we obtain $f(2) = 4$, since we are given that $f(1) = 2$. Now plug in $n = 2$ to find that $f(4) = 5$. Next try $n = 4$. You should eventually find that $f(2) = 4$, $f(5) = 7$, $f(8) = 10$, and so on. Prove that this pattern continues by induction.

114. To show that f is injective, suppose that $f(a_1) = f(a_2)$. Plugging a_1 and a_2 into the given equation shows that $f(f(a_1)) = a_1$ and $f(f(a_2)) = a_2$. But since $f(a_1) = f(a_2)$ it follows that $f(f(a_1)) = f(f(a_2))$ as well. Continue from here.

Chapter 7: Cardinality

7.1 Comparing Sets

EXERCISES

1. We could take D to be Disney dalmatians, and let E be the set of eggs in a carton.

2. The most obvious formula is to map $n \mapsto (n+1)/n$.

3. The formulas $f(n) = \frac{3}{4}(n-1)$ and $g(n) = \frac{4}{3}n + 1$ will do the job.

4. We could have $f(x) = 3x - 2$ or $f(x) = x^2$, among other possibilities.

5. One of the simplest bijections is $f(x) = 4/x$.

6. If P is a point in quadrant I, then rotate it by $90°$ around the origin to obtain a point in quadrant II. Alternately, map $(x, y) \mapsto (-x, y)$.

7. Given a horizontal line, rotate it by $90°$ clockwise about the origin to obtain a vertical line. Or match the horizontal line $y = c$ with the vertical line $x = c$.

8. If sets A and B have the same cardinality, and sets B and C also have the same cardinality, clearly we would want our definition to guarantee that $|A| = |C|$.

WRITING

9. To show symmetry consider the inverse function f^{-1}. For transitivity, suppose that $f : A \to B$ and $g : B \to C$ are bijections. How can we obtain a function from A to C?

10. Think about how we could describe the elements of A algebraically in order to obtain a formula for a bijection. Then show that your function is in fact a bijection.

11. Try using $f(n) = (n+9)^2$ as your bijection. Begin by noting that $f(n)$ is always a perfect square with three or more digits. Next argue that f is one-to-one, taking care to explain why we can ignore the negative root when taking square roots to reduce the equation $f(n_1) = f(n_2)$. Finally, show that f is onto.

12. A bijection which shows that $|\mathbb{N}| = |L|$ is obtained by mapping $b \in \mathbb{N}$ to the line having equation $y = -x + (b+1)$. To begin, show that $y = -x + (b+1)$ is in fact one of the desired lines. Then briefly explain why this mapping is injective. Finally, show that this mapping is surjective by explaining how to choose b if a given line passes through (m, n) where $m, n \in \mathbb{N}$.

13. Given a circle centered at the origin, what is the natural way to produce a horizontal line above the x-axis? Use this construction to define your bijection, then show that your proposed bijection really is one-to-one and onto.

14. One possible bijection is given by the formula $f(x) = \frac{2}{3}x + 7$.

15. Can you think of a simple function which accepts all real numbers as inputs but only gives positive real numbers as outputs?

16. Our bijection must turn subsets of $\{a, b, c, \ldots, y\}$ into subsets of $\{a, b, c, \ldots, y, z\}$ having an even number of elements. Try mapping $\{a, d, k, m, t, s\} \mapsto \{a, d, k, m, t, s\}$ and $\{s, k, y, l, i, g, h, t\} \mapsto \{s, k, y, l, i, g, h, t\}$, but send $\{q, u, a, r, t\} \mapsto \{q, u, a, r, t, z\}$ and $\{s, c, h, n, o\} \mapsto \{s, c, h, n, o, z\}$. Figure out the pattern in these examples, use it to define your bijection, then show that your bijection is one-to-one and onto.

7.2 Finite and Infinite Sets

EXERCISES

17. One answer would be to let $A = \{1, 2, 3, 4, 5, \ldots\}$ and let $B = \{3, 2, 1, 0, -1, \ldots\}$.

18. We could conclude that B is infinite, but we cannot say anything about A.

19. Let N be the largest number of digits appearing in the numerator or denominator of any of the fractions $r_1, r_2, \ldots, r_n$. Then the fraction $10^N/(10^N+1)$ does not appear in the list, since the numerator and denominator both have $N + 1$ digits.

20. Let N be the largest element appearing in any set. Then the set $\{4, 5, 6, \ldots, N+1\}$ satisfies the condition in the problem but does not appear in the list.

21. A simple example would be $g(n) = \pi + n$.

22. One such function is $g(n) = (2n + 1)/4$.

23. We could define $g(n)$ to be the word consisting of the letter l followed by n a's.

24. Let $h(\alpha)$ be the word obtained by appending a 'k' to the end of α, for instance.

WRITING

25. Assume to the contrary that such a function exists, so the elements of B can be numbered as $r_1, r_2, \ldots, r_n$ for some $n \in \mathbb{N}$. Let 7^N be largest denominator in the list. Now explain how to find a fraction that belongs to B which is not already in this list.

26. Define $g(n)$ as a rectangle two of whose vertices are $(0, 0)$ and $(n, 0)$. What must the coordinates of the other two vertices be?

27. Show that $h(x) = \frac{2}{3}x + 3$ has outputs in I, is one-to-one, but is not onto.

28. One approach would be to construct an injective function $g : \mathbb{N} \to S$. What might a set with 7 elements look like if its smallest element were n?

29. Consider the infinite list 7.01, 7.001, 7.0001, ... of rational numbers all located between 7 and 7.1. Now find a formula for the nth term of this sequence.

30. An infinite sequence of distinct elements of W might look like tt, tot, toot, tooot, toooot, ... Use this to create an injection $f : \mathbb{N} \to W$.

31. If A is infinite then there is an injection $g_1 : \mathbb{N} \to A$. Now consider $g_2 : \mathbb{N} \to \mathcal{P}(A)$ defined via $g_2(n) = \{g_1(n)\}$. Now show that if A is finite then $\mathcal{P}(A)$ is also finite.

32. Consider the images $g(1), g(2), \ldots, g(n), g(n+1)$ in A and argue that they cannot all be different, since A only has n elements.

33. We are assuming that $g : C_k \to A$ is one-to-one. If g were also onto then we would have a bijection, meaning that A would be finite, contradicting the fact that A is infinite. Hence g cannot be onto. Use this fact to define $g(k + 1)$.

7.3 Denumerable Sets

EXERCISES

34. The picture will consist of all points (m, n) in the plane for which $m \in \mathbb{N}$ and $n \in \mathbb{Z}$; i.e. all lattice points to the right of the y-axis. One way to number them is to start with the point $(1, 0)$ followed by $(1, 1)$, $(2, 0)$, $(1, -1)$, then $(1, 2)$, $(2, 1)$, $(3, 0)$, $(2, -1)$, $(1, -2)$, and so on in ever expanding $\rangle$ shaped sets of points.

35. Set A consists of the lattice points in the first quadrant along a sequence of parallel lines having slope -1 and y-intercepts 2, 5, 8, etc. Each line has only finitely many points along it, so we may number the points along each line before moving to the next. One numbering would be $(1, 1)$, then $(1, 4)$, $(2, 3)$, $(3, 2)$, $(4, 1)$, followed by $(1, 7)$, $(2, 6)$, $(3, 5)$, and so on.

36. The points in set B are located where the circles with radii 1, 2, 3, ... centered at the origin intersect the horizontal lines $y = 1$, $y = 2$, $y = 3$, etc. There are only finitely many such points around each circle, so number the points along each circle before moving on to the next larger circle to include them all.

37. Set C is infinite since it includes all the fractions of the form $(5n + 1)/5n$, where $n \in \mathbb{N}$. (Note that we can't just use the sequence $\frac{1}{5}, \frac{2}{5}, \frac{3}{5}, \frac{4}{5}, \frac{5}{5}, \ldots$, because the latter fraction reduces to $\frac{1}{1}$.) Since $\mathbb{Q}$ is denumerable, we are done.

38. Set D is infinite because it includes the integers 3, 30, 300, 3000, ..., a sequence of numbers given by the formula $3 \cdot 10^n$ for all $n \in \mathbb{N}$. This gives an injective function $f : \mathbb{N} \to D$, and we already know $\mathbb{Z}$ is denumerable, so we're done.

39. This set turns out to be denumerable.

40. This set turns out to be uncountable.

WRITING

41. Clearly D is a subset of $\mathbb{N} \times \mathbb{N}$, which is a known denumerable set. It remains to show that D is an infinite set. Consider the sums $10 + 7$, $20 + 7$, $30 + 7$, ...

42. One way to number all the elements of $A \cup B \cup C$ is $a_1, b_1, c_1, a_2, b_2, c_2, a_3, \ldots$

43. A sneaky segment has endpoints $(a, 0)$ and $(0, b)$ for $a, b \in \mathbb{Z}$. Use this to explain why we can view our set as a subset of $\mathbb{Z} \times \mathbb{Z}$. Then prove that there are infinitely many sneaky segments by considering the segment joining $(1, 0)$ to $(0, n)$ for $n \in \mathbb{N}$.

44. Let B_n be the set of all words of length n for $n \in \mathbb{N}$. Then each B_n is a finite set (in fact $|B_n| = 26^n$), so we can list all words of length 1, followed by all words of length 2, and so on in one long list.

45. It is relatively straight-forward to list all infinite stairways of height 1, ordered according to where the lone vertical segment occurs.

46. Let m and n be the x-coordinates of the first and second vertical segments. Hence $m, n \in \mathbb{Z}_{\geq 0}$ with $n \geq m$. It follows that there is a bijection between the set of all paths and a subset of $\mathbb{Z} \times \mathbb{Z}$, which is a known denumerable set.

47. One can proceed as in the previous problem. Alternatively, group all such infinite stairways according to where they first reach height h. Then argue that there are only finitely many stairways in each group. Hence we can include them all in a single long list. (As a challenge, the reader might try showing that there are $\binom{h+k-1}{k}$ paths that first reach height h at the point (k, h).)

48. The set of all ordered pairs (c_j, d_k) can be arranged in an array stretching infinitely far up and to the right, similar to level four of the Mathematical Outing. Now use the technique from that level to number all the ordered pairs.

49. Think of $D_1 \times D_2 \times D_3$ as $(D_1 \times D_2) \times D_3$. By the previous exercise we know that $D_1 \times D_2$ is denumerable. Invoking that result again, we conclude that $(D_1 \times D_2) \times D_3$ is also denumerable. Now prove the general result by induction.

50. The previous problem implies that $\mathbb{N} \times \mathbb{N} \times \mathbb{N}$ is a denumerable set. Now create a bijection between this set and functions $g : \{a, b, c\} \to \mathbb{N}$ by considering how we might assign values for $g(a)$, $g(b)$ and $g(c)$, as was done in the text.

51. Move steadily along the list $d_1, d_2, d_3, d_4, \ldots$ Each time we encounter an element of A, give it the next spot in our list of the elements of A. Then explain why this process is guaranteed to include every element of A in our list.

7.4 Uncountable Sets

EXERCISES

52. One possible formula is given by $g(x) = 0.1x + 4.6$.

53. We could map a real number $r \in (0, 1)$ to the rectangle resting against the x and y axes having width r and height $4 - r$.

54. A graph with vertical asymptotes at $x = 0$ and $x = 1$ could work, such as the graph of $y = (x - 0.5)/(x^2 - x)$.

55. The circle with center (r, r) and radius r will work for any $r \in (0, 1)$, which gives uncountably many circles.

56. Convert each infinite string of a's and b's to a sequence of x's and y's. This shows that S contains a known uncountable set as a subset.

57. Create a new sequence according to the following rule. If the nth letter of s_n is x then let the nth letter of the new sequence be y. But if the nth letter of s_n is not an x then let the nth letter of the new sequence be x. The new sequence differs from each sequence in our list in at least one place, therefore it cannot appear in the list.

58. The portion of the family tree "sprouting" from the seventh duck down in the fifth column (call him Al) is identical to the entire family tree. Since there are uncountably many paths beginning with the matriarch duck, there will also be uncountably many paths beginning with Al.

59. Given any infinite string using the letters w, x, y, z replace each w with aa, replace each x with ab, replace each y with ba, and replace each z with bb.

WRITING

60. Construct a new function $h : \mathbb{N} \to \{a, b, c, d\}$ which is different from each of the functions h_1, h_2, h_3, $\ldots$ by making sure that h_n and h map n to different letters.

61. Write out the decimal expansion for each of x_1, x_2, x_3, $\ldots$ and then create a new real number x that differs from each of the others in at least one digit.

62. We can encode an infinite stairway as a sequence of a's and b's, where a means draw a vertical segment up and b means draw a horizontal segment to the right. For instance, the stairway pictured in the problem begins $abbbabbbbaabb\cdots$.

63. We can obtain such permutations by swapping 1 and 2 (or leaving them in place), then swapping 3 and 4 (or not), and so on. Use this idea to show that S contains a known uncountable set as a subset.

64. Suppose to the contrary that the set of irrationals is actually countable. Since $\mathbb{Q}$ is also countable, what would this tell us about $\mathbb{R}$?

65. Note that the segment with endpoints $(3, r)$ and $(3, -r)$ has $(3, 0)$ as its midpoint.

66. Observe that any quadratic function of the form $(x-r)(x-2)$ satisfies the condition in the problem.

67. Interpret an infinite sequence of a's and b's as a code describing how to create a subset of $\mathbb{N}$, by letting a mean "include" and b mean "exclude." Hence the sequence $bbabaaabab\cdots$ would correspond to the subset $\{3, 5, 6, 7, 9, \ldots\}$.

7.5 Cantor's Theorem

EXERCISES

68. Clearly $n \mapsto 2^n$ is such an injective function. The formula $n \mapsto 2^{n-1000}$ also works.

69. In the case of finite sets, we can conclude that $|A| < |B|$. But for infinite sets we can only say that $|A| \leq |B|$.

70. Yes. According to Cantor's Theorem, $\mathcal{P}(\mathcal{P}(\mathbb{R}))$ is strictly larger than $\mathcal{P}(\mathbb{R})$.

71. Define $f(m) = m$ for $m \geq 1$, but let $f(m) = m - 1$ for $m \leq 0$.

72. One possibility is to let $0 \mapsto 1$, $1 \mapsto 2$, $-1 \mapsto 3$, $2 \mapsto 4$, $-2 \mapsto 5$, $3 \mapsto 6$, etc.

73. Any subset of $\mathbb{R}$ which contains 2 will do, such as $f(2) = \{x \in \mathbb{R} \mid 0 \leq x < 3\}$.

74. The set $\{1, 2, 3, 5\}$ is guaranteed not to appear on the volunteer's list.

75. The empty set.

76. The only simple function $f : A \to B$ that has a chance of working is $f(x) = x + 1$. But this is not a bijection, since $f(x) \neq 2$ for any $x \in A$, so f is not surjective.

WRITING

77. The base cases are easy to check. Now suppose that $k < 2^k$ for some k. Then it follows that $2k < 2^{k+1}$. (Why?) One need only explain why $k + 1 < 2k$ to finish.

78. The argument can closely follow the proof in the text that $|\mathbb{R}| < |\mathcal{P}(\mathbb{R})|$.

79. To illustrate, we'll explain why the set $\{1, 3, 4, 5\}$ could appear in the volunteer's list. Since 2 is not an element in this set, we place it second in the list, then create other sets to make sure that all of the volunteer's answers are NO; the list $\{2\}$, $\{1, 3, 4, 5\}$, $\{4\}$, $\{5\}$, $\{1\}$ will do. Now adapt this idea for sets other than $\{1, 2, 3, 4, 5\}$.

80. The simplest injection $g : B \to A$ is just $g(x) = x$. It remains to exhibit an injective function $f : A \to B$.

81. An injection $f : A \to B$ is given by $f(x) = \frac{1}{6}x + 2$, for instance. Now also find a different injection $g : B \to A$.

82. A function from $\mathbb{N}$ to $\{a, b\}$ is already a function from $\mathbb{N}$ to $\{a, b, c\}$, so the first set is clearly a subset of the second. Obtaining an injection going the other way is trickier. If $g(1) = a$ then set $f(1) = a$ and $f(2) = a$, while if $g(1) = b$ then set $f(1) = b$ and $f(2) = b$. Finally, if $g(1) = c$ then let $f(1) = a$ and $f(2) = b$. Now define $f(3)$ and $f(4)$ similarly based on the value of $g(2)$, and so on.

83. Given a set of four natural numbers, construct a set of five numbers by including a fifth number that is larger than the others, then explain why this gives an injection from A to B. There are many creative ways to construct an injection from B to A. One method would be to map the set $\{j, k, l, m, n\}$ to $\{2^j 3^k, 5^l, 7^m, 11^n\}$.

84. Interleave the digits of the natural numbers to form a real number. For instance, the sequence 1729, 88, 13676, 222, 5, ...can be displayed in an array as shown, so this sequence becomes .92878610720062500320 $\cdots$.

$$
\begin{array}{rccccccc}
n_1 & = & \cdots & 0 & 0 & 1 & 7 & 2 & 9 \\
n_2 & = & \cdots & 0 & 0 & 0 & 0 & 8 & 8 \\
n_3 & = & \cdots & 0 & 1 & 3 & 6 & 7 & 6 \\
n_4 & = & \cdots & 0 & 0 & 0 & 2 & 2 & 2 \\
n_5 & = & \cdots & 0 & 0 & 0 & 0 & 0 & 5 \\
& & & & & & \vdots & &
\end{array}
$$

7.6 Ordering Cardinal Numbers

EXERCISES

85. There are infinitely many, including $\mathbb{N}$, $\mathcal{P}(\mathbb{N})$, $\mathcal{P}(\mathcal{P}(\mathbb{N}))$, $\mathcal{P}(\mathcal{P}(\mathcal{P}(\mathbb{N})))$, $\ldots$.

86. The irrational numbers have the same cardinality as $\mathbb{R}$, and we know $|\mathbb{R}| = |\mathcal{P}(\mathbb{N})|$.

87. Because $|\mathbb{R} \times \mathbb{R}| = |\mathbb{R}|$, subsets of the plane have the same cardinality as $\mathcal{P}(\mathbb{R})$, and hence the same cardinality as $\mathcal{P}(\mathcal{P}(\mathbb{N}))$.

88. Create an infinite sequence 2, 2.3, 2.33, 2.333, etc. Let f map each term of the sequence to the next one, then define $f(x) = x$ for all other values of $x \in (1, 3)$.

89. One method is to define $f(x) = e^x$ unless e^x happens to be a positive integer, in which case we set $f(x) = e^x - 1$.

90. Replace each of a, b, c by 0, 1, 2, respectively, then place a decimal point in front.

91. First map $x \mapsto e^x/(e^x + 1)$ to obtain a real number between 0 and 1. Then write this number in base three, which looks like a decimal point followed by a string of 0's, 1's and 2's. Finally, convert each 0 to an a, 1 to b, and 2 to c.

92. If we work directly with all real numbers then we lose the one-to-one property we need. For instance, both $\frac{2}{3}$ and $2\frac{2}{3}$ would produce the set $\{1, 3, 5, 7, \ldots\}$, since in binary we have $\frac{2}{3} = .101010\cdots$ while $2\frac{2}{3} = 10.101010\cdots$.

93. The real number $x = \ln(\frac{1}{2})$ gives the set $\{2, 4, 6, 8, \ldots\}$.

94. We find that $(\sqrt{2}, \sqrt{3}) \mapsto 11.4713422015\cdots$ while $(\sqrt{3}, \sqrt{2}) \mapsto 11.7431240251\cdots$.

95. We calculate $25\frac{14}{33} = 25.42424242\cdots$, so the point $(2\frac{4}{9}, 5\frac{2}{9})$ maps to $25\frac{14}{33}$.

96. Since $\frac{13}{33} = .39393939\cdots$ we would need to have $x = .3333\cdots$ and $y = .9999\cdots$. In other words $x = \frac{1}{3}$ and $y = 1$. (Since clearly y is three times as large as x.) But the point $(\frac{1}{3}, 1)$ maps to $1.303030\cdots = 1\frac{10}{33}$ instead.

WRITING

97. We need only exhibit injective functions from each set to the other. Show that the functions $f(x) = \frac{1}{5}x$ and $g(x) = x + 1$ will work.

98. Use Schroeder-Bernstein, and try using $x \mapsto e^x/(e^x + 1)$ as one of your injections.

99. Let $g(n)$ be the positive integer obtained by placing a 7 in front of n. Show that this is an injection from the second set to the first.

100. Follow the proof that $|\mathbb{R}| = |\mathcal{P}(\mathbb{N})|$ laid out in the text, except convert to base four decimals instead of to binary. Alternately, continue to work with binary, but replace *pairs* of binary digits with letters via $a \leftrightarrow 00$, $b \leftrightarrow 01$, $c \leftrightarrow 10$, $d \leftrightarrow 11$.

101. Mimic the proof that $|\mathbb{R}| = |\mathcal{H}|$, except weave together the digits from three real numbers this time instead of just two real numbers.

102. A function $h : [0, 2] \to \mathbb{R}$ can be extended to a function $H : \mathbb{R} \to \mathbb{R}$ by letting $H(x)$ agree with $h(x)$ for $0 \leq x \leq 2$ and declaring that $H(x) = 1$ for all other x. (Now show that this process is one-to-one.) To obtain an injection in the other direction, find a bijection $G : (0, 2) \to \mathbb{R}$. Now given an $H : \mathbb{R} \to \mathbb{R}$, define $h = H \circ G$.

103. To create an injection from C to D, interpret the coordinates of a point as the slope and y-intercept of a line. (Thus the point $(3, -1)$ maps to the line $y = 3x - 1$.) This approach cannot be readily implemented to create an injection from D to C, though, since it leaves out vertical lines. So given a line, let θ be the angle of inclination, where $0 \leq \theta < \pi$. Then let b be the y-intercept, unless the line happens to be vertical, in which case let b be the x-intercept. Then each line maps to a unique point (θ, b).

104. Since $g : B \to A$ is injective, at most one element of B maps to $a_0 \in A$. Hence b_{-1} is unique, if it exists. Similarly, since $f : A \to B$ is injective, there is at most one element $a_{-1} \in A$ which maps to b_{-1}. Continue in this manner.

105. Suppose to the contrary that some element appears in both sequences. Then argue that all elements before and after these two must also be identical, and reach a contradiction since we assumed that $\tilde{a}_0$ was not part of the original sequence. For instance, if $\tilde{a}_1 = a_4$, then explain why it follows that $\tilde{b}_0 = b_3$ and hence that $\tilde{a}_0 = a_3$.

106. For each sequence group the elements of A appearing within that sequence into a subset. Since different sequences are disjoint and every element of A appears within some sequence (why?), these subsets partition A. Now do the same for B.

107. Simply pair up $a_{-1} \leftrightarrow b_{-2}$, $a_0 \leftrightarrow b_{-1}$, $a_1 \leftrightarrow b_0$, etc.

108. In this case we can pair up a_k and b_k for every $k \in \mathbb{Z}$.

109. If $a_5 = a_0$ then the sequence will begin to cycle, repeating every ten terms. Thus we will have $b_5 = b_0$, $a_6 = a_1$, $b_6 = b_1$, and so on. In this case we just pair up $a_0 \leftrightarrow b_0$, $a_1 \leftrightarrow b_1$, $\ldots$, $a_4 \leftrightarrow b_4$.

110. Every such sequence will either terminate to the left, will extend infinitely far in both directions, or will be cyclic. In each case we can pair up adjacent elements of A and B; usually a_k with b_k unless we have a sequence terminating with an element of B as above, in which case we pair up b_k with a_{k+1}.

Acknowledgments

The image of Bernhard Riemann is in the public domain. It is reproduced courtesy of the Smithsonian Institution Libraries. The image appears at `http://www.sil.si.edu/digitalcollections/hst/scientific-identity/fullsize/SIL14-R003-02a.jpg`.

The image of Pierre de Fermat is in the public domain. It is reproduced courtesy of the University of St Andrews, St Andrews, Scotland. The image appears at `http://www-groups.dcs.st-and.ac.uk/~history/PictDisplay/Fermat.html`.

The image of the crab nebula is in the public domain. It is reproduced courtes y of the National Aeronautics and Space Administration (NASA). The image appears at `http://antwrp.gsfc.nasa.gov/apod/ap091025.html`.

The author is extraordinarily grateful to Eunice Cheung for taking all of the other photographs appearing within the body of this text and especially for designing and creating the artwork appearing on the cover of this book.

References

1. Edward Barbeau, Murray Klamkin and William Moser, *Five Hundred Mathematical Challenges,* Mathematical Association of America, Washington, DC, 1997.

2. Albert Beiler, *Recreations in the Theory of Numbers,* Dover Publications, New York, 1964.

3. Paul Cohen, *Set Theory and the Continuum Hypothesis,* Dover Publications, New York, 2008.

4. Joseph Dauben, *Georg Cantor, His Mathematics and Philosophy of the Infinite,* Princeton University Press, Princeton, NJ, 1990.

5. Howard Eves, *An Introduction to the History of Mathematics,* Brooks/Cole, Pacific Grove, CA, 1990.

6. Malcolm Gladwell, *The Tipping Point,* Little, Brown and Company, New York, 2000.

7. Shay Gueron, A Game-Like Activity for Learning Cantor's Theorem, *College Mathematics Journal,* **32** (2001), 122–125.

8. Dava Sobel, *Galileo's Daughter: A Historical Memoir of Science, Faith, and Love,* Walker Publishing, New York, 1999.

9. Ian Stewart, *Taming the Infinite: The Story of Mathematics,* Quercus Publishing Plc, London, 2009.

10. David Wells, *The Penguin Dictionary of Curious and Interesting Geometry,* Penguin Books, London, 1992.

Index